Land Law and Disputes in Asia

Through an in-depth legal analysis by leading scholars, this book searches for the exact legal causes of land-related disputes in Asia within the histories, legal systems and social realities of the respective countries. It consists of four main parts: examining the relationship between law and development; land-taking in developmental stages; common ownership; and proposals for new approaches to land law and dispute resolution. With a combination of orthodox legal interpretations and the empirical approach of legal sociology, the contributors undertake an extensive comparative legal analysis across common and civil law traditions. Most importantly, they propose pathways forward for legal transformations in the pursuit of sustainable development in Asia.

This book is vital contribution to the study of comparative law, and especially property law, in East and Southeast Asia.

Kaneko, Yuka, LL.D., Professor, Kobe University Center for Social Systems Innovation. She is active in the field of Asian comparative law as well as in the sociology of law. She is the author of several books, including *Asian Crisis and Financial Law Reforms*, Shinzan-Sya in 2004; *Law Reforms and Legal Development in Asia*, Daigakukyoiku-Shuppan in 2010; *Asian Law in Disasters: Toward a Human-Centered Recovery*, Routledge in 2016; *Law and Development of Myanmar*, Koyo-Syobo in 2018; and *Civil Law Reforms in Post-Colonial Asia: Beyond Western Capitalism*, Springer in 2019.

Kadomatsu, Narufumi, LL.M., Dean and Professor at Graduate School of Law, Kobe University. He studies legal issues of administrative law and urban land law. He has published many articles in academic journals in Japanese, English and German. He is an editor or a contributor of several books, including Kadomatsu et al., *Legal Response to Vacant Houses: An International Comparison*, Springer 2020. He is also a member of the board of directors of the East Asia Administrative Law Association.

Tamanaha, Brian Z., John S. Lehmann University Professor, Washington University School of Law, St. Louis, U.S.A. He is a renowned jurisprudence and law and society scholar, and the author of nine books, including his latest book titled *A Realistic Theory of Law* (2017), which received the 2019 IVR Book Prize from the International Association of the Philosophy of Law and Social Philosophy for best legal philosophy book published in 2016–2018, as well as an Honorable Mention for the 2018 Prose Awards in Law by the Association of Univer
the Rule of Law (2004), has been translated into nine langu

Routledge Studies in Asian Law

Asian Law in Disasters
Toward a Human-Centered Recovery
Edited by Yuka Kaneko, Katsumi Matsuoka and Toshihisa Toyoda

Judicial Review of Elections in Asia
Edited by Po Jen Yap

Rethinking South China Sea Disputes
The Untold Dimensions and Great Expectations
Katherine Hui-Yi Tseng

Civil Unrest and Governance in Hong Kong
Law and Order from Historical and Cultural Perspectives
Edited by Michael H.K. Ng and John D. Wong

Writing Chinese Laws
The Form and Function of Legal Statutes Found in the Qin Shuihudi Corpus
Ernest Caldwell

National Identity and Japanese Revisionism
Abe Shinzō's Vision of a Beautiful Japan and Its Limits
Michal Kolmaš

Constitutional Remedies in Asia
Edited by Po Jen Yap

Chinese Legal Culture and Constitutional Order
Shiping Hua

Land Law and Disputes in Asia
In Search of an Alternative for Development
Edited by Yuka Kaneko, Narufumi Kadomatsu and Brian Z. Tamanaha

For more information about this series, please visit: www.routledge.com/asian studies/series/RSIAL

Land Law and Disputes in Asia

In Search of an Alternative for Development

Edited by Yuka Kaneko, Narufumi Kadomatsu and Brian Z. Tamanaha

Routledge
Taylor & Francis Group
LONDON AND NEW YORK

First published 2022
by Routledge
4 Park Square, Milton Park, Abingdon, Oxon OX14 4RN

and by Routledge
605 Third Avenue, New York, NY 10017

Routledge is an imprint of the Taylor & Francis Group, an Informa business

British Library Cataloguing-in-Publication Data
A catalogue record for this book is available from the British Library

Library of Congress Cataloguing-in-Publication Data
A catalogue record for this book has been requested

ISBN: 978-0-367-77278-9 (hbk)
ISBN: 978-0-367-77279-6 (pbk)
ISBN: 978-1-003-17060-0 (ebk)

DOI: 10.4324/9781003170600

Typeset in Galliard
By Apex CoVantage, LLC

Contents

Contributors

GILLESPIE John, Adjunct Professor (research) in the Department of Business Law and Taxation, Monash University. He is working on a research project exploring the role of emotions in judicial decision making in East Asia. He has also authored and edited eight books and published more than 60 articles and book chapters in journals such as the *Law and Society Review*, *International Law Quarterly Review*, *Harvard Human Rights Journal*, *Law and Social Inquiry*, *Stanford Journal of International Law and New York University* and *Journal of International Law and Politics.*

JIAO Shu, Doctor of Laws (Kobe University), Lecturer at Shanghai University of Engineering Science. She has been working on the nature of the public interest requirement in land expropriation laws of China and Japan.

KADOMATSU Narufumi, LL.M., Dean and Professor at Graduate School of Law, Kobe University. He studies legal issues of administrative law and urban land law. He has published many articles in academic journals in Japanese, English and German. He is an editor or a contributor of several books, including Kadomatsu et al., *Legal Response to Vacant Houses: An International Comparison*, Springer 2020. He is also a member of the board of directors of the East Asia Administrative Law Association.

KANEKO Yuka, LL.D., Professor, Kobe University Center for Social Systems Innovation. She is active in the field of Asian comparative law as well as in the sociology of law. She is the author of several books, including *Asian Crisis and Financial Law Reforms*, Shinzan-Sya in 2004; *Law Reforms and Legal Development in Asia*, Daigakukyoiku-Shuppan in 2010; *Asian Law in Disasters: Toward a Human-Centered Recovery*, Routledge in 2016; *Law and Development of Myanmar*, Koyo-Syobo in 2018; and *Civil Law Reforms in Post-Colonial Asia: Beyond Western Capitalism*, Springer in 2019.

LEE Ming-Chih, Ph.D. Candidate, Osaka University Graduate School of Law and Politics, Japan. She is also a recipient of a fellowship for doctoral candidate of Institutum Iurisprudentiae, Academia Sinica in Taiwan from July 2020 to June 2021, and JSPS (Japan Society for the Promotion of Science) Research Fellow from April 2018 to March 2020. She has served as a lawyer in land expropriation cases in Taiwan from 2011 to 2015 and has published five articles and book chapters in journals on land expropriation issues in Taiwanese Mandarin and Japanese.

MATSUMOTO Mikiko, Officer at Administrative Management Bureau, Ministry of Internal Affairs and Communications; Ph.D. Candidate in the Graduate School of Law, Kobe University and JSPS (Japan Society for the Promotion of Science) Research Fellow from 2019 to 2021. She has been working on a comparative legal study on public–private cooperation in Japan and China.

MUROI Sachihiko, Ph.D. Candidate, Kobe University. He is a member of the Japanese Association of Sociology of Law. He is exploring the contemporary contexts of the traditional rights of commons in Japanese society, from a comparative perspective involving other parts in Asia.

NGUYEN Hong Hai, Civil Code drafter, Ministry of Justice of Vietnam; former lecturer at the Hanoi Law University. He took the leading role throughout the drafting process of the 2015 Civil Code in Vietnam and was also the member of the permanent editorial team of the 2014 Law on Marriage and Family, the 2015 Civil Procedure Code, the 2015 Law on amendment, supplement of the Law on Civil Judgment Enforcement, the 2016 Law on Auction, 2020 Law on Securities and many other legal documents on the precedents of the Supreme People's Court, securities transaction, land, trade, dealing with bad debt and restructuring credit institutions, etc.

OKAWA Kenzo, Associate Professor, Setsunan University. He has been the legal advisor dispatched to Laos since 2014 by the Japan International Cooperation Agency (JICA) to support the drafting team of the Lao Civil Code, which was adopted in December 2018 and came into force in March 2020. He is the author of several academic articles written about legal reform cooperation, including "Issues of Japanese legal cooperation projects in Asia: viewed from the Assistance for Civil Code Drafting" in Yuka Kaneko eds., *Asian Civil Law in Economic Reforms*, Kobe University Publisher in 2019.

PHAM Duy Nghia, Professor, Fulbright University Vietnam, the former Dean of the Law Department of the University of Economics of Ho Chi Minh City. He is a leading legal scholar in Vietnam and is one of 12 members of the Case-Law Advisory Council at the Supreme People's Court. His recent research focuses on good governance, including perspectives on how to enhance the people's participation in policy making and enhance the efficiency, transparency and accountability of government.

RUDY Lukman, Associate Professor, Faculty of Law, Lampung University, Indonesia. He holds the positions of the Director of the Center for Law and Development and the Secretary of Institute of Research and Public Services of his university. He is also the legal counselor to the Legislation Making Committee of the Regional Representative Council (Dewan Perwakilan Daerah) of Indonesia since 2015 to present. He is a member of the drafting team on the Law on Customary Land Rights, the Law on Land, as well as the Law on Customary Rights.

SAKANO Issei, Legal Counselor, Ministry of Justice of Cambodia. He was stationed in Cambodia as a technical advisor sent by the Japan International Cooperation Agency (JICA) to the Ministry of Justice of Cambodia during the codification work of the Cambodian Civil Code from 1999 to 2011. He was also dispatched by JICA as a technical advisor to the Union Attorney General Office of Myanmar from 2014 to 2016.

SE NooRi, Ph.D. Candidate in the Graduate School of Law, Kobe University. She has been working on comparative legal study of disaster law in Japan and Korea. She is also a correspondent of the Constitutional Research Institute of the Constitutional Court of Korea.

TAKAMURA Gakuto, Doctor of Laws, Professor of Graduate School of Policy Science & College of Policy Science, Ritsumeikan University, Japan. He received the award for best academic book from the Japanese Association of Sociology of Law in 2008 as well as the Shibusawa-Claudel and Louis Vuitton Prize in 2008 for his book titled *Historical Sociology of Freedom of Association and State Imagery in France*, Keiso-shobo, 2007. He was also awarded the Prize of Fujita by the Foundation of the Tokyo Institute for Municipal Research in 2013 for his book titled *Urban Commons and City Revitalization: Community Management of the Commons and New Functions of the Law* (in Japanese), Minerva-shobo, 2012.

TAMANAHA Brian Z., John S. Lehmann University Professor, Washington University School of Law, St. Louis, U.S.A. He is a renowned jurisprudence and law and society scholar. He is the author of nine books, including his latest book titled *A Realistic Theory of Law* (2017), which received the 2019 IVR Book Prize from the International Association of the Philosophy of Law and Social Philosophy for best legal philosophy book published in 2016–2018, as well as an Honorable Mention for the 2018 Prose Awards in Law by the Association of University Presses. His book, *On the Rule of Law* (2004), has been translated into nine languages.

YANG Yashu, Doctor of Laws (Kobe University), Lecturer at Faculty of Law, Osaka Gakuin University. She has been working on the land expropriation and compensation for livelihood rehabilitation in China and Japan.

YE Naing Lin, Township Administrator of Oat-Twin Township, Taung-gu District, Bago Region, General Administration Department of the Ministry of Home Affairs of Myanmar. He is a Ph.D. candidate at the Law & Development Program of the Graduate School of International Cooperation Studies, Kobe University.

YOO Jin-Sik, Doctor of Laws (University of Tokyo). He is a professor at Jeonbuk National University Law School and specializes in administrative law, environmental law, and Japanese law.

Figures

Tables

Introduction

Purpose of this volume

Land law in Asia has faced numerous protests raised by the people claiming what they believe to be justice against the formal legal regime that institutionalize various state apparatus as a means of lawful deprivation of their land. Such formal law has been guided by the land law reform agenda of the leading development agencies such as the World Bank and the Asian Development Bank. Since as early as the rise of the development economics guided by the modernist economic theory, the land fluidization policy to promote the free transaction of land as a marketable commodity has been one of the central premises of the development policy agenda guided by these developmental financers. Modernist development economists such as Harold Demsetz, known for his epoch-marking thesis "Toward the Theory of Property Rights" (appeared in *the American Economic Review* 57(2), pp. 347–59 in 1967), have emphasized the system of absolute ownership as a fundamental institutional basis for the "development" by way of "taking-off" from a subsistence agriculture-based economy toward a high-growth economy led by industrialization. To urge developing countries to realize this catch-up, the development assistance has been focused upon land law reforms aimed at the mobilization of land from low-productivity uses to higher productivity, as typically expressed in the World Bank's policy agenda *World Bank Land Reform* in 1975.

Since the wake of neo-institutional economics in the 1990s, leading development agencies have further focused on the land law reform agenda through the structural adjustment programs that once failed in the 1980s but have revived in 1990s with a logic that the good governance and rule of law is the indispensable basis of successful adjustment, as emphasized by Ibrahim Shihata, vice president of the World Bank, in *World Bank in a Changing World* in 1991. The reform agenda often includes a typical set of state apparatus in guiding the land law design, namely, land titling via the so-called Torrens-style registration system, which finalizes the effect of land title once it is issued and excludes judicial review, the wasteland management method that enables nationalization of unregistered land without compensation, and the utilization of compulsory land expropriation procedures for private development projects, as described in the World Bank's policy agenda "Land Policy: Securing Rights to Reduce Poverty and Promote Rural Growth" issued in 2011.

The natural result is the uproar of claims by the subsistence farming populations, who are suffering from the loss of land as the result of the functioning of such state apparatus introduced by the land law reforms. A number of academic works have cast critical eyes on the phenomenon of "land grabbing" or the deprivation of land, often involving forced evictions without compensation. Many of them take an empirical approach to the problems, eventually reaching the door of the leading development agencies as the origin of the problem but are still short on pinpointing the exact legal designs in the donors' land law reform agenda, which are detrimental to sustainable land use by those who make a subsistent living on the land. This volume intends to fill this research gap, from the perspective of Asian scholars who have been the insiders of the actual scenes of law drafting and dispute resolution on land.

The ultimate aim of this volume is to identify the exact legal mechanisms causing land-related disputes in Asia, through a legal analysis on the formal designs of state apparatus established by the land law reforms that are constantly guided toward the "development" goal set by the modernist development economics aiming at the "takeoff" from the subsistence economy. Currently, under the new definition of "development" set by the "Sustainable Development Goals (SDGs)," an alternative to land law reform should be in our hand. By the collaboration of vanguard scholars who know the law, history and social reality of disputes from the inside of Asia, this volume aims at searching out such an alternative.

The authors of this volume have led at the front of comparative Asian law with a particular focus on land law, while most of them are colleagues of the Asian Law and Society Association (ALSA), an academic society that recently achieved its independence from the Law & Society Association and is one of the rare Asia-based academic associations in the field of law. In response to this joint attempt of the authors, Brian Z. Tamanaha, world-renowned for his erudite study of jurisprudence, has joined as a co-editor of this volume, as a result of his intensive interaction with these Asian authors during his stay as a visiting professor at Kobe University, Japan, in late 2019 through early 2020.

Methodology of this volume

A methodological strength of this volume lies in the combination of orthodox legal interpretation and empirical approaches of legal sociologists. This enables an extensive legal analysis across the comparative differences between countries whose formal laws follow the different legal traditions of common law and civil law. This is made possible particularly by the authors who are trained in the field of Asian legal studies, which is backed by each long historical path of "reception" of Western law since the 19th century.

Such "reception" has, however, not been a simple path of transplanting any given model but rather a "transformation" from the original models that contained certain exploitative apparatus of colonial law. Japan's modern legal history has been, for example, a typical "transformation," though it is often simply cited as one of the successful "receptions" of Western law in Asia aimed at Weberian capitalism. Particularly in the sphere of land law, Japan's legal history is characterized by modifications to the absolute nature of ownership that was once established by the formal code through the accumulation of case law, such as the prohibition of abuse of rights in order to protect customary rights, the protection of the rights of land and house lessees as the basis of their dwelling and livelihood, the denial of the legal effect of ownership registration obtained with malicious will, and the restriction of alienability of farmland and its use change toward the protection of small farmers. The public law apparatus for compulsory land acquisition have also been modified in the interface with small property rights, as well as the recognition of acquisitive prescription by private parties over national land that was once deemed as wasteland but later ceased to be publicly utilized. Behind the rapid economic growth of capitalist Japan, often known as the East Asian miracle, the works of jurists were indispensable for realizing a successful process of "transformation" of formal law.

When the same historical reflection is given to various other parts of Asia, we might be able to identify each path of legal transformation, which may suggest the opening of a door toward an alternative Asian land law for the pursuit of sustainable development.

Structure of this volume

This volume consists of four parts, each collecting the contributions by vanguard scholars from both East and Southeast Asia. Part I collects the works of scholars in the field of law and development led by Yuka Kaneko, with a particular focus on the inter-donor conflicts on land law agenda experienced by these Asian scholars during the civil code drafting in Asian socialist economic reform countries, such as Cambodia, Laos and Vietnam. Part II is the result of research collaboration led by Narufumi Kadomatsu on the issues of Asian public law with a focus on the changing judicial interpretation and scholarly opinions from the perspective of the rule of law in the developmental regimes. Part III is guided by legal sociologist Gakuto Takamura, who explores the dimensions of contemporary ownership, which deviates from the modern theory of property law. Part IV collects scholarly proposals for the future direction of land law and dispute resolution in Asia, starting with John Gillespie, who reconsiders the legitimacy of the land law agenda, and concluding with the volume's main editor Tamanaha. The following is a brief description of the contents of each chapter.

Part I contains contributions by authors who have studied the legal reforms in the socialist market reform countries such as Vietnam, Cambodia and Laos while actually taking part in legal assistance projects such as civil code drafting. In the course of Japanese legal assistance to these countries, Japan's own experience of a century-long implementation of a civil code naturally had an influence. While the Japanese civil code takes the Pandect form, with general principles providing the theoretical basis for the consistent interpretation of provisions throughout the lengthy code, such general principles have actually offered a flexible basis for judicial interpretation, acting as the cradle for case law formation that extends beyond the literal meaning of each provision, which has enabled a policy balance between the needs of capitalist land transactions and the protection of the basis of livelihoods. When such Japanese practical implementation of a code is brought to the socialist reform countries, conflict was inevitable in regard to the land law reform guided by the international development agencies toward capitalist land markets.

Chapter 1 by Yuka Kaneko first identifies the methodology of comparative law and society toward Asian land law, then goes on to a historical review of Japanese and other Asian experiences in each path of "reception" of and subsequent "transformation" from Western law. A hypothetical view is that the modern capitalist law, which started as a pursuit of the ideal of individual dignity in the early 19th century, at some later stage switched to a pursuit of the maximization of wealth, which probably occurred somewhere in the process of the formation of colonial law in Asia and Africa in the late 19th century and the process of re-importing it back to the home countries. Japan chose to receive such a model in an attempt at rapid industrialization, but case law accumulated in the later stages of emerging social conflicts that modified the formal provisions and gradually resulted in reformist legislation. Similarly, the postindependence sui generis laws in the colonized countries in Asia aimed to overcome the colonial legal apparatus of land exploitation. The contemporary land law reforms led by the international development donors reveal a fundamental resemblance to the colonial apparatus and tend to result in the same phenomena of land exploitation. The solution will be available through the search for alternative legal designs by jurists who are open to the social justice asserted in the forefront of legal disputes, to a degree that may be called the unwritten social constitution.

Chapter 2 by Issei Sakano presents the attempt made by the Japanese team to assist Cambodia's civil code drafting toward the realization of a property law regime that suits the local society, which, however, resulted in an unexpected compromise due to inter-donor conflicts in tandem with the 2001 Land Law drafting guided by the World Bank and the Asian Development Bank (ADB). One of the controversial points is the abolition of the acquisitive prescription of ownership by the Land Law after a five-year period from its coming into effect, which has resulted in the ambiguous status of the right of "*phokeah*," a traditional land right that was recognized even during the French Protectorate era and particularly utilized in the transition period after the 1989 Constitution, which is still held and transacted between the vulnerable people even after the Land Law denied its chance to be transformed into a full ownership upon the competition of prescription. The author Sakano was a member of the Japanese code drafting team and is presently the counselor to the Minister of Justice of Cambodia.

Chapter 3 by Kenzo Okawa, who joined the Japanese support for the drafting of the Laos 2020 Civil Code, describes the model conflict between donors similar to what was experienced in the drafting of the Cambodian Civil Code discussed in Chapter 2. While the Civil Code drafting team aimed at securing the land use rights of subsistence farmers by newly introducing the terminology of real property rights in the civil law tradition such as superficies and usufructs, the results are invisible due to the policy conflict with the leading donors such as the International Finance Corporation under the World Bank group, which guide the implementation of land law apparatus such as the Torrens-style title registration aimed toward the free transaction of land use rights, turning the rights into property that has the same exchange value as capitalist ownership.

Chapter 4 is by Nguyen Hong Hai, a leading member of the drafting committee of the 2015 Civil Code of Vietnam and a recipient of the Japanese legal assistance. A similar strategy to the aforementioned Lao Civil Code was suggested by the Japanese team, which intended to utilize the traditional continental terminology of emphyteusis and superficies that prevail over ownership, in order to secure the status of the "land use rights" of ordinary farmers and residents that are not clearly defined under the Land Law. Interestingly, Vietnamese code drafters took such traditional superficies for a different purpose: to rewrite the substance of "land use rights" that had been restricted under the Land Law and move them toward a new property right that is similarly alienable as capitalist ownership. Nguyen Hong Hai represents the stance of lawmakers who follow the basic policy orientation of the international development agencies that aim for industrialization through the promotion of alienation of land to higher-value added use, which is also the stance explicitly endorsed by the Communist Party's recent policy aiming at land concentration in the drive for industrialization.

Part II of this volume focuses on the land expropriation system of Asian countries, with the intention of reconsidering the legal limits of public restriction over private rights in the context of developing states, particularly by revisiting the definition of "public use/public interest" as a fundamental element of the state's lawful taking of someone's property.

Land expropriation in the classical sense of deprivation of private property by the state has a long history, since the early stage of capitalist economies that required the formation of a concretely framed formal system for the construction of infrastructure such as railways and roads as the basis of industrialization. In particular, the land expropriation systems in the civil law countries first firmly established private property rights and then legalized the deprivation of such confirmed rights, with the justification being "public use" or "public interest." It is remarkable that this system of deprivation of ownership was established in parallel with the establishment of the ownership itself.

Originally, the term "public interest" was conceptualized in tandem with a notion of use open to the general public such as railways or roads or the projects that clearly benefit the "unspecified and many" people such as dam construction. Up to the present, however, we have increasingly seen expropriation for "private use" or "private interest," which does not necessarily come under the classical concept of land expropriation. Given the variety of "private use" phenomena, a comparative approach would be meaningful.

Chapter 5 by Narufumi Kadomatsu refers to two categories of land expropriation both vigorously implemented for "private interest" in 1960s Japan. The industrial development park projects were introduced as a policy to diversify the concentration of industry away from Tokyo and was typical of state-led capitalism in terms of state expropriation for the benefit of "specific" businesses, in contrast to the "general" benefits of building infrastructure such as railways and roads. On the other hand, the New Housing and Urban Development Act, which aimed at the provision of residences to the working class population, should be deemed as a transformation of the capitalist expropriation system in the context of the welfare state. Though both of these expropriation systems for "private interest" gradually faded out in the rapid economic growth of Japan, now a new mode of expropriation systems is being revived in contemporary Japan in different contexts, such as the community welfare promotion project that intends to reactivate land use in response to the social issues that arise in the era of serious population decline. In a sense, a new context of "public interest" is being developed in postindustrial Japan toward the communization of social interests, beyond the past context of "private interest" guided by state-led capitalism.

In Korea, expropriations for "private interest" have been obviously increasing in recent years, many of which have invited lawsuits and been found illegal by the court. The tendency of the court is, however, divided according to the cases: while projects for industrial estate development similar to the aforementioned Japanese system in the 1960s have been found constitutional, the Balanced Regional Development Act was found unconstitutional. Scholarly critiques against such increase of expropriation for private purposes are recently active in Korea as well as in Taiwan, reminding us of the similar academic debates during Japan's rapid economic growth period. Chapter 6 by Jin-Sik Yoo and NooRi Se first identifies the structural characteristics of the Korean land expropriation law and then investigates a recent case of expropriation for "private interest" for the development of a resort on Jeju Island with reference to the precedents of the Constitutional Tribunal as well as scholarly debates.

Chapter 7 by Ming-Chih Lee considers the nature of "zone expropriation" in Taiwan, which has been widely applied to enable the government to comprehensively expropriate large land areas beyond the target area for a particular project with public purposes. While "zone expropriation" has been allegedly justified as a means of equal treatment among local owners, jurists have focused critical debate on the legality of such a system that inevitably includes the taking of land for "private interests" in regard to the areas taken outside the projects for public use. Lee first extends a historical review on the formation process of "zone expropriation" and then analyzes the trend of precedents and influential scholarly opinions.

Expropriation for "private interest" in mainland China has its own context of socialist ownership of the entire land. While urban land and agricultural land are put under separate systems, agricultural land is collectively owned by the farmers, which precludes nonagricultural individuals and legal entities. A private developer intending to develop rural land must first to seek a change to the land's status from collectively owned property to state-owned land, and then further seek to acquire the usage rights for such state-owned land. Such a procedure resembles land expropriation for "private interest." Concerning urban state-owned land, on the other hand, usage rights are frequently targeted by land expropriation in the same context as capitalist countries, for which "public interest" is required. However, legal control by the court seems less analytical in terms of the quality of the examination of the "public interest" requirement. Shu Jiao and Yashu Yang in Chapter 8 analyze the legislative trend and scholarly debates on this issue.

Kadomatsu in Chapter 5 and Jiao and Yang in Chapter 8 also pay attention to the issues of compensation for land expropriation based on trends, precedents and scholarly arguments, from the different perspectives of Japan and China. Compensation under capitalist law has mainly dealt with compensation for the market value of the land but has also involved different contexts, such as undervalued compensation in cases of drastic social reform as in the case of the post-WWII agricultural land redistribution in Japan; methods of calculating compensation amounts in areas where the land market does not operate; and the issues of compensation for lost livelihoods in the situation in which the market value is not sufficient to meet the requirements for the recovery of the livelihoods of the affected population.

Part III is an attempt to envisage an alternative land law regime toward a redefined "development" by way of investigating the communal property rights in Asia, held among various types of local groups of both traditional and contemporary forms, as an antithesis to the modern ownership concept (or its synonyms of individualized private property rights alienable for its exchange value, whether or not named as land use rights, superficies, or cultivation rights). Many such communal property rights show a volume of empirical evidence of successful outcomes in terms of mutual livelihood support, enhanced sustainability of environment, disaster management, etc.

Chapter 9 by Gakuto Takamura combines the historical viewpoint stemming back to the French civil revolution and the socio-legal observation of empirical facts in contemporary capitalist societies, in an attempt to establish that the modern ownership regime has included internal restrictions within the local community as an indispensable element since the very beginning. Even Japan, which is deemed as a typical example of a capitalist society that once intentionally abandoned the entirety of its pre-modern tradition and chose to implement an absolute ownership regime, has now turned to step into a new post-growth era with an emphasis on the roles played by communities.

Chapter 10 by Rudy Lukman details the tension between the judgments of the Constitutional Court and the Supreme Court in Indonesia in regard to the fate of the community-based customary rights or *adat* in general. Though the postindependence formal land regime guided by the 1960 Basic Agrarian Law has aimed at securing pre-modern *adat* rights by turning them into an individual title called *hak milik*, a form of modern individual property right, many populations in the various ethnic areas have maintained their traditional communal order, including the communal rights or *hak ulayat*, which are currently reviving due to the recognition by the Constitutional Court. The author is a legal advisor to the senators' law committee in the Indonesian parliament and has been involved in the drafting process of *adat*-related legislations.

Chapter 11 by Sachihiko Muroi offers a concise review of the historical stream of scholarly theories on the communal rights in Japan, or *Iriai-ken*, which have been succeeded from since the pre-modern period by local communities in rural areas nationwide. Despite continuous government attempts to minimize, change and ultimately eliminate the existence of such pre-modern forms of property rights, *Iriai-ken* have in fact been succeeded as the socio-economic reality up to the present, largely because of the efforts made by the scholars and jurists who devoted themselves to theoretical confrontations with hardcore capitalism and aimed toward the protection of *Iriai-ken* amid the economic growth period of Japan. The same role is expected to be played by the Asian jurists at the forefront of contemporary land dispute resolution.

Chapter 12 by Mikiko Matsumoto casts both a historical and empirical review of the transformation process of traditional rural communities in China, through the socialist collectivization by the People's Commune, the household farmland contracting system during the reformation period, and the recent corporatization under the General Provisions of Civil Law of the People's Republic of China. Her view is focused on the stable existence of the agricultural community at the bottom of the changing society, or the relationship between land and humans, that has been succeeded despite the periodic drastic changes to the formal institutions in China.

Part IV collects contributions by the leading scholars in the field of Asian land law as recommendations to guide the future directions of this field of study.

Chapter 13 is by John Gillespie, a leading scholar in the study of legal reforms in the Asian socialist reform countries. He explores the question of whether state-centered property law can create legal understandings of property that conflict with the social reality of customary land practices. By comparing two types of statutory land systems, the title registration system brought in Cambodia and the socialist land use rights in China, this chapter describes the limitation of the state-centered narratives of defining rights and duties on land, which is a sphere rather closely tied to a broad range of political, social and economic forces, and calls for an empirical search to understand how property rights are conceptualized in everyday practice.

Chapter 14 by Pham Duy Nghia, a prominent Vietnamese scholar in the field of law and development, casts a fundamental question of whether the judicial system in Vietnam, in the context of the rule of law in the party state, can offer an ultimate solution to the confrontation between the state policy and the civic claims in a rapidly changing society. By elaborating the characteristics of legal and political setting of the administrative court system in Vietnam, the author describes the limitation of the functioning of the judicial independence under the current institutional regime but holds a view that further reforms will be inevitable as the general public increasingly become aware of the implementation of their legitimate rights.

Chapter 15 by Yuka Kaneko and Ye Naing Lin looks back at the historical process of formal land law in a methodological attempt to identify the substantive nature of the "cultivation right" as the core private property right under the contemporary land law reform in Myanmar. Currently, at the front line of administrative land dispute settlement, the concept of the "cultivation right" tends to be flexibly interpreted by locally elected mediators in a setting similar to an open trial, at the interface with the social justice held within each locality. An implication is the chance that the normative substance of the formal property law can be redefined from the bottom of the society through a dispute settlement mechanism that involves public participation.

Chapter 16 by Brian Z. Tamanaha is the concluding chapter, which examines several themes raised across the chapters in this collection, guided by Karl Polanyi's *The Great Transformation* that described the fate of land as a market commodity serving for the capitalist economy. After casting the insights on the issues of subsistence versus productivity ideologies, socialist economic reforms, state expropriation of land for private use, survival of community and state law monism versus customary law, Tamanaha deliberates on the historical fallacy of land law. He then concludes with a handful of guidelines as a concrete alternative template for development organizations to replace the neoliberal land market paradigm, to help make the market for land serve society, rather than have society serve the dictates of the market.

Part I

Model conflict in land law and civil code drafting

1 Origin of land disputes

Reviving colonial apparatus in land law reforms

Yuka Kaneko

1 Introduction

Since the Asian economic crisis broke out in 1997, Asian countries have been increasingly bound by the policy dialogues led by the international development agencies such as the World Bank and the International Monetary Fund in the formulation of long-term socioeconomic development plans and in all aspects of their implementation. Legal and judicial reform has also been in this context. Its policy path is guided by the neo-institutional economics addressing the modification, instead of the abrogation, of the structural adjustment policy that was the target of criticisms in the beginning of the post-cold war period, due to its failure to solve the accumulated debts problem during the 1980s, in a good contrast to the successful economic results in Japan and other Asian countries that chose an interventionist approach referred to as the "East Asian miracle" or neo-structuralism during the same period.[1] With the slogan of "good governance" and "rule of law,"[2] the neo-institutional economics attributed the failure of the structural adjustment programs to the lack of institutional capacities in the recipient countries to fill the information asymmetry, without changing the other elements of the structural adjustment prescriptions. The result was the legal instrumentalism that reforms the law as a means of development. Even the prominent keynote speech by Amartya Sen titled "What is the Role of Legal and Judicial Reform in the Development Process?" presented at the World Bank Global Conference on Comprehensive Law and Judicial Development in 2000 was its endorsement.[3] Despite the enormous endeavors of redefining of the goal of "development" in the contexts of human development, poverty alleviation and sustainable growth pursued since the 1990s up to the present, the legal and judicial reform agenda has remained unchanged according to the Washington Consensus.[4]

The Asian economic crisis triggered a first case of the sovereign legislative power surrendered to the contract terms of the structural adjustment loans. In addition to the corporate finance, the land law was another target in such conditionalities. Land titling designed for the so-called Torrens-style registration system is, for example, the biggest focus of the donor-led land law reforms across Asia today. As emphasized by Hernando de Soto,[5] formalization of property rights has been considered one of the main pillars of the legal reform agenda that

DOI: 10.4324/9781003170600-2

invigorates the land market via land titling. Originally a British colonial creation completed in the South Australia (Torrens 1882), the Torrens-style registration system was a mighty institutional device to mobilize land as a commodity by separating the abstract title from the actual land use, by endorsing the governmental authority to finalize a title while excluding the future judicial contest. This system was often implemented in conjunction with the wasteland management method that nationalizes untitled land for the use of concession. During the colonial era, this British colonial device was also utilized in the colonies of civil law countries.[6] Even in Japan, which escaped colonial rule, the issuance of land titles (*chi-ken*) through the initial land tax reform (*chiso-kaisei*) implemented in the earliest stage of its Westernization during the 1870s was nothing other than a Torrens-style title registration system.[7] In Thailand too, the Chakri dynasty, which intended to operate large-scale plantation for export, implemented the 1901 Land Title Deed Act,[8] which was succeeded by the 1934 Civil and Commercial Code that made the Torrens-style title registration a requirement for validity of ownership.

After the colonies gained independence, more than a few countries abolished the Torrens-style title registration system and switched to a land record system that served as no more than a public notification function, as seen in the following discussion of Indonesia and Myanmar, the same as Japan. It must also be noted that most developed countries in Europe as well as the United States do not adopt a Torrens-style title registration system. In the U.S., it is implemented in only 12 of the 50 states, only as a voluntary system. Even in the United Kingdom, the Land Registration Act 1925 was implemented as a voluntary system of public notice, and even under the Land Registration Act 2002, exceptional overriding interests are still permitted without notice, which is inverse to what they introduced in Asia for the redemption of existing interests.

Today, the donors' land law reform agenda has guided many Asian countries to repeal the postindependence sui generis laws that attempted to overcome the colonial land law that separated the abstract title and actual use. Even though the Asian economic crisis was a result of a bust of speculative land market that triggered the sudden selling of Thai baht, and it could have been an opportunity toward a reregulation to prevent the recurrence of bubble and busts, the prescription provided by the development agencies was the opposite, oriented toward the deregulation for further vitalization of the land market.[9] The 2008 global financial crisis sounded another warning about this direction of legal reforms. However, the same agenda of neo-intuitionalist legal reforms have remained, and even accelerated in Asia and Africa, highlighting the relaxation of restrictions on land sales and mortgages by foreign capital, to follow the simultaneous land titling, and the promotion of wasteland grants of untitled land for foreign investments.[10]

A hypothetical view of the author is that the contemporary land law reform led by the donor agencies is a revival of the design features of colonial law. The modern capitalist law that had started a pursuit of the ideal of human dignity in the early 19th century was in some later stage swapped out to a pursuit of maximization of wealth, which probably occurred somewhere in the process of the formation of colonial law, and then reimported to the home countries.[11] A main feature was a series of state apparatus of lawful exploitation of land from actual users and passing it to higher economic value. Today, numerous land grabbing cases are tormenting the peasants around the world, and various attempts to establish the international law for their protection have resulted in nonbinding campaigns. If the contemporary land grabbing is a result of the very design of the land law reform guided by the donor agencies, and if such design is no other than the colonial model for land deprivation, it is something we can overcome by learning from the historical lessons as well as exploring the social norms asserted in the forefront of legal disputes.

Asian law scholars are entrusted to seek an alternative land law to catch up with the global trend of redefining the "development" by getting rid of the century-old model for the land mobilization as speculative commodity. It might also be an attempt to rediscover the goal once sought by the postindependence sui generis land laws in this region. This chapter intends to induce hints toward an alternative of legal reform to the donor-guided land law reforms through a quick comparative sketch. After presenting a methodological frame guided by previous studies (Section 2), the author first attempts to articulate the legal nature of the "Asian" property rights that were envisaged in the postindependence sui generis laws (Section 3); next, the common legal issues of contemporary land grabbing disputes will be investigated through a focus on the gaps between the formal apparatus of land law and the social norms asserted (Section 4); then, we will trace the changing policy ideologies in a historical axis of land law reforms (Section 5).

2 Implications from previous studies

Land law is a diverse sphere of law and necessitates the knowledge of comparative land law across jurisdictions. Comparativists have presumed a dichotomy of common law and civil law, aiming to categorize the laws of the rest of the world into either of the two. Merryman (1974) was a work among influential American comparativists who draw the common law scholars' attentions to the "ownership" concept in continental law, but he overly emphasized the absolute nature of such concept, though in the reality its modification started soon in the historical path following the initial codification. Van Erp (2008) seeks a more accurate introduction of the continental property law by focusing upon the common principles such as the separation of real rights and personal rights (*summa divisio*), the binding and exclusive effect of real rights upon third parties (*erga omnes*), and the closed list of real rights (*numerus clausus*) and its historical loosening, and the formalism in the alienation of properties. While facilitating a pragmatic comparison, however, it does not detail the policy reasons why these principles were extremely strengthened in the late 19th-century codification but then required significant modifications in the 20th century. On the other hand, Zimmermann, Visser, and Reid (2004) examined land law in Scotland and South Africa, where elements of both civil law and common law were mixed in a single country's law, but their consideration are not extended to Asian or African countries beyond the interests of "legal transplants and legal culture" where the laws of former colonized countries have been categorized according to the maps of the former suzerain countries.[12] Therefore, the essence of Asian colonial law, which converges elements of civil law and common law into what could be called an extreme capitalist law, has not been the subject of study in the mainstream of comparative law.[13]

Positioned at the opposite pole is the contribution to land law research from the viewpoint of legal anthropology. Benda-Beckmann, Benda-Beckmann and Wiber (2008) elaborated a methodology for redefining property rights that can encompass the diversity of rights, rooted in empirical observations of Asian and African societies. They criticize the instrumental use of simplified property right concepts by development economists since Demsetz (1967), and rather, consider the property rights as a dynamic relationship between property and social entities.[14] They propose a methodological framework to overcome the mistakes of development economics by reclassifying the diverse and layered nature of such relationships[15]: First, to start with an accurate comprehension of the static dogmatic designs of the formal property law, rather than simply arranging them as a "bundle of rights," they encouraged subdivisions of elements of each property right focusing on the subjects of property relation, the property objects and the substance of rights and obligations. Second, they intend to identify the dynamics of "concretized social relationships" when such formal legal systems are brought into real society by way of empirical observations of land disputes and their resolution processes. Third, they deciphered the ideology of the overall system.

This chapter, too, will strive to understand the substantive nature of Asian land laws from the viewpoint of dynamic relationships between land and social entities, as suggested by Benda-Beckmann et al. However, the following points are to be supplemented when implementing their methodology. First, there is a concern that, though a number of studies conducted on land conflict with a keen attention upon the specific contexts,[16] they tend to move into the second-stage description of the dynamic problems without necessarily gaining an accurate grasp of the characteristics of the substantive law in the first stage. The first step is to solidify the dogmatic design of property law, so that the understanding of the dynamics of the second step will become clearer.

Second, attention should also be paid to a historical background behind the current dynamics. Tracing the history of the static designs of formal law with political ideology behind them may help to refine the third-stage ideological studies. In this sense, Hooker (1986) was a monumental work in the historical Asian law study that cast a view to the process of elimination of pre-modern formal laws through the penetration of colonial law in the Southeast Asia, but it remained silent on the paths taken by the postcolonial independence nations in formulating each sui generis law up to the present. On the other hand, attention is drawn to the legal historical approach that modern Japanese jurisprudence has continually relied upon when investigating the origin of current social issues by tracing the process of reception of Western law and the modification thereto, such as the withholding of the once introduced Torrens-style title registration system for the early-modern land tax reform, a process of lease rights transformed into real rights, judicial precedents to articulate the commons rights, as pioneer works of Asian law that has confronted the ideologies included in modern Western law.[17]

Third, the base values for the third-stage ideological analysis of Benda-Beckmann et al. should be clarified. This is in other words a work to articulate the different definitions of the term "development" as the ultimate goal for the donors' intervention into the legal reform scenes of developing countries. The mainstream development economics has attempted to evaluate the results of land law reform based on the capital increase linked to the GDP growth; there are other studies that have focused on microeconomic indicators such as the households' income increase or agricultural productivity to evaluate the outcomes of land law reforms on individual level in the context of human development and poverty alleviation.[18] In either approach taken by these economists, the goals are set from the outside of the local society according to a modern view of socioeconomic "evolution." The value used in this chapter as the lawyer's standpoint is the "satisfaction" of the local population, reflecting the normative sense of justice of those who make actual living on the land disputed. This is a logical consequence of the Sustainable Development Goals (SDGs), where the term "development" cannot continue to be a uniform agenda of linear evolution toward a given value but can take a variety of satisfactory choices of those who are the addressees of the reforms.

3 Nature of Asian land rights – divergence from the modern ownership

3.1 Land as market commodity vs. subsistent use

As the first step of methodological approach guided by Benda-Beckmann et al. in the previously mentioned, the following attempts to articulate the substantive nature of the formal property rights of Asian countries as the result of each postindependence historical path, based on the language of comparative law as a means. Land law changes in Japan will be first reviewed to describe the changing characteristics of "ownership" concept since when it was brought in the Westernization era, and then the land law reforms in Indonesia, Cambodia, Myanmar, China and Vietnam will be reviewed to identify some common elements in the legal design.

The subjects of rights, or to whom the formal law privileges the control of land is already a clear reflection of policy ideology. As Benda-Beckmann et al. criticized, Demsetz (1967) divided property rights into four categories only based on the subject of rights, namely unowned land, state-owned land, group-owned land, and privately owned land, which is not only incomprehensive, but also useless, since it lacked the explanation of policy implications behind.

The early-modern capitalist ideology that was pioneered by the Napoleon Code was said to be started from the denial of an intermediate feudal power by contrasting the state and individuals. But did all traditional communal order disappear under the stigma of pre-modern? In the early stages of the civil revolution, the small farmers in France who established ownership by removing feudal rule, either with or without compensation, could maintain local customs for collective use at least in the context of inherent restrictions on ownership under art. 544 of the Civil Code, and the French Cour de Cassation approved customary laws.[19] When Italy adopted the Napoleonic Civil Code, common right (*usi civici*) was maintained. Communal lands also continued in the Stein-Hardenberg Reforms in eastern Germany, while some areas were redistributed to individual ownership. Thus, the modern law did not start with the thorough discard of the existing land regime that constituted an indispensable part of livelihood, or we may say that a "subsistence" ideology was embodied in the modern code, which centered on the "productivity" ideology based upon the competition between wealthy individuals.[20]

As the capitalism proceeded, in the latter half of the 19th century, policy priority shifted to the promotion of transactions between corporations, which guided the commercialization of codes in the European continent, and the codification in the Asian colonies. Such a commercial ideology was the very target that many Asian countries attempted to overcome through the introduction of each sui generis land law that introduced a new concept of land right whose core subject was the individual farmers, while excluding the corporations. Asian socialist countries attempted this "subsistence" goal by the collectivization of individual rights, but in the 1980s, households were restored as the subject of land rights, as in the contractual farming rights in China and Vietnam.

As for the object of rights, land has diverse nature by use as residential, agricultural or industrial land. The ex post facto approval of enclosure of farmland via legislation and precedents formation in 18th century England was indeed an example of forcible rewriting of the land use by formal law,[21] and similarly, colonial law legalized the enclosure of farmland through a series of institutional devices such as the wasteland nationalization of lands lacking a registered title,[22] and the same phenomenon is repeated in the contemporary land grabbing cases.

As for the substance of land rights, the absoluteness, exclusivity, and perpetuality of modern ownership was once established in Art. 1 of the French Declaration of the Rights of Man and of the Citizen. The distance from such a modern ownership concept is the axis of comparative examination, as the rights both named "ownership" can have differing legal effect, as well as the cases in which rights are established under a name other than ownership but have equivalent substance. "Absoluteness" of a right means to definitively enjoy the freedom to occupy, use and dispose of the property in the sense that it is not subject to contests or restrictions by others. There are some jurisdictions, including Japan, which have introduced certain control over the freedom of ownership (e.g., controls of sales, lease and use change) particularly for the sake of farmland protection. "Exclusivity" of a right is the exclusive control of property enforceable against others (*erga omnes*), accompanied by real right claims (*rei vindicatio*), which are invoked against infringements.

Rights that included absoluteness and exclusivity are referred to as real rights (*ius in re*, *droit des biens*, *Sachenrecht*, rights in rem). Especially the continental civil codes have adopted the closed number of real rights (*numerus clausus*) to maximize the freedom of ownership by narrowing down the categories of real rights that can restrict the ownership. The question is what kind of real rights should be included in such a closed list. Many of the civil codes have permitted certain static land relations that had been succeeded from pre-modern time, such as emphyteusis (perpetual tenant farming rights), superficies and servitudes, but with a variation. The right of possession is also included in the list in some jurisdictions, in connection to the system of acquisitive prescription, an equivalent system to the adverse possession in common law. A policy implication of expanding the target of these real rights against ownership is the protection of subsistent land users who failed to obtain the ownership. In France, since many small farmers gained ownership status, the 1790 decree prohibited the establishment of perpetual type of real rights that restrict ownership, while ordinary tenant farming were treated as no more than a personal right of lease. Also in areas where civil revolution took a path of compromise, such as under the Stein-Hardenberg Reforms in eastern Germany, use of ordinary tenant farming was frequent as the feudal lords embarked on agricultural business as a result of half of the land remaining with them as of the ownership redistribution to the farmers. Japan's modern land taxation reform in the 1870s established ownership based upon the ability to pay taxes, and many of the perpetual tenant farming rights that had flourished in pre-modern times were converted to ordinary tenant farming rights.[23] Thus, the civil codes attempted to make ownership absolute, by limiting the other property rights both in law and practice, turning the status of tenant farmers to a lessee as a mere personal right.

On the other hand, common law countries maintained the tradition of feudal system, and the concept of "ownership" does not appear. In the U.K., there are various types of title (such as perpetual freehold and periodic leasehold), and the definiteness of title is also diverse; in addition, unlike the *numerus clausus* principle of continental law, there are various types of interests that threaten the exclusiveness of title. Fee simple absolute under Anglo-American law is considered to be equivalent to "ownership" under continental law, but restrictions from a variety of interests can also remain. Conversely, even for a leasehold, titles with a strong level of definitiveness and a high degree of exclusivity function as a basis for economic activity comparable to ownership under continental law. Although reorganization of this complicated English land law is difficult, the role of the registration system is emphasized to facilitate searching by disclosing all information as-is (the mirror principle).[24] Thus, the Anglo-American law retains a static existing order that suggests a "subsistence" ideology in the base, while pursuing the "productivity" policy needs by developing the mobility of leasehold on the surface of statistic base order. Such multilayer construction is in contrast to the single-layered system of the ownership established by the continental codes, which have guided the ideology of "productivity" by minimizing other property rights to disturb the ownership.

It should be noted that the land law brought to Asia during the colonial era was a hybrid of continental law and Anglo-American law. In many cases, elements have been inherited from the continental civil codes, including the establishment of the ownership whose subject of rights included both individuals and corporations while excluding communal groups; the commoditization of both farmland and residential land as the object of transactions; the absolute freedom to dispose and the exclusivity as represented by *erga omnes* and *rei vindicatio*. Property rights that bind the freedom of ownership are minimized through the principle of *numerus clausus*. On the other hand, however, the colonial land laws rely on the Torrens-style title registration system that was developed in British colonies as a means to establish the ownership. If England's registration system is a publication of rights as-is with ambiguity regarding their absoluteness and exclusivity, the Torrens-style registration system in the colonies was a device that abstractly established the land rights that were raised to the heights of absoluteness and exclusivity by the continental style civil codes brought to colonies. This system design of colonial law was a sophisticated instrument that mobilized land as an abstract object of investment and encouraged capital accumulation and had more affinity with the "speculative" ideology than with the "productivity" ideology.

Land law in the postindependence Asian countries began with the aim of establishing a new land right concept breaking away from the abstract modern ownership that is separated from the actual use. This attempt has, however, not been free from the remaining influence of the colonial law. The former British colonial countries have embarked on the land reforms to overcome the layered construction of the Anglo-American land law by establishing the single-layered ryotwari proprietorship for the personal cultivators, but often resulted in producing new layers of tenants lack formal tenure. The 1960 Basic Agrarian Law of Indonesia replaced the volume on property rights of the Dutch Civil Code that has been applied since 1848 as the first arrived Napoleon Code in Asia, but its new regime centering on the individual right concept *hak milik* has only endorsed the governmental exploitation of the customary land regimes in the entire archipelago. Perhaps, by reinvestigating the legal nature of these Asian land rights, we may reach the original ideal envisaged in the postindependence reforms, as well as the obstacles in legal designs that have invited difficulties in realizing it.

3.2 Revising the numerus clausus*: Japan's Civil Code*

We would like to start with Japanese law, even though it is regarded as a rare example of an Asian country voluntarily accepting Western law, as a desperate attempt to avoid being colonized by catching up with the "productivity" ideology held among the Western powers. But the history of Japanese land law can be described as a process of transformation from the once established capitalist law for land mobility to a regime of land security incorporating the "subsistent" ideology. The initial system of land titles under the land tax reform carried out in the 1870s was nothing other than the Torrens-style title registration system, as the Asian colonial standard of the era, while on the other hand, many farmers fell to the status of ordinary tenant farmers, opening the gap between titles and reality.[25] Then, Part II of the current 1899 Civil Code, which later affected China's

1929 Civil Code and South Korea's 1958 Civil Code, introduced a continental property law regime of the absolute ownership (art. 206), with the principle of *numerus clausus* (art. 175). Superficies, emphyteusis, and easements were defined as real rights against ownership, but their substances are limited.[26] The fact that emphyteusis was designed as the target of sales and sublease (art. 272) impresses with the "productivity" ideology of the Asian colonial law.

However, the Civil Code has also left traces of compromise with the "subsistence" ideology. On the eve of the enactment of the current 1899 Civil Code, the former 1890 Civil Code drafted by the French scholar Gustave E. Boissonade had a crushing effect on the "subsistence" ideology and influenced some of the drafters of the current 1899 Civil Code.[27]

One example is that Boissonade's 1890 Civil Code excluded the Torrens system, and the current 1899 Civil Code succeeded his stance.[28] It chose the principle of intention-based transfer of real rights (art. 176), resulting in the limited effect of registration to the mere publicity effect to third parties (art. 177). This was even an obvious deviation from the German approach, that was exemplified by the Japanese drafters of the Civil Code, since the German law lets a bona fide purchaser who relies upon the registration prevail even when the original sales contract is invalid. The Japanese code drafters had already learned the severe outcomes of the Torrens-style title registration system, which had encouraged abstract land trading too remote from the actual fact of cultivation.

It is also noteworthy that the Japanese drafters of the current Civil Code specified the "right of possession" as one of the real rights (art. 180). This is often criticized as a mistake committed by Kenjiro Ume, one of the drafters, but it seems to be another influence of Boissonade. Ume (1896) argued that while there have been opposing opinions since ancient times concerning the nature of possession as a fact or as a right, the possessory right expressed in this Article summarizes all of the rights that can be entertained for the law to protect possession. As aforementioned, the gap between registered owners and actual cultivation was remarkable since the distribution of land titles carried out in the early Meiji land tax reform. Boissonade's 1890 Civil Code is known for certain deviations from the French Napoleon Civil Code, probably as the efforts to strengthen the status of vulnerable populations in social transition. He formed the lease as a real right. He also constituted the acquisitive prescription system as a presumptive evidence based on the possessory right of the possessor, rather than on the negligent management on the side of the owner. He also strongly asserted the need of a special law that recognizes a perpetual emphyteusis right, opposing the stance of French Code to limit its duration. Perhaps Ume noticed the radicality of Boissonade's acquisitive prescription as a bridge to ownership for ordinary tenant farmers who once failed to obtain an ownership title and were denied a perpetual emphyteusis right, but still may have a chance to establish ownership by way of the acquisitive prescription without proving the owner's negligence. It can be said that Ume chose to follow this "subsistence" ideology of Boissonade and dared to recognize the "possessory right" as a real right, a right in a transitional period toward the ownership.

In addition, two provisions must be touched on as points of compromise with the "subsistence" ideology in the current Civil Code: the rights of common that have the nature of co-ownership (art. 263) and the rights of common that do not have the nature of co-ownership (art. 294), which officially acknowledged the collective rights of customary communities (*Iriai-ken*). Japanese traditional villagers have jointly managed areas such as mountain forests, water sources, pastures, and coasts as the essential foundation of their livelihoods, which has been conceived as collective ownership that differs from the usual concept of joint ownership in the sense that it is not subjected to division into individual shares. The fact that the Japanese Civil Code explicitly recognized the concept of *Iriai-ken* against the spirit of modern Western law that stood to deny feudal institutions was one expression of the "subsistence" ideology. However, the Civil Code only mechanically applies the "joint ownership" provisions to the *Iriai-ken* and does not actively protect them, which implied an attitude of planning to eventually disassemble the *Iriai-ken*, due to the joint owner's right to demand the partition of property share (art. 256).

In this way, with a slight appeasement, Japan's modern law started with a "productivity" ideology, but it was soon exposed to severe social friction and gradually saw the revisions through the accumulation of judicial precedents and special legislations based on the "subsistence" ideology. One of the most fundamental revisions was the constraint of the freedom of disposal, a core element of modern ownership, by the 1952 Farmland Law to secure the principle of ownership by cultivators, which has constituted the fundamental basis of Japan's farmland management up to the present. It was to confirm the result of a bold land redistribution implemented immediately after the Second World War that expropriated the land of absentee owners and established the ownership of tenant farmers. The Law inaugurated a democratic control of farmland-ownership, in which the right to dispose of farmland was entrusted to the permit system by the farmland committees consisting of representatives from the local community.[29]

Another aspect of the revision by special legislations to the Civil Code has been the emergence of the concept of "leasehold" (*shakuchi-ken*) as a real right. Boissonade was aware of the painful social reality of tenants who were evicted from homes or farmland upon the sale of land-ownership, as discussed earlier. The drafters of the current Civil Code rejected Boissonade's idea to construct the lease as a real right, but still they introduced a registrable real estate lease that could be asserted against a new owner upon such registration (art. 605). In real practice, the landlord class rarely cooperated in the registration procedure of real estate leases, and the notorious phenomenon of "earthquake sales" that took advantage of tenants' distress in disasters and forced them to vacate became a social problem. The accumulation of case law for realistic relief from this problem prompted the appearance of a series of special laws.[30] In particular, the 1922 Land Lease Law established a new *shakuchi-ken* concept as a real right that treated real estate leases the same as the real right *superficies* by integrating them under its name, regardless of whether they were registered or not, imposed an obligation on landowners to provide "justifiable grounds" for evicting or refusing to renew a contract and granted the protection by *rei vindicatio* or real right claims. Indeed, the same "subsistence" ideology that was intended by Boissonade was, after the passage of several decades, able to revise from the outside the Civil Code that favored ownership.

On the other hand, however, it is ironic that *shakuchi-ken*, which had its position assertible against ownership, saw its value increase as a transferable right in the subsequent economic reality and became a hotbed for the "speculative" capitalism.[31] In the urban areas of Japan today, as speculative money accelerated transactions in these leaseholds rather than the ownership, the value of *shakuchi-ken* is said to range from 60 to 80 percent of the land value. Criticism of high land values provided grounds for the regression of leasehold protections since the 1992 Law on Land and Building Leases, but such arguments missed the fact that there are two coexisting contexts that are named *shakuchi-ken* but are completely different in substance. Even if the protection of leaseholds is regressed, speculative money will only return to ownership. As long as the system surrounding land transactions tolerates a "speculative" ideology, the turbulence in land prices will not be eliminated.

In sum, land law under Japan's Civil Code was the product of "productivity" ideology, which started with the acceptance of modern ownership concept of the Western law, but at the same time, the demand has been strong for a "subsistence" ideology that protects the foundations of livelihoods. It is true that such ideology has guided the hundred-year history of modifications to the substance of real rights, such as limiting the legal effects of the land registrations that deviate from reality, establishing the farmland-ownership regime under the mutual control, protecting the possessory rights that lead to acquisitive prescription, recognizing the collective right of *Iriai-ken*, and protecting *shakuchi-ken* or leasehold rights as the sustainable basis of living.

3.3 Indonesia's experiment: integrating the modern law and adat

Indonesia's land law has been a hard experiment to establish a formal land regime in the interface with varieties of traditional land orders often generally referred to as *adat*. Modern ownership concept arrived in the Dutch East Indies in 1848 through the introduction of the 1838 Dutch Civil Code, the earliest in Asia. Legal pluralism resulted first, with colonial law applied to the colonists and local laws applied to the local people, but the 1870 royal decree of land nationalization coupled with the Torrens-style land registration realized the enclosure by a wasteland management method that automatically deemed unregistered land as state land.[32] After independence, the National Law Development Agency was established with the aim of overcoming the legal pluralism, and after an aborted attempt of drafting a new civil code,[33] the 1960 Basic Agrarian Law was enacted to repeal the Part III of the Dutch-oriented Civil Code (excluding collateral provisions) as well as the 1870 Farmland Law. Although there is a criticism that the Basic Agrarian Law resulted in the succession of Western individual property rights and downplayed the customary land orders that have existed in vast areas of Indonesia, nevertheless, the attitude of trying to overcome the modern ownership by redefining its substance is noteworthy.

When we read the basic principles in Chapter I of the Basic Agrarian Law, the "productivity" ideology that aims at the nation's economic independence seems to override the "subsistence" ideology that values the customary orders. While it declares the prohibition of land concentration (art. 8), prohibition of foreign land-ownership (art. 9) and the principle of ownership by actual cultivators (art. 10), the orientation toward state-led economic development is also clear, such as in the declaration of the state's land management authority for the welfare of entire people as national family (art. 2), that land rights are subject to social functions (art. 6), and the aim of increasing production and improving livelihoods (art. 13). Though the government can delegate to customary communities the right of land administration (art. 2, (4)), the collective rights of such customary communities (*hak ulayat*) are recognized to the extent permitted by law (art. 3). Detailed policy balancing is left to the formulation of land use plans (art.14).

Chapter II of the Basic Agrarian Law has established seven categories of rights over land (art. 16), according to the *numerus clausus* principle (art. 53). They basically correspond to the real rights in the continental law but have certain peculiarities. They are *hak milik*, which corresponds to the ownership; *hak guna usaha*, which corresponds to an emphyteusis; *hak guna bangunan*, which corresponds to a superficies; *hak pakai* as a lease right for commercial use; *hak sewa* or a lease right for the construction of buildings; *hak membuka tanah* or a possessory right for clearers of land; and *hak menungut hasil hutan* or a right to collect forest produce.

Regarding the subject of rights, only Indonesian "citizens" are the subject of *hak milik* (art. 21 (1)), while corporations can only be the subject of such right to the extent defined by the State (art. 21 (2)), and the acquisition of such rights by foreign investors is prohibited (art. 21 (3)-(4)). The subjects of *hak guna usaha* or emphyteusis, and *hak guna bangunan* or superficies are limited to Indonesian citizens and corporations established in Indonesia (art. 30, 36). Foreign citizens and companies can only be the subjects of *hak pakai* and *hak sewa* (art. 42, 45).

The Basic Agrarian Law is firm on the individualism inherited from the Western law, while being silent on the legal status of the traditional family clans or customary communities. The Law explicitly refers to a path to converting customary land rights into a *hak milik* based on government regulations (art. 22), which reflect the policy stance to divide the communal collective regime into individual stakes (*hak milik adat*). Given the previously mentioned *numerus clausus* principle, the Basic Agrarian Law reveals an approach of eventually dissolving the collective rights *hak ulyat* into one of the individual property rights, while including only the traditional rights of land clearers' individual possession *hak membuka tanah* and an individual use of forest products *hak menungut hasil hutan* in the closed list of real rights.

Hak malik is, however, not a simple copy from an ownership. Its substance is expressed as a "hereditary right and is the strongest and fullest right one can have on land that may be possessed by a citizen" (art. 20 (1)), though the right of disposal is subject to government regulations (art. 20 (2) and art. 26). In addition, the use of land by persons other than the owner is restricted by government regulations (art. 24), which represents the "subsistence" ideology based upon the prohibition on land concentration (art. 8) and the principle of ownership by cultivators (art. 10).

We can notice that "productivity" ideology is envisaged in the other real rights rather than the main right *hak milik*. *Hak guna usaha* or emphyteusis on farmland, which deviates from the principle of ownership by cultivators, are only permitted over state-owned land (art. 28). It is a fixed-term cultivation right limited to the use for profit via agricultural, fishery or livestock purposes (art. 28 (1)). The period is normally 25 years, with a maximum of 60 years even if renewed (art. 29). The smallest area that can be subject to a right is five hectares, and it is also possible to set over areas exceeding 25 hectares if the capital and technology are available (art. 28 (2)). The *hak guna usaha* is transferable (art. 28 (3)). In view of the fact that the subject of *hak guna usaha* is open to corporations, but the object is limited to the state land, we can recognize this right as a basis for large-scale agricultural concession that is reminiscent of the forced cultivation system promoted during the colonial period when Dutch colonists developed an emphyteusis right (*erfpacht*) evoked from British colonial law as a method of expediting economic exploitation while mitigating local resistance to direct nationalization. *Hak guna usaha* inherited this approach, which has carried the risk of conflict between the state-led development and customary orders, as is evident in today's Sumatra land recovery conflict.

Hak guna bangunan also embodies the "productivity" ideology rather than the "subsistence" ideology of individual residential ownership. Its term is usually 30 years, and the maximum is 50 years after renewal (art. 35 (2)). The right is also transferable (art. 35 (3)) and is open to corporations (art. 37). On the other hand, the transferability of *hak pakai* is not envisioned in principle, but it is possible if agreed to in the initial contract (art. 43). Whereas, the *hak sewa* lease right for constructing buildings is a land use right that can only be established for the purpose of owning a building on private land (art. 44), lost along with the loss of the building, and its transferability is not envisioned.

To summarize, the two-sided policy ideology is remarkable behind the closed list of real rights under the Basic Agrarian Law. On the one hand, it raises a flag for the "subsistence" ideology by creating the concept of *hak milik* as a livelihood base for small farmers, but on the other hand, the other real rights such as *hak guna usaha* and *hak guna bangunan* are, conversely, transferable and designed as an instrument of a "productivity" ideology. Even though foreign investors lack the access to these transferable rights, if the deregulation of the *hak pakai* land-use right progresses, it becomes an opening for foreign investors to enter into land transactions.

3.4 Remaining layered land order in Myanmar: private rights subject to state's conditions

Postindependence land law reform in Myanmar under the 1953 Land Nationalization Act was another example of the ownership-by-cultivator approach, but its legal design feature has been scarred by the British colonial law. In particular, the legal nature of the land cultivation right established by the Act succeeded the vulnerable design feature of the colonial property right "landholder's right" under the 1879 Land and Revenue Act, which brought in the British multilayer structure of land regime to Burma, which is still inherited by the donor-guided contemporary land law reform under the 2012 Farmland Law.

The pre-modern Burmese legal code *Dhamatthat* during the dynasty era had had secured the definitive formal titles (*myay thay*) such as *Bo Ba Pain* or land title established by holding for generations, as well as various defeasible titles in the transition toward definitive ones (*myay sheng*),[34] but the colonial law made the farmers' status simply into tenancy-like "landholder's rights," instead of using the term "proprietor" (ownership) used in the Ryotwari system in India.[35] Individuals who continually occupied the land and paid taxes for 12 years were the subject of "landholder's right," either themselves or through employees or tenant farmers, and the object of the right was cultivated land, while the substance of the right was expressed as "inheritable, transferable, perpetual use and occupation right" (sec. 7–8 of the 1879 Act); the right was established as an exclusive title through the Torrens-style title registration system after the objection procedure within five years (sec. 15–17). On the other hand, landholder's right was a vulnerable right in the sense that it was easily forfeited to the state on the grounds of delinquency in land tax payments (sec. 8) or if occupation was abandoned (sec. 11). This could not be a modern ownership, nor "fee simple absolute" in British law, but more like a right of tenancy that carried various conditions of compulsory termination, which the state as the ultimate landowner in the multilayer structure of land regime imposed from policy purposes. However, since it was a transferable right, it invited the land mobility through sales and provided for mortgage and caused a remarkable concentration of lands into financial investors within a few decades.[36]

After Burma's independence, the 1953 Land Nationalization Act (sec. 4) restricted the transfer of land and imposed a prohibition on the land concentration (sec. 5), thus colored with the "subsistence" ideology. The registration system ceased its function as a means of establishing final titles and turned to be a new system called the "land record," which was equivalent to the publicity effect of registration that was chosen by Japan and Indonesia after abolishing the Torrens system registration as aforementioned. It also excluded the term "landholder's right" and instead created a new right for cultivation use (sec. 9). The subject of this new cultivation right was limited to farmers, the object of the right was farmland, and the substance of the right included freedom to occupy and profit from cultivation, and to dispose of land within the agricultural purposes under a system of permits from the local farmland management committee. While such restriction of farmland disposal was equivalent to Japan's 1952 Farmland

Act and the *hak milik* under Indonesia's 1960 Basic Agrarian Law meant for the title-by-cultivator principle, unlike the ownership-based structure of Japan and Indonesian laws, the legal nature of Burmese new right followed that of the British colonial landholder's right, in that it retained the skeleton of the British multilayered land regime in which the upper right of the state controls the individual cultivator's rights with various conditions of compulsory termination: namely, the forfeiture in cases of a violation of the restrictions on transfer, abandonment of cultivation, tax delinquency, ceasing agriculture or degradation of land (sec. 11 and 29–32). This limited nature of the cultivation right allowed the government's large discretion to implement the notorious compulsory production system during the Burmese-style socialist era.

After the transition to civilian rule under the 2008 Constitution, the 1953 Act was abolished by the 2012 Farmland Law, which initiated the nationwide simultaneous implementation of the land titling, and the 2012 Vacant, Fallow and Virgin Land Management Act, which reinstated the method for waste land management. The 2012 land law reform was indeed a revival of the British colonial era two-stage exploitation structure.

The 2012 Farmland Law devoted a chapter to the introduction of "cultivation rights" (*loat paing kwin*) and declared the basic principle that "the State as original owner of all lands, giving permission for farming in conformity with this law and bylaws, rules and regulations of this law so that agricultural production capacity is developed" (sec. 3 (d)), which explicitly emphasizes the "productivity" ideology. As for the subjects of the right, in addition to the heads of farmers' households who have legally occupied and cultivated land under the former 1953 Land Nationalization Act, juridical entities such as government agencies and companies are newly admitted (sec. 6), as well as the joint ventures with foreign investors (sec. 9(f)). A question here is how to prove the "lawful occupation and cultivation" for households to establish *loat paing kwin*, while such burden of proof is not required for newly admitted investors. The conflict between the cultivation rights of farmers and investors is simply left to the judgment of the farmland management committees (sec. 22–25). The substance of *loat paing kwin* is characterized by the rights of possession, use and profit from cultivation, and dispose via sale and purchase, security, lease, and transfer (sec. 9(a) and (b)); however, the state may rescind the right on the grounds of nonpayment of tax, abandonment of cultivation, breach of registration obligations, violation of permits for nonagricultural uses, or violation of permits for changing crops (sec. 12, 13 and 19). Thus, the design framework of a British layered land regime with the state control through compulsory termination has been inherited from the 1876 Land and Revenue Act and the 1953 Land Nationalization Act to the 2012 Farmland Law.

Thus, both colonial law apparatus of the difficult land titling system coupled with wasteland management system and the layered construction of a cultivation right under the state control through compulsory termination were succeeded from the British colonial law to the 2012 land law and have resulted in the numerous land disputes raised by the farming population in the present time.

3.5 Clashing urban and rural land regimes: socialist market economies

As Asian socialist countries gradually progressed to market economies from the end of the 1980s, a feature has been the duality on the admission of land alienability between rural and urban areas. China promoted the farmland management contract system by farming households in rural villages under the land regime of collective ownership; in urban areas, the concept of a "land use right," which referred to the British fixed-term leasehold, was first introduced in areas such as the Shenzhen Special Economic Zone as an expedient method for mobilizing land under the socialist system. This concept of "land use right" reminds us of the colonial utilization of a multilayered land regime as aforementioned, such as *Erfpacht* in Dutch East Indies and the landholder's right in British colony Burma. But as the gap between urban and rural systems enlarged, the fierce clashes between two systems gradually occurred at the borders between cities and farming villages.[37] This conflict finally led to China's 2007 Property Law, which systematically placed, under its *numerus clausus* list, a series of real rights to be created over the state or collective ownership, namely, the farmland contract management right, the right to use land for construction and the right to use land for residence. However, in real practice, the conflicts between private rights are continuing at the borders between urban and rural lands, where urban land use rights drive out the contract management rights.

Vietnam also has the same contradiction. In response to the 1992 Constitution's reference to "land use rights" as a banner head of reform, the 1993 Land Law provided for a dual system of "land use right" for farmers and "land lease" for commerce and industry. However, the legal nature of this "land use right" was confused by expectations about whether it was synonymous with the Chinese-style freely transferable fixed-term leasehold. The 1993 Land Law was originally intended as a binary structure to maintain restrictions on the transfer of "land use rights" over agricultural land, but the confusion was added by the 1998 amendment of Land Law, which recognized a "land lease" on farmland that is transferable to corporations. The 2003 Land Law reduced the difference between "land use rights" and "land leases" over liberalized transfers, which is continued by the current 2013 Land Law.

Japan's official assistance for the Vietnam's drafting of Civil Codes in socialist reform countries has experienced a series of policy conflicts.[38] Vietnam's 2004 Civil Code was unable to keep pace with this rapid development of the Land Law and barely incorporated the German style general provisions and a special chapter on land use rights into the basic Institutiones code structure that was inherited from the French colonial era. Then, the 2014 Civil Code centered on the introduction of Pandekten system, which separates real rights from personal rights, and regarded the "land use right" under the Land Law as a "superficies," one of the real rights created over the state-owned land. A unique attempt by the drafters of Vietnam's Civil Code was to utilize the concept of "superficies" to cover all existing concepts under the Land Law: land use rights of farming households over farmland, farmland lease rights for corporations and land lease rights in cities. Such an attempt of integration of plural legal concepts seems to be the reflection of the aforementioned Japan's experience of developing the *shakuchi-ken* concept to strengthen the status of subsistent land users.[39] But the intention of the Vietnamese code drafters was driven more by "productivity" ideology as introduced in Chapter 4 of this book. The evaluation on the validity of this reform should await the outcomes in the real practice as to whether these newly defined private rights will lead to the resolution of land disputes.

4 Land conflicts – subsistence ideology in defense

After identifying certain common characteristics of the postindependence Asian land rights, next, this section intends to detect the origins of roaring land disputes in today's Asia. Due to the constraint of space, a focus will be on Cambodia in the aftermath of the introduction of the 2001 Land Law supported by the ADB's agricultural policy reform loan (TA2591-CAM) extended together with the World Bank and Germany, known as resulting in a wide-scale deprivation of lands.

4.1 Land titling

Today, the land law reforms in Asia promoted by the international donors have an aim of first and foremost implementing the land titling through the establishment of the Torrens-style title registration system. The core of this is a device for effectively transferring title with definiteness and exclusiveness. The definiteness of title is expected to exclude future disputes regarding the validity of title. Even if there is an error in a registry entry, subsequent transactions will be validly established as if the right had existed as the effect of the registration ("statutory magic"). This is contrasted with the perfection effect in German registration law, which is a protective system that validates transactions by bona fide third parties who trust the appearance of the registration, but Torrens-style registration in Asia since colonial time has been a system that creates new title through the formative power of the administrative act of making entries in the registry, eliminating the discrepancies between the registry and actual land use, and the subjective knowledge of third parties are irrelevant. The exclusivity of title has the effect of eliminating any preexisting interests in the land unless they are publicly notified in the registry. Mistakes in the state's management of the registry are dealt with through a compensation system.

Torrens-style title registration has been a difficult hurdle for the farming class who have continued cultivation for generations but do not have documentary evidence, and on the contrary, it is beneficial to the applications by investors who possess deeds such as purchase contracts. The 2001 Cambodian Land Law is a typical example, where the land titling project, despite its redistributive policy slogan of "Land of Their Own," resulted in the roaring protests. This was a result of the design of the Land Law (art. 29, art. 30, art. 38), which lays down alternative requirements as the hurdles for obtaining a title registration, namely, either five years of continuous, peaceful, uncontested and explicit possession of the land, or the purchase with consideration. Investors can easily prevail by presenting a land purchase contract. Since the Land Law does not recognize the acquisitive prescription, which reminds us of a revival of the colonial law,[40] a farmer who once failed to establish his title can have no further chance to claim his title as the effect of the Torrens-style registration and destined to be evicted as an unlawful occupant.

Though common law lawyers argue that farmers can instead claim the possessory right that the Land Law constituted as a real right (art. 29), such an argument lacks an understanding of the limited nature of a possessory right under the Law, which is deprived of the chance to be developed into ownership due to the abolition of the acquisitive possession system.[41]

4.2 Enclosure by waste land management

Waste land management is a method in which land that was not registered during a land titling project is automatically regarded as state-owned land and offered as concessions to private investors. It was a means of colonial land exploitation utilizing the feudal regalian doctrine.[42] But in the contemporary donor assistance for land law reforms, waste land management is endorsed as a means of advancing land use from subsistent to industrial uses, and even preferred to the compulsory land expropriation procedure that necessitates a legal compensation, since the waste land management method enables a cost-saving means of land eviction without compensation payment.

However, the legitimacy of this method is seriously questioned. Quite a few cases of land conflicts in Asian countries are attributable to waste land management, or known more as "land grabbing," where the government, military or police physically remove farmers from the land, or through criminal trespass charges, which should be called a modern version of enclosure.[43]

The 2001 Cambodian Land Law was a typical example of the donor-oriented introduction of the wasteland management, by stipulating that the land untitled for private ownership is deemed as the state land (art.12). A part of such nationalized land is categorized as the "state private land," which is transferable to the private sector (art. 16) and can be put into great concessions up to 10,000 hectares (art. 59) for 99 years (art. 61). The result was roaring protests.

The mechanism of waste land management, which determines land to be wasteland by consciously not granting title under the Torrens-style registration system, in itself lacks constitutional legitimacy. While public debate on "land grabbing" tends to mix the contexts of the compensated land expropriation and the uncompensated waste land management method, the two topics need to be clearly separated. Otherwise, it may start and end with the reform of land expropriation laws, which may never lead to the solution of the problem.

4.3 Land expropriation law for private interests

Whereas the waste land management is the uncompensated deprivation of land through the denial of the existence of private rights, land expropriation law is the public taking with compensation of an established private right, which has been a firmly established rule under modern capitalist law. Before the question of what is just compensation as a part of the doctrine of expropriation, there has been repeated debates on the preconditions for a lawful expropriation, such as the requirement of public interest, the need for proportionality and the distinction from police purpose regulations where uncompensated restrictions are conducted for the community's own benefit.

The trend of land expropriation laws in Asian countries is in the direction of expanding the concept of "public interest," by utilizing the wider categorization list of projects eligible for expropriation. Today, within the trend toward post-authoritarian democratization, a common theme of the land conflicts is the question of expropriation for private interests, namely, whether land expropriation law applies to private projects such as industrial estates and housing developments. Japan during its high economic growth period saw a series of legislation as well as the stream of academic theories that have justified the expanded utilization of expropriation for private projects.[44] Socialist countries have also been in the trend to guarantee the private property rights in recent constitutional amendments. China's 2004 Constitution attracted attention as the country's first to define provisions for the protection of private property rights (art. 13), even though the separate system is applied between "expropriation" and "requisition" of land (art. 10 (3)), which was retained in the 2018 Constitution.

International donors have emphasized the participatory planning process and the increased loss compensation in consideration of "proportionality."[45] Many Asian governments follow this line: Indonesia enacted the 2012 Land Expropriation Law that introduced a participatory procedure into the process of determining the public interest and the amount of compensation. India's 2013 Right to Fair Compensation and Transparency in Land Acquisition, Rehabilitation and Resettlement Act also avoided arguments on the publicness of projects by emphasizing the proportionality principle, such as requiring that 40 percent of project revenues be returned to residents. This law also had an effect upon Myanmar's 2019 Land Acquisition, Resettlement and Rehabilitation Law.

However, it should be remembered that the question of proportionality is not the substitute for the question of public interest. The question of whether the relevant project possesses a keen "public interest" for the general public to the extent that it needs to be realized by utilizing the general taxpayers' resources should be determined on the will of the taxpayers as a whole in the democratic processes and cannot be substituted by the participation of local people. Thus, the path recommended by the development agencies in substituting the issues of public interest by the issues of proportionality is a logical contradiction.

4.4 Registration of collective ownership

The nationalization of wasteland emerges not only as a conflict with the private rights of individuals on fallow land, but also as a conflict with collective rights. International donor agencies have recently begun to recommend a registration system for communal rights. However, highly systemic structure of such registration systems can only result in the elimination of communal rights due to the increased hurdles for such a registration.

This is largely different from the simple filing mechanism such as the U.K.'s Commons Registration Act 1965, under which anybody can assert and register a customary right, which is then established through the dispute resolution process. There are concerns that, depending upon how the system is operated, such collective ownership registration functions only as a way of disregarding collective rights and turning to development use.

The "collective ownership of the traditional community" under the 2001 Cambodian Land Law was a donor-led model that incorporated a series of quite difficult hurdles for local communities: first, a community is required to be registered under the law on community by establishing the sociocultural "unity," the existence of a traditional way of living, the existence of a collective-style agricultural method and the actual continuation of this communal existence and land usage (art. 23); second, each individual member of the community has to prove himself or herself to be such a member (art. 24); and third, the community has to establish the geographical land area that is used for the traditional agriculture (art. 25). After all these meticulous requirements are met, the right that the community can secure is, however, not different from an ordinary joint ownership, which is vulnerable to the division by individual members claiming for his or her share for free disposal (art. 27). Thus, the donor model of "collective ownership" is a procedural mechanism for ultimate extinguishment of communal rights and its merger into the ownership regime. The Law uses the logic of "social evolution" as the justification for such an elimination of customary land regime (art. 27).

The Japanese assistance team for Cambodian Civil Code-drafting repeatedly advised the Cambodian government to amend the 2001 Land Law to ensure the systemic consistency with the code, which designed the registration system that only gives a notice and priority effect instead of the Torrens-style registration, treated the possessory right as a real right linked to the acquisitive possession system (art. 162) and also explicitly accepted the customary law as an integral part of the code's normative order (art. 306),[46] but such amendment to the Land Law never took place. This seems to be a case of the failure of the Japanese attempt to reflect its own historical experience of modification to the Western capitalist law toward the consideration for "subsistence" policy ideology.

4.5 Land use conversion in rural–urban border

Land laws in many Asian countries adopt a dual structure for farmland and urban areas. Japan is a typical example of this, in which the 1952 Farmland Act is applied to agricultural areas where the freedom of disposal of landowner is restricted under the self-regulation of rural communities, while on the other hand, urban development is promoted in the cities under the Urban Planning Act. The problem is the border between rural and urban areas. During Japan's high-growth era, the erosion of the rural order due to the urban sprawl phenomenon and land speculation was a problem. Even though zoning regulations were adopted under the Urban Planning Act to establish urbanization control areas at the edge of cities, it produced various loopholes such as the disorderly development outside such urbanization control areas.

Today, many parts of Asia are experiencing the same problem of rural areas being eroded by cities and facing the difficulties in implementing the regulations on farmland use-conversion.[47] In China, farmers' contract management rights were originally exclusive to farming households and could not be held by investors, but many local governments had connived it via public taking. The central government has tightened regulations since the 1990s that allow the land use-conversion only after a process of converting the land from collective to state-owned land, which is approved by the central government. In Vietnam, deregulation at the end of the 1990s recognized farmland lease for investors, which was separate from the land use rights of farming households, and its land use change has been formally made possible since the 2003 Land Law. Similarly, in Myanmar, the agricultural land use-conversion system under the 1953 Land Nationalization Act (sec. 39) was said to be a breeding ground for land speculation and corruption involving investors, but the problem still continues because the 2012 Farmland Law (sec. 30) maintains the same procedure.[48]

This common problem of erosion of farmland due to urban expansion is a direct result of the development policy guided by the Asian governments. To avoid the dissent among farming population, the governments often prefer to use the micro-level administrative intervention to individual land transactions via the land use-conversion permit system, instead of conducting wide-scale expropriation of farmland for the purpose of industrialization and urban development. However, if this individual approach follows the path of deregulation, market failures such as unbridled urbanization and corruption will be unavoidable. A series of study call for the harmonized policy framework that respects the principle of farmland conservation.[49]

5 Ideological axes of state apparatus

5.1 Contests on legal design

Today, many Asian governments embrace the land law reforms bringing to land mobilization mechanisms such as Torrens-style title registration, waste land management, expropriation for private interests and use conversion, but the people do not submissively accept these statutory mechanisms. When we visit the scenes of conflicts, we are made aware that the parties are voicing their objections based on their firm convictions that could be called a sense of social justice. We recognize the common nature of conflicts in the background to such diversity: the assertion of "right to live" on land in chorus. They are not fighting over the exchange value of a piece of land. Land and its surrounding integrated ecosystems are the foundation of subsistence that the people have continued to protect for generations, and their rational lifestyle compatible with such ecology is asserted as the basis of survival. If we call this an ideology, it may be an ideology that concerns the minimum of human dignity.

It is possible to design the formal law to recognize such "subsistence" ideology. After escaping from colonial control, the postcolonial independence land laws raised the principle of cultivator's ownership and froze the two-tier methods of Torrens-style title registration and waste land management. This was the law reform that formalized the social norms of subsistence since before colonization.

To the opposite to this, there is the modernist ideology that affirms the role of colonial law that liberated individuals from outdated social binds, which regards the subsistence social norms of harmonization with the ecosystem as a relic of the pre-modern era. Today, the international development agencies led by thoughts of development economics are denying the results of the Asian postindependence sui generis laws, reviving the Torrens-style title registration system, removing restrictions on the farmland sale, promoting waste land management and pushing for reforms that legalize land expropriation for private interests; this is precisely the reinstatement of colonial law.

When we look at the history of Asian land law in this way, it is the history of struggles that have gone back and forth between two ideological axes. The future direction of formal land law also may depend upon political decisions.

5.2 *Conflict behind the state apparatus: individual vs. investors*

In doing so, lawyers should not lose sight of the legal axis of conflict between private rights, namely between the subsistent land users and the investors, behind the public law context of a confrontation between the state authority and private rights. Even though the economics since Demsetz (1967) has put these two categories of subjects into one "private ownership" and ignored their difference, the essence of land disputes lay in between them. Today, under the contemporary development of constitutional norms on property rights protection, the land law reform guided by the Washington Consensus cannot simply reinstate the same pragmatic designs of public law that allowed the state to intervene in the conflicts with a constant affirmation to the investors.

In today's land titling projects in Asian countries, just as in the colonial period, investors are able to apply for Torrens-style title registration even using forged purchase contracts without directly facing farmers to negotiate the purchase of farmland and protected by short objection periods that stifled the claims made by true rights holders. Instead of adjusting the register to match reality, they were able to establish title by changing reality to match the register. The courts are expected to respect the definitive effect of registration by public authority and reject the claims of farmers. However, turning to the courts of developed countries, the situation is the opposite. In the United States, the court once decided that the title registration system that finalized by the administrative decision was unconstitutional due to a violation of the U.S. Constitution's due process clause; this led to the repeal of the 1895 Illinois law, and a shift occurred to a titling system governed by the judiciary. There is also an accumulation of equity precedents that deny title claims by mala fide parties.

Today, the colonial method of waste land grant is reinstated by international donors in developing countries. In developed countries, however, the courts never permit the nationalization of wasteland based solely upon the absence of registered title. In Japan's judicial precedents, the theory of natural determination of ownership is widely accepted, in which the absence of land certificates issued under the Torrens-style title registration system during the Meiji modernization era is not regarded as absolute, and the criterion for determining the existence of ownership is whether there is the strongest substantive control over the land.[50] There is also a trend in Japanese precedents to recognize the acquisitive prescription by a private party of abandoned state-owned land under the theory of implied abolition of public use.[51] Instead of being captured by the public domain theory, the Japanese court has applied empirical attitude in identifying the actual control of land, backed by the constitutional guarantee of private property rights (art. 29).

International donors encourage Asian governments to utilize the land expropriation law, as well as the farmland use-conversion procedure, which enables the transfer of the investor's cost of land acquisition to the state authority. However, in the developed countries, the expropriation for private interests is clearly a constitutional matter. American judicial precedents adhere to the "public use" requirement of the Fifth Amendment, and, although there is a trend of deregulation in the context of the public purpose of an overall plan, such context is not extended to merely incidental types of public interest.[52] If these standards in developed countries are applied to the cases of farmland expropriation for foreign investment promotion in Asia, legality would not be easily asserted. A mere participatory procedure targeted for local sacrificed population, as promoted by the recent land law reforms guided by the international development agencies, would not substitute for the approval of taxpayers on such degree of public interests.

Thus, even though the conflicts triggered by the contemporary land law reforms in Asia are often put in the confrontational setting between public authority and local residents, we should not lose sight of the investors as core actors who utilize the state apparatus designed for neo-liberal orientation. They are a conflict fought between the gap of ideologies on land use.

6 Conclusion

As an attempt to consider the origins of Asian land disputes that increase rather than mitigate as the donor-led land law reforms are implemented, this chapter started with the debates of legal anthropologists who dispute the simplified definition of ownership as a tool of economic development. To supplement accurate recognition of the legal nature of land rights in Asian countries, this chapter first utilized the languages of modern property law in the comparative jurisprudence as the axis. Many of them, such as the farmland-ownership in Japan and *hak milik* in Indonesia, are the main rights comparable to modern ownership in exclusiveness and perpetuity but are distinguished in the agrarian restriction on the land transactions as commodity, which has an implication toward a redefinition of land rights harmonious with the goals of sustainable growth.

A related issue is the way how to bridge the actual land use order into the formal law. Myanmar's 2012 Farmland Law requires the element of "cultivation" for establishing the main right *loat paing kwin*, but its substance is unclear since the repeal of the former 1953 Land Nationalization Act. The system of acquisitive prescription under the Japan-supported Civil Code of Cambodia could have acted to bridge a traditional right of possession to the ownership, but the ADB and World Bank-supported 2001 Land Law prohibited the acquisitive prescription.

Another related question was whether the local community groups may be regarded as the subject of real rights. Many formal laws take the modernist stance and deny the legal personality of customary communities. *Iriai-ken* in Japan, *hak ulyat* in Indonesia and the communal ownership in Cambodia formalize the communal rights, but their relation with the main ownership right is unclear. This seems to be the bottleneck to envisage new design of land law for the alternative development beyond the modern ownership regime, and perhaps an integrated legal design between them should be studied from the facts in reality.

Also noted is the protection of a series of real rights such as emphytheusis and superficies that restrict the absolute freedom of ownership, which is applicable for the protection of subsistent land users in the jurisdictions where a rigorous land redistribution cannot easily take place. Among such examples, there are the attempt of civil code drafters in the socialist reform countries heading for the state-led capitalism, to introduce the right of superficies in the recent civil code drafting to secure the land use rights of farmers.

On the other hand, we also recognized the revival of transferable leasehold in the contemporary land law reforms, such as *hak guna bangnan* in Indonesia, "land use rights" in the market reform economies such as China and Vietnam, as well as *shakuchi-ken* as target of speculation in urban areas in Japan, which remind us of the remaining influence of the multilayered colonial land regime that developed the transferable leasehold such as "Erfpachtin" in the Dutch East Indies and "landholder's right" in British colony Burma.

Turning our focus to the typical land conflicts, we find that the very state apparatus introduced by the donor-oriented land law reform are the origin of land disputes, including the objections to land titling projects, land-grabbing via waste land management, compulsory expropriation for private projects, and farmland use-conversions. When today's land conflicts are reviewed from the historical axis, they are the revival of colonial land law designs, as if a continuous battle of formal law has swayed between the interests of capital investors and rural population.

When the essence of Asian land conflicts is exposed as a struggle between competing private rights behind the state apparatus of formal law, the direction of jurists' involvement in the scene begins to be apparent: lawyers are entrusted a legal argumentation by removing the hidden cloak of "public interest" embellished by the land law reforms in the strong drive of investment promotion guided by Washington Consensus, and instead, returning again to the legal setting of the constitutional and civil code-oriented private rights protection as the starting point. Within the human rights catalog, it is the raw confrontation between the private rights of the investors seeking economic value embodied in a single title certificate and the local population defending their basis of survival. When put in this legal context, then, Asian land disputes are no more an exotic topic for anthropologists but turn to a familiar context that has similarly been pursued in both developed and developing countries: a hopeful fight toward the realization of a sustainable mode of the world's socioeconomy, through perpetual efforts of legal argumentations.

Notes

1 World Bank (1993) was in high esteem of the results of neo-structuralism in East Asian economies.
2 World Bank legal vice presidency initiated a series of legal and judicial reform policy agenda guided by the thought of neo-institutionalist Douglas North. See Shihata (1991), World Bank (2003, 2005).
3 See Sen (2000).
4 Trubek and Santos (2006) is known among the critical works uncovering the nature of legal reforms led by the Washington Consensus as the second wave of law and development movement.
5 See de Soto (2000), and UNDP (2008) edited by de Soto.
6 For example, the Dutch royal declaration of land nationalization in 1870 in the East Indies, the 1920 Civil Code art. 74 in French Indochina, and the 1902 Public Land Act in the U.S. colony of the Philippines followed by the 1931 Civil Code.
7 See Matsuo (2018).
8 See Kitahara (2002).
9 IMF's initial response was to tighten the regulations, but the World Bank took the lead of "rescue." See Kaneko (2009, 2021).
10 See World Bank (1975, 2011), Bruce et al. (2006), Deininger and Feder (2009), etc.
11 Said (1993) is suggestive in this view.
12 See Cordero (2012).
13 See Kaneko (2012).
14 Benda-Beckmann, Benda-Beckmann, and Wiber (2008: 10–14).
15 Ibid. at pp. 16–22.
16 There is a great deal of research on African land law, but Peters (2008) and others provide an overview.
17 In particular, this chapter took much suggestion from Masao Fukushima's series of works, such as Fukushima (1975).
18 For a review of measure works of economic evaluation on land law reforms, see Trebilcock and Veel (2008: 416–427).
19 See Van Erp (2008: 1054) regarding a French Court of Appeal case (*Caquelan v. Lemoine* 1834) on the Normandy customary law.
20 Tamanaha in Chapter 16 of this volume attributes such an ideology of "subsistence" to Karl Polanyi, which may also relate to the term "vernacular" of Ivan Illich.
21 Kingston-Mann (2008), Upham (2018), etc.
22 Benda-Beckmann (1979), etc.

23 Pursuant to the Japanese government's 1875 directive on land tax reform, the pre-modern perpetual tenant farming right was abolished (except for the purchase of reclaimed land by tenants) and converted to ordinary tenant-farming (lease as a personal right) of terms of no more than 20 years. Tenant-farming rents have been raised to 68 percent to support land tax collection and the exploitation of farmers has progressed. Fukushima (1975).
24 See U.K. Land Registration Act 1925, and Land Registration Act 2002.
25 See, for the in-depth investigation into the legal historical facts of Japan's Meiji land tax reform, Fukushima (1962, 1975).
26 The duration of the superficies was limited to 50 years in principle (art. 269). The length of the emphyteusis was limited to 50 years with a renewal of 50 years (art. 278), which was not much different from the personal right of real estate lease (art. 604), and implied the code drafters' intention to eventually abandon the traditional tenant farming rights.
27 There is a series of considerations in Hironaka and Hoshino (1998), Hoshino (2015), etc.
28 However, subsequent judicial cases turned to trade promotion and protected a bona fide purchaser, by analogy to the provisions of misrepresentation by conspiracy in the Civil Code, Article 94, paragraph 2.
29 For the essence of farmland reform in Japan, see Kurumisawa (2016).
30 They included the 1909 Building Protection Law, the 1922 Land Lease Law and the House Lease Law, and the 1949 Act on Temporary Treatment of Rental Land and Housing in Disaster Stricken Cities.
31 See Mizumoto (1988).
32 For details, see Benda-Beckmann (1979).
33 See Lev (1965).
34 Okudaira (1986).
35 See Saito (1985).
36 See Furnivall (1956).
37 Fu and Gillespie (2014), Upham (2018: 53–58), etc.
38 See Kaneko (2010b).
39 See Kaneko (2021).
40 See Jaluzot (2019).
41 See Chapter 2 of this volume by Sakano, and also Fitzpatrick (2014).
42 See Peters (2008) for an overview.
43 See, for example, Carter and Harding (2014).
44 See Chapter 5 of this volume by Kadomatsu.
45 For example, regarding Vietnam's 2013 Land Law, see World Bank (2012), and regarding Myanmar's Land Acquisition, Resettlement and Rehabilitation Law 2019, see Chapter 15 of this volume.
46 See Chapter 2 of this volume by Sakano, as well as Kaneko (2010a, 2010b, 2012).
47 Fu and Gillespie (2014) candidly conveys the current status of land conflicts in China and Vietnam.
48 See Chapter 15 of this volume by Kaneko and Ye.
49 Kurumisawa (2016) refers to Japan as well as some advanced cases in Europe, such as Switzerland, Austria and Germany, which have maintained the laws restricting farmland transactions based on the constitutional principles, guided by agricultural policies focused upon sustainability.
50 The Mita aqueduct case (Supreme Court decision dated December 18, 1947, reported in *Shoumu Geppo* Vol. 15, No. 12, p. 1401) and the Dotonbori case (Osaka District Court decision dated 19 October 1976, reported in *Hanrei Jiho* No. 829, p. 13), etc.

51 Supreme Court decision dated December 24, 1976, reported in *Minshu* Vol. 30, No. 11, p. 1104.
52 For example, the concurring judgment of Kennedy J in the United States Supreme Court decision of *Kelo v. City of New London*, 545 U.S. 469 (2005).

References

Benda-Beckmann, Franz von (1979) *Property in Social Continuity: Continuity and Change in the Maintenance of Property Relationships through Time in Minangkabau, West Sumatra*, Martinus Nijhoff

Benda-Beckmann, Franz von, Benda-Beckmann, Keebet von and Wiber, M. G. (2008) "The Properties of Property," in F. von Benda-Beckmann, K. von Benda-Beckmann and M. G. Wiber, *Changing Properties of Property*, Oxford University Press

Bruce, John W., et al. (2006) *Land Law Reform: Achieving Development Policy Objectives*, World Bank Law, Justice, and Development Series, World Bank

Carter, Connie and Harding, Andrew, eds. (2014) *Land Grabs in Asia*, Routledge

Cordero, Santos J. A., eds. (2012) *Legal Culture and Legal Transplants*, Vol. I & II, International Academy of Comparative Law

Deininger, K. and Feder, G. (2009) "Land Registration, Governance, and Development: Evidence and Implications," *The World Bank Research Observer*, 24(2), pp. 233–266

Demsetz, Harold (1967) "Toward the Theory of Property Rights," *The American Economic Review*, 57(2), pp. 347–359

de Soto, Hernando (2000) *The Mystery of Capital: Why Capitalism Triumphs in the West and Fails Everywhere Else*, Black Swan

Fitzpatrick, Daniel (2014) "The Legal Design of Land Grabs: Possession and the State in Post-Conflict Cambodia," in Connie Carter and Andrew Harding (eds.), *Land Grabs in Asia*, Routledge

Fu, Hualing and Gillespie, John (2014) *Resolving Land Disputes in East Asia*, Cambridge University Press

Fukushima, Masao (1962) *Research on Land Tax Reform*, Yuhikaku

Fukushima, Masao (1975) "Land Tax Reform and Land Ownership – In Particular the Comparative History" in Professor Sakae Wagatsuma Memorial Essay Collection (eds.), *New Developments in Private Law* (in Japanese), Yuhikaku

Furnivall, J. S. (1956) *Colonial Policy and Practice: A Comparative Study of Burma and Netherlands India*, The Cambridge University Press

Hironaka, Toshio and Hoshino, Eiichi, eds. (1998) *A Hundred Years of the Civil Code I-IV* (in Japanese), Yuhikaku

Hooker, M. B. (1986) *Laws of South-East Asia, Volumes I & II*, Butterworths

Hoshino, Eiichi (2015) *Civil Code Essays Vol. 10*, Yuhikaku

Jaluzot, Beatrice (2019) "Civil Law in French Asian Colonies," in Yuka Kaneko (eds.), *Civil Law Reforms in Post-Colonial Asia: Beyond Western Capitalism*, Springer

Kaneko, Yuka (2009) "A Review of Model Law in the Context of Financial Crisis: Implications for Procedural Legitimacy and Substantial Fairness of Soft Laws," *Journal of International Cooperation Studies*, Kobe University, 17(3), pp. 1–16

Kaneko, Yuka (2010a) "An Alternative Way of Harmonizing Ownership with Customary Rights: Japanese Approach to Cambodian Land Reform," *Journal of International Cooperation Studies*, Kobe University, 18(2), pp. 1–21

Kaneko, Yuka (2010b) "A Procedural Approach to Judicial Reform in Asia: Implications from Japanese Involvement in Vietnam," *Columbia Journal of Asian Law*, 23(2), pp. 315–358

Kaneko, Yuka (2012) "Accompanying Legal Transformation: Japanese Involvement in Legal and Judicial Reform," in J. A. S. Cordero (eds.), *Legal Culture and Legal Transplants*, Vol. I & II, International Academy of Comparative Law, 2012

Kaneko, Yuka (2021) *Insolvency Law Reform in ASEAN Developing Countries: An Epitome of Post-Asian Economic Crisis Legal Transplants*, Kobe University Springer Brief Series

Kaneko, Yuka (forthcoming) "Reconsidering the Contemporary 'Legal Transplant': A Review from the Land Law Reforms in Vietnam and Myanmar," *Asian Journal of Law & Society*, Cambridge University Press

Kingston-Mann, Esther (2008) "The Romance of Privatization and Its Unheralded Challengers," in F. von Benda-Beckmann, K. von Benda-Beckmann, and M. G. Wiber (eds.), *Changing Properties of Property*, Oxford University Press

Kitahara, Atsushi (2002) "The Road to Land Policy for the Creation of Small Farmers in Modern Thailand (Parts 1 and 2)" (in Japanese), *Keizai Kagaku*, 50(2), pp. 21–40 and (3), pp. 21–39

Kurumisawa, Yoshiki (2016) *What Is the Protection of Farmland?* (in Japanese), Nobunkyo

Lev, D. S. (1965) "The Lady and Banyan Tree: Civil-Law Change in Indonesia," *The American Journal of Comparative Law*, 14(2), pp. 282–307

Matsuo, Hiroshi (2018) "The Formation of Land Ownership in Japan – From the View of Development Jurisprudence" (in Japanese), *Keio Hogaku*, No. 41

Merryman, John Henry (1974) "Ownership and Estate," *Tulane Law Review*, 48, pp. 916–945

Mizumoto, Hiroshi (1988) *Conversion Periods in the Act on Land and Building Leases* (in Japanese), Nippon Hyoron Sha

Okudaira, Ryuji (1986) "Burmese Dhammathat," in M. B. Hooker (ed.), *Laws of South-East Asia, Volume I*, Butterworths

Peters, Pauline (2008) "Beyond Embeddedness: A Challenge Raised by a Comparison of the Struggles Over Land in African and Post-Socialist Countries," in F. von Benda-Beckmann, K. von Benda-Beckmann, and M. G. Wiber (eds.), *Changing Properties of Property*, Oxford University Press

Said, Edward (1993) *Culture and Imperialism*, Vintage Books

Saito, Teruko (1985) "The Initial Land Systems in British Burma 1826–1876" (in Japanese), *Southeast Asian Studies*, 23(2), pp. 142–154

Sen, Amartya (2000) "What Is the Role of Legal and Judicial Reform in the Development Process?" presented at *the World Bank Global Conference on Comprehensive Law and Judicial Development*, June 2000, Washington, DC

Shihata, Ibrahim (1991) "World Bank and 'Governance' Issues in Borrowing Members," in I. Shihata (eds.), *World Bank in a Changing World*, World Bank, 53–95

Torrens, Sir Robert (1882) *An Essay on the Transfer of Land by Registration: Under the Duplicate Method Operative in British Colonies*, Cassell (MOML edition)

Trebilcock, Michael and Veel, Paul-Erik (2008) "Property Rights and Development: The Contingent Case for Formalization," *University of Pennsylvania Journal of International Law*, 30(2), pp. 397–481

Trubek, David M. and Santos, Alvaro (2006) *The New Law and Economic Development: A Critical Appraisal*, Cambridge University Press

Ume, Kenjiro (1896) *Essence of the Civil Code Vol. 2 Real Rights* (in Japanese), Japanese-French Law School, Meihodo

United Nations Development Programme: UNDP (2008) *Making the Law Work for Everyone Volume I & II*, UNDP

Upham, Frank (2018) *The Great Property Fallacy*, Cambridge University Press

Van Erp, Sjef (2008) "Comparative Property Law," in M. Reimann and R. Zimmermann (eds.), *Oxford Handbook of Comparative Law*, Oxford University Press

von Benda-Beckmann, Franz, von Benda-Beckmann, Keebet, and Wiber, M. G. (2008) "The Properties of Property," in F. von Benda-Beckmann, K. von Benda-Beckmann, and M. G. Wiber (eds.), *Changing Properties of Property*, Oxford University Press

World Bank (1975) *World Bank Land Reform*, World Bank Sector Policy Paper Series, World Bank

World Bank (1993) *East Asian Miracle: Economic Growth and Public Policy*, World Bank Policy Research Report, World Bank

World Bank (2003) *Initiatives in Legal and Judicial Reform*, World Bank

World Bank (2005) *World Development Report 2005: A Better Investment Climate for Everyone*, World Bank

World Bank (2011) *Land Policy: Securing Rights to Reduce Poverty and Promote Rural Growth*, World Bank

World Bank (2012) "Compulsory Land Acquisition and the Land Law to Enable Sustainable Development in Vietnam," *World Bank Policy Paper 64891*, World Bank

Zimmermann, Reinhard, Visser, Daniel, and Reid, Kenneth (2004) *Mixed Legal Systems in Comparative Perspective: Property and Obligations in Scotland and South Africa*, Oxford University Press

2 Registration of land-ownership in Cambodia

Protection of private rights in development

Issei Sakano

1 Introduction

Since the collapse of the Democratic Kampuchea regime in 1979, Cambodia has experienced three different constitutional orders: the People's Republic of Kampuchea, seeking gradual advance of socialism; the State of Cambodia, which allowed private ownership of land under the state-controlled economy; and the current Kingdom of Cambodia, which adopted the market economy system after the provisional rule of the United Nations. The economic system and land policy also changed in accordance with these constitutional orders. Regarding laws and regulations concerning land rights, land registration and management, etc., they began to be developed in the latter half of the 1980s, when the Constitution of the State of Cambodia officially recognized private ownership over land, and the Land Law was enacted in 1992 and fully amended in 2001. However, unclear hierarchy of the existing laws and regulations and lack of explicit revision and abolition of the existing laws and regulations make the transition from the former land regime to the new one difficult. In addition, as the market economy progresses and the value of land rises, land has become more important not only as a base for agricultural production and residence, but also as an asset and a commodity, and disputes over registered and unregistered land frequently occur due to inadequate registration or delays in registration.

As a premise for understanding the land issues in Cambodia, this paper tries to sort out a brief history of the land regime in Cambodia since 1979, with a particular focus on the ownership and the *phokeah*.[1] "*Phokeah*," which literally means "property," is, different from the ordinary possessory right that protects a state of actual occupation of a thing as a right, a traditional right legitimized by the old Civil Code promulgated in 1920 during the French Protectorate era[2] and has succeeded in the present Cambodian society, which is expected to become ownership right in the future, or in other words, it is the right in a process of acquisitive prescription. It can be also registered under the 2001 Land Law (Article 40), at the request of the right holder, and in this sense, it can be said that this right is as close to ownership as a certificate is issued and the right holder can use, make profit from and dispose of such thing. In this chapter, the possessory right provided in the Land Law is referred to as "*phokeah*" and is distinguished from the ordinary possessory right (*sett kankap*).

DOI: 10.4324/9781003170600-3

2 Cambodia before land law

The People's Republic of Kampuchea, which was established in January 1979, promulgated the Constitution in June 1981 and declared all land as state property (Article 14 of the Constitution of the People's Republic of Kampuchea). Citizens were granted with the right to use land allocated by the state for residence and home farming (Article 15), and agricultural workers are granted the right to use land for residence and farmland for private consumption, the right to collectively use the land allocated to the production solidarity group[3] and the right to lease land for agricultural production from the state (Article 16). Transactions such as purchase, sale, leasing and use for tenant purposes were not permitted for such land, and conversion of farmland and forests to land for other purposes without permission was prohibited (Article 17). Therefore, the right to use land was not to be transferred except by succession, and the mobility of land remained quite low.

In terms of specific legislation, the State Council Ordinance No. 06 on Land Management and Use was issued in May 1985, and the previously mentioned right to use farmland of the production solidarity group was stipulated in detail in addition to the provisions on state-owned farms, land for school construction and Buddhist temples. It also provided the land distribution method and sets the upper limit of land possession, while system and method of registration, filing or management of the land were not covered. In reality, the allocation of land to the production solidarity group was done by commune/sangkat.[4,5]

Unlike the original plan, the co-cultivation system by production solidarity groups became unworkable from the early 1980s, and the land allocated to each group was in fact divided to each household of the group for individual cultivation.[6] In addition, there were many cases in which farmland parcels were transferred from parents to children by gifts, not by succession.[7]

On the other hand, the Kampuchean People's Revolutionary Party established a working group on economic reform and a sub-working group on land policy under it in 1987.[8] In addition, at the Standing Committee meeting in April 1989, economic reform including land policy became the main agenda. After spending two years for preparation to recognize private ownership of land, the State Council Ordinance No. 25 on the Granting of Housing Rights to Cambodian Citizens was issued on April 22, 1989. This stipulates private ownership of residential land and was the first official document to recognize private ownership over land since 1979. It also states in its Article 1 that no one can claim ownership of pre-1979 residential land or other types of residential land so that it became clear that the state adopted a policy to avoid complicated legal issues related to land before 1979. Despite official recognition of private ownership over land in general, however, as the first sentence of Article 2, Paragraph 1 of the Ordinance provided that the state should grant households of Kampuchean citizens with the ownership over residential land where such households live and the authorities of the respective communes or sangkats allow, private ownership was not recognized based on actual fact of living and recognition of the authority was essential requirement for acquisition of ownership. In fact, each household needed to apply for recognition of ownership to the respective commune or sangkat authority and the state or city's People's Revolutionary Committee was to issue a certificate (Article 4, Paragraphs 1 and 3 of the Ordinance). It also stated that once the ownership is recognized, the land can be transferred without any restriction as long as the transferee is not a foreigner (Article 2, Paragraph 2). In addition, while a right holder to which the ownership is granted by the state is a "household" and there is no definition of a "household" as legal entity, the Ordinance provides that ownership may be transferred to "children-grandchildren," "relatives," and "other persons" due to succession and other transfer (Article 2, Paragraph 2), and this causes confusion on whether the subject of ownership is the household or the individual as a natural person. However, since Cambodia has been maintaining the common property system for married couples, it seems that there was an idea that the initial ownership was, in principle, recognized as common property for each household of a married couple in principle except for single-person households. There also seems to be confusion in the relationship between the residential land and the buildings built on the land as to where a building on land is subject to independent ownership (i.e., Article 5). Furthermore, at the time of its issuance, the Constitution of the People's Republic of Kampuchea, as the supreme law of the country, did not allow private ownership of land so the Ordinance was also suspected of being unconstitutional. In reality, as will be described later, no single ownership of residential land was recognized based on this Ordinance.

The Constitution of the State of Cambodia was promulgated on April 30, 1989. The 1989 Constitution clearly recognized the private ownership of land by providing that it grants Cambodian citizens with "the right to own and use land" and "the right to inherit land granted by the state for the purpose of residence and clearing for cultivation" (Article 15) and that the detailed substantial provisions on ownership and other real rights are delegated to the legislature by providing that the right to own and use land shall be stipulated by law (Article 17).

In June 1989, the government, which was renamed as the State of Cambodia due to the constitutional amendment, issued the Instruction No. 03 on Policy Implementation on Land Management and Use. Despite the previously mentioned provisions of Article 17 on the delegation to law in the Constitution, the preamble of the Instruction clarified that the Instruction was only to be applicable during the absence of the Land Law. It recognized the ownership of the residential land up to 2,000 square meters and if a household actually possesses the residential land of which the area was more than 2,000 square meters, *phokeah* was to be recognized for the part exceeding 2,000 square meters.[9] In addition to recognizing ownership and *phokeah* over residential land, the Instruction also provides that *phokeah* is granted for agricultural land up to five hectares for the farmland that has been continuously cultivated for more than one year and that such *phokeah* was transferable. The chairpersons of the District People's Committee were authorized to issue the certificates for *phokeah*. In addition, it was stipulated that even over five hectares of land could be used by individuals as a concession for specified time period for the cultivation of important crops that contribute to the national economy, and the concession permit was under the authority of the Minister of Agriculture.

Although private ownership of land was officially permitted as a consequence of the previously mentioned set of reform, the object of private ownership was limited to residential land under the Instruction No. 03 on Policy Implementation on Land Management and Use, and the 1992 Land Law also follows this principle. It should be noted that although the Instruction stated that ownership of residential land was to be recognized by the Provincial or Municipal People's Committee, it provided that ownership certificates should not be issued until the Land Law is enacted and *phokeah* certificates were expected to be instead issued for residential land in the same way as agricultural land. Therefore, the recognition of ownership of both residential and agricultural land with issuing ownership certificates did not happen at all. Moreover, the Instruction (Section II) limited the application period for *phokeah* certificates for residential and agricultural land by the end of 1989, and if the application was not made within this deadline, the land was considered *terra nullius*.

3 *Phokeah* under 1992 land law

The Land Law promulgated in 1992 (hereinafter referred to as the "1992 Land Law") was drafted by then Department of Cadastre, the Ministry of Agriculture, Forestry and Fisheries,[10] and the substantive part was originated from the old Civil Code. Although it almost follows the old Civil Code, an obvious difference is that the 1992 Land Law (Article 19, Paragraph 2) provides that ownership is granted only to residential land while such a provision did not exist in the old Civil Code. Thus, it can be considered that the policy judgment of the Cambodian government was reflected in such provisions in line with the Instruction No. 03 Policy Implementation on Land Management and Use. It also declares that the state does not recognize the land property right existing before 1979 (Article 1). Ownership of the residential land can be acquired by possession for five years and registration (Articles 74 and 75). If anyone possesses an unregistered land parcel peacefully, honestly, publicly without ambiguity for five consecutive years (Article 74), a certificate of ownership will be issued once the registration is made. However, in reality, there is no single case in which the ownership was recognized based on the 1992 Land Law due to lack of infrastructural arrangement. In addition, the ownership can be also acquired by converting the agricultural land for which *phokeah* has been reregistered to the residential land and registering such conversion (Article 59), although this provision remained unapplicable throughout the period of application of the 1992 Land Law. Therefore, the ownership officially recognized by the Constitution and the 1992 Land Law was literally existing on paper only. Many Cambodian officials say that the reason for the lack of registration of ownership was that Cambodia did not have the technology to create cadastral maps at the time. As a result, even under the 1992 Land Law, only *phokeah* were registered not only for agricultural but also for residential land.

The *phokeah* can be obtained by occupying the land with good faith, notorious to the public, without interruption and fraud and clearly without violence (Article 62). Of these requirements, "notorious to the public" requires application for possession and tax payment to commune/sangkat (Article 66). The chief of the commune/sangkat who received the application is required to enter the area, land type, and boundary of the land in the certified document (Article 67), but the relation between this certified document and the *phokeah* register provided in Article 211 is not clear. It can be literally interpreted that one shall acquire *phokeah* at the time of application, that is, before the issuance of certificate. Although any time of registration shall be carried out within 30 days from certification by the chief of commune/sangkat (Article 203), in reality, it took much longer time to register *phokeah* and issue a certificate of the right to possess and use land[11] due to administrative delay in registration procedure. There were applications for about 4.5 million parcels and certificates were issued for about 520,000 parcels by the end of 2000.[12]

Under the 1992 Land Law, even though it did not accept the application to realize the registration of ownership, the status of those who actually had held and used residential and/or agricultural land and met the requirements for *phokeah* were divided into the following two categories: those who received certificates of *phokeah*, and those who applied for issuance of certificates but have not received them. For those who had not applied for issuance of certificates, it is difficult to recognize the right to land under the 1992 Land Law as application is one of the requirements for *phokeah* (Article 66), while those who applied and are waiting for issuance of certificates do not have means to prove their *phokeah*. However, in reality, many people continued to use the land without certificates (even without applying for issuance of certificates), and *de facto* land transactions were also carried out.[13]

The 1992 Land Law is also ambiguous regarding the transfer of *phokeah*. Taking transfer of rights by sale, for example, registration is a requirement for transfer of ownership that was not actually recognized as mentioned earlier (Article 182), while Article 60 stipulates that the formulation of an authentic document[14] and registration are the requirements for perfection[15] against a third party regarding the transfer of ownership, of *phokeah* and other real rights, and the relationship between these two articles are unclear and complicated. One can interpret that registration is a requirement for the transfer of ownership in case of sale and exchange to which the provisions on sale shall apply *mutatis mutandis* (Article 190), while for gifts, ownership transfer occurs when the parties prepare a certified document (Article 194), and registration is a perfection requirement (ibid.). In any case, these provisions and the previously mentioned interpretations are for the transfer of ownership. Regarding *phokeah*, the 1992 Land Law only states that it is transferable and that transfer shall be effective when the document for transfer is made in authentic formula (Article 73), and registration is not required as a requirement for the validity of the transfer. Rather, registration is, together with an authentic document, only a requirement for perfection of *phokeah* against a third party (Article 60). Therefore, it is possible to interpret that the *phokeah*, of which the certificate has not yet been issued, can be transferred if a sales contract is concluded in authentic formula.[16] In fact, the sales were often carried out without registration so that the seller who has been issued the certificate could evade the tax on the sale[17] or avoid the complicated registration procedure. In many cases, the certificates of *phokeah* were handed over to the buyers to effectuate *de facto* transactions without registration.[18]

4 2001 Land Law: coexistence of ownership and *phokeah*

The revised Land Law (hereinafter referred to as the "2001 Land Law") was promulgated in August 2001. It was originally drafted in 1996 as part of a technical support project called the Agricultural Policy Reform Support by the Asian Development Bank. In the 2001 Land Law, the grounds for ownership over agricultural land were finally provided (Article 4), and the Ministry of Land Management, Urban Planning and Construction, with the support of the World Bank and other donors, established a system of comprehensive land registration under which initial registration of ownership started in 2002. The requirement for acquiring ownership is possession unambiguous, nonviolent, notorious to the public, continuous and in good faith (Article 38) for no less than five years (Article 30). In addition, if the possession started before the promulgation of the Land Law but the period of the possession did not reach five years at the time of the promulgation of the 2001 Land Law, the possessor is authorized to extend the possession until he or she fulfills the requirement of five-year-long possession (Article 31). However, no new possession was allowed after the promulgation of the Land Law (Article 30), and the method for private individuals to acquire original ownership on the land of the state is limited to a five-year social concession (Articles 48, 51 and 52) of which the details are provided in the Sub-decree No. 19 on Social Concession. According to the statistics of the Ministry of Land Management and Urban Planning and Construction, the registration procedure for the recognition of the original ownership was completed and certificates were issued for approximately 5.8 million parcels by July 2020, equivalent to 83.1 percent of the estimated number of land parcels nationwide.[19]

On the other hand, regarding *phokeah*, the application for issuance of certificate to commune/sangkat and tax payment, which were the elements of the requirement of being "notorious to the public" under the 1992 Land Law, were removed from the relevant provisions in the 2001 Land Law. This is the result of a series of consultation on the draft 2001 Land Law draft continuously held between the government and non-governmental organizations (NGOs) such as human rights organizations between 1998 and 2000,[20] and the 2001 Land Law stipulates that "any person who, due to ignorance or negligence, failed to register his possession has the right to protection of Article 29, Article 30 and Article 31" so that even those who did not apply for issuance of *phokeah* certificates may acquire *phokeah* and ownership subsequently. In other words, under the 2001 Land Law, *phokeah* holders can be divided into two categories: those with *phokeah* certificates (those whose *phokeah* who have been registered) and those without such certificates (regardless of whether they have applied for issuance of such certificates). Article 39 further recognizes *phokeah* as real right even before the ownership is recognized and that it is transferable. In addition, the authority shall continue to issue certificates of *phokeah* while waiting for the reconstitution of cadastral map and land register (i.e., initial registration of ownership) even after the promulgation of the 2001 Land Law (Article 40). Therefore, the system of registration of *phokeah* continues to exist, but the number of applications remains small. Regarding the registration of *phokeah*, the procedure has been completed and certificates have been issued for approximately 600,000 parcels as of July 2020.[21] If the number of certificates issued under the 1992 Land Law is correct, the number of certificates issued after the promulgation of the 2001 Land Law is approximately 100,000 parcels.

Regarding registration method, under the 2001 Land Law, there are two types of registration procedures: systematic registration and sporadic registration, which separate sub-decrees provide the respective procedures in detail. The former is a procedure for registering ownership, and the latter is for ownership and *phokeah*,[22] while ownership and *phokeah* are registered in separate registries. Once ownership or *phokeah* is registered, subsequent changes in rights (e.g., transfer, creation of hypothec, etc.) will be recorded in registry of such ownership or *phokeah* at the request of parties.

Regarding the relation between the transfer of rights and registration under the 2001 Land Law, as for ownership, Article 65 stipulates, "the transfer of ownership can be enforceable as against third parties only if the contract of sale of immovable property is made in writing in the authentic form drawn up by the competent authority and registered with the Cadastral Registry Unit," while Article 69 provides, "the transfer of ownership shall be considered valid upon the registration of the contract and if not, the contract shall be considered null and void." There seems to be confusion in legal implication between the effect of the transfer of ownership and perfection against a third party and between validity of transfer of ownership and validity of contract. However, it can be interpreted that registration is a requirement for the transfer of ownership. On the other hand, since the 2001 Land Law does not provide any provisions regarding the effect of the transfer of *phokeah*, it is unclear whether registration is a requirement for effective transfer of registered *phokeah*, and there is no clue in the text as to what the requirements are for effect and perfection of the transfer of unregistered *phokeah*.

5 Transition from Land Law to Civil Code: remaining challenges

The Civil Code promulgated in 2007 incorporates almost all the substantive private law provisions of the 2001 Land Law. As a result of the application of the Civil Code, those provisions of the 2001 Land Law were declared to be repealed in accordance with the provisions of Article 80 of the Law on the Application of Civil Code, promulgated in May 2011. However, since *phokeah* is regarded as a right of provisional character recognized in the process toward acquisition of ownership through initial registration that is a function from the public law perspective and thus, it is considered not appropriate to stipulate in the Civil Code, which is a general law of private laws, the provisions on *phokeah* were not incorporated in the Civil Code and left in the 2001 Land Law.[23] Therefore, the requirements for *phokeah* are still subject to the provisions of the 2001 Land Law. In addition, according to Article 14 of the Law on Application of the Civil Code, with respect to the registered *phokeah*, the provisions of the Civil Code shall apply by deeming such right as ownership unless provisions of the Civil Code are contradictory with the characteristics of the possession. Regarding transfer, the Civil Code clarifies that registration is a requirement for the transfer of ownership by agreement (Article 135). and the same rules apply to registered *phokeah* as mentioned earlier. Therefore, the rules for transfer of registered ownership and registered *phokeah* became clear with the start of application of the Civil Code. The remaining issue for the registered land is how to ensure registration of subsequent transfer and other dispositions of registered land.[24,25]

As for *phokeah* without registration, Article 39 of the 2001 Land Law stipulates that it constitutes a right *in rem* and thus, the general rules on creation, transfer and alteration of real rights (Article 133 of the Civil Code) shall apply and transfer etc. of *phokeah* shall become effective by agreement. However, since there is no registration, it is not possible to meet the perfection requirements stipulated in Article 134, Paragraph 1 of the Civil Code. Therefore, even after the application of the Civil Code, the situation remains unstable for unregistered *phokeah* holder unless such *phokeah* or ownership is registered.[26] Due to the efforts of the Ministry of Land Management and Urban Planning and Construction, initial registration of ownership has progressed to a large extent, and although there is a system to continue accepting applications for registration of *phokeah*, there is still a considerable number of vulnerable people living on unregistered land without adequate legal safeguard.[27]

Notes

1 In the current Civil Code of Cambodia, promulgated in 2007 and started its application in 2011, the ordinary possessory right is referred to as "*sett kankap.*"

2 It was promulgated by the Royal Ordinance No. 17 of King Sisowath on February 25, 1920 and enacted by the Decree of Résident Supérieur on the same date. Prior to the colonization by France, there was a set of codes on Buddhist clergy, the governing structure of the kingdom, rights and responsibilities of the people, rules related to family, succession, properties and transactions, which was called "*Krom Khmae* (Khmer Codes)." Those codes were compiled as "*Les codes cambodgiens,*" translated into French by Adhémard Leclère. The first volume and the second volume of the codes were published in 1881 and in 1898, respectively. Volume 1 contains *Loi sur les terrains* (Land Law), but the footnote states that only six articles were extracted from another code due to an error in transcription. There were no provisions related to *phokeah* in those six articles. The author confirmed that the National Archive of Cambodia possesses the original Khmer handwritten version of the codes. By the time this chapter was written, however, it has not been confirmed that *Krom Khmae* contains provisions related to *phokeah.*

3 In the People's Republic of Kampuchea, the system of joint/communal cultivation was adopted as the center of agricultural policy, and the unit of joint/communal cultivation was named "*krom samaki bongkoeurn phal* (production solidarity group)." *See* Amakawa (2001) and Sekiguchi and Hatuskano (2013: 438).
4 Commune/sangkat is the smallest administrative unit in Cambodia. Level of local administration at that time was divided into three: "city-khan-sangkat" for the capital city and "province-district-commune" for the rest of the country.
5 According to an interview with HE Lim Vorn, then Director of the Land Registration Department of the Council of Ministers in September 1998, the chairperson of the Commune-Sangkat People's Revolutionary Committee exercised the authority to allocate land, while its legal ground was not clear.
6 Amakawa (2001: 162), Takahashi (2001: 238).
7 Amakawa (2001: 182).
8 This policy reform is believed to have been influenced by the introduction of the Doi Moi policy in Vietnam, which supported the Cambodian People's Revolutionary Party administration at the end of 1986.
9 Yotsumoto (2001: 120).
10 The cadastral sector was under the Ministry of Agriculture, Forestry and Fisheries from 1989 to 1994, and under the Office of Council of Ministers from 1995 to 1999, before it was transferred to the Ministry of Land Management, Urban Planning and Construction at the Ministry's establishment in 1999.
11 It was renamed to a certificate of right to possess immovable in 1994.
12 Chan et al. (2001). However, this figure of 4.5 million is doubtful. According to the 2001 census, the number of households in Cambodia is less than 2 million, so there may be cases in which one household is applying for several parcels of land, and even considering that there are applications from juristic persons such as corporations, it is unlikely that there will be applications for registration of 4.5 million parcels.
13 For example, land was often sold from one person to another by handing over the receipt of application for issuance of a certificate as if such receipt was considered as a certificate.
14 The 1992 Land Law does not provide the definition of an "authentic document" and "authentic formula," and thus, it is unclear whether "authentic document" refers to a "notarized document" or a "document certified by cadastral officer or other authorized person such as commune/sangkat chief."
15 "Perfection" in this chapter refers to a state able to assert legal effect of the creation, assignment and alteration of a real right against a third party as provided in Article 134 of the Civil Code.
16 However, in that case, the certificate of *phokeah* to be issued would bear the name of the original right holder (the seller); registration under the name of the new right holder (the buyer) is still required for the perfection purpose.
17 A trading tax of 6 percent of the sale's price of the land was levied from 1991 and 4 percent from 1995. However, the seller and the buyer often conspired to avoid tax by writing the sale's price on the contract document lower than the actual agreed amount. The Cambodian government has been trying to establish a land evaluation system so the tax amount can be calculated based not on the sale's price but on the actual land price.
18 *See* Kaneko (2010: 13) and Adler et al. (2008: 2). A similar phenomenon can be seen in the transaction of land for which ownership has been granted. *See* Un and So (2011: 304) and Trzcinki and Upham (2014: 64).
19 The Ministry's Monthly Report July 2020 (in Khmer). http://mlmupc.gov.kh/items/7.%20July_.pdf (accessed on August 31, 2020).
20 Cooper (2002: 18).

21 Ibid.
22 Some misunderstand that sporadic registration is only for registration of *phokeah*. Although sporadic registration had been used mainly for registration of *phokeah* and there had been no case in which ownership was recognized by sporadic registration until recently, it refers to registration upon individual application in contrast to systematic registration under which all land parcels in a certain area are subject to survey and registration.
23 However, to protect *phokeah* in the transitional period of restoration of ownership, *phokeah* shall be deemed as ownership for application of certain provisions in the Civil Code. For example, Article 242 of the Civil Code provides that the *phokeah* holder shall be deemed to be the owner with regard to claims based on real rights.
24 *See* So (2010: 4, 6) for the challenges faced.
25 Inter-ministerial Ministerial *Prakas* (ministerial ordinance) on subsequent registration was issued in 2013. *See* Isoi (2014) for details.
26 One can still seek protection by exercising rights to demand protection of (ordinary) possession (Articles 234–241 of the Civil Code), and according to Article 243 of the Civil Code, the period of exercising such rights will be extended to three years if the requirements for *phokeah* are met.
27 According to the Ministry of Land Management, Urban Planning and Construction, it is reported that 83.1 percent of the total estimated land parcels have been registered. *See supra* note 20.

References

Adler, Daniel, et al. (2008) Legal Pluralism and Equity: Some Reflections on Land Reform in Cambodia, *Justice for Poor* Vol 2, No. 2, World Bank.

Amakawa, Naoko (2001) Nouchi shoyu no seido to kouzou: Pol Pot seiken houkai go no saikouchiku katei [System and Structure of Ownership Over Agricultural Land: Process of Reconstitution after Collapse of Pol Pot Regime], in Amakawa, Naoko, ed., *Kambojia no hukkou kaihatu* [Reconstruction and Development in Cambodia], Institute of Asian Economics, Japan External Trade Organization, pp. 151–211.

Chan, S., Tep, S., and Sarthi, A. (2001) *Land Tenure in Cambodia: A Data Update*, Cambodia Development Resource Institute.

Cooper, George W. (2002) *Land Policy and Conflict: The Cambodia Portion of an Eight-Country Study by North-South Institute for the World Bank*, Unpublished.

Isoi, Miha (2014) Kambojia no fudousan touki ni tsuite [On Immovable Registration in Cambodia], *ICD News No. 60*, Ministry of Justice (Japan), pp. 33–43.

Kaneko, Yuka (2010) An Alternative Way of Harmonizing Ownership with Customary Rights: Japanese Approach to Cambodian Land Reform, *Journal of International Cooperation Studies* Vol. 18, No. 2, Kobe University, pp. 1–18.

Leclére, Adhémand (1881) *Les codes cambodgiens Tome 1*, Ernest Leroux.

Leclére, Adhémand (1898) *Les codes cambodgiens Tome 2*, Ernest Leroux.

Sekiguchi, Nanami and Hatuskano, Naomi (2013) Land Conflicts and Land Registration in Cambodia, in Unruh, Joh and Williams, Rhodri C., eds., *Land and Post-Conflict Peacebuilding*, Routledge, pp. 437–449.

So, Sokbunthoeun (2010) Land Rights in Cambodia: An Unfinished Reform, *Asia Pacific Issues No. 97*, East-West Center.

Takahashi, Miwa (2001) Kambojia inasaku nouson ni okeru kazoku shinzoku no kouzou to saiken; Tako shu no jirei [Structure and Restitution of Family and Relatives in Cambodian Rice Farming Village], in Amakawa, Naoko, ed., *Kambojia no hukkou kaihatu* [Reconstruction and Development in Cambodia], Institute of Asian Economics, Japan External Trade Organization, pp. 213–274.

Trzcinki, Leah M. and Upham, Frank K. (2014) Creating Law from the Ground Up: Land Law in Post-Conflict Cambodia, *Asian Journal of Law and Society* Vol. 1, No. 1, Cambridge University Press, pp. 55–77, http://www.law.nyu.edu/sites/default/files/upload_documents/CmbdnLawIRLE%20FNL%20draft%207-28-13%20reformated%20AJS.pdf

Un, Kheang and So, Sokbunthoeun (2011) Land Rights in Cambodia: How Neopatrimonial Politics Restricts Land Policy Reform, *Pacific Affairs* Vol. 84, No. 2, University of British Columbia, pp. 289–308.

Yotsumoto, Kenji (2001) Kambojia no hukkou kaihatu to houseido [Reconstruction and Development in Cambodia and Legal System], in Amakawa, Naoko, ed., *Kambojia no hukkou kaihatu* [Reconstruction and Development in Cambodia], Institute of Asian Economics, Japan External Trade Organization, pp. 111–149.

3 Civil Code and Land Law debate in Laos

Kenzo Okawa

1 Introduction

1.1 Overview of Lao PDR

Laos was incorporated into the French Indochina Federation in 1898, passed through the period of Japanese occupation, and became independent in 1949 within the framework of the French Union. Finally, it became completely independent by the Treaty of Franco-Lao on October 22, 1953. After the civil war, the Lao People's Democratic Republic was established as a socialist nation in December 1975, and it continues to this day.

The land area of Laos is approximately 240,000 square kilometre and is composed of Vientiane City and 17 provinces (eight provinces in the north, five provinces in the central part and four provinces in the south). Some districts are established under these provinces, and lots of villages are located under these districts. Laos has a population of 7,062,000 and 50 ethnic groups (The Ministry of Foreign Affairs of Japan 2020) and is a one-party dictatorship socialist state by the Lao People's Revolutionary Party.[1] Despite being a socialist nation, the "New Thought (Chintanakan Mai)" policy was adopted at the 4th People's Revolutionary Party Convention in 1986 and is promoting a market economy.

The Lao economy is in a relatively stable and continuous developing state. The nominal GDP (US$) was about $15,920 million in 2016, about $17.07 billion in 2017, about $18.120 billion in 2018, and the nominal GDP per capita was about $2,325 in 2016, about $2,455 in 2017 and about $2,566 in 2018 (IMF 2020). Laos has joined the Association of Southeast Asian Nations (ASEAN) since 1997 and officially joined the World Trade Organization (WTO) since 2013. Therefore, reforms of banking systems, tax system, economic structure, etc. have been implementing and enacting laws related to transactions and adjusting between various rules and laws. As part of that effort, Japanese bilateral assistance has also been involved in various legal fields, including the drafting of the Lao Civil Code.

1.2 Status of Japanese legal technical assistance to Laos and the legal status

Laos has adopted a market economy and is promoting economic reforms since 1986, and the first constitution came into effect in 1991. Before and after the

DOI: 10.4324/9781003170600-4

constitution was enacted, civil-related and land-related legal systems and laws have been enacted in various forms. For example, the Property Law 1990, the Contract Law 1990, the Law on Heritage and Basis of Inheritance 1990 (revised in 2008), the Family Law 1990 (revised in 2008), the Tort Law 1990 (on December 8, 2008, was integrated with the Contract Law to be the Contractual and Non-Contractual Obligations Law 2008), the Family Registration Law 1991 (revised in 2008 and 2018), the Law on Civil Procedure 1994 (revised in 2004 and 2012), the Law on Secured Transaction 1994 (revised in 2005) and the Land Law 1997 (revised in 2003 and 2019) were enacted (Matuo & Okawa 2015:11). After that, the Lao Civil Code was drafted in the form of inheriting the contents of these laws, passed the Parliament on December 6, 2018, and became effective from May 27, 2020.

Thus, in Laos, individual laws were prescribed in various forms until the Lao Civil Code has been enacted. These laws were provided with the support of the World Bank, the United Nations Development Program (UNDP), the Swedish International Development Cooperation Agency, Asian Development Bank (ADB), the German International Cooperation Agency, etc. In other words, after the foundation of the Lao PDR, the World Bank provided legal assistance; after "New Thought," UNDP took the initiative; and since 1992, the Swedish International Development Cooperation Agency began providing the assistance (Kaneko 2001:1). Moreover, the International Finance Centre (IFC) assisted in drafting the Law on Secured Transaction 1994 and the Prime Minister's Ordinance on the Law on Secured Transaction 2011, which are closely related to the land legislation. The Law on Secured Transaction 1994 was amended in 2005, and it is greatly affected by the Uniform Commercial Code (UCC) in the U.S. (Kodumi 2007:67). The Land Law 1997 was drafted with the support of the U.S. (USAID), Germany (then GTZ, now GIZ) and Australia (AUSAID). While developing the law, a Laotian group went to Australia to study and learn about the Torrens system with the support of ADB. The Land Law 1997 was amended in 2003. In the amendment, the procedure such as land registration procedures were changed, and the management of land registration has been transferred from the Ministry of Finance to the Land Management Bureau under the jurisdiction of the Ministry of Natural Resources and Environment (Matuo 2012:162). These supports sometimes caused inconsistencies among the laws because the individual laws were enacted without considering the actual conditions or customs of the economic and social situation in Laos (Kaneko 2001:5).

Japan has also been providing legal technical assistance in Laos since 2003. Regarding the Lao Civil Code, JICA's Legal Human Resource Development Project Phase 1 was started in June 2010, and the drafting support for the Lao Civil Code was started from the project. The Lao Civil Code draft respected the existing law and Lao customs. The drafting method was carried out in such a way that the Lao side first made a draft; the Japanese side interrogated the contents or the meaning, accepted questions and provided necessary legal information for them. When drafting the Lao Civil Code, references were made by the Lao drafting committee to not only Western laws such as the French Code Civil, German Bürgerliches Gesetzbuch and Anglo-American law, but also laws of neighboring Asian countries such as the Japanese Civil Code, Vietnam 2014 Civil Code, Thailand 1934 Civil and Commercial Code, Cambodia, etc. (Irie 2019a:34). Especially, the relationship with Vietnam, which is a neighboring country as well as a socialist country, and its influence are very significant for the Lao Civil Code.[2] Japan has also assisted Vietnam, Cambodia and Nepal in drafting the code, and the Lao Civil Code became the fourth such one.

Since Laos was a French colony, the law of Laos is influenced by French law. For example, as a requirement for a contract to be validly concluded, the Contract Law 1990 had a provision "Cause," which is introduced in the Civil Code. The Law on Secured Transaction 1994 and the Prime Minister's Ordinance on the Law on Secured Transaction 2011 were supported to make the drafts, and when the contract law was amended in 2008, it introduced a discipline in line with United Nations Convention on Contracts for the International Sale of Goods. Thus, the laws of Laos have been culled from various foreign origins. Japan provided advice so as not to lose the consistency of its contents.

The Lao Civil Code is composed of nine parts: Part 1, "General Provisions"; Part 2, "Person and Juristic Person"; Part 3, "Family"; Part 4, "Things, Ownership and Other Rights to the Thing"; Part 5, "Contractual Obligations"; Part 6, "Non-Contractual Obligations"; Part 7, "Security"; Part 8, "Inheritance"; and Part 9, "Final Provisions." Most of the articles follow the provisions of the precious laws and those articles are assigned to each of the mentioned parts. Of course, there are new and amended systems in the Lao Civil Code. In principle, these new systems have been written by the drafting members with reference to the systems of foreign countries, international conventions and trading practices.[3] The Japanese side supported the drafting of the Lao Civil Code by asking questions about the contents and pointing out any inconsistencies in the draft.

Although lots of provisions of the previous laws has been taken over in the Lao Civil Code, not all provisions have been transferred. In this connection, Art. 630, Para. 3 of the Lao Civil Code provides: "This Code replaces the civil-related provisions stipulated in the provisions of the Contractual and Non-Contractual Obligations Law, the Family Law, the Property Law, the Law on Heritage and Basis of Inheritance, and other laws." In Laos, when amending an existing law, in general, the final Article of the new law has a provision such as "Provisions conflicting with this law will be invalid." (e.g., Art. 87, Para. 3 of the Land Law 2003, Art. 40, Para. 3 of Contractual and Non-Contractual Obligations Law, etc.). However, the Lao Civil Code does not have such an article. Therefore, if the contents of the provisions conflict between the Lao Civil Code and the previous laws, the contents of the Lao Civil Code will be given priority. However, it is unclear how provisions and customs that are implemented in practice but are not adopted as provisions in the Lao Civil Code will be dealt with after the Lao Civil Code is enforced. This problem is still under discussion as of September 1, 2020.

1.3 Purpose of this paper

As mentioned earlier, although the Lao Civil Code has been put into effect, various problems of ambiguity and contradictions on the terminologies still remain. The purpose of this paper is to consider the conformity of the land-related systems stipulated in both the Lao Civil Code and the Land Law 2019 in Laos, and to present the current problems and issues left for future improvement. As for the amended Land Law, although it passed the parliament in June 2019 and has been enforced on August 28, 2020, some articles have somehow been revised between the time of enactment at the parliament and the time it came into effect. However, I have not confirmed the content of the revision version of the Land Law yet. Therefore, this paper has no other choice but to depend on the contents of the Land Law at the time of passing the parliament.

2 Land Law overview

2.1 Land system and policy change

In Laos, after the market economy policy was adopted since 1986, the 1991 Constitution of Lao PDR confirmed such policy in 1991 (*see* ICD 2002:67). Art. 14 of that stipulated that "The state protects and expands all forms of state, collective and individual ownership, as well as private ownership of domestic capitalists and foreigners who make investments in the Lao People's Democratic Republic." Art. 15 provided that

> The state protects the right to ownership (rights to governing, rights to using to transferring) and the rights to inherit property of organisations and individuals. As for the land which is under the ownership of the national community, the state ensures the rights to using, transferring, and inheriting it in accordance with the law.

The private ownership system is recognized, and the land is owned by the state only in the Constitution. Similar provisions were made in Art. 16 and Art. 17 of the Constitution 2003 (*see* ICD 2004:147), and the contents are maintained in Art. 17 of the Constitution 2015 (Kawamura 2016:49).

In accordance with the contents of the Constitution, state ownership of entire land was also stipulated in Art. 4, Para. 2 of the Property Law 1990 as well as Art. 3, Para. 1 of the Land Law 2019. As a result, the people could only have the "use right" of the land recognized by the state, and Art. 4, Para. 3 of the Property Law 1990 and Art. 3, Para. 2 of the Land Law 1997 prohibited the sale and purchase of the land. However, since the Land Act 2003, buy and sell land use rights have been made possible (Art. 53 and Art. 57 of the Land Law 2003, Art. 134 and Art. 138 of the Land Act 2019).

These contents are maintained in the Lao Civil Code and the Land Law 2019. This state ownership means the ownership of state property by a national institution (Art. 262, Art. 263 of the Lao Civil Code). A person who has obtained the land use rights from the state has the right to protect the land (or possessory right in the Lao Civil Code), the right to use it, the right of usufruct, the right to transfer the land use right, and the right relating to inheritance of the land use right (Art. 250 of the Lao Civil Code, Art. 134 of the Land Law 2019). Note that Art. 4 of the Property Law, which prohibited the sale and purchase of the land, was not revised until the Lao Civil Code was established. As described in the following 1.4 of this article, Art. 87, Para. 3 of the Land Law 2003 has a provision that "Provisions conflicting with this law will be invalid." Based on this provision, it is probable that the conflicting part of Article 4 of the Property Law 1990 was invalidated.

The rules regarding ownership of a condominium and its registration system are not provided in the Lao Civil Code, but these are first introduced as a clear statement in the Land Law 2019.

2.2 *Relationship between land and building*

Legal relationship between land and buildings is not clear in the Laotian law whether a building is an independent real estate or integrated with land. The Law on Secured Transaction 2005 provides that

> A security contract over immovable property must include an assessment of the value and a clear description of the characteristics of the immovable property, such as the category, type, size, quality, quantity, and location of the immovable property used as security rights.

The object of the security rights is ambiguously stipulated. Art. 48 of the Decree on the Implementation of the Law on Secured Transactions 2011 states that

> Immovable assets which can be used as a security rights include: 1. Construction land, industrial land, or agricultural land which an individual or legal entity holds the right to use; 2. Land and structures such as houses and buildings; 3. Offices in buildings; and 4. Land concessions.

However, for example, when security right is set on a parcel of land on which a building is built, it is unclear how the building will be dealt with when the security right is foreclosed. The author, along with other members, conducted a field research on this issue in the cities of Vientiane, Luang Prabang and Pakse in Laos in August November 2019.[4] This survey clarified that the way to treat the buildings in practice differs in each region. In some areas, when hypothec is set on the land on which the building is built, the fact is registered on the back of the land title deed. Whether the hypothec is effective in the building varies depending on each region and the contents of transaction contracts. How to secure the "legality" of this variety under the formal law is an issue for the future.

2.3 Registration and transfer of land use rights

Land transactions refer to the activities of individuals, legal entities and organizations, and the transfer of land use rights, including the purchase and sale of land use rights, the setting of collateral, the exchange of land use rights and the capitalization of land (Art. 111 of the Land Law 2019). The contents of land registration are not only the land use right, but also the contents of transactions and the transfer of land. This registration is classified into four categories: cadastre registration, land title deed registration, land use right activity registration, and land use right change registration (Art. 92 of the same law). Cadastre registration is made for basic information such as tracking the activity status and changes in the purpose of use of land, issuing rights certificates and paying taxes on land (Art. 93 of the same law). Land title deed registration is made to prove the contents of the land use right of individuals or legal entities (Art. 94 of the same law). The land use right activity registration is to record and certify the lease of land use rights and the setting of rights for them, or the renting, security rights setting and sale of assets that are established on the land (Art. 104 of the same law). The land use right change registration is to record and prove the transfer of the land use right when the land use right is transferred due to inheritance or sale of the land use right (Art. 105 of the same law).

As a general rule, the title of land is transferred as of the time it is delivered or received. When determined by contract, it depends on the contents of the contract. The property that is required registration is transferred from the time it is registered (Art. 28 of the Property Law 1990, Art. 292 of the Lao Civil Code).

2.4 Usufructs (servitudes and superficies)

The Civil Code has introduced two concepts of property rights on land that were not provided in Lao law before: servitude and superficies. Before the enactment of the Lao Civil Code, the only way for citizens to use the land of others was by lease contracts. Therefore, the two systems have been introduced for the purpose of increasing the methods of using other people's land, regulating the land use methods and agreements in the contract and clarifying the contents of that externally by registration. It is also intended to encourage investment by foreign investors.

Servitude is a right that makes lands belonging to others available for the benefit of their own lands in accordance with natural conditions, laws and contracts (Art. 339 and Art. 340 of the Lao Civil Code). By registering the servitudes through a contract or a juristic act, the owner of the dominant land will be able to use the servient land (Art. 341 of the Lao Civil Code).

Superficies is a right to use another person's land within the scope of the land use right by contract or juristic act so that the right holder can construct something that is his or her property on that land, grow trees and make profit through other things the right holder will make (Art. 350 of the Lao Civil Code). It is effective only when it is registered (Art. 352 of the Lao Civil Code). There is also the right of lease whose function is similar to the surface right (Art. 434–438 of the Lao Civil Code), but registration is not required to establish a lease. There is no specific provision in the Lao Civil Code regarding the duration of the lease. On the other hand, superficies right requires registration to obtain it, and the duration can be freely set by contract. If it is not set, it is supposed to end in 20 to 30 years depending on the purpose of use (Art. 359 of the Lao Civil Code). It is assumed that the superficies is established to use overhead space or underground for the future construction of expressways and construction of subways. Moreover, it is considered necessary for those who want to use all or part of the land definitely for a certain period of time without needing to acquire the land use right (Irie 2020:70).

In addition to these systems, there is a concession contract between a legal entity entrusted by the government and the state (Art. 439 of the Lao Civil Code). This is a contract that is made to use the land of the nation and to carry out investment projects etc. there.

2.5 Relationship between land and security rights

The security rights include both the security rights pursuant to law (statutory lien) and the security right pursuant to a contract (Art. 511 of the Lao Civil Code). The latter is important in relation to land. There are two types of security rights pursuant to a contract: a security right pursuant to a contract secured by assets and a security right pursuant to a contract with another person or legal entity (Art. 520 of the Lao Civil Code). The previous system allowed the establishment of pledges only for movable assets. However, the Lao Civil Code allows it to be set for land and rights such as claims (Art. 527 of the Lao Civil Code). Although hypothec was allowed only for real estate, the previous system provided the pledge for movable things. Moreover, a system of "pledge of documents" has prescribed and it has transferred into the Lao Civil Code. A pledge of documents refers to a contract in which the debtor assigns documents of title over movable property to the creditor to guarantee the repayment of a debt. However, the debtor retains the right of ownership and the right to use such property. In a pledge of documents, the debtor retains the right of ownership and the right to use such property. However, he shall not have the right to sell, transfer or put the material items under another pledge. In addition, the debtor shall protect the material items in the same condition (Art. 533 of the Lao Civil Code).

In the previous system, to establish hypothec real estate, the debtor had to place documents that certify the right of ownership or the right to use the property in the possession of the creditor or an appointed party. To give a security over the right to use immovable property, prior consent had to first be obtained from the owner (Art. 20 of the Law on Secured Transaction 2005). Therefore, although it is permitted to take out hypothec on a parcel of land for multiple debts (Art. 50 of the Prime Minister's Ordinance on the Law on Secured Transaction 2011), the establishment of the second and subsequent hypothec was not able to be set. According to an interview survey, the method of actually setting up a second hypothec is to have the person who first made the hypothec return the documents from creditor, and then use the documents again when setting up the second hypothec. However, it is highly unlikely that the person will return the documents. When there are multiple creditors to a single immovable asset, the creditor who registered the security rights in the form of an immovable asset first shall hold preferential rights and receive compensation for the debt before the other creditors. When there are multiple creditors who have not registered the security rights, the creditor that provided the loan first shall hold preferential rights over the other creditors (Art. 51 of the same Ordinance). However, the hypothec registration system is not implemented in practice.

As mentioned earlier, this registration system was established with the support of the IFC. It was introduced to improve the liquidity of funds and assets by changing the practice of handing over documents. However, it did not lead to a change in practice. However, this hypothec registration system has also been introduced in the Lao Civil Code. This registration is made at the Natural Resources and Environment Office in the district. Moreover, to set the second and subsequent hypothec, the land title is to be provided there (Art. 562 of the Lao Civil Code). How well this system works will be an issue for the future.

3 Suggestion by IFC on the revision of Lao Civil Code

3.1 Outline

As previously mentioned, the IFC has provided various support for improving the security rights system and for some other legislations to Laos. As part of IFC support, the Registry Office for Security Interests in Movable Property has been established for the purpose of promoting the secured transaction on movable properties, and in parallel to this, the IFC proposed to abolish the pledge of movable property system as well as the pledge of documents in order to improve the integrated implementation of the aforementioned Registry on movable properties. From around October 2017, the IFC began to submit comments to the Lao Civil Code Drafting Committee[5] requesting revision of the security provisions of the Lao Civil Code. Here, we will briefly confirm the contents pointed out by the IFC (Irie 2019b:40).

3.2 Contents of indication by IFC

In introducing the Registry Office for Security Interests in Movable Property, the IFC emphasized a series of changes to the provisions of the Lao Civil Code, which was once adapted at the Lao National Assembly: for example, the introduction of a unified movable property hypothec system through movable property registration and abolishment of the pledge of movable property system and pledge of documents that are utilized by general citizens in daily transactions. In addition to supporting the enactment of legislation, the IFC has been assisting the revision of "the Law on Bankruptcy of Enterprises 1994" for reforming the bankruptcy proceedings. The IFC also recommended that security rights procedures should be aligned with bankruptcy procedures. What is notable is that these recommendations by the IFC to change the contents of the Lao Civil Code were made after the formal submission of the Civil Code to the National Assembly, based on the draft unilaterally composed by the IFC. It is reported that the IFC informed the Laos side that the Strength of Legal Right score, which is one of the indicators of Doing Business, would go from six points to zero if the IFC's suggestion is not adopted,[6] knowing that this score has become a very crucial issue for the Lao government, which aims to improve the investment environment quickly and raise the ranking of Doing Business.

3.3 Response to the suggestion

The IFC's proposal was sent at the final stage of the Lao Civil Code drafting work and included a major amendment to provisions of the draft. Moreover, knowing that the Lao government attaches great importance to Doing Business, the IFC demanded to revise the draft of the Lao Civil Code while it informed that adopting the Lao Civil Code draft would affect the score of Doing Business. Therefore, the Lao side did not fully adopt the IFC suggestion. Many drafting members showed displeasure with the IFC method.[7] Although the Lao Civil Code regulates not only business issues but also the lives or transactions of ordinary citizens, the IFC suggestion aimed to improve only business transactions. If the pledge of movable property system and pledge of documents are abolished, the actual situation of daily transactions and of financial transactions in civil society will be significantly changed. In addition, little consideration is given to issues regarding the procedure for executing security rights and their effectiveness.[8]

However, for the Lao Civil Code draft to be deliberated in the National Assembly, the consent of the top of the Lao government is required first. Therefore, the Lao Civil Code drafting committee had to be modified for some parts toward the acceptance of certain points of the IFC proposal. The following are some of the main amendments part.

(1) In the Lao Civil Code draft, the pledge of claims system was originally prescribed as follows:

> The pledge of claims is set by agreement to guarantee repayment of a debt or contractual performance from debtor's claims or claims under the possession of other person, other rights, business profits or income based on project that will surely occur in the future.

The IFC insisted on widespread recognition of the pledge of unwritten rights, such as accounts receivable. Since the Lao Civil Code draft didn't assume only written claims, the pledge of claims provisions has been amended as follows in line with the content of IFC proposal (Art. 540 of the Lao Civil Code):

> The pledge of claims is to guarantee repayment of a debt or contractual performance from claims, other rights, business profits or income based on project.

By the time of enforcement in May 2020 after passing the parliament, the previously mentioned text "that will surely occur in the future" (underlined part) will be deleted. The reason for this is currently unknown.

The IFC also insisted on the abolition of the pledge of documents provisions. However, in view of the actual social situation, confusion will occur if the provision is not provided in the OCC. Therefore, the provision is provisionally kept until the improvement of a unified movable property security system by registration.

(2) IFC emphasized that sellers of installment sales of goods contract (Art. 408 of the Lao Civil Code), hire-purchase contract (Art. 414 of the Lao Civil Code),[9] and sale-purchase contract with special agreement on redemption (Art. 427 of the Lao Civil Code) should have preferential position on third parties, since those contracts have a function similar to security rights. Therefore, the sellers of these contracts should be allowed to register as security rights of movable property in order to ensure the transparency of the transaction.

In response to this proposal, the Lao Civil Code draft has been amended. Movable property, which is the object of installment sales of goods contract, must be registered as security rights under the security rights registration system (Art. 427, Para. 4 of the Lao Civil Code). Since the seller of the hire-purchase contract is the owner of the product until the full price is paid, it is not necessary to register as security rights of the movable property. However, in the sale-purchase contract with special agreement on redemption, since the ownership of the object is transferred to the buyer, the registration system of that wasn't stipulated at the discretion of the drafting committee, in spite of the fact that it was possible to put a provision for registration of movable property as security rights.

(3) Security rights pursuant to contract has the following provision of security rights object:

> The object of security rights shall be comprehensively written in the contract in terms of its character and price in accordance with the consent of both parties to the contract. For example, the type, character, size, quality, quantity and location of the object set as security rights.

The IFC argued that the requirement to state the price of the object would hinder the establishment of future claims and liquid security rights. Therefore, the provision has been modified as follows:

> The price of the object can be stated arbitrarily, and the stated amount can be the price agreed by the parties rather than the market value that requires appraisal.
>
> (Art. 522 of the Lao Civil Code)

In this article, the word of rights or claims regarding the "future," as in (1), was not prescribed. The reason is unknown. The Lao government may dislike to set security rights for unstable things such as future rights.

(4) Previous provision regarding the transfer of claims was as follows:

> Creditors may transfer their claims *based on the contract* to new creditors; provided, however, that, this doesn't apply when transfer is prohibited by law or contract.
>
> Since IFC requested the deletion of the word "based on the contract" that limits the scope of the transfer of claims, it was deleted and the range has been expanded.
>
> (Art. 401, Para.1 of the Lao Civil Code)

4 Issues left for the Lao Civil Code: ambiguity as a result of donor intervention

Drafting of the Civil Code has been a long winding path with enormous patience and accumulation of various debates, but even after the Code has come into force in practice, the debates are also still continuing, particularly on the issues on which the inter-donor coordination sees difficulties as previously described. The following are the major lessons learned in this difficult path.

4.1 Abolished articles and statutes

As mentioned in Section 1.2, the Lao Civil Code doesn't take over all provisions from the previous laws and doesn't prescribe such provision in Lao Civil Code as "Provisions of the previous articles or statutes conflicting with this law will be invalid." Therefore, if problems related to some articles that were previously stipulated but deleted in Lao Civil Code occur, it is whether previous articles can apply.

4.2 Legal relationship between land and building

Many of the provisions of the Lao Civil Code are considered to be the default rules; however, they lack specific articles for legal relationship between land and building built on the land, and the relation between the Lao Civil Code and the varieties of local customs is unclear. In the practice of some areas of the hypothec, for example, it is unclear whether the relationship between the building and the land is considered an integrated real estate. Therefore, some issues arise as seen in the author's survey: First, when mortgage is taken out on a parcel of land and the security rights are exercised, a problem occurs whether the security rights include the building. Second, after superficies are established and a building is built on it, a question arises when the superficies are extinguished. If it is a single real estate, unless otherwise agreed, it is just a matter of accession (Art. 308 of the Lao Civil Code), and the building and the land are dealt with as co-owned thing. If they are independent real estate, landholders can claim for the discontinuation of the disturbance (Matuo 2016:79). Third, when a building is built on another person's land without land title, the legal treatment of the building is also different.

4.3 Registration of usufructs

Servitudes and superficies are newly introduced in the Lao Civil Code, and how to register them and the building is unclear in the Code. The contents of these registrations have been provided in the Land Law 2019. However, discussions on the detailed procedures are still ongoing. The intention of the Japanese drafting support on this point was to increase the methods of using other people's land, regulating the land use methods and agreements in the contract and clarifying the contents of that externally by registration, but it will take some time before such expectation is to be met.

4.4 Security rights on land

There are various remaining problems with the security rights system on real properties due to the last-minute change to the Lao Civil Code upon the intervention by the IFC. First, the biggest problem is that the practice of placing hypothec documents in the possession of a creditor will be changed to the system of hypothec registration in the Lao Civil Code. However, this is unlikely to be implemented immediately. In fact, it has not been put into practice despite the provisions regarding registration in the Prime Minister's Ordinance 2011. Second, the method of valuing the price of objects is also unclear (Irie 2020:89).

Bearing in mind all the lessons learned by being involved in the Lao Civil Code drafting, the author wishes to conclude this Article by emphasizing the need for a policy dialogue between the donors, instead of a unilateral imposition of any single model, in order to share a common goal of the donors' involvement in the legal reforms in Asian developing countries.

This work was supported by JSPS KAKENHI Grant Numbers JP19H01405, JP19K01243.

Notes

1 Article 3 of the Lao Constitution 2015 provides that "The rights of multi-ethnic people to be the masters of country are exercised and ensured through the functioning of the political system with the Lao People's Revolutionary Party as its leading nucleus."

2 On February 26, 2018, the "Lao Civil Code Law Forum" was held in Vientiane between Vietnam and Laos, and the Japanese side also participated (the author also participated).

3 There are the following new concepts and systems to be introduced: First, juristic act concept, which did not exist in the Laos Law, is introduced. The concept exists in Article 149 of the Thai Civil and Commercial Code of the neighboring country, too. Laos refers to the Code, and the term in Lao is the same as in Thailand. Second, the statutory of limitations system has been changed to the negative and positive prescription system. Third, the provisions for Agency, which didn't exist

until enacting the Lao Civil Code, have been introduced. Fourth, personal rights provisions have been provided. It is placed in part 2 and it includes two provisions: personal rights (Art. 48 of the Lao Civil Code) and protection of personal rights (Art. 49 of the Lao Civil Code).

4 The members of the research are Hiroshi Matsuo (professor at Keio University), Katsunori Irie (attorney-at-law, Japan), Legal Expert of JICA project (Lao PDR), Hiromichi Onishi (International Cooperation, Department of Ministry of Justice in Japan), and Hitomi Fukazawa (research fellow of Keio Institute for Global Law and Development).

5 The drafting committee consists of the Minister of Justice, the Deputy Minister of Justice, the former Chairman of the Legal Committee of the National Assembly, the Vice Chairman, the former Deputy Secretary of the Supreme People's Court, the Deputy Secretary of the Supreme People's Prosecutor, the Director of the Ministry of Justice, and the drafting members in practice belonging to Ministry of Justice, the Supreme People's Court, the National University of Laos, the National Assembly, the Ministry of Foreign Affairs and the Ministry of Commerce and Industry.

6 Katsunori Irie, *supra* note 15, p. 40. For Laos Doing Business scores, see *Topic Scores (0–100) – Lao PDR*, *www.doingbusiness.org/en/data/exploreeconomies/lao-pdr#DB_gc*

7 Katsunori Irie, *supra* note 15, p. 47.

8 Katsunori Irie, *supra* note 15, p. 47.

9 The hire-purchase contract is defined in the Lao Civil Code as "when the provider lends the product to the user, and when the user finishes paying the price of that according to the agreed number and time of payment, the user takes ownership of the product."

References

International Cooperation Department in Ministry of Justice of Japan (ICD; 2002), *ICD NEWS* No.3, pp. 61–97.

International Cooperation Department in Ministry of Justice of Japan (ICD; 2004), *ICD NEWS* No.13, pp. 147–154.

International Monetary Fund (IMF) (2020), *World Economic Outlook Database*, www.imf.org/external/ns/cs.aspx?id=28 (last visited Aug. 30, 2020).

Irie, Katsunori (2019a), "Laos minpoutenn no gaiyou-sou so ku (Outline of the Lao Civil Code – General Provisions)", in *ICD NEWS* No.79, pp. 29–40.

Irie, Katsunori (2019b), "Laos minpoutenn kisou ni okeru donor kan tyousei jirei no syoukai (Introduction of Donor Adjustment Cases in the Drafting of the Lao Civil Code)", in *ICD NEWS* No.81, pp. 40–50.

Irie, Katsunori (2020), "Laos minpoutenn no gaiyou-kaku ron (Outline of the Lao Civil Code – Special Provisions)", in *ICD NEWS* No.80, pp. 78–93.

Kaneko, Yuka (2001), *Laos no keizaikannrennhousei no genjyo to kyouryoku no syouten (Focus on the Current Situation and the Cooperation of Lao Economic Related Legislation)*, Japan: Japan International Cooperation Agency, JICA.

Kawamura, Hitoshi (2016), "2015nen laos kenpou kaisei no youten (Key Points of Lao Constitutional Revision 2015)", in *ICD NEWS* No.68, pp. 49–68.

Kodumi, Kenzaburou (2007), "Laos minpou kyoukasyo sakusei sien ni tsuite 3. tanpohou (Lao Civil Law Textbook Creation Support)", in *ICD NEWS* No.30, pp. 67–70.

Matuo, Hiroshi (2012), "Laos ni okeru minpou no hatten (Development of Civil Law in Laos)", in *Asia hou kenkyu*, pp. 161–179.

Matuo, Hiroshi (2016), "2015nen Vietnam minpou to zaisan touki seido no kadai (Issues of Property Registration System under Vietnamese Civil Code)", in *ICD NEWS* No.69, pp. 74–85.

Matuo, Hiroshi & Okawa, Kenzo (2015), *Laos ni okeru minjikankeihousei ni kamsuru chousa kenkyu* (Survey and Research on Civil Laws in Lao P.D.R.), www.moj.go.jp/content/001147824.pdf

The Ministry of Foreign Affairs of Japan (2020), *Lao People's Democratic Republic Basic Data*, www.mofa.go.jp/mofaj/area/laos/data.html#section1 (last visited Aug. 30, 2020).

4 Land Law reform and Civil Code drafting in Vietnam

How to balance the conflicting needs for land

Nguyen Hong Hai

1 Introduction

1.1 Controversies in the Land Law regime in Vietnam

Unlike the majority of the countries in the world, in Vietnam, land belongs to the all-people's ownership with the State acting as the representative thereof and performing the unified management of all assets under such ownership.[1] Organizations and individuals are allocated land use or land lease by the state and have their "land use right" recognized by the State.[2] This "land use right," however, has a similar function to the ownership in the capitalist system, in the sense that the land users can transfer the land use rights in accordance with the law.[3] This gives rise to rather complicated legal relationships, including the legal mechanisms under which the State exercises the ownership rights over land, the legal relationship between the State and the other entities, and the legal relationship among the entities having land use rights.

Such a complicacy of the land relations in Vietnam is regulated by a Land Law regime headed by the Constitution, detailed by the Land Law and the Civil Code as fundamental laws, together with a series of laws and sub-laws.[4] Currently, both the 2013 Land Law and the 2015 Civil Code basically recognize the "land use right" granted to the land users through the issuance of a certificate of such right, which is separated from the certificate of ownership of houses and land-attached assets. Basically, land users can enjoy the right of occupation and the right to use, namely, to enjoy the fruits of their labor and results of their investment on land, and enjoy the benefits from state works serving the protection and reclamation of agricultural land; and they also can exercise the right of disposition, namely, to exchange, transfer, lease, sublease, inherit, donate, pledge or contribute a land use rights as capital as prescribed by the law.[5] All land-related changes must be registered to become effective.

The Land Law regime of Vietnam has, however, plenty of complexities and controversies reflecting policy conflicts. For example, land user is defined by the Land Law in a complicated manner: the term "land users" includes organizations without legal personality (e.g., households and cooperative groups) in addition to the individuals and the legal persons, but in the provisions on the land-related

DOI: 10.4324/9781003170600-5

transactions, the organizations without legal personality are excluded from the subjects of such transactions. There are also numbers of debated issues on the regulations under the Land Law on the land users, in terms of the land area limit,[6] the land use purpose control[7] and the limited duration of land use.[8]

The Land Law, on the other hand, lacks detailed provisions on the rights and obligations of the land users. Particularly, while the land belongs to the all-people ownership, the status of land users toward the State is only touched on slightly under the Land Law. Basically, the rights and obligations that the organizations that are allocated the land by the State with land use levy or the organizations lease land from the State with a one-off land rental payment for the entire land lease term have the similar rights and obligations toward the State as in the relationship between the owner and its contractors. Article 174 of the Land Law states as follows, including a plenty of vagueness:

1 *Economic organizations that are allocated land with land use levy or leased land with full one-off rental payment for the entire lease period by the State have the following rights and obligations prescribed in Articles 166 and 170 of this Law.*
2 *In addition to the rights and obligations defined in Clause 1 of this Article, economic organizations that are allocated land with land use levy or leased land with full one-off rental payment for the entire lease period by the State have the following rights:*

    a/ To transfer land use rights and land-attached assets under their ownership;
    b/ To lease land use rights and land-attached assets under their ownership in case of being allocated with land use levy by the State and to sublease land use rights and land-attached assets under their ownership in case of being leased land with full one-off rental payment for the entire lease period by the State;
    c/ To donate land use rights to the State and communities for construction of facilities for common public interests of the communities and donate land-attached gratitude houses in accordance with law;
    d/ To mortgage with land use rights and land-attached assets under their ownership at credit institutions which are licensed to operate in Vietnam.

1.2 Civil Code drafting as the solution for policy conflict

The 2015 Civil Code has been an attempt to provide further elaborations for the debated aspects of the Land Law. The author was a member of the drafting team of the 2015 Civil Code at the Ministry of Justice of Vietnam and has been involved in the efforts to deal with varieties of the policy conflicts on land. As a result, in terms of the ownership regime, the 2015 Civil Code was a compromise, providing for three different forms of ownership, namely, all-people ownership, private ownership, and common ownership. However, in terms of the introduction of a series of new property rights over the land, a unique attempt was achieved by the drafting process of the 2015 Civil Code to overcome the systemic complicacy of the Land Law regime.

In its Book 2 on the property relations, in addition to providing for the ownership rights, the 2015 Civil Code acknowledged three types of other property rights directly related to the land and land-attached assets: the easement,[9] the usufruct,[10] and the right of superficies.[11] These three rights are vested with the real right claims (*rei vindicatio*), which are invoked against infringements: namely, the subject of such rights directly holds or controls the property owned by another subject;[12] such rights are not illegally restricted or deprived of; the subject of such right may, with the own free will, protect and prevent anyone else from infringing upon his, her or its rights by measures not contrary to the law.[13] Such rights take effect for all individuals and legal persons unless otherwise prescribed by the law and remain effective even in case the base ownership right is transferred, unless otherwise prescribed by the law. The owner may not reclaim the property possessed by the subject of such new rights.[14] The subjects of such new rights may perform any disposition on the property within their scope prescribed by the law as far as not causing damage to or affecting the national interests, people's interests, public interests or lawful rights and interests of owners of property or of other persons.[15] A subject having such rights shall bear risks to the property within his, her or its scope of rights, unless otherwise agreed upon with the property owner or otherwise prescribed by the law.[16]

Thus, in an attempt to realize a systemic consistency of Land Law regime and provide for the detailed substance of the "land use rights," including the alienability of "land use rights" despite that it is created on the land belonging to the all-people's ownership, the 2015 Civil Code introduced a new series of property rights, by utilizing the traditional terminologies of the continental civil law traditions.

1.3 Land Law remaining as the source of restrictive land policies

However, it should be noted that these provisions still contain numbers of reservations by the law, which mostly refers to the Land Law, which is the fundamental law of socialist land regime of policy considerations. Without the mandates by the Land Law, even the Civil Code that is the fundamental code in the sphere of civil and commercial law cannot realize its substance.

For instance, while the Land Law prescribes that land-related changes must be subject to the registration, the aforementioned new type of property rights under the 2015 Civil Code cannot be registered under the Land Law and therefore unable to ensure the publicity as a property tight.[17]

Another example is the land recoveries by the State under the Land Law. The Civil Code generally provides that the ownership rights and other property rights are restricted by the State in emergency cases or for environmental protection, assurance of social order and safety, etc.[18] Apart from such restrictions, in case of the extreme necessity for reasons of national defense and security, national interests, state of emergency or natural disaster prevention and control, the State may effect a compulsory purchase or requisition of the property of organizations and individuals, upon the compensation at the market price.[19] In addition to these general principles given by the Civil Code, the Land Law contains the details of provisions that the State shall recover land currently used by organizations or individuals for the reasons of national defense and security and socioeconomic development[20]; violations of the land law[21]; or termination of land use as prescribed by law.[22]

2 Debated issues for the further liberalization of land regime

2.1 *Social expectations for the land mobility*

According to the statistical data on the situation of land allocation in Vietnam as of December 31, 2017, under Decision No. 3873/QD-BTNMT of December 25, 2018, of the Minister of Natural Resources and Environment, as shown in Table 4.1, an overview of the land regime in Vietnam is largely agriculture-oriented, and the majority of such agricultural lands are allocated for the agricultural households. There is the policy debate that more land should be shifted from the agricultural use toward the industrial and commercial uses, to achieve the modernization and industrialization of the national economy.

2.2 *Recommendation by the Ministry of Justice*

Ministry of Justice Report No. 251/BC-BTP of October 26, 2018, which was submitted to the Prime Minister, described the results of a review of problems and overlaps in regulations on the right to access land of the people and businesses for implementation of investment and production and business projects. The essence of this report will be summarized in the following.

First, as for the definition of land users, the present Land Law recognizes the organizations without legal personality as the subject of property rights, which has resulted in risks in transactions, due to the unclearly defined subjects lacking legal personalities. On the other hand, the Land Law does neither regard the foreign entities as land users nor stipulate the grant of land use rights certificates to foreigners. While the increasing numbers of foreigners take part in the land-related investments or the business projects involving land, the discrepancies between the law promoting such business transactions and the Land Law have caused problems. For instance, the Housing Law states that foreigners may own homes in Vietnam and are granted by competent state authorities certificates of land use rights and ownership of houses and land-attached assets under the law.

Second, there are discrepancies between the relevant laws on the range of target assets categories, which may cause impediment to the investment attraction and implementation of business projects on land. For example, the Land Law lacks provisions on the future land use rights, while the Civil Code prescribes that assets may include immovable and movables, which may be either

Table 4.1 Basic data on land use in Vietnam (unit of calculation: thousand hectares)[23]

	Total area	*Of which*	
		Land allocated for users	*Land allocated for different entities for management*
THE WHOLE COUNTRY	**33,123.6**	**26,818.6**	**6,305**
Agricultural land	**27,268.6**	**24,437.3**	**2,831.3**
Land for agricultural production	11,508	11,397.2	110.8
Land for annual crops	6,969.3	6,909.5	59.8
Paddy land	4,126.4	4,108	18.4
Land for other annual crops	2,842.9	2,801.5	41.4
Land for perennial crops	4,538.7	4,487.7	51
Forest land	14,910.5	12,197.6	2,712.9
– Production forests	7,479.4	6,078.4	1,401
– Protection forests	5,239	4,014.6	1,224.4
– Special-use forests	2,192.1	2,104.6	87.5
Water surface land for aquaculture	796.1	789.2	6.9
Land for salt production	17.2	16.7	0.5
Others	36.8	36.6	0.2
Nonagricultural land	**3,749.7**	**1,868.3**	**1,881.4**
Residential land	714.9	712.9	2
– Urban residential land	158.9	158.0	0.9
– Rural residential land	556	554.9	1.1
Special-use land	1,874.3	926.5	947.8
– Land used by offices and nonprofit agencies	95.6	93.2	2.4
– Land for national defense and security	297.6	297.4	0.2
– Land for nonagricultural production and business	274.5	272	2.5
- Public land	1,206.6	263.9	942.7
Land for religious purpose	18.6	18.6	
Land for cemeteries, funeral houses for crematoriums	103.9	93	10.9
Rivers and special-use water surface	986.7	66.4	920.3
Others	51.3	50.9	0.4
Unused land	**2,105.3**	**513**	**1,592.3**
Unused flat land	213.9	17	196.9
Unused mountainous land	1,722.8	488.8	1,234
Non-tree rocky mountains	168.6	7.2	161.4

existing or future assets. The Housing Law also acknowledges future houses as objects of housing-related transactions. Another example is the discrepancy between the Land Law that treats the land and the land-attached assets (such as houses) in an integrated way, while the Civil Code has a separated treatment between the land use rights and the rights over land-attached assets. This may cause difficulties or legal risks to the people and enterprises in their efforts to prove their rights over property and detrimental to the business transactions over assets.

Third, the Land Law makes the registration of land use rights compulsory while the registration of ownership rights over land-attached assets is optional. This fails to create a separate legal mechanism for the land use rights and the land-attached assets, thus causing obstacles to the transaction practices separating them, especially in cases in which the land use right holder is not the owner of land-attached assets, or in which they are put in separate transactions, etc.

The Land Law is also short in detailing the transfer of land use rights. It says a transfer of a land use right must be notarized or certified, and such transfer becomes legally effective from the time of registration. However, it fails to explain the separation between the contractual transaction giving rise to the rights and obligations between the two parties to such transaction (as of the time of notarization or certification), and the property transaction that establishes the *erga omnes* effect of the transfer of a land use right (as of the time of registration). The lack of explicit provision on such a separation of two spheres of transactions may cause confusion; for instance, in determining the timing of the mortgage to take effect over a land use rights, etc.

Fourth, the limited access to the land-related information is also a critical issue, especially in regard to the information about changes in land use rights and land-attached assets, land use master plans and plans, land recovery, compensation, support or resettlement. In addition, the interpretation of connotations related to the land information system is also insufficient. The Land Law only generally refers to the "land information system" without defining what are such "land information," which causes the gaps in both the State land management and in the private business transactions.

As for the issues of land recovery, and the compensation, support and resettlement upon land recovery by the State, the Land Law still lacks a stable legal mechanism. Particularly, more attention should be paid to the land recovery for promoting the business investment activities, especially for the projects to develop concentrated agriculture or hi-tech agriculture, thereby exploiting to the utmost land use values, stabilizing land use-related relations, implementing land-using investment projects, limiting legal risks, increasing sustainable efficiency for the people and businesses and increasing competitiveness of the economy.

Regarding the issues of land pricing, the Land Law states that the setting of land prices must conform to the common prices in the market of the land type with the same use. But the Law lacks a mechanism for rational setting of land prices, leading to the tendency that the land prices decided by the State are always lower than market prices and depend on land price consultants, thus causing losses of state budget revenues in case of designated sale of land or change of land use purpose. This is one of the causes for complaints and corruption in land management and problems in implementation of investment or production and business projects upon land recovery by the State and compensation, support and resettlement.

Lastly, the Land Law fails to distinguish the disputes concerning the state management of land from the disputes on transactions irrelevant to the state management of land. As the Land Law provides that a party who lacks documentary evidence of a land use right can still resort to a dispute settlement by submitting a request for dispute settlement at the People's Committee, administrative interventions occur in the civil relations between the civil parties. The disputes concerning civil cases should come within the competence of courts and should be separated from the administrative disputes on the issues of state management of land.

2.3 *Utilizing the novel rights under the 2015 Civil Code*

The 2015 Civil Code has introduced a series of novel provisions as aforementioned, including the usufruct and the right of superficies. These rights shall be further established in the real economy, through an agreement or a testament with a longer and more stable term with more transparent provisions on ownership over property in investment and business activities. These rights are definitely different from the existing land lease rights that are a mere contractual personal right. Accordingly, the subjects having the usufruct or the right of superficies on land can perform all conducts within the scope prescribed in the Civil Code and relevant laws. None of them are deprived of his or her rights over property; even in cases of transfer of the base rights, the usufruct and the right of superficies remain effective.

Particularly, the status of the "land use rights" under the Land Law can be confirmed by the Civil Code as the right of superficies on the land belongs to the all-people's ownership, and thus, could be secured even in any changes brought by the State on the fate of the land, including the land recovery. The businesses of investment projects can also secure their sustainable basis of business on their land use rights, unless otherwise prescribed by the Civil Code and relevant laws.

Therefore, the Land Law and the Housing Law should include the specific provisions recognizing these novel rights of usufructs and superficies under the Civil Code. Also, the Land Law should explicitly recognize the consistency of these rights even in cases of the transfer and any other changes to the basic rights.

The Land Law also prescribes in detail the registration of changes in land use rights and the writing of establishment of easement, usufruct or right of superficies on land use rights of other persons in certificates of the rights to use land, houses and land-attached assets. Otherwise, it is difficult for the people and businesses to establish these rights under the Civil Code until the Land Law has insufficient relevant provisions.

3 Policy forecast toward the Land Law reform in Vietnam

3.1 Resolution of the 5th plenum of the Party Central Committee

The Resolution of the 5th plenum of the Communist Party Central Committee (the 12th tenure) in 2017 on improvement of the socialist-oriented market economic institutions declared to fully institutionalize the rights of the State, organizations and individuals to own assets as prescribed in the 2013 Constitution, so as to ensure publicity and transparency in administrative procedures and public services for facilitating the transactions of rights over property, ensuring the effect and effectively protecting property ownership rights.

Such Resolution emphasized the improvement of the Land Law and related laws to facilitate the mobilization, distribution and effective use of land and natural resources, reducing disputes, complaints, corruption and waste in this sector; to ensure public and transparent management and use of public land areas; to create favorable conditions for the transfer or lease of "land use rights" or contribution of "land use rights" as capital; and to support the land accumulation and concentration for the development of industries and services in rural areas and large-scale and hi-tech commodity agriculture in parallel with job creation and generation of sustainable incomes for farmers, thus ensuring sociopolitical stability in the countryside.

The Resolution also emphasized the improvement of regulations on contracts and settlement of civil disputes in a uniform and comprehensive manner; to renew and raise the effect and efficiency of institutions for settlement of civil disputes with simple, public and transparent processes and procedures; and to develop a transparent, interagency and easily accessible registration system, especially for real estate.

Also emphasized was a single legal regime to businesses, regardless of their forms of ownership or economic sectors. All businesses of all economic sectors operate under the market mechanism in an equal manner and healthy competitive environment in accordance with the law.

The Resolution encouraged to improve the laws on promotion of investment and business, especially those on public investment and bidding; to ensure the freedom of business and fair competition of economic entities as prescribed in the Constitution; and to remove barriers to investment and business activities.

Another focus was to improve the legal institutions on competition as well as increasing the transparency on the State monopoly in order to eliminate the mechanism whereby the State exercises direct administrative interventions in and provides subsidy for businesses of all economic sectors.

The emphasis was made to improve laws, mechanisms and policies for development and smooth operation of the real estate market; to focus on formulating and improving regulations on development of the primary and secondary markets on the "land use rights," even on agricultural land; to ensure the public and transparent operation of the market of "land use rights" in an order; to develop and raise the operational efficiency of the market for the lease of agricultural land; and to improve tax laws on the use of assets, especially land.

Based on the criteria of "ownership" and "use" separation, the Party Resolution gave the classification of the real estate markets into three types:

- The real estate trading market: the ownership rights are transferred to the buyer.
- The real estate lease market: the ownership rights belong to the owner while the right to possession and use rights are transferred to the lessee.
- The real estate pledge and insurance market: the ownership rights do not belong to the owner, while the right to possession and use rights do.

Particularly for the land, the Resolution emphasized that the supreme right of disposition belongs to the State. Chronologically, the real estate markets are classified into three types:

- Primary market: this is the market for transfer, lease or allocation of land use rights. Primary market is the market of the State with all strata of people. This market is public and involves no "underground" transactions.
- At present, the national land areas for allocation or lease are almost exhausted. For land allocation or lease, the State must recover land or change land use purposes or invest in land (especially mobilize unused land areas).
- Secondary market: this is the market for construction of real estate works for sale or lease.

Tier-III market: this is the market involving the State and private sector. These two entities may build real estate works for sale or lease. This is the market of all strata of people. The transfer of land is in substance the purchase and sale of land use rights. Based on land use purposes, the real estate markets are classified into five types:

- Houses of residents.
- Real estate for trade and service activities.
- Officetels.
- Real estate for industries.
- Real estate for agriculture.

3.2 Party Resolution No. 39-NQ/TW of January 15, 2019

Resolution No. 39-NQ/TW of January 15, 2019, of the Political Bureau of the Communist Party of Vietnam was issued to raise the efficiency of management, exploitation, use and promotion of resources of the economy.

Resolution No. 39 emphasized that managing, exploiting, mobilizing, distributing, using and effectively promoting resources of the economy for national development are the responsibility of the entire political system and people of all strata.

It also declared to diversify the forms of mobilization and uses of resources; to promote socialization and attract non-state investment resources; to apply the market principle in the management, exploitation and use of resources for development; to turn material resources into economic values, focusing on natural resources; to concentrate the efforts on fully exploiting scientific and technological potential for socioeconomic development.

It aims to improve the legal system promoting the building of the national geo-spatial data infrastructure up to international standards; to formulate mechanisms, policies and solutions concretizing the viewpoint on turning mineral resources into economic values.

It encourages to change plant, animal and product structures as suitable to the advantages and market demands in adaptation to climate change; to diversify resources for disaster prevention and control and response to climate change and sea level rise.

It especially mentions to revise the laws, mechanisms and policies forming a legal framework regulating the land area limits and the land accumulation and concentration for restructuring agriculture, and developing agricultural intensives and specialized farming on a large scale with application of high technologies; to review existing land areas and land areas allocated to users, especially large-sized state enterprises and enterprises with state capital; to thoroughly settle problems in land management and use by agriculture and forestry companies, especially land encroachment, land transfer, change of land use purpose, lease, lending or contracting of land in contravention of law.

3.3 Policy conflicts remaining in the Land Law

In response to the aforementioned Resolutions by the Communist Party, the Ministry of Justice Report No. 251/BC-BTP of October 26, 2018, further referred to the policy on land accumulation and concentration for the development of commodity agriculture, clean agriculture and hi-tech agriculture, which has been affirmed in the series of recent resolutions by the Political Bureau, Party Central Committee and Government.

In this regard, a reference was made to the policy conflicts remaining in the present Land Law, which lacks clear provisions for promoting the land accumulation and concentration for the development of commodity agriculture, clean agriculture and hi-tech agriculture. Some specific provisions of the Land Law have not yet encouraged or even have created significant increase of expenses or risks in land accumulation and concentration. For instance:

- The Land Law sets the limits for the transfer of agricultural land use rights.
- The Land Law particularly sets the limit for the economic institutions to receive the transfer of land use rights for rice cultivation, land of protection forests or land of special-use forests. At the same time, households and

individuals not directly engaged in agricultural production may not receive the transfer or donation of rice cultivation land use rights. The exchange of agricultural land use rights must be conducted within the same commune-level locality. In addition, the interpretation of the term "directly engaged in agricultural production" in the Land Law only covers the cases in which households and individuals are the subjects directly engaged in agricultural production but has not touched upon other entities, especially those in relations on land accumulation and development of hi-tech agriculture and clean technology.

Similarly, the Land Law is cautious about the protection of the residential land for stable and permanent use, and it allows only for the limited use for tourism, commercials and service activities. As a result, there is a branch of law on the multifunctional works, such as the owners of "condotel" or "officetel" projects that lease land for a term of 50 years from the State (in the form of apartments or offices where they can live but which do not form residential places). The Land Law and any other relevant laws (such as the Housing Law, Construction Law and Tourism Law) have no specific provisions so far, causing problems in management of investors and in the identification of the nature of legal relationship between project owners and transferees of condotels or officetels, in their determination of land use term and grant of land use rights certificates, etc.

4 Challenges and recommendations

Over the past years, Vietnam has faced numerous problems in the increase of productivity and economic value of the same land parcels. People and businesses have been suffering from limited access to the production resources, leading to fewer investment opportunities and poor development of economic relations based on natural resources, thus making Vietnamese economy lag behind. Even though Vietnam has huge demands for large-scale commodity production, investors have difficulties in their access to land, largely due to the shortage of land areas and conflicts of interests between investors and people over the "land use rights."

In this setting, the Communist Party of Vietnam has issued the aforementioned major policies concerning the reform of the Land Law.

To ensure the sustainable development and social stability, people should have optimal and safe choices when they invest in land, particularly from the claims by different entities on the same land parcels. Also, the legal regime on land-attached assets should be developed separately from that of the land. The improvement of the regulations on the asset registration system should be made public.

The Communist Party's policy on the land accumulation and concentration is directed toward the development of agriculture and services in rural areas as well as large-scale and hi-tech commodity agriculture, aiming to create jobs, ensure stable incomes for farmers and ensure the sociopolitical stability in rural areas.[24] In parallel to this goal, the regulations on property rights of foreigners over land use rights and land-attached assets should be improved, and the efficiency of settlement of land-related disputes should be developed.

Notes

1 Article 53 of the 2013 Constitution says: "Land, water resources, mineral resources and resources in the sea areas and airspace, other natural resources and assets invested and managed by the State are public assets under all-people ownership with the State acting as the owner representative and performing the unified management," referenced in Article 197 of the 2015 Civil Code, Article 4 of the 2013 Land Law.

2 The State recognizes land use rights of the entities receiving the exchange, transfer, lease, inheritance, donation or contribution of land use rights as capital.

3 As provided in Articles 15 and 54 of the 2013 Constitution; Article 4 of the 2013 Land Law; Articles 197 and 198 of the 2015 Civil Code.

4 The 2014 Investment Law (revised in 2016); the 2014 Law on Enterprises; the 2014 Law on Real Estate Business; the 2014 Housing Law; the 2014 Construction Law; the 2017 Law on Forestry; the 2014 Law on Environmental Protection; the 2014 Law on Marriage and Family; the 2018 Law on Tourism, etc. In addition, the Government, the Ministry of Natural Resources and Environment, the Ministry of Justice, etc., have issued many sub-law documents to guide the implementation of land-related laws, for example, Decree No. 102/2017/ND-CP on registration of security measures.

5 Article 125 of the 2015 Civil Code; Articles 166, 167 and 170 of the 2013 Land Law.

6 Land area limit is the limit of agricultural land area based on which households and individuals are allocated land by the State or permitted to receive the transfer of land use rights, including "land allocation limit" and "limit of receipt of the transfer of agricultural land use rights" (Articles 129 and 130 of the Land Law). For example, the limit of land area for growing annual crops, aquaculture or salt making for each household or individual directly engaged in agricultural production is three hectares for provinces and centrally run cities in the Southeastern Vietnam, or 30 hectares for provinces and centrally run cities in the Mekong River delta region.

7 Article 10 of the Land Law Classification of land types: Land for agricultural production is land used for agricultural production, including land for cultivation of annual crops and land for growing perennial crops. Forest land means land with forests (including natural forests and planted forests up to forest standards prescribed by the law on forest protection and development, and land on which forests are just planted or forests are planted in association with natural zoning). Special-use land includes land for offices of state agencies; land for construction of nonbusiness works; land for national defense; land for security; land for nonagricultural production and business; and land for public purposes. Residential land means land for construction of houses and works serving daily life; land of gardens and ponds in association with houses within the same land parcels in a residential quarter (including gardens and ponds attached to individual houses). Residential land includes residential land in rural areas, residential land in urban centers; unused land for which use purposes are not yet determined, including unused flat land, unused hilly land; and rocky mountains without trees.

8 Including land for stable and permanent use, land for definite term use; use term upon land use change purpose; and use term upon the receipt of land use purpose change.

9 Civil Code Articles 245 through 256 provide for the "easement" as a right to be exercised on an immovable property (referred to as servient estate) with an aim to serve for the benefit of another immovable property owned by another person (referred to as dominant estate). Easement still exists as long as relevant immovables and the demand for enjoyment of rights still exist, despite the fact that servient estate and dominant estate have been transferred to another subject.
10 Civil Code Articles 257–266 provide for the "usufruct" as a right of an entity to exploit the utilities of, and enjoy yields and profits from, property under the ownership of another entity within a specified period, and shall last until the first usufructuary being an individual dies, or until the first usufructuary being a legal person ceases its existence, which must, however, not exceed 30 years.
11 Civil Code Articles 267–273 provide for the right of "superficies" of an entity over the ground, water surface, space above the ground or water surface, and the underground space of the land whose use rights belong to another entity. The entity having the right of superficies has the ownership rights over property created under the law. In case the right of superficies is transferred in part or in whole, the transferee may inherit the right of superficies according to the conditions and within the scope corresponding to the transferred part of the right of superficies.
12 Civil Code Article 159.1.
13 Civil Code Articles 160.1 and 163.2.
14 Civil Code Articles 160.1 and 166.2.
15 Civil Code Article 160.3.
16 Article 162.2.
17 In the view of the Ministry of Justice of Vietnam, such new propety rights that are established under the law or depending on natural geographical locations (for easement) are not subject to registration because the law or natural geographical locations guarantee the publicity of rights; whereas such rights established under agreements or testaments must be registered to publicize the establishment at the will of the subjects and the effect from the time of registration of rights.
18 Civil Code Articles 2.2, 160.2, 160.3 and 163.1.
19 Articles 2.2, 163.2, and 171 thru 178 of the Civil Code.
20 Articles 61 and 62 of the Land Law.
21 Article 64 of the Land Law.
22 Article 65 of the Land Law.
23 Statistical Yearbook of 2018, General Statistics Office, Ministry of Planning and Investment of Vietnam. The data are based on the situation as of December 31, 2017, under Decision No. 3873/QD-BTNMT of December 25, 2018, of the Minister of Natural Resources and Environment.
24 Trinh Dinh Dung (2017) "Minutes of the Speech Delivered by Deputy Prime Minister Trinh Dinh Dung," in the proceedings at *the Conference Discusses Measures to Accumulate Land for Large-Scale Agriculture*, April 14, 2017, Vinh Yen City, Vinh Phuc.

References

General Statistics Office, Ministry of Planning and Investment of Vietnam (2015–2018) *Statistical Year Books of Vietnam 2018*, Statistical Publishing House, Hanoi.

Ministry of Justice of Vietnam (2018) "Report No. 251/BC-BTP of October 26, 2018 Submitted to the Prime Minister, on Results of the Review of Problems and Overlaps in Regulations on the Right to Access Land of the People and Businesses for Implementation of Investment and Production and Business Projects," Ministry of Justice of Vietnam.

Trinh Dinh Dung (2017) "Minutes of the Speech Delivered by Deputy Prime Minister Trinh Dinh Dung," in the proceedings at *the Conference Discusses Measures to Accumulate Land for Large-Scale Agriculture*, April 14, 2017, Vinh Yen City, Vinh Phuc.

Part II

Land taking for "development" and beyond

5 Takings for private use/ private interest and livelihood compensation in Japan*

Narufumi Kadomatsu

Preface

Article 29, Paragraph 3 of the Constitution of Japan stipulates that "private property may be taken for public use upon just compensation therefor." Given that the Constitution recognizes the land-ownership rights of private individuals, the underlying rule is that ownership rights to land cannot be acquired (expropriated) in a manner contrary to the will or intent of the owner. However, the land expropriation system makes allowances for the state acquisition of land rights in exceptional cases for "public use" such as the construction of railways and roads.

Although the legal system of land expropriation (eminent domain, takings) has a long history, it was established as a system with clear parameters during the development stage of capitalism for the construction of railways, roads, etc. as an industrial base ("classical expropriation"). At least in civil law countries, the legal system of land expropriation is premised on the establishment of capitalist land-ownership and supported by the notion of public use or public interest that justifies the deprivation of such ownership. The establishment of the right to land-ownership and the recognition of the public interest as grounds for a deprivation of this right are inextricably linked. Public interest is linked to the notion of public use, which is open to use by an unspecified number of people, as seen in the case of railways and roads.

However, in many countries and jurisdictions, this "classical expropriation" has experienced turmoil, especially as the phenomenon of "takings for private interest" does not necessarily fit the concept of public use has appeared. The approaches to this issue have not been uniform, and thus the topic merits comparative legal examination (Kim et al. 2017).

In one famous case in the U.S. Supreme Court,[1] it was contested whether the appropriation of land for urban redevelopment, which included facilities for pharmaceutical manufacturer Pfizer, violated the constitution. In a case before the German Constitutional Court, the question was whether the creation of a special city planning zone for a test circuit for the automotive manufacturer Daimler-Benz and the achievement of that plan by expropriation violated the constitution.[2] Similar issues have occurred in South Korea[3] and Taiwan.[4] In

DOI: 10.4324/9781003170600-7

China, where private land-ownership is not recognized, issues of expropriation for private interest occur for reasons entirely separate from those in Western countries.[5]

This chapter begins by reviewing the structural makeup of Japan's Expropriation of Land Act[6] (hereafter "ELA") (1). It then reflects on the discourse surrounding the introduction of two legal schemes in the 1960s that recognized the "takings for private interest": (i) the conferral of expropriation rights for a project involving the creation of an industrial development park following the period of rapid economic growth in the 1960s, and (ii) the enactment of the New Housing and Urban Development Act (2.1). Finally, it examines the discourse on the theory of "publicness by planning" (2.2).

With the end of Japan's rapid economic growth, the previously mentioned two legal schemes of "takings for private interest" have almost been forgotten. Today, however, against the backdrop of the "underuse" problem brought about by a declining population, there is a renewed legislative trend toward the use of eminent domain. The newly enacted "Unclaimed Land Act" introduced the special procedure of land expropriation in the case of "land of unknown owner" (2.3.1). In addition, the Act introduced the scheme of "community welfare promotion projects," which allowed the right of use for local public purposes while the landowner retained ownership. In today's age of population decline, the question of how to maintain local regions in a sustainable way appears to have sparked a reappraisal of the issue of "publicness" (2.3.2).

This chapter also deals with the issue of compensation for land expropriation. Takings compensation under the capitalist legal system is centered on compensating for the market price of land. However, the problems of compensation for below-market prices in large-scale social reform (e.g., postwar agricultural reform in Japan) and of calculating the price for land where there is no market are discussed. After introducing the debate on the meaning of "just compensation" as required by the constitution (3.1), this chapter analyzes the provision on compensation for loss in the ELA and examines whether the element of "livelihood compensation" for the expropriated who have difficulty in reconstructing their livelihood solely through market price compensation is included (3.2). Finally, the issue of livelihood compensation is considered from a justice theory perspective (3.3).

1 Basic structure of the ELA and undertakings eligible for expropriation

The basic procedures set forth in the ELA are:

(1) Delineating specific types of undertakings eligible for expropriation by law (Article 3).
(2) Conducting a review and approving an individual undertaking by the Minister of Land, Infrastructure, Transport and Tourism or the prefectural governor (Article 16).

(3) Utilizing the stand-alone authority (Article 51) of prefectural expropriation committees (Article 47, Paragraph 2) to render a ruling on (i) the zoning and plot details of the land to be expropriated, and compensation for rights-related losses other than property rights to the land (Article 48); and (ii) compensation for other losses, the date of vacation and other details (Article 49). However, expropriation based on other individual statutes other than the ELA is also permitted.

In other words, in (1), the parliament as the legislator renders a resolution on whether the public nature of a specific *type of undertaking* is sufficient to justify expropriation. In (2), a government agency reviews the public nature of *a specific undertaking*. Note that the public nature of the undertaking is not subject to scrutiny in (3).

Article 3 states that "An undertaking for public interest for which land may be expropriated or used must be for any of the following." It then lists 49 types of undertakings eligible for expropriation. Many of the entities operating these businesses or undertakings, that is, entrepreneurs ("expropriators") such as national bodies, the local government, independent administrative corporations, etc., are "entities that have a public nature," an admittedly ambiguous phrase. However, enterprises in the private sector such as railroad companies and electric and gas utilities are included in this scope. In principle, a private entity as an expropriator is only permitted where they pertain to basic societal infrastructure that directly and/or indirectly satisfies the usage needs of an unspecified large number of people.

2 Taking for private interest

2.1 "Taking for private interest" in the context of legal systems created in the postwar period of rapid economic growth

As seen earlier, the ELA has a logic whereby the criteria for "public interest" sought undertakings eligible for expropriation that "satisfied the needs of an unspecified large number of people." However, in the period of rapid economic growth in the early 1960s, two statutes were enacted that applied expropriation to large-scale area-level development projects. Given that the ultimate beneficiaries of these statutes were not the public at large but specific private sector companies or individuals, the constitutional validity of taking for private interest was brought into question.

2.1.1 Industrial development park projects

The Act Concerning the Development of the Suburban Consolidation Zone and Urban Development Zones of the National Capital Region in 1958[7] was amended in 1962[8] with additional provisions concerning the construction of industrial development park projects, recognizing the expropriation of land or other facilities necessary for the implementation of the project. The original infrastructural conceptualization at the time was to create several urban development precincts (industrial satellite cities) on the periphery of Tokyo and absorb the growing population and industries there. However, given the inherent limitations of securing vast tracts of land through at-will purchases and land zoning, an amendment was made to authorize the use of eminent domain.

Developers of industrial development park projects were limited to municipal bodies and the Japan Housing Corporation, a public entity. However, the resulting plots were ultimately assigned to private companies. The Diet discussed whether this satisfied the requirements for "public use" set forth in Article 29, Paragraph 3 of the Constitution.

Isao Satō, a public law scholar who appeared as an expert witness at the hearing, gave three reasons justifying the amendment bill as constitutional. First, he discussed the premises of concurring opinions in a judgment of the Supreme Court in 1953[9] that ruled that the Act on Special Measures for the Establishment of Landed Farmers, which was the central legal scheme for the postwar agricultural reform, was constitutional. The agricultural reform measures ultimately involved the acquisition of farmland for the benefit of individual tenant farmers. However, the opinions stated that given that "democratizing the farm system is a public purpose," the measures could be reasonably construed as "public use." Satō stated that the same interpretation applies to industrial development park projects. Second, the amendment sought to shore up the metropolitan area and prevent the overconcentration of the population, a measure Satō stated was "a new interpretation of publicness" that differed from foregoing interpretations of public interest undertakings in the ELA. Third, the amendment bill stipulated the provision of the preferential assignment of land to parties spreading out from existing precincts in the metropolitan capital to ensure that public purposes would be met.[10]

Jōji Tagami, also a public law scholar and expert witness, stated that the Constitution could be interpreted not from the standpoint of stand-alone individualism or liberalism, but rather in terms of allowing the vitalization of the citizenry's economic life or imposing significant restrictions on property rights. He used this interpretation as a starting point to indicate that the proposed bill, which sought to disperse and reallocate the population, contains the premise that a new form of special expropriation of land is necessary.[11]

2.1.2 *The New Housing and Urban Development Act*

The New Housing and Urban Development Act[12] enacted in 1963 was primarily concerned with the creation of so-called "new town" developments. This was the result of a residential system council opinion, which found that "we must demonstrably pursue projects to systematically provide, and on a large scale, quality residential plots at reasonable rates in order to provide for the struggling populace." However, given the limitations of the currently available methods, the "most effective and optimal means of satisfying the requirements above is allowing for the compulsory acquisition of land for residential development through wholesale purchase."

Expropriation requires identifying the zone or precinct in which the undertaking is enforced. In the case of road construction projects, one can physically identify a suitable area. In residential development projects, however, it is exceedingly difficult to physically identify a specific area (Shimura 1963:37). Therefore, the aforementioned opinion sought to establish specific criteria (population density etc.) and to render urban planning decisions for the zones in which residential development undertakings would be implemented. Moreover, given that the residences, stores and other buildings constructed on the residential land would be offered for private use, the opinion recommended allocating plots via an open call and only to those struggling to attain a better residential standard; creating a land usage plan for the given zone; restricting recipients' use and disposal of the property (imposing an obligation to erect a residence and prohibiting resale); and that the business operator retain buyback rights.

With the help of expert witnesses, the Diet deliberated on the constitutionality of allocating expropriated land to individuals in the context of Article 29. Expert witness Yoshio Kanazawa stated,

> In expropriation carried out under plans pertaining to a pronounced need to comprehensively achieve a public purpose, even if land is ultimately used by an individual, the provision of the land for the use of said individual is in general not the result of merely providing the land for that individual's interest, but a result of the inherent public nature of the plan itself.[13]

Expert witness Jōji Tagami (see 2.1.1) stated that (1) given that this was not an issue of attracting factory operations but one concerning residential problems, and the expected large numbers of applicants, "It is clear that the current bill exhibits a public nature"; (2) given that speculative buying and selling, and the unplanned construction of residential plots was occurring because of population density, "This is not only a question of erecting a home as such, but an issue that exhibits a marked public aspect in terms of politics"; and (3) given that the legal requirements of city planning decisions, construction obligations and resale restrictions guaranteed "the erected plots to follow comprehensive plans and are clearly used for public purposes and residential policy, this is not mere private interest, but corresponds to public use as set forth in the Constitution."[14]

2.2 *The theory of "publicness by planning" and criticisms thereof*

2.2.1 *From "points and lines" to "wholesale" expropriation (Ogawa)*

The industrial development park projects and the new residential development projects, as discussed in Section 2.1, were the attempts to integrate expropriation and the large-scale development of urban areas. These attempts brought into relief the question of how to reconcile the fact that the system ultimately led to the beneficiaries being private individuals with the classic "public use" requirement in expropriation law.

At a general meeting of the Japan Public Law Association in 1966, Ichirō Ogawa stated that as the classical land expropriation system exhibited an "individual and coincidental character" in terms of the way it targeted specific businesses, it was ill-equipped to accommodate the acquisition of large tracts of land such as those used for the development of major electric power projects and cities. These large-scale projects require the coordination of multiple stakeholders' interests in a more wide-ranging way. He continued that given the large numbers of persons seeking residence today, there is a social need for "the acquisition of land necessary for the erecting of residences by national or local governments – with the land ultimately being moved into and used by private individuals for private purposes." He elaborated that times called for "a shift from individual expropriation in the context of 'points and lines' to 'wholesale' land expropriation systems that coordinate a wider range of interests." (Ogawa 1988:534–537, 541).

2.2.2 *"Publicness by planning" (Endō) and "two lines of logic" (Fujita)*

Administrative law scholars proposed the concept of "publicness by planning" as a means of explaining and justifying these systems for the wholesale acquisition of land. Regarding the industrial development park projects and the new residential development projects, Hiroya Endō states the following:

> The current law does allow expropriation for industrial and residential cities, but this does not imply that it allows it for the benefit of individual factory lots or residential areas. . . . The publicness of [*the industrial development park and the New Housing and Urban Development Act*] is neither the result of publicness of individual facilities, nor publicness as a result of city-building as a whole; rather, the publicness of such legal schemes is based upon the fact that through the use of overall city planning, the legal schemes promote the maintenance and promotion of city functionality through dispersion; this in turn contributes to the resolution of residential issues, and in the end the resolution of other problems as they pertain to large cities. In this way, the publicness is found in the *rationality of the plan itself* (emphasis added).
>
> (Endō 1980:215–216)

Endō elaborates on this logic, stating,

> In cases where the publicness of an administrative activity that would serve as the basis for restricting the exercise of rights is not concretely (or in abstract form but unambiguously) codified in the law, only the rationality of the plan serves as a reasonable alternative. . . . This forces one to conclude that this new publicness seen in the abovementioned statutes is in fact the result of and imparted by these plans.
>
> (Endō 1976:50)

Thus, we can interpret the plan itself as functioning to create publicness.

According to Tokiyasu Fujita, the discourse on "publicness by planning" incorporates two lines of reasoning:

> The first line of reasoning posits that in contexts in which an attempt is made to intuit publicness in residential complex construction projects, there must be a clear and rational basis for justifying why a given project is deemed inevitable for that particular tract of land. In this approach, the compliance with a plan is equivalent to the substantive validity of the project's content and objective. In other words, this logic seeks an approach that would secure substantive publicness. For example in the context of the New Housing and Urban Development Act, this logic demands enumerating limited criteria used to determine the precincts in which undertakings would be made. . . . Moreover, it bears out the necessity of wide-area comprehensive land use plans, which serve as the basis for these criteria. In contrast, the other line of reasoning posits that in contexts in which publicness is obtained as a result of formulation within these plans, the compliance with the plan itself seems to function as a justification of the publicness of the venture.
>
> (Fujita 1988:172–173)

Fujita's argument is that the second line of reasoning – the justification of publicness – is open to criticism. The reasoning presumed a standard of procedural rationality, namely, "avoiding standards based on substantive interests and instead seeking to find these through procedural assurances in regard to the formulation of plans." He continues that the "specific criteria to put into place regarding the rationality of a given plan" and the "criteria used to compare and evaluate the balancing of interests" must be further considered (Fujita 1988:175–176).

2.2.3 Residential land acquisition and its public nature (Watanabe)

In contrast, some discourse did not center on emphasizing "publicness by planning," but (in the context of the New Housing and Urban Development Act) that the publicness was found in the acquisition of residential land and in the transfer of ownership rights in itself.

Yōzō Watanabe criticizes an approach that would attempt to posit private interest and public interest as diametrically opposed. According to him, it is the government's responsibility to secure food, clothing, and shelter; therefore, new residential development projects are equivalent to imposing a duty to farmers to sell rice to the government and then allocating it to consumers for private use, under the then-extant rice regulation system. Watanabe states that be it rice regulation or agricultural reform, "allowing the assignment through government power of goods owned by an individual to another individual is valid provided – and only when – there is a public benefit in said assignment." Therefore, his position is that

> Regulations concerning city plans and land use are themselves undergirded by the public nature seen in the acquisition of residential land. Such regulations themselves do not serve to rationalize the publicness. The publicness of residential land acquisition must be logically presaged on the publicness of land use after its planning or disposal.
>
> (Watanabe 1973:209–211)

There is a clear distinction here with Endō's argument, which emphasizes that industrial development park projects and new residential development do not allow for the benefit of individual factory lots or residential areas (Endō 1980:215).

According to Watanabe, the criteria for coordinating benefits are the number of citizens expected to receive such benefits and a qualitative comparison of the benefits that would be restricted and conferred. Watanabe uses the term "publicness" but eschews the inherent meaning of the concept and instead simplifies it as the bare alignment of interests. From this angle, Watanabe posits that if the system acquires residential plots and constructs large-scale, low-cost rental housing and provides it in large quantities "to workers truly struggling to find homes, especially low-income workers," it is more than sufficiently public in nature. However, the New Housing and Urban Development Act principally satisfies the demands of those with the ability to erect a residence – that is, those with relative financial leeway; thus, it exhibits only "minimal publicness." Conferring expropriation rights in said cases raises doubts (Watanabe 1973:215).

As seen in the remarks by Fujita in 2.2.2, "publicness by planning" as a justifying logic evades the fundamental question of whose benefits are to be sacrificed for the benefits of whom, and may hinder autonomous and responsible decision-making (Fujita 1988:175). In that sense, Watanabe's point is correct. However, stripping the inherent meaning from the concepts of publicness and simplifying the equation to a quantitative and qualitative alignment of private interests seem to impede the making of meaningful and practical recommendations from a legal perspective.

2.2.4 Summary

The previous considerations can be summarized in two points.

First, the issue of taking for private use in Japan's ELA has almost exclusively been looked at from the vantage point of the type of undertakings or businesses subject to such measures. Moreover, the act presumes that a private entity may also be an expropriator such as in the case of a private railway company (which is natural considering the historical origin of expropriation). Thus, the issue of taking for private use as debated in the context of industrial development park projects and new residential development hinged not on "who" the expropriator was, but on the "ultimate beneficiary" of these measures. However, if a private entity is the expropriator, this is limited to facilities that directly or indirectly satisfy some use by an unspecified large number of people. In this sense, the attribute of the expropriator is also put to the test.

Second, the classical example of taking for private use, namely, industrial development park projects and new residential development, emerged out of the need for a wholesale land expropriation in the period of rapid economic growth. One line of reasoning justifying private individuals or companies as beneficiaries revolves around "publicness by planning." However, this logic avoids the fundamental question of whose interest is to be sacrificed for whose benefit. In contrast, simplifying the equation to an alignment of private interests produces a new question: What should the role of legal discourse here be? Jurisprudence does not appear to have provided a clear and demonstrable basis for answering the questions that arise: How should interests be coordinated and what kind of interest coordination would yield publicness in the context of land expropriation? The only basis we currently have is the criterion of "the usage needs of an unspecified large number of people" as discussed in Section 1.

As seen earlier, the concept of taking for private interest ultimately problematizes the question of who is to be the ultimate beneficiary. However, it is often difficult to pinpoint who the beneficiary might be. Since this was relatively easy to do with industrial development park projects and new residential development, and the differences with classical forms of expropriation were clear, this point was highlighted and its conformity with the Constitution was debated.

Today, industrial development park projects and new residential development are seldom carried out. However, with type-2 urban redevelopment projects,[15] which are still often carried out today, land is first expropriated across a wide range, after which the new rights to the floors of a newly constructed building are allocated to the previous landowners and new business operators. If we interpret those who are allocated rights to floors as ultimate beneficiaries, this could rightly be categorized as "taking for private interest." However, the legal scheme is seldom discussed in this context.

In a previous paper analyzing a German Federal Constitutional Court judgment on the aforementioned test circuit,[16] this author stated the following:[17]

> The intended "purpose of expropriation" in the context of systems for expropriation of land for construction in cities is frequently observed or identified by critics merely through reading into the matter. The point at issue in this judgment on the test circuit was the structural improvement of the local economy and creation of work opportunities. This would not ordinarily – at least in the context of Article 85, Paragraph 1, Item 1 of the federal construction code – come to the fore as a basis for justifying expropriation.
>
> (Kadomatsu 2004:539)

The previously mentioned analysis pertains only to a special example of expropriation in German law; however, could we not say that in general – be it for the "purposes of expropriation" or "the ultimate beneficiaries" – that these factors are discovered and identified only by reading into these issues? For these reasons, we should question the framing of these issues. In this regard, the benefits afforded by comparative law are considerable.

2.3 *Eminent domain in an age of population decline: handling land whose owner is unknown*

In contrast to the industrial development park projects and new residential developments, which occurred against the backdrop of legislation in the period of rapid economic growth, today's declining population in Japan is leading to "underuse" (Takamura 2015), which is driving the application of a new type of legislation that differs from the prevailing expropriation system in that it does not focus on the acquisition of property rights, but on the configuration of usage rights.

2.3.1 *The Unclaimed Land Act (1) special cases of land expropriation*

The Act on Special Measures Concerning Facilitation of Use of Land of Unknown Owner (hereafter "Unclaimed Land Act" (ULA)),[18] enacted in 2018, stipulates special cases of procedures for land expropriation, and systems for the configuration of usage rights for regional welfare promotion projects as concern the "land of an unknown owner," described in Article 2, Paragraph 1 of the act as "land, in whole or in part, the owner of which cannot be identified following methods prescribed by ordinance and where substantial effort is deemed to have been made in said search." (See Kadomatsu 2020.)

The special cases for land expropriation procedures describe how a ruling ("*Saitei*") by a prefectural governor can be made on land expropriation for the "specified land of an unknown owner" (Article 2, Paragraph 2) on which no building is currently erected and which is not being used for a particular business purpose or otherwise. This ruling allows the governor to make the ruling of expropriation without referring the matter to an expropriation committee. This has two implications.

First, it relaxes the requirement of finding the owner. The ELA already employs a system for rendering judgments on land whose owner is unknown. Where the expropriator is unable, without negligence, to ascertain the name and address of the landowner, some procedural requirements may be exempted. In contrast, as mentioned, the ULA states that for land "on which no building is currently erected and which is not being used for a particular business purpose or otherwise," provided a search is made "by the methods prescribed by Cabinet Order," the land can be classed as "specified land of an unknown owner." The requirements of "without negligence" clause is relaxed, with a search satisfying the patterned survey methods deemed to suffice (Hiramatsu 2019:38).

Second, expropriation by the ruling of the governor can be carried out without the intervention of the expropriation committee. The justification for this is that (i) having limited dates to convene an expropriation committee, a council system by outside experts, causes a bottleneck in the ruling proceedings; (ii) compensation for the specified land of an unknown owner can be easily calculated; and (iii) the nonexistence of rights holders objecting to the details of compensation can be confirmed in advance through the use of public notice (N. Tanabe 2018:64). However, (i) and (iii) in some respects correspond to the usual "owner unknown" ruling system in the ELA. Therefore, (ii) appears critical. Where the expropriator is a prefectural governor, parties with direct interests engage in a ruling, which to some extent impairs the neutrality and fairness of the procedure. There is room to debate whether the circumstances in (ii) justify this or not.[19]

2.3.2 The Unclaimed Land Act (2): community welfare promotion projects and publicness from a local community standpoint

Next, "community welfare promotion projects" refers to the undertakings enumerated in Article 2, Paragraph 3 of the ULA as "those that contribute to the increased common welfare and/or convenience of local residents and other parties." Even if the undertaking does not correspond to one of the undertakings eligible for expropriation as defined in Article 3 of the ELA, if it corresponds to any of the "community welfare promotion projects," this allows for configuring usage rights for the specified land of an unknown owner. The act enumerates undertakings such as parks, public squares, and shopping facilities, for which provisional or temporary land use is expected. In other words, this system looks at undertakings that lack sufficient publicness to justify expropriation, but in which a certain level of publicness as concerns the welfare and convenience of local residents is found. For such undertakings, in lieu of assigning ownership rights through expropriation, this system allows for provisionally configuring usage rights. How should we interpret this system?

First, this differs from taking for private interest, as seen in the strictures of land supply during the period of rapid economic growth (see 2.1). The land of an unknown owner is today the result of decreased economic demand for said land, causing the owners to lose economic incentives to manage or dispose of it properly. Moreover, in many cases, the transactional costs of inheritance exceed the benefits accrued from the land. Thus, the estate is not allocated, producing a legal anti-commons situation in which the shared state of the heirs continues (Kadomatsu 2020:72–73).

To accommodate this, some arguments suggest eschewing the requirement of "a certain level of publicness" by the ULA for community welfare promotion projects. For example, a joint proposal by several academic associations suggests a legal system to encourage the use of unclaimed land. Even if the use is entirely of a private dimension, the party seeking to use the land can make a filing and a public body execute by proxy the presumed intent of the owner of the unclaimed land, imposing terms of sale or rental.[20] If we consider cases in which the owner does not evince interest in the land and it is not being used in any practical way, it is true that the need to protect the property in terms of personal freedom (as one basis for justifying property rights) is minimal, thus such a proposal is intriguing. However, this is a challenging question in view of ownership rights system as a whole. In my view, at least at this stage, one must adhere to the principle that some kind of "publicness" is required for the compulsory acquisition of and configuration of the use rights for land. The next question is whether there is any difference in cases of the land of an unknown owner from the usual standard of publicness required for expropriation (Kadomatsu 2020:79–80).

As seen earlier, the ULA employs a system requiring the ruling of the prefectural governor to approve not the acquisition of ownership rights, but the usage rights as concern community welfare promotion projects. How does this system properly and sustainably achieve publicness, and what type of publicness might that be? While the types of businesses prescribed by Article 2, Paragraph 3 of the ULA include elements similar to those in Article 3 (undertakings eligible for expropriation) of the ELA, such as facilities for roads (1) and schools (2), unique items are also enumerated, such as residences for the victims of disasters (7) and shopping/cultural/educational facilities prescribed by Cabinet Order (8). In addition, the act imposes the requirement of "those that contribute to the increased common welfare and/or convenience of local community residents and other parties." Compared to the forms of publicness used to justify land expropriation, these could be considered "weaker," but of interest is the mention of the "local community" in these requirements. Here, a form of publicness revolving around the "shared welfare of local residents" is recognized, an aspect not necessarily front and center in the ELA.

In contrast to the changes to publicness following the need for wholesale land acquisition in the period of rapid economic growth, as seen in the cases of industrial development park projects and new residential development, in today's age of population decline the question of how to sustainably maintain local regions seems to produce a new form of publicness. At least insofar as the land of an unknown owner is concerned, this publicness is not presaged on inherent or internal dimensions of the concerned plot, but on external factors. However, the publicness presupposes the "commonality" of the local region, which relates to the commons nature of the land and space above it. To achieve that publicness, the ULA employs a system whereby usage rights to the land are configured for up to a maximum of ten years. Given the weaker publicness here, the act did not provide for the acquisition of property rights but instead employed a system whereby usage rights are configured through a specialized ruling (Kadomatsu 2020:77–79). This system cannot be appropriately discussed outside the context of the commonality of "local communities."

A criticism of the usage rights scheme in the ULA states that since the land must be restored to its original condition after the end of the term, the undertakings economically eligible for use will be limited, impeding active use. Thus, the system should be extended to acquiring ownership rights (Tomita 2017:27).[21] Admittedly, community welfare promotion projects fail to function in the event that an entity to operate such a project does not appear. To that end, a reasonable amount of time to turn a profit is likely needed for private sector firms. On the other hand, requiring the parties undertaking projects to periodically renew their usage rights after a given length of time is significant as it provides a framework for ensuring that publicness (albeit weak) can be maintained.

3 Compensation for loss, with an emphasis on livelihood compensation

3.1 "Just compensation" under Article 29, Paragraph 3 of the Constitution

Article 29, Paragraph 3 of the Constitution stipulates that "private property may be taken for public use upon just compensation therefor." There is a classic conflict between the "full compensation" argument and "appropriate compensation" argument regarding what constitutes "just compensation." The former treats the expropriated party as "eligible for full compensation at the objective market value of the asset," while according to the latter, "provided the amount is reasonably calculated and appropriate for the given asset, it can be lower than market rates" (Ashibe/Takahashi 2019:249).

However, caution is advised when making such simple contrasts. First, the "appropriate compensation" argument is derived from an interpretation of a Supreme Court judgment concerning the postwar agricultural reform. The main point at issue in the judgment was determining what calculation method to use for farmland, disposition of which was heavily restricted and therefore market rates virtually do not exist in the first place.[22] The ruling found that "just compensation" as used in Article 29, Paragraph 3 of the Constitution "is based on amounts deemed valid given the economy at the time and represents a reasonably calculated appropriate amount, which need not match the corresponding amount in full." It added that the acquisition amounts set forth in the Act on Special Measures for the Establishment of Landed Farmers represent "just compensation." In addition, as previously mentioned, for farmland with no established market value, calculating the price based on "rates that would be deemed valid given the economy at the time" is the point at issue, even before the question of whether the price and the amount of compensation "match."[23]

Second, the "full compensation" logic argues that the aforementioned full "objective market value" is constitutionally supported, but this alone may not be enough to compensate the party subject to expropriation for all losses. The underlying premise is that psychological losses and other damages, namely the "affection value" one has for the land, are not included. First, if we assume that the owner is a "rational economic player" in possession of complete information, then he or she continues to retain the land because the perceived value accrued from retaining it (the subjective value) exceeds the market value for that land (more accurately, the amount after transactional and transfer/assignment fees are deducted) (Iwahashi 2000:189). Therefore, at least theoretically, the above market rate (the objective value) should under no circumstances represent "full compensation" for the owner. To compensate for this, the ELA employs the concept of "loss ordinarily incurred" (Article 88) and measures for livelihood rehabilitation (Article 139–2).

3.2 Compensation for loss under the ELA and "livelihood compensation" in a broad sense

Compensation for loss for the expropriated land under the ELA is primarily (1) a fair value at the time of public notice of approval of the undertaking for public interest, calculated by taking into account the market value of similar neighboring land (with adjustments corresponding to fluctuation in commodity prices until the time of determination of the acquisition of rights) (Article 71), and (2) loss from expropriation or use of land ordinarily incurred (Article 88). The details of "loss ordinarily incurred" are set forth by Cabinet Order (Article 88–2) (hereafter the "Details Order"). In addition, voluntary acquisition is stipulated in a similar way as in the guideline by cabinet decision (hereafter "Criteria Guidelines"), and more detailed criteria by the Land Consultation Liaison Group, an organization of expropriators.

A 1973 Supreme Court judgment uses the term "full compensation" with respect to the compensation sought under the ELA, which differs from its interpretation of Article 29, Paragraph 3 of the Constitution. Specifically, it states that "parties subject to expropriation must be indemnified in a manner equivalent to the asset value; where indemnifying in cash, said amount must be sufficient for the party to be able to acquire substitute land commensurate to the value of the expropriated land in a neighboring area."[24] Can it be said that the "full compensation" argument incorporates this element of "*ensuring that the livelihood and business of those subject to expropriation is maintained at an equivalent standard to that they once enjoyed on the land prior to expropriation*"? (This is referred to later as "livelihood compensation in the broad sense.")

3.2.1 Compensation for land and rights thereto: the concept of "commensurate substitute land"

The Supreme Court found that the ELA seeks not necessarily compensation for the market value of land, but "an amount sufficient for the party to acquire substitute land commensurate to the value of the expropriated land in a neighboring area." Of course, if the real estate market functioned ideally, the two would coincide, but if not, the latter is called for.

This logic is also consistent with the 2002 Supreme Court judgment.[25] As stated earlier, the ELA stipulates that the amount of compensation for land must not be the value at the time the land-ownership rights are ultimately assigned after a ruling by an expropriation committee, but calculated based on "the value at the timing of the approval of the undertaking+ adjustment corresponding to changes in commodity prices" (Article 71, fixed price system). The judgment found the use of the fixed price system to be constitutional.

By right, the amount of compensation for the land must first be calculated based on the timing of ruling for acquisition of rights. The computation method used in the current law does not always correspond to fluctuations in trade prices after the approval of the undertaking in neighboring areas.

However, the judgment lists three items:

(1) "In general, changes in the transaction price of similar land in the neighboring area are deemed to be due to the influence of the project concerned. There is no reason to necessarily allow the owner, etc. of the expropriated land to enjoy the benefit that is equal to any increase due to the project in the value of the similar land in the neighboring area. Any changes in the value of the expropriated land that may arise from the influence of the project are attributed to or borne by the expropriator."

(2) "Furthermore, the final decision to expropriate land is made by the determination on the acquisition of rights. Upon public notice of project approval, it becomes certain that a determination on the acquisition of rights will be made at the petition of the expropriator and the land will be expropriated unless the landowner, etc. agrees to voluntarily sell the land. After that, the land will no longer be subject to any ordinary transaction, and hence the transaction price of the land would not change in the same manner as the prices of ordinary land.

(3) "In the case of the voluntary sale of land, a sales contract may be concluded based on a reasonable price calculated at the time of the public notice of project approval considering factors including the transaction price of similar land in the neighboring area."

It uses this to justify not incorporating fluctuations in trade prices for neighboring land occurring between approval of the undertaking and the ruling to acquire the rights. The judgment then concludes the following:

> The ELA provides that after the public notice of the project approval, the landowner, etc. may demand payment of compensation from the expropriator even before a determination on the acquisition of rights is made, and the expropriator so demanded must pay an estimated amount of compensation within two months, in principle (Articles 46–2 and 46–4). Accordingly, it is possible for the landowner to acquire substitute land commensurate to the expropriated land in the neighboring area by using this compensation system.
>
> Based on these points, it is reasonable for Article 71 of the ELA to include provisions concerning the amount of compensation as described above. These provisions enable the owner of the expropriated land to receive compensation by which the owner can retain possession of the same property value before and after expropriation.

One major premise to determine if this is constitutional is whether the system for seeking compensation guarantees the possibility of a party subject to expropriation obtaining *substitute land commensurate to the value of the expropriated land* in a neighboring area.

How should we interpret this notion of a substitute land "commensurate to" the value of the expropriated land? Treating "commensurate to" as meaning "commensurate to the market value" for the expropriated land is of course, redundant. Should this not be interpreted to mean "commensurate to" in the sense of *the expropriated party being able to maintain on the substitute land the same conditions of use by prior to the expropriation on the expropriated land*? If we consider that one reason property rights exist is to guarantee the stable livelihood of the property owner and ensure that it meets the physical requirements to personal freedom, then critical here is the maintenance of the expropriated party's way of life and business, is it not?

3.2.2 "Loss ordinarily incurred": understanding relocation costs

Article 88 of the ELA stipulates,

> Beyond compensation for loss under the provisions of Articles 71, 72, 74, 75, 77, 80, and 80–2, compensation must be made for payment for separation from farming, operating loss, rental loss from building relocation, and other loss from expropriation or use of land ordinarily incurred by Landowners or Interested Persons.

Of the previously mentioned, compensation per Articles 71 and 72 (Amount of Compensation for Land), 74 (Compensation for Remaining Land), 80 (Compensation for Articles), and 80–2 (Compensation for Use Where There are Difficulties in Restoration) is understood as "commensurate value for the taken land (or for the rights thereof)," while all other compensation is understood in the broad sense of "loss ordinarily incurred." Compensation for these "loss ordinarily incurred" has been explained as "that amount deemed necessary for compensation from the standpoint of fair burden that . . . is in line with the actual livelihood of the original landowner." In this way, "livelihood" or "lifestyle" is emphasized (Ozawa 2019:289).

Moreover, compensation in the broad sense of "loss ordinarily incurred" as seen for the items enumerated in Article 88 of the ELA has led to an intriguing debate surrounding the legal positioning of property relocation costs (Article 77).

Article 77 of the ELA states that "if there are articles on the land to be expropriated or used, the articles must be relocated and the relocation costs of the articles compensated for." This is not an "expropriation-centric logic" as concerns properties on a given tract of land – that is, expropriating both the land and the buildings upon it and paying the parties subject to expropriation compensation for the value of the property – but a "relocation-centric logic." Legislative examples of this relocation-centric logic are in the minority worldwide. The majority of countries in Western Europe employ a rule where the buildings on the land are also expropriated (Ozawa 2019:174), based on the expropriation-centric logic.

Where buildings exist on the land and they are not useful to anyone but the expropriated, the value of the land is generally perceived to decrease (i.e., construction depreciation). Article 1, Paragraph 3, Item 1 of the Details Order states that "appropriate value" for the expropriated land (Article 71 of the ELA) should be calculated "when there are structures on the land to be expropriated, without considering the existence of the structures." Unlike normal land transactions in the open market, this approach ignores construction depreciation and attempts to evaluate the land based on the value of the empty plot. This can be understood as a consequence of relocation-centric logic. This is because if the expropriator cannot acquire the site as a vacant lot, relocation (i.e., the entirety of removal, transport and reproduction) cannot be performed (Ozawa 2019:76).

Aiichi Tanabe attempted to describe the relocation-centric logic of the current ELA from the vantage point of understanding the entirety of expropriation compensation with "livelihood compensation."

> For landowners who are forced to relocate as a result of the implementation of a public undertaking, such a change is quite unexpected, and it would be no exaggeration to call it misfortune. Misfortune because the indemnified person will be forced to change their standard of living regardless of his or her own life plans. Ordinarily, when a landowner seeks to sell off a piece of real estate, they have a life plan in mind prior to selling the asset. This is a major difference. . . . If the landowner voluntarily sought to sell the property, it would suffice that the value of the asset was consistent before and after letting it go. However, when one's land is expropriated, one's way of life is also called into question, so simply restoring the equivalent value of the asset to one commensurate to a condition in which no expropriation would have occurred does not suffice. Rather, the individual's way of life must be restored to the state it would have been in the absence of expropriation.
>
> (A. Tanabe 2003:40)

Tanabe relates the relocation-centric logic of the ELA to the idea of livelihood compensation.

> When a landowner is to sell the land and buildings of his or her own accord, the landowner does not seek relocation expenses from the buyer. However, with expropriation, the land and buildings must be given away against the owner's original will, so it does not suffice to seek out substitute land and relocate the buildings and resume their way of life; rather, the original lifestyle prior to the change must be restored. This is why, as a rule, a duty of relocation is incorporated in measures for the acquisition of public land.
>
> (A. Tanabe 2003:71)[26]

3.3 Livelihood compensation and theories of justice

Taking this line of reasoning, that expropriation compensation should be configured such that the original landowner is guaranteed an equivalent standard of livelihood and business commensurate to that held prior to expropriation of the land ("livelihood compensation in the broad sense"), it is implied that the asset compensation could also be understood as part of livelihood compensation. If the objective value inherent in the property was to "enable the security of living and business," the value would be reflected in the market price of the property, preventing a large divergence between compensation for the property value and compensation for lifestyle security. Nevertheless, the diversity of individual lifestyles and values and social capital as they relate to the assets in question tend to produce a divergence between these two elements.

The latter issue of social capital reached a head in relation to compensation following a dam submersion project. When expropriation causes a community to collapse, the internal community relationships and other social capital, one necessary condition for the formation of a particular way of life prior to expropriation, are lost, and the landowners who lost this fundamental basis are unable to maintain their standard of living. This issue seems to have first emerged in the history of Japan's ELA in a dispute surrounding the Shimouke and Matsubara dams (Research group on Shimouke and Matsubara dams 1972). Economist Yuzuru Hanayama conducted an empirical survey of compensation using the dam case, finding compensation that relies solely on the appraised value of the asset to be insufficient. Instead, he advocates the need to incorporate livelihood compensation that includes everyday expenses for a given period, and administrative measures for the livelihood reconstruction and development of the affected region (Hanayama 1969:373).

In terms of constitutional and administrative law studies, "just compensation" has come to be argued in the context of the necessity of including livelihood compensation and living rights.[27] Some believe that the constitutional basis for livelihood compensation should, in addition to Article 29 (property rights), include Articles 25 (right to life) and 14 (equality). While space constraints prevent providing more detail here, what remains to be clarified in these arguments is whether livelihood compensation should be, insofar as the person is an individual, *the minimum standard of wholesome and cultured living* guaranteed by the Constitution as a right to life, or sufficient to guarantee *a livelihood commensurate to that they maintained prior to expropriation*. This point also pertains to the constitutional basis question discussed earlier.

The discourse around compensation for living rights was not directly incorporated into the practice of expropriation. The Cabinet Understanding annexed to the aforementioned Criteria Guidelines in 1962 stated that "If compensation is properly made per these guidelines, additional compensation such as 'living rights compensation' is deemed unnecessary." The opinion of the Losses Compensation Inspection Committee in 1997 declared that property compensation and livelihood reconstruction are not entirely different in terms of their purposes.

The method of compensation generally employs the property value as the most objective and rational means of easily calculating the amount, but its purpose is still to ultimately restore the original landowner's way of life. The opinion further says that "*We must revise individual standards toward shoring up to the extent possible the original asset value compensation* (underlined in original document) such that the way of life of the original landowners can be restored" (Research group on compensation practice 1999:4–5). However, a 2001 ELA amendment led to the inclusion of Article 139–2, Paragraph 1, which states that people who lose the basis of their livelihood as a result of providing land may apply through the expropriator for livelihood rehabilitation measures to be taken, such as the acquisition of substitute land and a new residence or shop, or employment placement. However, this is not codified as a legal obligation but only calls for a reasonable effort of the expropriator.[28,29]

The issue of compensation for living rights can be analyzed from various angles. First is how this relates to theories of justice. Large-scale land expropriation is often carried out in regions where land prices are relatively low and in underdeveloped regions. This invariably leads to certain structural imbalances such as those resulting from income stratification or ethnic differences. This brings to mind the Nibutani Dam Incident judgment[30] in Japan, where a dam project was found illegal because it has failed to exercise "maximum care" in relation to the potential changes the project would cause to the Nibutani region's environment, considered the cradle of Ainu culture. At times, expropriation is implicated in structural imbalances. Is justice regarding expropriation compensation strictly a matter of corrective justice, or does it incorporate elements of distributive justice? The constitutional basis for livelihood compensation and how it pertains to theories of justice may become a contentious point.

Second, in terms of equity, which is the basis of corrective justice, various issues of development interests emerge. Hanayama enumerated the "problem of not allocating any development benefit obtained from the business to the original landowner" in three ways: (1) unfairness between the landowner and expropriator (or beneficiary), (2) incomplete compensation for loss on the part of the landowner (he lists the case of charcoal manufacturers), and (3) strong resistance from the landowner so that compensation negotiations can run into problems (Hanayama 1969:11–19). He places the two issues of full compensation for those subject to expropriate on and unfairness associated with the allocation of development benefits side by side. In addition to the perspective of ensuring the livelihood of the original landowners, the traditional discourse on livelihood compensation has arisen out of an awareness of injustice between beneficiaries of projects – in addition to the expropriator, such beneficiaries might include neighboring landowners who enjoy increased asset value – and the original landowners.

Third, in terms of ensuring the livelihood of the expropriated, another issue is (as discussed earlier) the loss of community relations and other forms of social capital. However, emphasizing this point leads to a certain tension with individual lifestyles and diverse individual values, as mentioned in the first paragraph of this section.

(1) As previously discussed, the Supreme Court seeks that the compensation amount under the ELA be "sufficient for the party *to be able to* (emphasis added) acquire substitute land commensurate to the value of the expropriated land in a neighboring area."[31] Whether or not the person is to acquire an alternative plot in the vicinity is left to the individual's free choice. If the measures for compensation for livelihood rehabilitation seek to reconstruct the community in a separate town, this leads to a certain tension in terms of individual choice.

(2) This paper examined the question of livelihood compensation in the broad sense from the angle of "ensuring that the lifestyle and business of those subject to expropriation is maintained at an equivalent standard to that they once enjoyed on the land prior to expropriation." However, there remains room to question whether it would truly be just to fully compensate values pertaining to all lifestyles and businesses formed through personal preferences prior to expropriation. Katrina Wyman highlighted issues of "objectionable preferences" and "expensive tastes."

> Imagine a white takee who highly values his home at least partly because it is in a homogeneously white neighborhood. Paying this takee and others with similar racist preferences enough to make them subjectively indifferent would entail compensating these takees for objectionable racist preferences.
>
> (Wyman 2007:268)

> Why, for instance, should individuals who choose to prefer elaborate swimming pools and garden statues receive the large amount of funds required to satisfy these costly preferences?
>
> (Wyman 2007:269)

Wyman emphasizes the notion that expropriation compensation is ultimately an issue of realizing corrective justice (not distributive justice) – in other words, "what it means to make somebody whole." However, here, "making somebody whole" does *not* refer to "paying the person sufficient compensation to enable her to feel subjectively indifferent to her losses" (Wyman 2007:250–251), the assumption taken by many theories.

Instead, Wyman proposes her unique theory of "objective criteria."

> The metric for assessing whether a takee has been made whole under a subjective measure is whether she is indifferent to the taking. In contrast, under an objective measure, whether a takee has been made whole is determined by reference to the considered judgments of others about what makes a person whole.
>
> (Wyman 2007:274)

When discussing compensation, we generally employ a lexicon in which the market value of a given asset is referred to as "objective," and contrast this with the "subjective" evaluations of the party subject to expropriation. However, according to Wyman, the fair market value standard employed by the U.S. Supreme Court is "ultimately rooted in individual preferences, including those of the takee" and is an "aggregation of individual preferences" (Wyman 2007:254, 265) making it merely a "subjective measure." Her argument reverses the usual logic of objective value and subjective value.

Her approach is rather rhetorical and radical, but the attempt to interrogate the matter of compensation from the view of what people need to go about their lives, and doing so not from the standpoint of distributive justice, but corrective justice, is exceedingly intriguing. Wyman attempted to explore the possible creation[32] of an objective "schedule" based on an "objective list theory" and Amartya Sen's notion of "capability" (Wyman 2007:278, 275).

Attempting to compensate the expropriated based on their standard of living prior to the change perforce requires analyzing each individual's specific way of life. This "observational" process is inevitable, even if we assume it to not represent "intervention" by the state. However, does this not imply a certain tension regarding the diversity of individual values and formation of a free lifestyle?

Let me add a very short note, though considerations of time and space mean a full and proper treatment of this issue must await another occasion. In the suits for damages arising from the evacuation following the Fukushima nuclear reactor incident, the plaintiffs' claim calls for compensation for "loss of one's homeland."[33] There have been several judgments that admitted the claim.[34] One theoretical issue emerging out of this case will be whether the damages shall be treated as psychological damage, or as damage to livelihood and property. These arguments bear some similarity to the livelihood compensation argument as discussed in this paper. However, we must also note that the suits seek compensation for tort damages, not compensation for loss as in taking compensation, so its theoretical dimensions differ.

Notes

* This work was supported by JSPS Kakenhi Grant Number JP 18KK0033 and JP 18H00796. The author would like to thank Gengo (https://gengo.com) for the draft translation and Editage (www.editage.com) for English language editing. The Japanese version of this chapter was published in *Kobe Law Journal* Vol. 69 No. 2 pp. 195–242 (2019).

1 *Kelo v. City of New London*, 545 U.S. 469 (2005). See Somin (2017).
2 Boxberg Teststrecken Urteil.BVerfGE 74, 264 (1987). See Schäfer (2017).
3 See Chapter 6 in this book.
4 See Chapter 7 in this book. See also Chang (2017).
5 See Chapter 8 in this book. See also Peng (2018).
6 土地収用法 (Act No. 219 of 1951).
7 首都圏の近郊整備地帯及び都市開発区域の整備に関する法律 (Act No. 98 of 1958).
8 Act No. 137 of 1962.
9 Judgment of the Supreme Court, December 23, 1953. 13–7 *Minshu* 1523.
10 40th Diet House of Representatives Construction Committee Minutes, Volume 19, pp. 6–7.
11 Ibid., 7–9.

12 新住宅市街地開発法 (Act No. 134 of 1963).
13 43rd Diet House of Representatives Construction Committee Minutes, Volume 18, pp. 2–3.
14 Ibid., at 4–5.
15 For the legal scheme of type-2 urban redevelopment projects, see www.urca.or.jp/english/pdf/e-urban_redevelopment_in_japan.pdf www.toshiseibi.metro.tokyo.lg.jp/pdf_e/023.pdf.
16 Supra n. 2.
17 BVerfGE 74, 264 (1987).
18 所有者不明土地の利用の円滑化等に関する特別措置法 (Act No. 49 of 2018).
19 Hiramatsu 2019:42 strongly criticizes this point.
20 www.jares.or.jp/dl/0425_suggestion.pdf. Based on the same idea, Tomita proposed the use of some sort of a "rule of occupation" for the properties of an unknown owner (Tomita 2017:29–30).
21 This was a criticism of the drafting stages, that is, the setting of a maximum of five years for usage rights, which was later revised to ten years in the subsequent bill.
22 The plaintiff's argument emphasized a landowner-computed value, while the defense emphasized the "landed farmer income value" set forth in the Act on Special Measures for the Establishment of Landed Farmers.
23 Supra n. 9.
24 Judgment of the Supreme Court, October 18, 1973. 27–9 *Minshū* 1210.
25 Judgment of the Supreme Court, June 11, 2002. 56–5 *Minshū* 958. www.courts.go.jp/app/hanrei_en/detail?id=1492
26 However, there are also convincing criticisms of this position. Even when structures or buildings retained for investment purposes, the ELA applies the relocation-centric logic. If they are to be relocated, the land will be evaluated as a vacant lot. According to the criticism, because such structures or buildings for investment purposes that do not bear on considerations of the restoration of the person's livelihood are also evaluated as vacant lot, the relocation principle and evaluation as a vacant lot do not relate to the idea of livelihood compensation. See Ozawa (2019: 77).
27 Yang (2018) provides a comprehensive survey of livelihood compensation theories in Japan.
28 Article 139–2, Paragraph 2 ("endeavor to").
29 Japan now has far fewer large-scale expropriation projects such as dam development than it once did. However, this is a serious issue in developing countries and in terms of Japan's aid to these countries (Takesada (2012) examines this problem based on field surveys in Japan and Sri Lanka).
30 Sapporo District Court Judgment of March 27, 1997, 1598 *Hanrei Jihō* 33.
31 Supra n. 24.
32 A hypothetical example is shown at Wyman (2007:285).
33 Cf. Yokemoto (2015). Note that this "loss of homeland" argument cites the argument of Hanayama (1969).
34 Cf. Fukushima District Court Iwaki Branch Judgment of March 22, 2018. LEX/DB 25560651.

References

Ashibe, Nobuyoshi (芦部信喜) (revised by Kazuyuki Takahashi (高橋和之)) (2019), *Constitutional Law* (憲法), 7th ed., Iwanami Shoten.

Chang, Yun-chien (2017), Eminent Domain Law in Taiwan: New Law, Old Practice? in: Kim et al. (2017), pp. 93–117.

Endō, Hiroya (遠藤博也) (1976), *Administrative Planning Law* (計画行政法) Gakuyō Shobō.

Endō, Hiroya (遠藤博也) (1980), *Fifty Lectures on City Planning Law* (都市計画法50講) Yūhikaku.

Fujita, Tokiyasu (藤田宙靖) (1988), Compulsory Acquisition of Public Land and Contemporary Public Law (公共用地の強制的取得と現代公法) in: *Land Law in West Germany and Japan* (西ドイツの土地法と日本の土地法), Sōbunsha, pp. 158–184.

Hanayama, Yuzuru (華山謙) (1969), *Theories of Compensation and Reality* (補償の理論と現実), Keisō Shobō, p. 373.

Hiramatsu, Hiromitsu (平松 弘光) (2019), Land of Unknown Owner and "Owner Unknown" Ruling System in the ELA (所有者不明土地と土地収用法の不明裁決), 68 *Evaluation* 1–45.

Iwahashi, Takesada (岩橋健定) (2000), The Meaning of "Publicness" in Pollution Civil Litigation (公害民事訴訟における公共性の意義), in: Mitsuaki Usui (碓井光明) et al. (eds.), *Kōhōgaku no Hō to Seisaku* (公法学の法と政策), Yūhikaku, pp. 179–204 (189).

Kadomatsu, Narufumi (角松生史) (2004), Re-examining "Publicness Through Planning" (「計画による公共性」再考), in: Natsuo Sambe (三辺夏雄) et al. (eds.), *Hōchi Kokka to Gyōseihō* (法治国家と行政法), Yuhikaku, pp. 513–549.

Kadomatsu, Narufumi (2020), The Tragedies of the Commons and Anticommons in an Era of Underuse, in: Kadomatsu et al. (eds.), *Legal Responses to Vacant Houses: An International Comparison*, Springer, pp. 61–81.

Kim, Iljoong/Lee, Hojun/Somin, Ilya (eds.) (2017), *Eminent Domain: A Comparative Perspective*, Cambridge University Press.

Ogawa, Ichiro (雄川一郎) (1988), The Development of Public Requisition Jurisprudence and Land Use Planning (公用負担法理の動向と土地利用計画), in: *Gyōsei no Hōri* (行政の法理), Yūhikaku, pp. 533–551.

Ozawa, Michikazu (小澤道一) (2019), *Commentary of the Expropriation of Land Act (II)* (逐条解説土地収用法(下)), 4th ed., Gyosei.

Peng, Chung (2018), *Rural Land Takings Law in Modern China: Origin and Evolution*, Cambridge University Press.

Research group on compensation practice (1999), *Amendment of the Loss Compensation Criteria* (改正損失補償基準), Taisei Shuppansha.

Research group on Shimouke and Matsubara dams (1972), *Public Works and Fundamental Human Rights* (公共事業と基本的人権), Teikoku Chihō Gyōsei Gakkai.

Schäfer, Hans-Bernd (2017), Taking Law from an Economic Perspective with Reference to German Law, in: Kim et al. (2017), pp. 8–37.

Shimura, Seiichi (志村清一) (1963), On the Opinion of the Residential System Council (宅地制度審議会の答申について), 272 *Jurist* 36–39.

Somin, Ilya (2017), Eminent Domain in the United States, in: Kim et al. (2017), pp. 38–66.

Takamura, Gakuto (高村学人) (2015), Reconsidering Property Right Theories in the Era of the Underuse of Proprieties (過少利用時代における所有権論・再考), 81 *Hōshakaigaku* (法社会学) 64–75.

Takesada, Naruhiko (武貞稔彦) (2012), *Development Intervention and Compensation* (開発介入と補償), Keisō Shobō.

Tanabe, Aiichi (田辺愛壱) (2003), *Loss Compensation System* (損失補償制度), Seibunsha.

Tanabe, Naoki (田邊直樹) (2018), Overview of the Act on Special Measures Concerning Facilitation of Use of Land of Unknown Owner (所有者不明土地の利用の円滑化等に関する特別措置法の概要), 71–8 *Hōritsu no Hiroba* 60–72 (64).

Tomita, Yu (富田裕) (2017), On the Proposal by the National Land Development Council on the Usage Right for the Land of Unknown Owners and Discussing Introduction of the Rule of Occupation for Properties with No Owner (国土審議会の提案する所有者不明土地利用権設定制度の問題点とその解決としての無主不動産に一定の先占権を認める制度の考察), 31–3 *The Japanese Journal of Real Estate Sciences* 23–30 (29–30).

Watanabe, Yōzō (渡辺洋三) (1973), The New Housing and Urban Development Act (新住宅市街地開発法) in: *Zaisan to Hō* (財産と法), Tokyō Daigaku Shuppan Kai, pp. 205–218 (209–210).

Wyman, Katrina Myriam (2007), The Measure of Just Compensation, 41–1 *UC Davis Law Review* 239–287.

Yang, Yashu (楊雅舒) (2018), *Expropriation Compensation in Japan and China – With an Emphasis on Livelihood Reconstruction Compensation* (収用補償の日中比較ー生活再建補償を中心に), unpublished LL.D. thesis at Kobe University.

Yokemoto, Masafumi (除本理史) (2015), Is the "Loss of Homeland" of the Evacuee Compensated? (避難者の「ふるさとの喪失」は償われているか), in: Takehisa Awaji (淡路剛久) et al. (Eds.), *Fukushima Gempatsu Jiko Baishō no Kenkyū* (福島原発事故賠償の研究), Nihon Hyōron Sha, pp. 189–209.

6 What enables a private party to expropriate an individual from an estate in Korea?*

Jin-Sik Yoo and NooRi Se

1 Introduction

Since the 1970s, the legal system of land expropriation (taking) in Korea has been continuously deregulated under the influence of national land development policy, which overemphasizes the importance of economic growth through the development of industrial complexes. Under the present legal situation, private takings (i.e., cases when a private corporation exercises its power through eminent domain) are prevalent but lack enough safeguards for the protection of private properties and securing public interest. This situation has instigated many conflicts between the user, the landowner and the residents. This paper examines the structure and content of the legal system related to land expropriation in Korea and also examines the current issues.

To begin, the paper introduces the Constitutional clause related to expropriation (Art. 23 Sec. 3) and its "public necessity" requirement (2.1). It then examines two judgments of the Constitutional Court related to the requirement and discusses how the court's position on private takings is changing (2.2, 2.3). It also introduces the legal scheme related to land expropriation and identifies a large loophole – namely, the possibility of the abuse of individual special acts (3). The danger of such a loophole is illustrated using an example of the Jeju Special Act (4.1) and a case study of a Supreme Court judgment related to the Act and its aftermath (4.2). Lastly, a summary is provided (5).

2 The "public necessity" requirement of the Constitution

2.1 Art. 23 Sec. 3 of the Constitution as a basis for expropriation

The Constitution of the Republic of Korea Art. 23 Sec. 3 provides as follows:

> Expropriation, use, or restriction of private property from public necessity and compensation therefor shall be governed by the Act: Provided, That in such a case, just compensation shall be paid.

DOI: 10.4324/9781003170600-8

As in other countries, the meaning of "public necessity," as described in the previous paragraph, is highly controversial in Korea. The controversy is closely related to the discussion of whether a private taking – the case in which a private corporation is allowed to exercise its power of eminent domain – should be allowed and, if it is, whether there should be special requirements for the case. This point was a central issue in two cases presented before the Constitutional Court of Korea.

2.2 *The Industrial Sites and Development Act case judgment*

The first judgment of the Constitutional Court on September 24, 2009,[1,2] concerned the constitutionality of the Industrial Sites and Development Act (hereinafter, "ISDA").[3] Art. 22 Sec. 1, which stipulates that private corporations may expropriate properties that are necessary for industrial complex development, was contested in this case. The petitioners insisted that the provisions infringed upon their right to property.[4]

2.2.1 *Background of the case*

On July 31, 2004, the Governor of Chungnam Province approved and announced the development project of the "Second Tangjeong General Local Industrial Complex" in Tangjeong-Myeon, Asan City. The governor designated an electronic company A, which is part of a large conglomerate, as the project operator[5] according to Art. 16(1)3 of the ISDA.

Petitioners were owners of land located in the development area. Company A attempted to purchase the land with petitioners. When the negotiation failed, the corporation initiated the condemnation proceeding with the Chungnam Province Land Tribunal and applied for an adjudication.[6] On May 22, 2006, the Land Tribunal ruled to condemn the lands and buildings (taking disposition).

The Petitioners filed a case seeking to revoke the disposition of the Tribunal in the Daejeon District Court. While the case is pending, petitioners also filed a motion to request a constitutional review on the part of "project operator" of Art. 22 Sec. 1 with regard to Art. 16, Sec. 1, Item 3 of the ISDA, alleging the contested provisions that permit private corporations to expropriate lands necessary for industrial complex developments infringed on the right to property. After the motion was denied, petitioners filed a constitutional complaint.[7]

The Constitutional Court, in an 8 to 1 vote,[8] held that the contested provisions do not infringe on the right to property, thereby not violating the Constitution.

2.2.2 *The opinion of the Constitutional Court*

A. *On whether private taking is allowed*

Art. 23 Section 3 of the Constitution stipulates the possibility of the expropriation of properties under the condition of just compensation, not limiting the eligibility for expropriation. This provision focuses on whether the taking complies with public necessity, and whether the compensation for the taking is just, not on whether the person exercising eminent domain power[9] should be a governmental body or a private corporation. There would be no significant differences in determining public necessity and condemnation scope in the event of either a public institute, such as the State, may directly take properties or a private corporation may take properties under the condition of the permit of a public institute. Therefore, there would be no reasons to limit the eligibility for takings into public institutions, such as the State.

As long as public institutions, such as the state, have the leading role and final decision-making authority in the overall process of determining the public necessity of the project and reviewing whether or not to accept it, this is only a concrete implementation of the decisions of the State or others, even if the private enterprise is the subject of expropriation.

(. . .)

The development of industrial complexes may require a large-scale capital investment. If a project operator of industrial complex development is limited only to the state or local governments, limited budgets may cause difficulties in promoting the development project. If the public development system is the only available option, the development of an industrial complex is likely to end up wasting resources due to an imbalance of demands for development. On the other hand, if a corporation is allowed to develop an industrial complex directly, it would promote the participation of corporations. Therefore, it would be implied that it is not unconstitutional to stipulate that a private corporation can be qualified as a project operator, and it is reasonable for legislators to enact the contested provision that allows private corporations to take land required to implement the project.

B. On what "public necessity" means

The legislative purpose of the contested provisions to contribute to the sound development of the national economy by promoting balanced national land planning and steady industrial development through the smooth supply of industrial location and reasonable industrial arrangement (Art. 1 of the ISDA), proposing to stimulate industrial decentralization and to activate the local economy (Art. 25(b)(i) of ISDA). If the industrial location is smoothly supplied, it would promote the construction of industrial complexes that would lead to economic development and growth. Besides, economic growth through the development of industrial complexes has been the fundamental foundation of the social and cultural development of our society. Considering that economic growth has significantly improved the living standards of the national community, the importance of industrial complex developments would be ascertained.

It should be considered that the provisions of the Act regulate the project operator that conducts the industrial complex development project lest the

> initial public interests that are expected to be achieved through the construction of industrial complexes can be neglected because of overfocusing on the profits of private corporations. Therefore, the contested provisions would satisfy the requirement of "public necessity under Art. 23 Section 3 of the Constitution."

2.2.3 Dissenting opinion

There was also a dissenting opinion expressed by Justice Kim Jong-Dae as follows:

> The expropriation of private corporations demands intensive legislative measures to secure the public necessity of the taking and to revert the benefits from taking to the public in order to justify such expropriation because it is more difficult to promote public interests through private taking, compared to a public taking where the State leads the condemnation to benefit the public. For instance, some institutional arrangements, such as measures to guarantee continuous restitution of the development benefits caused by such expropriation or public use the business profit derived from such expropriation or the mandatory job quota system providing for local residents should be added, thereby sharing the fruits of expropriation with all members of the community, including those taking and being taken. Without these legal and systematic remedies, private takings pertinent to the contested provisions would not comply with the value of the guarantee of the right to property of our Constitution.[10]

2.2.4 Comment

In the authors' view, it is controversial whether economic development can be included within the scope of the "public necessity" cited in Art. 23 Sec. 3 of the Constitution. Notwithstanding, the majority opinion of the Constitutional Court overemphasized the importance and meaning of economic growth through the development of industrial complexes while making light of the other various points that should be necessarily considered in the land expropriation system.

In the previously mentioned case, the petitioners contended that a stricter standard must be stipulated in the Act that provides for a private taking, because the ultimate goal of the private sector is the pursuit of profit. However, the opinion of the Court rejected the petitioners' argument and responded:

> Art. 23 Sec. 3 of the Constitution states that "public necessity" and "just compensation" as legal requirements, eligibility for expropriation shall be determined by whether the above two requirements are met. (. . .) The need for a stricter standard in expropriation should be understood in a political context to facilitate the process of expropriation based on the will of the wider public or to prevent abuse of the authority to expropriate. Therefore, it is hard to call the law unconstitutional merely because of its lack.

In Korea, most scholars are inclined to admit that private taking is allowed. Many of them, however, emphasize that there should be strict limitations to it so that it meets the requirement of "public necessity" prescribed in Constitutional Law Art. 23 Sec. 3. Naturally, there is academic discussion about what "public interest" or "public necessity" mean, including a notable opinion that focuses on what the enterprise engages in.[11] It states that only if the enterprise serves to provide goods and services that are necessary for human existence, which is concerned with transportation, electricity, gas and water service, etc. (*Daseinsvorsorgeunternehmen* in German[12]), may it take private property. However, there should be stricter limitations for takings by a private enterprise that undertakes pursuits only pertaining to private interests.[13] Even when enterprise business activity may result in enhancing public welfare through industrial development or creating job opportunities, this is only an incidental benefit of seeking private profit.[14] In addition, we cannot ensure that public welfare is sustainably guaranteed in the case of private takings. Therefore, the prevailing view in the academic field is that some special legal-institutional guarantees will be necessary in case of private takings.[15]

In this case, the opinion of the Constitutional Court did not mention what kind of activities the enterprise was engaged in nor how the benefit derived from the development would be shared. Needless to say, private taking would bring a sizable profit to the enterprise with the increase in land price and the operation of the would-be factory. At the very least, the Court should have considered how the benefit would be shared. However, it failed to do so because the Court prioritized economic development. In this respect, dissenting opinion is much more persuasive.

2.3 *The Balanced Regional Development Act case judgment*

On October 30, 2014, the Constitutional Court rendered another judgment concerning private taking.[16] It ruled that the Balanced Regional Development and Support for Local Small and Medium Enterprises Act (hereafter the "Balanced Regional Development Act (BRDA)") violates Art. 23 Sec. 3 of the Constitution.

Under the Act, a private party can also be designated as the project operator of a district development project (Art. 16(1)4), and the manager may expropriate or use such land as is needed for the execution of the said project (Art. 19). The dilemma is that among the district development projects prescribed by this Act, "the preparation of tourist resorts" includes projects such as luxurious golf courses and resorts. The Constitutional Court, in a 6 to 3 vote,[17] deemed the contested provisions of the Act as unconstitutional.[18] This judgment can be appraised as one step forward for the regulation of private takings, but it still has its shortcomings.

2.3.1 *Background of the case*

On October 26, 2009, the head of a Gun ("county" in Korean) designated Company B as the project operator for the regional development project according to the BRDA. The project aimed at the development of a golf course and resort area. The Act endows the power to the project operator, which may include private corporations, to expropriate the land necessary for the implementation of the regional development project. Because Company B didn't acquire the plot of the appellants by negotiation, it applied for adjudication on the expropriation. On December 21, 2010, the Local Land Tribunal ruled to condemn the lands and buildings (taking disposition). After the other court proceedings were exhausted, the Petitioners filed a constitutional complaint.

2.3.2 Opinion of the court

2.3.2.1 Public necessity

The Court first renders the interpretation of "public necessity" in Art. 23 Sec. 3 of the Constitution. The judgment analyzed the concept based upon two elements: "public interest" and "necessity."

> ***"Public Interest"***
>
> The scope of projects that are in the public interest for which expropriation is permissible, i.e., "public works," must be clearly defined by law according to the principle of reservation of laws on expropriation. (. . .) The scope of public works is a matter to be determined by legislative policy, which may change depending on the goals of the state and the circumstances of the time. In the past, public works that were allowed to be expropriated for public use began with specific projects such as road construction, railroad construction, power plant construction, and canal construction, but have been expanded to include nonspecific projects. In addition, the scope of public works is defined by the administrative demands of the time and changes in the socio-economic environment. The undertakings that are currently available for public expropriation are enumerated in the Act on Acquisition of and Compensation for Land, etc. for Public Works Projects and also in each individual Act.
>
> (. . .) In light of today's legislative tendency to expand the scope of public works, it is necessary to consider the "public necessity" requirement in order to assure harmony with the existence guarantee of property rights. As to the "public necessity" requirement, it is reasonable to view the concept as requiring a significant public interest beyond the abstract public interest in general or the state's interest in particular, and more narrowly than "public welfare," which is the reason for limiting fundamental rights in general. To determine the degree of public interest, the legislative purpose of the individual law authorizing public expropriation, the nature of the project, the extent to which the project contributes to the legislative purpose as well as the possibility of use and accessibility of the general public to the project facilities, especially if the business targets the general

public, must be taken into account [Underlines are inserted by authors of this chapter].

"Necessity"

Takings not only directly deprive others of their property rights, but also threatens to bring about de facto restrictions on a number of constitutional values, such as freedom to relocate freedom of contract, which is derived from Art. 10 of the Constitution. Therefore, even if the expropriation is provided for in the Constitution, it must be found to be so necessary that the property of the people must be acquired, even forcibly against their will, and in order for that necessity to be found, the public interest that is sought to be achieved through the expropriation of public property and the interests of private persons whose property rights are thereby infringed. In the balance between the two, the superiority of public interest must be found to justify an infringement of the private party's property rights.

In particular, when the project operator is a private person, in addition to the superiority of the public interest mentioned above, there should be institutional discipline to ensure that the public interest obtained by executing the business is not significantly omitted, taking into account that the basic purpose of the private person's economic activity is to pursue profit.

2.3.2.2 Unconstitutionality of the Balanced Regional Development Act

Based on the previously mentioned interpretation of the "public necessity" requirement, the Court moves on examining whether the BRDA violates the constitutional requirement. The Act enumerates the possible executers of "regional development project" including a private corporation. When the project implementation plan is approved by the relevant administrative authorities and the corporation is designated as the executor, the corporation will be endowed with the power to exercise expropriation. The "project for preparation of tourist resorts" is one of the "district development plans" enumerated by the Act (Art. 14 Sec. 7 item 4).

The Court stated as follows and concluded that the Act violated Art. 23 Sec. 3 of the Constitution.

Some projects for the preparation of tourist resorts, such as large-scale amusement park projects, contribute to the legislative objectives in terms of increasing the income of residents in areas where the level of development is significantly low. In addition, some projects are open to the public and readily available in terms of cost, hence in public interest in terms of public use of and accessibility. On the other hand, in the case of luxurious golf courses and resorts (hereinafter referred to as "luxurious golf courses, etc."), the average number of employees is small, even though they are built on large sites and cost a lot of money, and they have a self-sufficient business model in which all the consumption activities are carried out within the facilities. The contribution to the legislative objectives, such as balanced development and increase in residents' income, is low. In addition, although these businesses are operating for the public, they are inaccessible to a small number of people due to excessive financial burdens associated with the use of business facilities, which means that public use and accessibility are low and the public interest is low.

We must weigh the public interest achieved through the expropriation of the business of luxurious golf courses against the interests of private persons whose property rights are infringed by the expropriation. As the characteristics of the business of luxurious golf courses show, the public interest in securing the local tax revenue and revitalizing the local economy is achieved only incidentally. Compared to the basic rights violated by the residents who are forcibly expropriated by the business, this level of public interest is not superior enough to justify the violation of such basic rights. Therefore, in the case of a luxurious golf course project, it is not necessary for private developers to be able to acquire the property of others against their will by coercion. It is not necessary to examine whether there is an institutional discipline to ensure that the public interest that can be obtained through the implementation of the business is not seriously impaired.[19]

2.3.3 Comment

The BRDA Case Judgment of the Constitutional Court is remarkable in that it states that the "public necessity" requirement of Art. 23 Sec. 3 must be a "significant" public interest beyond the abstract public interest and concludes that the Act be rendered unconstitutional because it may allow the expropriation even for a luxurious golf course, as happened in the case in point.

However, this judgment is subject to several criticisms. First, academics question the judgment that divides the concept "public necessity" into two elements – "public interest" and "necessity." The critics argue that the concepts should be considered indivisible.[20]

Second, the judgment distinguishes between the "public necessity" of the Art. 23 Sec. 3 and "public welfare" of the Art. 37 Sec. 2[21] of the Constitution. The latter stipulates the restrictions on fundamental human rights in general.[22] The Constitutional Court has required the principle of "prohibition of excessiveness (*Übermaßverbot* in German)" in judging whether a statutory act violates Art. 37 Sec. 2. However, as the judgment separated Art. 23 Sec. 3 from Art. 37 Sec. 2, there is a danger that the Court will abandon the principle of "prohibition of excessiveness" and merely resort to the general proportionality principle.

Third, the judgment mentions the requirement of special "institutional discipline" in the case of private takings but does not convey the actual contents of the discipline. Moreover, the judgment focused on the nature of the project itself, and the conclusion of unconstitutionality does not seem to be dependent upon the fact that this was a private taking. The "institutional discipline" argument remains *obiter dictum* in the opinion of the court.[23]

Fourth and foremost, the criterion of "significant" public interests, by its nature, is very vague. It is very doubtful whether this criterion can function effectively to control individual Acts that allow private takings. In this particular case, it was easy to establish that there was very weak public interest in the development of a luxurious golf course. However, the scope of this finding is unclear (can we draw a clear distinction between a luxurious golf course for the wealthy and a sports facility for the general public?).[24,25] However, in more subtle cases, it would be very difficult to judge the constitutionality.

All in all, even with the BRDA Case Judgment, it would be too optimistic to expect effective control of takings legislation by the Constitutional Court.

3 Land Expropriation Act (AACL)

As mentioned, Art. 23 Sec. 3 presupposes that the statutory act regulates the details of taking and compensation. Based on this article, the Land Expropriation Act has been enacted, with the official name: "Act on Acquisition of and Compensation for Land, etc. for Public Works Projects" (hereafter, AACL).[26] The AACL prescribes the process of land expropriation as follows:

3.1 Project approval and its loophole

The first step for project operators to expropriate land from others according to the AACL is to obtain project approval from the Minister of Land, Infrastructure and Transport (Art. 20(1)). Project approval means the determination of any public works as a project to expropriate or use land, etc. (Art. 2 Item 7).

To obtain project approval, the planned project must belong to the categories of undertakings enumerated in Art. 4, such as the undertakings for national security, railways, roads, etc. In addition, the "public necessity" (Art. 19(1)) of the specific project must be recognized.

In granting the project approval, the Minister should consult the heads of related central administrative agencies and the Special Metropolitan City Mayor, a Metropolitan City Mayor, a Do Governor, and a Special Self-Governing Province Governor (hereinafter referred to as Mayor/Do Governor) and hear in advance the opinions from the Central Land Tribunal established under Art. 49 and persons interested in such project approval, as prescribed by Presidential Decree (Art. 21(1)). As such, the project approval system of the AACL aims to regulate substantial requirements as well as a process to guarantee that there is a public necessity for the project.

However, there is a significant issue in this step, related to the "exceptional case" admitted under the AACL. Art. 4 Item 8 of the law stipulates that taking is not only possible for the undertakings enumerated in the same Article Items 1 to 7, but also possible for projects based on individual special Acts as prescribed in the Attached Table.[27] This works as a large loophole to allow private taking easily.

The number of the Acts prescribed in the Attached Table amount to 110. Some of them – that is, the Tourism Promotion Act, the Act on Building and Managing Marina Port, the Act on Developing and Utilizing Station Influence Area and the Act on Promoting Taekwondo and Building Taekwondo Park – allow private taking. In addition, many such special Acts ease the strict process required for obtaining project approval. Today, most of the land expropriations in Korea have been accomplished based upon the special Acts prescribed in the Attached Table. For a long time, it has been said that this is the biggest problem in Korean land expropriation.

3.2 Application for adjudication

When a consultation held under AACL Art. 26 yields no agreement, a project operator may file an application for adjudication with the competent Land Tribunal, as prescribed by Presidential Decree, within one year from the date project approval is publicly notified (Art. 28(1)). There are two land tribunals that render adjudication on the expropriation. One is the Central Land Tribunal, established under the Ministry of Land, Infrastructure and Transport, and the other is a local land tribunal, established under the Special Metropolitan City, a Metropolitan City, Do or Special Self-Governing Province.

4 Special individual acts

As mentioned earlier, according to AACL Art. 2 Item 8, there are 110 special individual acts prescribed in the Attached Table, many of which allow private takings and ease the expropriation process and laws, which prescribe different expropriation procedures from those of AACL.

Let us consider the "Special Act on The Establishment of Jeju Special Self-Governing Province and the Development of Free International City" (hereafter the "Jeju Special Act" or JSA) as an example and examine how they are different from the original rule of the AACL.

4.1 Jeju Special Act

4.1.1 Purpose of the Act

The purpose of this Act is to contribute to national development by establishing the Jeju Special Self-Governing Province and guaranteeing substantial devolution to its local government in order to maximize the geographical, historical and cultural traits of its preceding local government, Jeju-do, with highly guaranteed autonomy based on self-regulation, accountability, creativity, and diversity, and also by developing Jeju-do into a free international city through extensive administrative deregulation and application of international standards (JSA Art. 1).

4.1.2 The process through which project operators obtain project approval

In Jeju Island, according to the Jeju Special Act, it is easy to obtain project approval. The Act stipulates that a project operator must obtain approval from the Governor to implement a development project. However, the project operator is the State or the Jeju Free International City Development Center (hereafter "JDC"), which is established according to JSA Art. 166, only the opinion of the Governor, and not the approval, is required (JSA Art. 147(1)). [28]

When the project operator attains approval from the governor, it shall be deemed as the project approval prescribed in AACL Art. 20(1) (JSA Art. 147(1), 148(1) Item 5). Furthermore, the procedure to obtain the governor's approval is simple. The project operator should formulate a project plan and submit it to the governor, along with accompanying documents, as prescribed by Provincial Ordinance.

In such cases, the project plan and accompanying documents to be submitted to the governor should include the details for preferential employment of residents of the Jeju Self-Governing Province (JSA Art. 147(3)). After receiving those documents, the Governor shall seek the opinions of local residents, interested experts, etc., as prescribed by Provincial Ordinance, and if such opinions are deemed valid, he or she may grant approval to implement the project plan on condition that such opinions shall be reflected in the project plan (JSA Art. 147(4)).

After obtaining approval, he or she consults with landowners and persons concerned. If there is a failure to reach an agreement with them, he or she may file an application for adjudication to the competent Land Tribunal.

Although the requirements and the process of the previously mentioned approval differ from the project approval scheme under the AACL, the approval shall be "deemed as" the project approval and will have the same legal effect. This legal technique is commonly called "project approval as legal fiction" and is quite prevalent in special individual acts that provide for expropriation. This technique makes the problem of special individual acts serious.[29]

4.2 Case of Jeju-do's Ye-rae Healing Style Housing Site

4.2.1 Background of the case

On November 5, 1997, the mayor of Seoguipo, Jeju-do made a city planning decision for an amusement park project based on the National Land Planning and Utilization Act (before the amendment on December 7, 2005, hereinafter, "NLPU"). Amusement parks belong to one of the categories stipulated in NLPU Art. 2,[30] for which expropriation is possible. As of 2001, the amusement park had not been implemented and a Healing Style Housing Site Formulation Project was proposed, which included housing (condominium and farmland-style dwellings) and leisure (golf course and sports center). On October 14, 2003, Jeju-do decided to implement the Healing Style Housing Site Formulation Project (hereafter, the Formulation Project) on the site of the previously mentioned city planning facility area. It designated JDC as the project operator of the Formulation Project. The mayor of Seoguipo amended the city planning facility area on October 14, 2005, to incorporate a larger area for the Formulation Project. The size of the project was 743,700 m^2 in total, but 51.5 percent of the area was designated as the "Healing Facility," which comprises healing housing facility (condominium) and tourist hotel. On November 14, 2005, the mayor of Seoguipo, Jeju-do approved the Formulation Project as the implementation of the city planning facility based on NLPU Art. 86 and Art. 88. Based on this provision, the JDC was endowed with the power to exercise expropriation.[31]

The project operator, JDC, failed to form an agreement with the landowners about buying the project site. JDC had applied for the adjudication of the Central Land Tribunal to expropriate their land. The tribunal delivered an adjudication that accepted JDC's application. The landowners then protested against it and, in turn, submitted an appeal to the tribunal. However, the tribunal overruled their appeal on November 22, 2007. Finally, they filed a suit to revoke the tribunal's adjudication.[32]

4.2.2 Summary of the decision

The Supreme Court[33] declared the adjudication of the central land tribunal void. The reason for this was very simple. It ruled that the Implementation Project on which the adjudication was based was illegal. The main factor of illegality was that the size of the Healing Housing Facility was larger than that prescribed in the law. That is, the mayor authorized the Implementation Project based on the city planning facility decision to build an "amusement park," but the Healing Style Housing, which comprised 51.5 percent of the entire project, cannot be regarded as such.

> This Healing Style Housing Complex is designed to be used by a specific class of people, such as the elderly with high incomes, and the main purpose of the complex is to make profit by selling the complex to them. In addition, as the main facility is for residences or long-term stays, the availability to the general public is limited, and in light of the overall structure of the facility, the use by the general public is only incidental. In light of the above, it is clear that this Healing Style Housing Complex is far from an amusement park, which is a city-planned facility that is required to have a public character as "a facility for entertainment and rest, established mainly to contribute to the improvement of the welfare of the residents" as stipulated in Art. 56 of the Urban Planning Facilities Regulations.[34]

In the end, the Authorization of the Implementation of Urban Planning Facility Projects was ruled void and it followed that the Adjudication of the Central Land Tribunal was also declared void.

Through the examination of this case, we can observe how it is easy for the head of a local government to approve an implementation project and designate the executor. Even prior to the amendment in 2017 (see 4.2.3), it was easy and probably even easier after the amendment.

In the case cited earlier, the illegality was very clear so that the Supreme Court could easily declare the mayor's authorization of the implementation project to be void and, accordingly, the taking adjudication. However, if the mayor had more seriously tried to meet the formal requirements, we do not know how the Supreme Court would have decided on the issue.

4.2.3 Aftermath

After the taking adjudication had been declared void, the former landowners filed a suit to reclaim their property.[35] Land owned by those landowners amounted to 61 percent of the entire plot.

On the other hand, the National Assembly amended the Jeju Special Act in an effort to legalize the development project in 2017. Specifically, the amendment has introduced a special provision of the Act on Planning and Utilization of National Land that includes "facilities for recreation and healing that contribute to the improvement of residents' welfare and facilities for tourists' sightseeing and rest" to the definition of "amusement facilities."[36] Following this amendment, we cannot clearly establish that the Healing Style Housing Complex is not an amusement park, so whether the Supreme Court would evaluate the project as illegal under the present law is uncertain. In addition, as mentioned earlier (4.1), the amendment has introduced the scheme of project approval as legal fiction.

The former landowners filed a constitutional complaint against this amendment of the Jeju Special Act, contending that the amendment infringes upon their right to sue in order to recover their properties. However, the Constitutional Court rejected the petition for lack of standing because the petitioners did not meet the requirement of Constitutional Complaints based on Art. 68 of Sec. 1 of the Act on Constitutional Court[37] and did not concretely describe the possibility of the infringement of their constitutional rights.[38,39]

This overall process demonstrates the danger of abuse of special individual Acts for takings, which can even legalize private takings after the fact, and the Constitutional Court may not provide an effective remedy against abuse.

5 Conclusion

This paper aimed at examining the structure and content of the legal system of land expropriation in Korea and examines where the problem lies, with a special focus on private takings.

First, we established that the main reason a private party can obtain a landowner's land easily is the "loophole" in the AACL. The Constitution and the AACL in Korea have normal (or "global standard") prescriptions (substantial and procedural requirements), similar to other countries. However, a large loophole, namely, the expropriation based on individual special Acts stipulated in the Attached Table, circumvents the functions of the formal procedure prescribed in the AACL. According to such individual special Acts, if the head of the local government authorizes the project implementation and designates a project implementer, he or she may expropriate a landowner's land (project approval as legal fiction). It does not matter if he or she is a private or public party. Unfortunately, most of the land expropriations have been undertaken based on individual special acts in Korea, resulting in a lack of safeguards for the protection of private property and securing public interest. The Jeju Special Act and the aftermath following the Supreme Court judgment illustrate this danger.

Second, we cannot help lamenting the Constitutional Court's weak stance in interpreting the constitutional requirement of "public necessity" for the expropriation. The Industrial Sites and Development Act Judgment allowed for too much economic development and provided the legislator with an excessive amount of flexibility to provide for private takings in an individual special Act. The judgment did not consider the unique danger of private takings and the necessity of safeguards against it. The Court is much to blame for easy private taking in Korea. The BRDA Case Judgment is one step forward, but it still has shortcomings. The judgment is not only academically debatable in its distinction between "public interest" and "necessity" but is also largely unclear in the scope of its finding. It remains to be seen whether the judgment may function as an effective safeguard against the abuse of individual special acts that provide for private takings.

Notes

* This work was supported by JSPS Kakenhi 18KK0033.

1 21–2(A) KCCR 562, 2007Hun-Ba114, September 24, 2009. English summary can be found at: http://search.ccourt.go.kr/ths/pr/eng_pr0101_E1.do?seq=1&cname=%EC%98%81%EB%AC%B8%ED%8C%90%EB%A1%80&eventNum=23571&eventNo=2007%ED%97%8C%EB%B0%94114&pubFlag=0&cId=010400. When quoting this judgment, the author relied primarily on this English summary but made necessary supplements and modifications.

2 This judgment is mentioned in I. Kim (2017, pp. 180–183).

3 Industrial Sites and Development Act (Revised December 29, 1995 by Act No. 5111).

4 Art. 22 (Land Expropriation) of the ISDA [Enforcement Date July 1, 2001.] [Act No. 6406, January 29, 2001.] (1) A project operator (. . .) may expropriate or use land, buildings, things fixed to the land, rights thereto excluding ownership, mining claims, fishery rights, or rights concerning the use of water (. . .), which are necessary for executing the industrial complex development project concerned.

Art. 16 (Operators of Industrial Complex Development Projects)

(1) An industrial complex development project shall be implemented by a person who is selected according to the development plan as designated by the authority to designate industrial complexes from among persons falling under any of the following subparagraphs:

1.~2. (omitted)

3. A person who wishes to install facilities adequate for the relevant development plan and to move therein, or a person who is deemed capable of developing an industrial complex in accordance with the relevant development plan, if such person meets the requirements prescribed by Presidential Decree;

5 This designation as a project operator is an example of "project approval as legal fiction" as explained later (4.1.2).
6 See 3.3.
7 Constitutional Court Act Art. 68–2.

> If the motion made under Art. 41 (1) for adjudication on the constitutionality of statutes is denied, the party may file a constitutional complaint with the Constitutional Court. (omitted).

8 When the Constitutional Court declares a statutory law unconstitutional, it requires the assent of at least six justices out of nine.
9 When taking is allowed for the benefit of a project by a private enterprise, there is a discussion on whether the "subject" of the taking is the state, which makes an expropriation decision, or the enterprise, which enjoys the legal effect of the expropriation (see Jang (2013, pp. 82–85)). The Industrial Sites and Development Act Case Judgment is not clear on this point. On one hand, the judgment states that a private corporation may "exercise" eminent domain power and admits "eligibility for takings" to such a corporation. On the other hand, however, the judgment states: "Even if the private corporation is the subject of the expropriation, it is only a concrete implementation of the state's decision." Here the judgment reduces the role of the corporation to "implementing" the decision of the state.
10 He also warns as follows: "If the subject of expropriation and the object of expropriation are both equally positioned private party, such expropriation would be tantamount to forcing the property of one person to be transferred to the property of another."
11 Chung (2015b, pp. 176–178).
12 As is well known, the founder of this concept is Forsthoff (1938).
13 Chung (2015b, p. 177).
14 N. Kim (2004, p. 595).
15 Some statutory laws that allow private takings do stipulate such special legal-institutional guarantees. The requirement to voluntarily acquire a certain ratio of the plot of the undertaking before the takings adjudication (hereafter "land acquisition requirement") is one such example (e.g., Special Act of the Development of Enterprise Cites, Special Act on Private Rental Housing, Special Act on the Establishment of Jeju Special Self Governing Province and the Development of Free International City (for the last act, see 4.1)). The ISDA, however, did not stipulate such a requirement. The petitioners contended that the lack of land acquisition requirement would lead to the unconstitutionality of the law, but the Court rejected the argument. The Court contended that the decision to impose certain land acquisition requirements on eminent domain should be left to the policy judgment of the legislator based on the public need for the project in question (however, due to later legal revisions after the Constitutional Court judgment, the land acquisition requirement was inserted into the ISDA).
16 26–2(A) KCCR 639, 2011 Hun-Ba 172, October 30, 2014. This judgment is mentioned in I. Kim (2017, p. 199).
17 The judgment barely met the minimum requirement (see supra n. 8).

18 Basically, "(t)hree types of decisions are made by the Constitutional Court; rejection, dismissal and upholding. Rejection is made when the request of adjudication does not have rationale; dismissal is made when the request was made unlawfully; and upholding is made when the request has reason" (https://english.ccourt.go.kr/site/eng/03/10301020000002020081101.jsp).

However, to avoid the possible legal vacuum and turmoil by nullifying the Act because of unconstitutionality, the Court declared the Act to remain in force until the legislator revised it (Suspended Unconstitutionality).

19 As mentioned earlier, this judgment was a 6–3 split decision. Three justices contended that the Act is constitutional stating that:

> Even if the clause restricts the property rights, it cannot be said that the degree of restriction is more important than the public interest guaranteed by the clause of the law in this case. (. . .) The legal provisions in this case also provide an institutional device to ensure that the public interest is not impaired, and thus are considered to provide the "public necessity" as required by Art. 23 Sec.3 of the Constitution.

20 Chung (2015a).

21 Art. 37 Sec. 2 The freedoms and rights of citizens may be restricted by the Act only when necessary for national security, the maintenance of law and order, or for public welfare. Even when such a restriction is imposed, no essential aspect of the freedom or right shall be violated.

22 Regarding the relationship between Art. 23 Sec. 3 and Art. 37 Sec. 2, see Hong (2016).

23 On the other hand, the dissenting opinion appears to admit rather easily that there is enough "institutional discipline" incorporated in the Act. This also cast doubts on the effectiveness of "institutional discipline" criterion in controlling private takings.

24 There is a judgment of a lower court that admitted "public necessity" for a golf course available to the general public (Suwon District Court 2008 GuHap6418).

25 The dissenting opinion views that the "institutional discipline" of the BRDA is sufficient. The opinion also shares the view that projects such as luxurious golf courses are not in the public interest that may legitimize expropriation. However, the opinion does not view this as a problem of statutory provision itself. According to the opinion, it is an issue of administrative authorities that designated the project operator and approved the implementation plan.

26 English translation can be found at: https://elaw.klri.re.kr/eng_mobile/subjectViewer.do?hseq=48465&type=subject&key=03&pCode=49&pName=Housing%20Re-development

27 After the 2015 amendments of the AACL, it was made impossible to allow takings by an individual act not based on Art. 4 and the Attached Table. In other words, if an individual law would allow private takings, it became necessary to amend Art. 4 and the Attached Table at the same time. It was said that this amendment provided for "stricter control" of takings considering the reality that "individual laws have allowed for indulgent public expropriation." However, as will be shown later, "stricter control" has not been achieved in practice.

28 The JDC is a national public corporation under the Ministry of Land, Infrastructure and Transport. See https://english.jdcenter.com/about/aboutdetail.cs

29 Regarding the issue of "project approval as legal fiction," see J. Kim (2015). The 2015 amendment of the AACL stipulated that in the case of expropriation under special individual acts, the administrative authority must hear the opinion of the Central Land Tribunal before the project approval. One must see whether this regulation will be effective. It should be noted that other procedural requirements in the AACL (Article 22 (Public Announcement of Project Approval), Article 23

(Invalidation of Project Approval) etc.) are still omitted in the case of special individual acts.

30 More specifically, it was prescribed by the Enforcement Decree.

> Enforcement Decree of the National Land Planning and Utilization Act
> Art. 2 (Infrastructures) (1) The term "facilities as prescribed by the Presidential Decree" in subparagraph 6 of Art. 2 of the National Land Planning and Utilization Act (hereinafter referred to as the "Act") means the facilities falling under each of the following subparagraphs (including incidental facilities and convenience facilities necessary for the display of functions and utilization of the relevant facilities):
> 2. Space facilities: Squares, parks, green areas, amusement parks, and public vacant lands;

31 This approval as the implementation of the city planning facility based on the NLPU has the same legal effect as the project approval under the AACL. As mentioned later (4.2.3), the Jeju Special Act was amended after this Supreme Court judgment. Whereas the main text in 4.1 discusses the present law, the background of the case and the judgment in 4.2 naturally presupposes the legal situation under the Act before the amendment, where the power to exercise expropriation is based on the NLPU and not on the Jeju Special Act.

32 As mentioned earlier, because the JDC is a national public corporation, it is debatable whether we can regard this as "private takings." However, because the situation is still different from the takings for the benefit of the state or local governments, we treat this example as private takings in a broader sense.

33 Because Korea employs a Constitutional Court system similar to Germany, the primary role of the Supreme Court is not constitutional interpretation, but the interpretation and application of statutory laws and regulations. However, the Supreme Court does retain some roles in constitutional issues. See https://eng.scourt.go.kr/eng/judiciary/introduction.jsp#t103

34 Supreme Court Decision 2011 Du3746 Decided March 20, 2015 [Revocation of Adjudication on Land Expropriation, etc.]

35 Forty-three landowners whose property was expropriated and most of the landowners who transferred their property after negotiation following the project approval filed lawsuits for the cancellation of registration of transfer of ownership.

36 Art. 406 Sec. 2 of the Jeju Special Act (2) Notwithstanding Articles 43 (2), 77, and 78 of the National Land Planning and Utilization Act, matters concerning the guidelines for the determination, structure, and installation, and the building-to-land ratio, floor area ratio, etc., of amusement facilities (including amusement and recreation facilities to be installed for the improvement of residents' welfare and convenience and tourist facilities to be installed for the tourism and recreation of tourists) among urban and Gun planning facilities to be established in Jeju Self-Governing Province, may be prescribed by Provincial Ordinance: Provided, that no area for tourist accommodation shall exceed 30/100 of the total area. (Amended by Act No. 14190, May 29, 2016.)

37 See Constitutional Court Act Art. 68. https://english.ccourt.go.kr/site/eng/03/10301020000002020081101.jsp.

38 Constitutional Court 2016. September 27, 2016 Hun-Ma727, Decision [rejection (4th)].

39 In addition, there were legal conflicts (an Investor-State Dispute Settlement procedure as well as a lawsuit) between the JDC and the Malaysian Corporation that had invested in the Formulation Project (Berjaya Land Berhad) because the project was suspended as a result of the Supreme Court judgment (Yonhap News 2020).

References

Chung, Nam-Chul (2015a), On Whether Private Taking Is Constitutional or Not, and How the Concept of Public Necessity Should Be Translated (민간기업에 의한 공용수용의 위헌성 판단과 공공필요의 개념해석), *Lawtimes* (법률신문), 2015.4.15.

Chung, Nam-Chul (2015b), Eminent Domain for Privater (사인을 위한 공용수용), *The Basic Principle of Administrative Relief* (행정구제의 기본원리), *bobmunsa* (법문사), pp. 172–198.

Forsthoff, Ernst (1938), *Die Verwaltung als Leistungsträger*, Stuttgart/Berlin: Kohlhammer.

Hong, Gang-Hun (2016), A Study on the Relationship between the Public Welfare (Constitution of the Republic of Korea Article 37(2)) and the Public Necessity (Constitution of the Republic of Korea Article 23(3)) (헌법 제37조 제2항의 "공공복리"와 제23조 제3항의 "공공필요"에 관한 연구), *Public Law Review* (공법연구), vol. 45, no. 1, pp. 177–202.

Jang, Eun-Hye (2013), A Study on the Possibility and Limitation of Private Takings in the View of Public Law (사인수용의 가능성과 한계에 관한 공법적 연구), doctoral dissertation at Ajou University, pp. 1–262.

Kim, Il-joong (2017), Who Exercises the Eminent Domain Power in Korea? A Focus on Private Takings, in: Iljoong Kim et al. (eds.), *Eminent Domain: A Comparative Perspective*, Cambridge: Cambridge University Press, pp. 177–207.

Kim, Jong-Ha (2015), A Study on the Unconstitutionality of the Acts Governing Large-scale Urban Development Projects (대규모 도시개발사업 관련 법률의 위헌성에 관한 고찰), *Public Land Law Review* (토지공법연구), vol. 71, p. 190.

Kim, Nam-Chul (2004), Legal Problems Concerned with Eminent Domain in the Enterprise Cities (기업도시에서의 사인을 위한 토지수용의 법적문제), *Public Land Law Review* (토지공법연구), vol. 24, pp. 573–596.

Yonhap News (2020), https://www.yna.co.kr/view/AKR20200701090100056?input=1195m, 2020.7.1.

7 Public-interest requirements of zone expropriation in Taiwan*

Ming-Chih Lee

1 Introduction

In Taiwan since the 1980s, the government has widely used a system of "zone expropriation" to seize a wide range of private lands for urban development. The system is widely regarded as a comprehensive land-improvement measure.[1]

As it turns out, the Taiwanese government has routinely abused zone expropriation, leading to public outcry in recent years. One particularly notorious case came to light in 2009. Known as the "Dapu Incident," it involved the confiscation of arable farmland in central Taiwan for two development projects: a science park and a residential area. Many Taiwanese criticized what they regarded as a lack of regard for the public interest. This case has raised concerns about just how much public interest is actually satisfied in zone-expropriation projects. My focus in the present study is this very issue: Does zone expropriation meet the public-interest requirement associated with land expropriation?

First, I look back at the history of zone expropriation in Taiwan and the system's relationship with capitalism. I then review the system of zone expropriation as it exists today in Taiwan. Afterward, I clarify the quality of public-interest requirement that accompanies zone expropriation and confirm whether zone expropriation satisfies the public interest.

2 The history of zone expropriation

2.1 Sharing the benefits of zone expropriation with the general public (1930–1977)

In the legal system in the Republic of China (ROC), zone expropriation first surfaced in the Land Law of 1930, which was enacted only in mainland China, as imperial Japan ruled Taiwan until 1945. After the government established certain undertakings, land prices of the surrounding land rose, and the surrounding landowners, despite having done nothing extra to improve the value of their own land, benefited from this government-triggered inflationary pressure. Therefore, the ROC government instituted zone expropriation to expropriate land on a large scale while trying to preserve a degree of equality in land rights and to

DOI: 10.4324/9781003170600-9

avoid excessive concentrations of land-based wealth in landowners. Pursuant to Article 343 of the Land Law of 1930, zone expropriation meant the compulsory purchase of all land within a given area, where replanning and consolidation were required. (This Article became Article 212 in the Land Law of 1946, which took the place of the 1930 law and is still in effect today in Taiwan.)

To implement urban land reform, the Taiwanese government promulgated the Statute for the Equalization of Urban Land Rights on August 15, 1954. (It was reenacted as the Equalization of Land Rights Act on February 1, 1977.) This law stipulated that "Municipal and County (City) Governments may choose appropriate areas to implement zone expropriation for the needs of urban construction and development," a stipulation that effectively expanded the scope of zone expropriation. In general, the law's regulations concerning zone expropriation followed the provisions of the Land Law.[2]

During this period, the purpose of zone expropriation was to prevent private-land monopolies from forming, to place limits on the concentration of land-based wealth among private landowners and to share the benefits of rising land prices with the general public.[3]

2.2 *The development of zone expropriation and mandatory cooperation (1977–2000)*

In the 1970s and 1980s, limited public funds, coupled with objections from landowners, resulted in a notably low number of actual zone expropriations.[4] Meanwhile, real estate prices and demand for developable land were increasing. To expand the implementation of zone expropriation, the government enacted the aforementioned Equalization of Land Rights Act (1977, known at the time as Article 54). This provision, which affected the original landowners concerning their preferential right to purchase expropriated land in proportion to its original value,[5] essentially served to protect their rights by allowing them to share in the development benefits.[6]

Nevertheless, because compensation for expropriation was too low, and the land being set aside for repurchase by the original landowners was too little, the implementation of zone expropriation remained difficult at best.[7] Therefore, in 1986, improvement measures such as the "land for compensation" provision were added to the Equalization of Land Rights Act. This provision, in particular, meant that now the original landowners could choose cash compensation or compensation in land (Article 54).[8] In principle, the total area of lands set aside for compensation was now to be 50 percent of the total zone expropriation area (Article 54).[9] In this way, the government sought to avoid costly monetary payouts while permitting the original landowners to share in the post-development benefits.[10]

The function of zone expropriation gradually evolved into a promotion of land development and land use. Likewise, the nature of zone expropriation evolved into a kind of mandatory cooperative development project, requiring the government and original landowners to share in the benefits of development.[11] To increase residential land area and prevent the formation of private land monopolies, the Executive Yuan in 1989 and 1990 declared that when national or local governments establish or expand urban planning, zone expropriation should be the basis for any related construction development ("The Letter of 1989," No. 24460, and "The Letter of 1990," No. 23088, issued by the Executive Yuan). This declaration was made in response to housing shortages and inadequate urban development, and as a result, after 1990, the government dramatically increased its use of zone expropriation to obtain land for the planning and building of public housing.[12]

2.3 *The emergence of zone expropriation for public–private cooperation since 2000*

In addition to the Equalization of Land Rights Act, regulations such as the New Town Development Act and the Statute for Encouragement of Private Participation in Transportation Infrastructure Projects promoted zone expropriation for the acquisition of developable land. Owing to differences in procedural and compensatory land-expropriation standards, the Legislative Yuan promulgated the Land Expropriation Act of 2000 to integrate all relevant regulations. The zone-expropriation provisions stipulated in the Land Expropriation Act generally followed those of the Equalization of Land Rights Act. Nevertheless, the new provisions now allowed competent authorities at various levels to entrust certain zone-expropriation matters to individuals, business-sector organizations and academic organizations (Article 55 of the Enforcement Rules of the Land Expropriation Act). Also, these provisions authorize the Executive Yuan to transfer or sell certain lands to specific persons (Article 44 of the Land Expropriation Act). Therefore, when the government obtains developable lands, it may sell part of them to a developer to offset the development expenses that the government has already incurred in its partial development of the land. This approach promotes public–private cooperation for development-oriented zone expropriation[13] but could trigger land speculation leading to an economic crisis.[14]

In summary, the purpose of zone expropriation has been to prevent the concentration of landownership and land interest. However, because of opposition from landowners, and the inherent complexity of zone expropriation, the Taiwanese government gradually implemented regulations promoting public–private cooperation. As a result, the guiding principle of "sharing the rising prices of land with the general public" ceded place to co-sharing the land-development benefits between government, developers and landowners. An important point is that zone expropriation, because it serves the development of specified swaths of land, is currently considered a means of land development,[15] especially in urban settings. However, because zone expropriation is a method of compulsory land acquisition that falls under the category of land expropriation,[16] it is recognized that zone expropriation shall follow public-interest requirement for land expropriation according to Articles 15[17] and 23[18] of the Constitution and to Judicial Yuan (JY) Interpretations of the Constitution, and it should follow that land-expropriation requirements, such as those concerning the public interest and compensation, should apply to zone expropriation.[19]

In the following section, I review Taiwan's system of zone expropriation as stipulated in the Land Expropriation Act. I then discuss the issue of public interest as it relates to zone expropriation.

3 Taiwan's system of zone expropriation

Pursuant to Article 1 of the Land Expropriation Act, land expropriation shall be governed by the act, and matters not provided in the act shall be governed by other applicable acts. In short, the Land Expropriation Act should be – and is – the basis for my discussion of Taiwan's system of zone expropriation. I have divided the discussion into two parts: the first part delves into the specific reasons for Taiwan's zone expropriation, and the second part explores land use after zone expropriation.

3.1 The reasons for carrying out zone expropriation

According to Article 4 of the Land Expropriation Act, zone expropriation may be carried out when any of the following six circumstances apply: (1) all or part of a newly established urban area is to undergo development; (2) an old urban area is to undergo renewal to meet public-safety, sanitation, or transportation needs or to promote reasonable land use; (3) an agricultural zone or protection zone of urban land is being changed to construction land or an industrial zone is being changed to a residential zone; (4) any nonurban land is to undergo development; (5) a rural community is to undergo renewal to improve infrastructure, public health, or to coordinate with agricultural development planning; or (6) zone expropriation is to be carried out according to other acts. Zone expropriation in the Land Expropriation Act generally follows the provisions laid out in the Equalization of Land Rights Act.[20] However, Subparagraph 6, which states that zone expropriation may be carried out according to other laws, was newly added to the Land Expropriation Act in 2000, and this provision is not contained in the Equalization of Land Rights Act.

According to the current pertinent acts, zone expropriation may be widely used for development, and some of the reasons for zone expropriation are so vaguely defined as to open themselves to remarkably broad interpretations.

3.2 Land use after zone expropriation

Land, after it is obtained through zone expropriation, becomes public. However, the Land Expropriation Act sets aside parts of the expropriated land for private use. This stipulation has injected great controversy into the zone-expropriation system. For this reason, we should explore the seven main ways in which zone-expropriation lands are to be handled according to the Land Expropriation Act: (1) competent authorities in charge of the expropriation shall uniformly plan and allocate the public land (Article 43); (2) competent authorities may create a special agricultural zone where the original landowners, if they apply for it, may farm (Article 43–1); (3) competent authorities shall distribute lands for compensation back to the original landowners (Article 44); (4) lands used for roads, ditches, parks, green space, children's playgrounds, public squares, car parks, public athletic grounds and primary schools shall be registered, on a gratuitous basis, under the ownership of the appropriate municipality, county (city), or village (township) (Article 44); (5) competent authorities may, according to their financial plans, allocate lands designated for certain public facilities to government agencies that need such lands or either sell those lands to public enterprises (Article 44); (6) lands used for public housing, settlement of the original residents, or for special projects approved by the Executive Yuan, may be transferred or sold (Article 44); and (7) other construction lands may be sold or leased through bidding, or be created with superficies (Article 44).

The post-expropriation guidelines previously mentioned reveal that parts of expropriated lands are used for compensation and that other parts are sold or leased, the latter parts being the land finally transferred to private persons or enterprises other than the original landowners. In other words, zone expropriation involves expropriated land for "public use" and expropriated land for "private use."[21] As mentioned earlier, zone expropriation should meet certain requirements that attach the idea of public interest to the general practice of land expropriation. Does the system of zone expropriation meet these requirements? Or does it just serve private interests? In the next section of this study, I clarify the types of public-interest requirements that accompany general land expropriation, I assess their quality and I discuss them in the context of zone expropriation.

4 The public-interest requirements of zone expropriation

4.1 The public-interest requirements of general land expropriation as interpreted through the Constitution

Articles 15, 23 and 143[22] of the Constitution guarantee the right of property but stipulate that government can still expropriate property for certain purposes. Controversy surrounds the question of just to what extent the government can expropriate land, with much of the debate centering on the necessity of "public use" projects[23] and on the connection between these projects and the "public interest." JY Interpretation recently ruled that the government can expropriate land not only for "public use," but also in the "public interest" (JY Interpretation Nos. 400, 516, 579, 652, 731 and 732). Therefore, if land expropriation meets the public-interest requirement, the expropriated land may be set aside for private use. However, no constitutional interpretation has clearly established the nature of the public interest in land expropriation when the expropriated land is for private use.

JY Interpretation No. 732 is considered to be the first case in which the court addressed the private use of "general land expropriation,"[24] which means the state's seizure of private land to establish certain undertakings for the public interest. This interpretation is, in essence, a response to the question, "Is it unconstitutional that the provisions allow competent authorities to expropriate adjacent lands, which are not necessarily required for transportation, in accordance with applicable laws for the purpose of land development?"[25] This interpretation treats "the disputed law"[26] as unconstitutional. The JY Interpretation recognizes that harnessing "general land expropriation" for the promotion of effective land use, for the establishment of local development and for the expansion of state construction-designated funding is inconsistent with the constitutional principle of proportionality[27] and with the constitutional guarantees of people's right to property (Article 15 of the Constitution) and people's freedom of residence (Article 10 of the Constitution[28]).

However, the Justices did not explain the minimum requirements for the quality and quantity of the public interest in land expropriation for private use,[29] nor did they clarify whether land development, in general, serves the public interest in private-use land expropriation. Although Interpretation No. 732 leaves unaddressed the issue of how much public interest must be satisfied by land expropriation for private use, the concurring opinions submitted by several Justices suggested an important criterion: clarify the concept of public interest. Because the public interest is generally an indefinite concept, authorities can easily claim that any compulsory acquisition of private land satisfies the "public interest."[30] A strict examination and a formal clarification of the concept[31] would go far in preventing misuse of the term. Thus, land expropriation for private use must serve a "compelling and advantageous public interest"[32] or an "extremely important public interest,"[33] or must "significantly enhance public welfare,"[34] or must have a purpose "equivalent to the purpose of public utilities for common use by the whole people."[35] Some Justices argued that treasury revenue garnered from the sale of expropriated land does not, in itself, satisfy a strictly defined public-interest criterion.[36] Also, because land expropriation promoting local development can result in redistribution or a transfer of the good of the resources of the land to some other private persons, land expropriation satisfies the private interest of select individuals.[37] As a consequence, if the government uses land expropriation to increase government revenue, to extract resources from land or to promote local development, one person's property rights will be sacrificed just because of others' property interests (usually commercial interests). In turn, expropriation will victimize people who lack social resources whereas people possessing substantial social resources (most notably, in this case, investors) will benefit extensively from the redistributed property.[38] Thus, it is difficult to argue that land expropriation for promoting local development meets the public-interest requirement for land expropriation.

4.2 *The standard of the public-interest requirement in zone expropriation*

What kinds of public interest – and how much of them – should be satisfied by land expropriation? To answer this question, we have to discuss which rights are violated when expropriation is undertaken. JY Interpretation No. 732 clearly asserts that "the expropriation of private land by the State not only imposes a restriction on people's right to property, but also has a serious impact on the freedom of residence of persons."[39] The same interpretation goes on to note that the constitution protects people's right to property in order to "guarantee each individual the freedom to exercise their rights to use, profit by, and dispose of their property during the existence of the property, and to prevent infringements by the government or any third party, so as to guarantee individual freedom, personal development, and maintain personal dignity" (also see JY Interpretations Nos. 400 and 709).[40]

Moreover, Taiwan signed the International Covenant on Civil and Political Rights and the International Covenant on Economic, Social and Cultural Rights on May 14, 2009. The two covenants were officially implemented on December 10 of the same year. According to Articles 2 and 3 of the Act to Implement the International Covenant on Civil and Political Rights and the International Covenant on Economic, Social and Cultural Rights, the human-rights protection provisions in the covenants have domestic legal status, and any application of the covenants to a given matter should make reference to their legislative purposes and to the United Nations Human Rights Committee's general comments. Pursuant to Article 11 of the International Covenant on Economic, Social and Cultural Rights (a multilateral UN treaty adopted in 1966), the participating states shall "recognize the right of everyone to an adequate standard of living for himself and his family." Also noteworthy in the treaty are General Comment No. 4 and General Comment No. 7, both of which concern "The Right to Adequate Housing": one passage explains that "forced evictions are *prima facie* incompatible with the requirements of the Covenant," and another passage explains that "the practice of forced evictions may also result in violations of civil and political rights, such as the right to life, the right to security of the person, the right to non-interference with privacy, family and home and the right to the peaceful enjoyment of possessions."

Expropriation is a means by which government can completely deprive people of their property. In addition, forced evictions, privacy violations, and other assaults on landowners' personal dignity may arise from expropriation. Hence, if society is to avoid these intrusions on people's rights, the public interest that is served by land expropriation must be exceedingly clear. Especially in situations in which expropriated lands are for private use, the boundary between public interest and private interest is blurred, and it is reasonably easy to brand private interest as public interest. Therefore, strict standards for clarifying the public interest are needed. In other words, government authorities should authorize land expropriation for private use only when they can conclude, with confidence, that the outcome will greatly benefit a compelling public interest.[41]

As mentioned earlier, zone expropriation is a type of land expropriation that deprives landowners of their property rights. It is a mandatory expropriation of these people's land, which constitutes a serious imposition on their property rights and their freedom of residence and will cause a large-scale forced eviction.

Given these facts, I argue that zone expropriation shall meet the requirement of compelling public interest and use the strict criterion to examine the issues of zone expropriation.[42] Moreover, zone expropriation is proposed for and often undertaken in rural areas for conversion of undeveloped land into urban real estate.[43] However, Article 143, Paragraph 4 of the Constitution emphasizes the importance of government assistance for land-holding farmers,[44] and Article 153, Paragraph 1 of the Constitution obligates the government to ensure improvements in the livelihood of farmers.[45] Because zone expropriation for private use may damage the livelihood of farmers and agricultural resources, the public interest that the zone expropriation serves must be highly important.

One may argue that, in zone expropriation, the original landowners of expropriated land can choose to receive other land for compensation and that the protections afforded to original landowners in zone expropriation are better than the protections afforded to original landowners in general land expropriation. However, the right to property functions to protect the existence of the property (JY Interpretations Nos. 400, 709 and 732). For this reason, the government must first identify the sufficient public interest that is satisfied in a proposed instance of land expropriation and must then identify what constitutes "fair compensation" for the people whose private property the government will expropriate. These two "stages" are sequential. In the second stage, "property-rights protection" (*Eigentumsgarantie*) shifts to "property-value protection" (*Eigentumswertgarantie*).[46] In zone expropriation, because the government uses a lottery when determining the allocation of compensatory land to original landowners, the original landowners must move to the other place where the land is located. Compensation for lands is intimately bound up with the issue of "property-value protection," and no amount of compensation can change the fact that the government, on the basis of zone expropriation, has deprived a citizen of his or her private land. We should avoid making the logical mistake of using the compensation in the second stage as the basis for judging whether the government has used zone expropriation to damage the property rights of original landowners.

4.3 The issues of public-interest requirement in zone expropriation

A major challenge is determining whether a particular public interest is "compelling." Nevertheless, as Chen, Chung-Lin study contends, promoting local development and assisting construction projects are by no means necessarily compelling public interests.[47] These objectives can easily turn a "land expropriation" project into a "land commercialization" project, which in turn can trigger land speculation benefiting a handful of private actors or a single government agency.[48] These dangers are real, as is spelled out in the previously mentioned General Comment No. 7, which concerns the right to adequate housing. The General Comment requires participating states to provide information relating to

> measures taken during, *inter alia*, urban renewal programmes, redevelopment projects, site upgrading, preparation for international events (Olympics

> and other sporting competitions, exhibitions, conferences, etc.), "beautiful city" campaigns, etc. which guarantee protection from eviction or guarantee rehousing based on mutual consent, by any persons living on or near to [sic] affected sites.

In other words, forced eviction caused by land expropriation may occur in the name of development, and the treaty's participating states have an obligation to prevent evictions or to guarantee rehousing based on the residents' consent in many cases. When the government prioritizes the expansion of local development and of government revenue, land gets commercialized and financial benefits accrue to the privileged few, be they people or enterprises. These outcomes are difficult to regard as compelling public interests being satisfied.

As mentioned earlier, the primary function of zone expropriation is the development of specific tracts of land, especially for new or ongoing urban planning. Current Taiwanese law permits wide use of zone expropriation for development projects, some of which rest on remarkably abstract and ill-defined rationales. It is doubtful that these rationales actually meet the "compelling public interest" requirement, which itself requires concrete, empirically verifiable justifications. Second, zone expropriation as a "land development" method creates a revenue stream for the treasury through a kind of mandatory cooperative relationship between public and private entities. However, private lands that the government seizes and transfers to private persons or to firms for revenue purposes typically fail to meet the public-interest requirement. And this process may trigger land speculation and tend to accumulate specific persons' private capital. In short, the public interest of most zone-expropriation projects is ambiguous but easily satisfies the private interest of select actors.

Also doubtful is the long-held notion that zone expropriation is necessary, particularly in this era of a declining population. The structure of Taiwan's zone expropriation often changes as the country's political, social and economic circumstances change. From the history of zone expropriation, we can realize that zone expropriation gradually became a contributor to high economic-growth periods. But, according to the official government report "Population Estimation, ROC (Taiwan): 2018–2065,"[49] Taiwan's total population is expected to peak at approximately 23.5 million people between 2020 and 2027.

Table 7.1 Demographic indicators[50]

Variant	*Item*	*2020*	*2027*	*2028*	*2065*
High	Total population (persons)	23,619,633	23,715,285	23,711,361	18,802,188
Medium	Total population (persons)	23,610,230	23,541,926	23,510,973	17,352,644
Low	Total population (persons)	23,599,410	23,397,557	23,338,005	16,005,981

Thereafter, the population will decline. By 2065, the total population is expected to be between 16 and 19 million people. Taiwan is facing a crisis of population decline, so the old policy centered on urban expansion and regional development needs to be reviewed. The problem of overdevelopment has become apparent even in recent years, when residential projects, industrial zones and science parks built on expropriated lands have actually been left abandoned. "The Amended National Regional Plan," published in 2017, states that there is no current need for Taiwan to pursue new urban planning.[51] Development may prove to be an undertaking with uncertain outcomes, and land expropriation may yield more drawbacks than benefits.

5 Conclusion

In this study, I have looked back on Taiwanese zone expropriation and have shown that its original purpose was to prevent private-sector entities from monopolizing the island's lands and to grant the general public many benefits of land use. Over time, zone expropriation became, somewhat paradoxically, a kind of mandatory cooperative endeavor for development. Zone expropriation has thus changed for various political, social and economic reasons, evolving into its current form as a means of land development, especially for urban expansion. From this, we can recognize the close relationship between the state and capitalism.

I have examined the system of zone expropriation up close and have noted the diverse reasons, some of which are quite abstract, for zone-expropriation projects. Because many projects allocate land for private use, I have argued that the degree to which these projects serve the public interest should be of great concern. Only those projects that serve "compelling public interests" should merit approval by the state. My conclusion is that zone expropriation today operates mainly in the service of urban development as a revenue generator that simultaneously improves the private interests of a few individuals or firms, thus violating the public-interest requirement in land expropriation. As Taiwan faces its declining population, the entire system of zone expropriation, centered as it is on urban expansion and regional development, may need to be thoroughly reconsidered.

Notes

* This work was supported by JSPS Kakenhi Grant Number JP 18KK0033 and JP 18J10690.

1 Agenda Related Documents of the Legislative Yuan, No. 285, 1999. Proposal of Bill No. 6564, 83–84.
2 For a detailed review of the provisions, please refer to Chung (2009: 91).
3 Ibid., 90.
4 Ibid., 93–94.
5 Because the calculation methods for "receiving land for compensation" and for "preferential right to purchase" differed from each other, unfair treatment of original landowners was a very real possibility. Thus, the government abolished

the rule of "preferential right to purchase" in the Equalization of Land Rights Act in 2000.

6 Agenda-Related Documents of the Legislative Yuan, No. 248, 1976. Proposal of Bill No. 15556, 45.
7 Reasons for the Amendment of Article 54 of the Equalization of Land Rights Act (1986). Retrieved August 9, 2020, from Legal System of Legislative Yuan, R.O.C (立法院法律系統) https://lis.ly.gov.tw/lglawc/lglawkm.
8 This provision is still valid today.
9 According to Article 54, Paragraph 1, "the government at various levels shall compensate with land value, according to the provisions of Article 10 of this Act, for the lands subject to zone expropriation. The compensation may be paid in kind, if so applied for by the landowner, with the construction land after zone expropriation of which the land value is equivalent to compensation in cash. In principle, the total area of lands in lieu of compensation shall be 50 per cent of total zone expropriation area, unless approved by the superior authorities due to special conditions. But it shall not be less than 40 per cent."
10 Supra note 7.
11 Yang (1994: 12).
12 Research, Development, and Evaluation Commission of the Executive Yuan (2012: 148).
13 Supra note 2, 98–99.
14 Supra note 12, 151, 154–159.
15 Chen, Li-Fu (2002: 293).
16 Chen, Li-Fu (2007: 355).
17 Article 15 of the Constitution guarantees the people's right of existence, right of work and right of property.
18 According to Article 23 of the Constitution, "all the freedoms and rights enumerated in the preceding Articles shall not be restricted by law except by such as may be necessary to prevent infringement upon the freedoms of other persons, to avert an imminent crisis, and/or to maintain social order or to advance public welfare."
19 According to Article 48 of the Land Expropriation Act, the provisions of Chapters II (Expropriation Procedures) and III (Compensation for Expropriation) shall, mutatis mutandis, apply to the procedure of and compensation for zone expropriation not provided in Chapter IV (Zone Expropriation).
20 The Second Session of the Fourth Legislative Yuan, 1999, Meeting Minutes of the Second Joint Meeting regarding the Land Expropriation Bill Proposed to the Interior Affairs and Ethnic Groups Committee, the Economic and Energy Committee and the Finance Committee for Review, 40, 42.
21 Chen, Chung-Lin (2011: 1066).
22 According to Article 143, Paragraph 1 of the Constitution, "all land within the territory of the Republic of China shall belong to the whole body of citizens. Private ownership of land, acquired by the people in accordance with law, shall be protected and restricted by law. Privately-owned land shall be liable to taxation according to its value, and the Government may buy such land according to its value."
23 Article 108, Paragraph 1, Subparagraph 14 of the Constitution delegates the power of eminent domain to the central government, which "shall have the power of legislation and administration," but which "may delegate the power of administration to the provincial and Hsien governments." JY Interpretation No. 236 addresses not only Articles 23 and 143 but also Article 108 of the Constitution and declares that "the right of property shall be guaranteed to the people, which is made explicit in Article 15 of the Constitution, whereas the state can condemn private land for public purpose under the authority."

24 Justice Chen, Shin-Min's concurring opinion in part and dissenting in part of JY Interpretation No. 732, 1.
25 JY Interpretation No. 732, translated by Chen, Yen-Chia. Retrieved August 12, 2020, from https://cons.judicial.gov.tw/jcc/en-us/jep03/show?expno=732
26 Article 7, Paragraph 4, of the Mass Rapid Transit Act amended on May 30, 2001, provides: "The land required for . . . the development of areas adjacent to the Mass Rapid Transit system . . . may be expropriated by competent authorities in accordance with applicable laws." Article 7, Paragraph 3, of the Mass Rapid Transit Act promulgated on July 1, 1988, provides: "Lands used for joint development . . . may be expropriated." Article 9, Paragraph 1, of the Regulations for the Joint Development of Land Adjacent to or Contiguous with the Mass Rapid Transit System provides: "Lands used for joint development . . . may be acquired by competent authorities in accordance with applicable laws." Ibid.
27 The constitutional principle of proportionality first received clarification in JY Interpretation No. 476, which stated that the principle involves the "due purposes," "necessary means" and "proper restrictions" required by Article 23 of the Constitution.
28 According to Article 10 of the Constitution, "the people shall have freedom of residence and of change of residence."
29 Supra note 24, 4.
30 Supra note 24, 5–6. Justice Li, Chen-Shan's concurring opinion in JY Interpretation No. 732, 3–4.
31 Justice Lo, Chang-Fa and Tsay, Ching-You's concurring opinion in JY Interpretation No. 732, 3–4.
32 Supra note 24, 2–25.
33 Justice Yeh, Pai-Hsiu's concurring opinion in JY Interpretation No. 732, 10–11. Justice Li, Chen-Shan, supra note 30, 3–4.
34 Supra note 31, 6–7.
35 Justice Chen, Beyue Su's concurring opinion in JY Interpretation No. 732, 5–6. Supra note 24, 2–25.
36 Supra note 24, 20. Justice Li, Chen-Shan, supra note 30, 4. Supra note 35, 7.
37 Supra note 31, 6–7. Supra note 35, 6.
38 Supra note 35, 6. Also refer to supra note 21, 1060–1062.
39 Supra note 25.
40 Ibid.
41 Chen, Chung-Lin also believes that general land expropriation for private use shall meet compelling interests. Supra note 21, 1065–1066.
42 Same opinion, please refer to supra note 21, 1066.
43 Supra note 20, 40.
44 According to Article 143, Paragraph 4 of the Constitution, "in the distribution and readjustment of land, the State shall in principle assist self-farming landowners and persons who make use of the land by themselves, and shall also regulate their appropriate areas of operation."
45 According to Article 153, Paragraph 1 of the Constitution, "the State, in order to improve the livelihood of laborers and farmers and to improve their productive skill, shall enact laws and carry out policies for their protection."
46 Supra note 24, 7.
47 Chen, Chung-Lin advocated that economic development cannot be used as a reason for general land expropriation. Supra note 21, 1067–1070.
48 Supra note 21, 1064–1065.
49 National Development Council. 2018. "Population Estimation, ROC (Taiwan): 2018–2065," 4.

50 National Development Council. Population Projections for the ROC (Taiwan): 2018–2065 (Last update: 2018.08.30). Retrieved August 24, 2020, from www.ndc.gov.tw/en/cp.aspx?n=2E5DCB04C64512CC&s=002ABF0E676F4DB5
51 Ministry of the Interior. 2017. "Amended National Regional Plan," 75.

References

Chen, Chung-Lin (陳仲嶙) (2011), Constitutional Restraint on the Exercise of Eminent Domain for Private Use (徵收之憲法拘束：以「私用徵收」的違憲審查為中心), *National Taiwan University Law Journal* (國立臺灣大學法學論叢), Vol. 40, No. 3, pp. 1029–1088.

Chen, Li-Fu (陳立夫) (2002), The Land Use Zoning Control and the Land Expropriation System in Taiwan, in T. Kotaka and D. Callies (Eds.), *Taking Land: Compulsory Purchase and Regulation in Asian-Pacific Countries*, University of Hawai'i Press, pp. 286–304.

Chen, Li-Fu (陳立夫) (2007), *A Study of the Land Law* (土地法研究), Xin Xueli Press (新學林出版).

Chung, Li-Na (鍾麗娜) (2009), A Retrospective of and Prospects for the Transformation of Zone Expropriation (區段徵收法制變遷之回顧與展望), *Land Issues Research Quarterly* (土地問題研究季刊), Vol. 8, No. 3, pp. 89–109.

Research, Development, and Evaluation Commission of the Executive Yuan (行政院研究發展考核委員會) (2012), *Evaluation of the System of Land Expropriation in Taiwan* (我國土地徵收制度之評估), Research, Development, and Evaluation Commission of the Executive Yuan Press.

Yang, Song-Ling (楊松齡) (1994), Analysis of the Equity and Distribution of Zone Expropriation (區段徵收制度之公平性與分配內涵之分析), *Taiwan Di Zheng* (臺灣地政), No. 101, pp. 10–16.

8 Land expropriation and compensation in China

Shu Jiao and Yashu Yang[1]

1 Introduction

As the scope, scale and speed of land expropriation expanded and accelerated in China as a result of economic development, serious conflicts and disputes concerning land also increased. China's current system of land expropriation has a number of problems, including deficiencies in the expropriation procedures, inadequacy of compensation and a lack of measures for the relief of those affected.

In this chapter, we briefly explain the dual structure of landownership rights (urban and agricultural) under China's socialist market economy and the historical development of the land expropriation system (Part 1). We pay particular attention to the positioning of "public interest" as a prerequisite for expropriation and examine this separately as it pertains to land owned by rural collectives and state-owned urban land (Part 2). We also consider payments of compensation for expropriated land in a similar manner, as it pertains to rural and urban situations. It is noteworthy how compensation paid for urban land is premised on the market value of the land, whereas payments for rural land are calculated based on a (frequently insufficient) livelihood guarantee welfare allowance (Part 3). Part 4 summarizes our findings.[2]

2 Public interest and the historical development of the land expropriation system

Reforms in the land and housing systems were very important in the process of the "reform and opening-up" national policy since 1979. Under the 1982 Amendment of the Constitution ("the '82 Constitution"), the system under which two forms of landownership existed side by side, that is, the state ownership and the ownership by rural collectives, was confirmed at the constitutional level for the first time. Generally, while "land in the cities is owned by the State," "land in the rural and suburban areas" is owned by rural collectives (Article 10) (such types of land are referred to as "state-owned land" and "collective-owned land" in this chapter). Under this dual structure, land expropriation was differentiated into two forms: the expropriation of collective-owned land and the expropriation of buildings on state-owned land (which expropriates the ownership rights to

DOI: 10.4324/9781003170600-10

buildings simultaneously with the reclamation of usage rights to the plot of land on which the building was constructed).

Having demarcated each period in history, we now examine the two patterns of expropriation previously described, distinguishing between historical periods.

2.1 The initial land expropriation system

2.1.1 Requisition of collective-owned land

The '82 Constitution stipulates that the state may requisition land in accordance with the law in public interest. The term "requisition" (徵用), used in the constitution, typically refers to an alteration not of ownership, but of usage rights (Ye, B. et al. 2004, 28). In 1982, the Regulation for State Construction and Requisition of Land ("Regulation on Requisition") was enacted. This regulation serves as the legal ground for land requisition and stipulates that "the state will possess ownership rights to requisitioned land and businesses will possess only usage rights." Thus, it defined the term "requisition" to mean the alteration of usage rights.

With the enactment of the Land Administration Law (土地管理法, "LAL") in 1986, the Regulation on Requisition was abolished. The LAL adopted the substance of the Regulation on Requisition in the section on "Land to Be Used for State Construction." Although brief, the section stipulates the projects for which expropriation is permitted, the authority that can approve such expropriation and the compensation payment system. Whereas the first two are discussed next, compensation payments are discussed in Part 3.

(1) The LAL mentions the projects for which expropriation is permitted and stipulates that "when the state seeks to expropriate collective-owned land for economic, cultural, national defense, or public works projects, it may do so pursuant to the provisions of this section" (Art. 21). Any project, be it the construction of a dam or a factory, could justify land expropriation as long as it was carried out by the state or with state investment. Consideration was not given to whether or not the project served a public interest (Research Team of the Ministry of Land and Resources on the Land Expropriation Reform 2003, 50). The "reform and opening-up" era had scarcely begun at this point. The public ownership system continued to apply to most other forms of ownership and the legacy of the planned economy remained the foundation for it.[3]

(2) The LAL stipulates that the State Council has the power to approve land expropriations for farmland exceeding 1,000 *mu*[4] or other land exceeding 2,000 *mu*. In contrast, for "land within provinces, autonomous regions, or directly state-controlled municipalities," the approval of people's governments at the provincial level, for "farmland not exceeding 3 *mu* or other land not exceeding 10 *mu*," the approval of people's governments at the county level was considered sufficient. The assignment of authority to the county level gave rise to issues as the reform and opening-up process progressed.

2.1.2 Eviction from and demolition of urban buildings

During the planned economy era, urban state-owned land could be used free of charge. At the end of the 1980s, a fee-based system for land use was established and large-scale urban construction began based on it. As urban land was state property, the seizure of ownership rights for urban construction was not considered a problem. However, problems did arise with regard to the buildings constructed on state-owned urban land. During the planned economy era, not only urban land, but also buildings constructed on it were the property of the state and were accessible either for free or at a low rental fee. With the beginning of the reform and opening-up period, the concept of private property for the buildings emerged, and the 1982 constitution declared the protection of property rights. However, such protection was only in abstract terms and not specifically defined. Private ownerships, on which the idea of expropriation is premised, were not clear concerning those buildings. For such urban buildings, the Regulation on the Administration of Urban Housing Demolition and Eviction ("Regulation on Demolition and Eviction") was enacted in 1992, which should be distinguished from the expropriation system, which presupposes the concept of ownership. This regulation stipulated that those who evicted tenants from and demolished buildings had a duty to provide compensation and resettlement.[5] Ultimately, the regulation served to ensure the progress of construction in cities.

2.1.3 Characteristics of the initial land expropriation system

Dual land expropriation systems were still significantly influenced by the planned economy. As the state had a role in cooperative socioeconomic development under the planned economy, interested parties were obliged to submit to the supreme authority of the state, whether for the expropriation of land or eviction from and demolition of buildings. The concept of property rights was weak in Chinese society, which still carried the legacy of socialist transformation (1953~) and the people's commune movement (1958~). Little thought was given to the necessity of placing various limits on the state's ability to seize property or of establishing rigorous procedures for doing so. Neither system was furnished with the essential elements of an expropriation system.

2.2 The land expropriation system in transition

As economic reforms proceeded, state ownership ceased to be the sole form of ownership and other forms including private ownership emerged. The planned economy era was drawing to a close and the transition to a socialist market economy began (Amendment of the Constitution in 1993). The initial system for land expropriation could not withstand such serious socioeconomic fluctuations.

2.2.1 Expropriation of collective-owned land

2.2.1.1 Formation of the land expropriation system

With the Amendment of the Constitution in 1988, it became constitutionally permissible to transfer usage rights to land. The LAL was revised accordingly that year, stipulating that "usage rights to state-owned land and collective-owned land may be transferred in accordance with the law" (Art. 2). The enactment of regulations for the enforcement of this law was delegated to the State Council. However, no enforcement regulation sanctioning the transfer of land usage rights to collective-owned land has been enacted to date. The LAL, after the 1998 amendment, stipulated that the usage rights to collective-owned land "shall not be transferred, retransferred, or rented out for non-agricultural construction" (Art. 63).

Because the massive loss of arable land due to the abuse of land requisition had become a problem, the LAL was revised in 1998 under the banner of "establishing the strictest land administration system in the world." To remedy the abuse of authority in expropriation, in addition to the prohibition on the transfer of usage rights for nonagricultural construction as a general rule, an overall plan for land use ("overall plan") and a system for regulating land usage were established. The state had to formulate an overall plan that would determine the amount of land allocated for three specified types of land use, namely arable land, land for construction and unused land. Businesses had to use land according to the usage category determined by the overall plan. The area to be converted on an annual basis from agricultural land to land for construction had to follow the quotas specified in the annual plans that were a constituent of the overall plan. The land system during this period was characterized by limitations on property rights concerning collective-owned land and planned control of land usage.

With the 2004 revision of the constitution, "land requisition" (土地征用) was changed to "land expropriation" (土地征收), a term that clearly meant the right to possess land. The LAL was revised and the land expropriation system was established. However, the details were not substantially different from the initial land requisition system – only the conditions under which it was to be applied differed.

2.2.1.2 Exerting the power of expropriation

Through the revision of the LAL in 2004, limitations were placed on the transfer of usage rights to collective-owned land (only transfers for agricultural construction were permitted) and if one needed to use land for other kinds of construction, they were obliged to use state-owned land. However, state-owned land for construction use was limited and was not adequate to meet the sharp rise in demand for land necessitated by economic development. The only way to achieve this was for the state to exercise its power to expropriate, convert collective land into state-owned land for construction and transfer the usage rights to businesses for a fee ("land usage rights transfer fee"). For collective-owned land, land expropriation served as a substitute for the acquisition of a site by an agreement between the business and the owner of the land. Until now, the function of the land expropriation system in China is considerably larger when compared to that in capitalist countries, where site acquisition by mutual agreement is the general rule.

The exercise of expropriation was also related to government finance. The transfer fees paid for land usage rights constitute a substantial source of revenue for regional governments (Research Team of the Ministry of Land and Resources for Land Expropriation Reforms 2003, 51–52). In contrast, the compensation paid to farmers by these governments was based on low standards. For this reason, regional governments tended to conduct land expropriation at a large scale in pursuit of enormous financial gains. The overall land use plan described earlier was a primary measure developed to resolve this problem. However, it did not function as anticipated. First, the overall plan did not have substantial binding force. Second, the quota of land for construction as specified by the overall plan was distributed by each level of governments. As a result of the lower levels of government seeking to secure larger quotas from the higher levels in any way they could, the quotas of land for construction use were distributed evenly among local governments (Chen, Y. et al. 2006, 32; Gu, J. et al. 2005, 11), While land shortages restrained urban development in localities experiencing an influx of population because of economic growth (Chen et al. 2006, 32), in localities that did not experience such population growth, large amounts of land were expropriated and "ghost cities" appeared.

The 2004 revision of the LAL, enacted with the purpose of specifying the substance of "public interest" and limiting the exercise of expropriation power, did not alter the initial system of land expropriation substantially. However, there were important alterations made during this period to the authority to approve expropriation. According to the 1998 amendment of the LAL, people's governments at the county level no longer had the authority to approve expropriations. As private entities (such as businesses) could obtain approval from people's governments at the county level relatively easily, this revision placed a certain degree of constraints on the exercise of their powers of expropriation. Still, this was not useful in solving the broader problem. Thus, by implementing the socialist market economy, two patterns that we will discuss next appeared on a large scale in the practice of land expropriation, which remained heavily influenced by the planned economy.

2.2.1.3 Planned expropriation and expropriation in isolation

Land expropriation can be either planned or conducted in isolation. First, under the Implementing Regulation of the LAL, collective-owned land may be expropriated for supply to specific businesses as needed for such use as energy resources, transportation, water supply, mining and/or military affairs (Art. 23). This is described as "expropriation in isolation."[6] Except for the difference between the transfer of land-ownership rights and of land use rights, expropriation in isolation is largely the same as land expropriation in most countries with private land-ownership.

In contrast, "planned expropriation"[7] is conducted irrespective of whether there is a specific business or not. It takes place for the sake of urban planning, and within the scope of urban land for construction as designated by the overall plan (Art. 20 of the Implementing Regulation of the LAL). We provide a brief description of planned expropriation here. The overall plan sets out the extent of urban land to be used for construction for the next 15 years. The annual plans that constitute the overall plan specify quotas for the area of agricultural land that is to be converted to land for construction during each applicable year. A local government specifies the future extent of a city according to the extent of urban land for construction use as specified by the overall plan and then uses this to devise urban plans. These urban plans are then implemented and collective-owned land is expropriated each year in accordance with the specifications of the overall plan, and eventually, the city expands. In the past, whereas some expropriated land was provided for the use of housing development and industrial parks, in many cases, such land was also held in reserve.

2.2.2 Expropriation of buildings constructed on state-owned land

Awareness of the property value of buildings on state-owned land sharpened. Under the eviction and demolition system that did not adequately protect private property rights, one incident after another occurred, involving the malicious infringement of rights surrounding eviction from and demolition of buildings. The system was finally abolished through the enactment of the Regulation on the Expropriation of Buildings on State-Owned Land and Compensation ("Regulation on Expropriation and Compensation" or REC) in 2011.[8]

2.2.2.1 The expropriation decision and its prerequisites

According to Article 8 of the REC, governments are required to make an expropriation decision whenever they seek to take control of buildings on state-owned land. This Article also stipulates the prerequisites for such expropriation decisions.[9] First, we summarize the requirements in the regulation for the expropriation decision:

Requirement 1: The project must fulfill the eligibility requirements listed in Article 8 of the REC.

Requirement 2: Expropriation must be necessary for the sake of preserving or advancing public interest, such as preserving national security, enhancing the national economy and facilitating the development of society.

Requirement 3: The project must comply with the National Plan for Economic and Social Development ("Development Plan") and, for the construction of public housing for low-income earners or redevelopment of derelict districts, must be incorporated into the Development Plan at the city or county level.

Requirement 4: The project must comply with urban planning rules.[10]

This way, the REC lays down the specifics of the public-interest requirement. This marks the first time that the specifics of the requirement have been codified into law in China. As an expropriation decision is an administrative act, it is subject to administrative litigation. This means that courts can, while investigating whether a project fulfilled the practical and procedural requirements necessary for making an expropriation decision, make judgments on that project's fulfillment of the public interest requirements. In this sense, the REC can be described as ground-breaking. However, various problems arose when the requirements for expropriation were applied. These problems are detailed next.

2.2.2.2 Problems with the system for expropriation of buildings on state-owned land

2.2.2.2.1 REQUIREMENT 1 (ELIGIBILITY OF THE PROJECT) HAS LOST ITS SUBSTANTIAL SIGNIFICANCE

While listing specific types of projects that are eligible for expropriation, Article 8 of the REC lists out broad categories such as "infrastructure" and "public utilities," and vague concepts with wide scopes, such as "science and technology projects" or "cultural projects." These categories caused problems when it came to determining whether a project fulfilled the eligibility requirements. A case concerning a "science and technology park"[11] addressed this issue. The court determined that a "science and technology park project," which included the launch of a business and the construction of an office building, hotel and public square fell under the ambit of "public works project related to science and technology" as specified under Article 8 (3) of the REC. One may be able to accept, for example, the construction of a science and technology museum with the aim of educating the public about and popularizing science, technology and industry as being carried out in the public interest. However, the "science and technology park" in question was considerably different, as it included the establishment of a business and construction of an office building and hotel as well. It raised questions on why it was being treated as a "public works project related to science and technology." Even though the court could have excluded this "science and technology park" from the category of "public works project for science or technology," based on the project's details and nature, it did not do so in this judgment.

2.2.2.2.2 DECISIONS CONCERNING REQUIREMENT 2 (NECESSITY)

The REC does not define the kinds of facts that should be considered. It does not prescribe the methods that can be used while judging the necessity of expropriation. In administrative and judicial practice, a particular project is deemed necessary when it is specified in the development plan or when it accords with macro-level development goals that are specified in a development plan. For example, in the previously mentioned judgment on the "science and technology park," the court accepted the necessity of the expropriation decision, deciding that the "science and technology park" met the criteria of "adjustment of industrial structures or the development of a high-tech industry" as stipulated in the city's development plan. However, there are a variety of other means for accomplishing the goal of "adjustment of industrial structures or development of high-tech industry," such as tax abatements or exemptions, or the simplification of administrative approval and authorization procedures. It is questionable why the court did not choose to examine why it was necessary to exercise the power to expropriate in this situation.

2.2.2.2.3 DETERMINATIONS CONCERNING THE PUBLIC NATURE OF REDEVELOPMENT PROJECTS FOR DILAPIDATED DISTRICTS

There were more lawsuits that argued on the public nature of expropriations that were intended for the purpose of redevelopment projects in dilapidated areas. Article 8 of the REC lists the project that is "necessary for the rebuilding of an old urban area where dilapidated buildings are concentrated and infrastructure lags behind as organized and implemented by the government according to the relevant provisions of the Urban and Rural Planning Law" as one category of projects that are eligible for expropriation. The main focus of the previously mentioned litigations was on the legality of designating specific individual buildings as targets for dilapidated district redevelopment. These lawsuits challenged the legality of a given determination to expropriate land in cases in which a certain building was not dangerous in itself or a certain district had adequate infrastructure[12] but was nevertheless marked to be included in a dilapidated district redevelopment area and designated for expropriation.

On this point, the Supreme People's Court set forth the standard that "if a project has undergone due process [the social stability risk assessment – supplemented by this author], that decision should be upheld." The court determined that "projects that have been approved by the local people's congress, its executive committee, or by a majority of those subject to expropriation should be regarded as necessary for the public interest," and it elaborated that

> concerning projects for redevelopment of dilapidated districts, the intentions concerning land to be expropriated of the parties subject to expropriation should be given particular weight and, if a majority of these parties approve of a proposed development, we may conclude that the development is necessary for the public interest.[13]

However, such an adjudication standard, based on the vote of a majority, may obstruct the path to seeking judicial relief for minorities. It raises questions on whether the justice system effectively fulfills its functions and how the constitutional rights of individuals can be protected. This standard for a majority decision also permits the boundaries for dilapidated district redevelopment projects to be drawn wider than necessary.

2.3 Characteristics of the land expropriation system in transition

Both the land expropriation system for collective-owned land and that for buildings on state-owned land each accomplished a certain development in the transition phase. For state-owned land, the status of property rights (ownership rights to buildings and usage rights to land) was defined under law and the substantial and procedural requirements for expropriation were regulated systematically. However, as these requirements lacked precision, they did not prevent the abuse of the power of expropriation sufficiently. In contrast, property rights as applied to collective-owned land were limited (such as by the impermissibility of the transfer of usage rights for nonagricultural purposes), and these lands were subject to control by planned economy-style mechanisms. In the socialist market economy, planned expropriation emerged, wherein a large area of collective-owned land was expropriated, and the speed at which cities expanded exceeded the rate at which peasants who lost their land could be guaranteed jobs, welfare, education for their children and healthcare. Peasants who lost their lands, as rural collective-owned land was converted into urban land for construction, suffered profound discrimination when compared to urban residents. This became one of the most severe problems in the course of China's economic development.

2.4 Current tendencies in the land expropriation system

With another revision of the Constitution in 2018, the text was amended to read thus: "[t]he right to use [collective and state-owned] land may be transferred in accordance with the provisions of law." Consequently, the LAL was revised in 2019. Two points are most significant. The first is Article 63 of the LAL, which permits market transactions concerning the usage rights of collective-owned land for construction.[14] It also notes that the method for the transfer of such usage rights will be based on those used for state-owned lands having the same purpose. The second point is that "public interest" has been defined as it pertains to the expropriation of collective-owned land. Article 45 of the LAL lists projects that are eligible for expropriation. Although stipulations in Article 45 are more precise than those concerning eligible projects in the REC, there are some broad categories and vague concepts with a wide scope, and there is still a risk that the requirements for the eligibility may lose substance. For example, the "tract development" (成片開発) projects[15] specified in Paragraph 5 of the Article are not at all clearly defined.

Other requirements stipulated in the REC are also specified in the LAL, but as opposed to the REC the decision to expropriate is not stipulated an administrative act. Therefore, it is not possible to use administrative litigation to dispute the element public interest in the expropriation of collective-owned land.

Following the revision of the LAL as previously discussed, planned expropriation (see 2.2.1.3) was eliminated. The revision also systematically specified the practical and procedural requirements for the expropriation of collective-owned land, on the lines of the requirements specified for buildings on state-owned land. However, given that this new LAL has only just come into effect, it is still unclear as to whether it will solve all the aforementioned problems.

3 Compensation for expropriation

We now discuss the current state of compensation for land expropriation in China based on whether it is for agricultural collective-owned or urban state-owned land.

3.1 Compensation for agricultural land owned by collectives

Compensation for agricultural land comprises a land compensation payment made to the rural collectives that owns the land, and a resettlement subsidy[16] and compensation for crops and immovable property on the land paid to individuals subject to expropriation.

3.1.1 Provisions of the Constitution, Civil Code[17] and Land Administration Law

Provisions concerning the expropriation of and compensation for agricultural land under current Chinese law are scattered across multiple legal documents. As mentioned in Section 2.2.2, the 2004 revision of the Constitution stipulated that compensation was mandatory if private property was expropriated to serve public interest (Article 13 of the Constitution). The Civil Code that came into effect on January 1, 2021, stipulates that in the event that collective-owned land is expropriated, the payment of land compensation, resettlement subsidies and compensation for peasant housing, immovable property and crops on the land will be made promptly and fully; social welfare will be allotted to peasants subject to the expropriation of land, their basic living will be ensured and their legal rights will be protected (Article 243). However, no provision articulates the details of the standard by which amounts of compensation are to be calculated. Therefore, stipulations under the previously enacted LAL (third amendment 2019) will be applied. One of the main components of the 2019 amendment is that it mandates that peasants subject to expropriation should be maintained at their prior living standard and that fair and reasonable compensation should be granted to them to guarantee their long-term basic living standards in the event that their land is expropriated (Article 48).

Before the revision, the LAL contained the stipulation:

> Land compensation for expropriated arable land will be between six and ten times the annual average production of the land over the three years prior to expropriation, while the basis for the resettlement subsidy will be between four and six times the average production of the land over the three years prior to expropriation. The total amount of compensation will not exceed thirty times the average production of the land over the three years prior to expropriation of the land.
>
> (Article 47 of the 2nd amendment in 2004)

This provision was removed by the revision.

The revised LAL further stipulates that, in the event land is expropriated, the payment of compensation, including land compensation, resettlement subsidies and compensation for peasant houses, immovable property and crops on land, should be made promptly; that social welfare payments be distributed to those subject to expropriation; and that categories of compensation be established other than those solely for the value of the land to be expropriated, including resettlement subsidies and other categories of compensation distinctive to farmland (Article 48).

3.1.2 Stipulation of compensation when agricultural land is expropriated

Article 48 of the revised LAL states thus:

> In the event that agricultural land[18] is expropriated, provinces, autonomous regions, and directly-controlled municipalities will determine the basis for land compensation and resettlement subsidies through official announcement of the appraisal of the overall price of the parcel of land. The appraisal of the overall value of a parcel of land should be made in consideration of all relevant factors including the original purpose of the land, the presence of resources on the land, the productivity of the land, the location of the land, conditions of supply and demand for the land, and development level of the population and economy and should be adjusted or re-announced at least once in every three year period.

It abolishes the annual value of the productivity standard given in the old law and has provinces, autonomous regions and directly controlled municipalities that set the standard for land compensation payments and resettlement subsidies.

3.1.3 Provisions addressing compensation for expropriation of nonagricultural land

Article 48 of the revised LAL stipulates that "provinces, autonomous regions, and directly-controlled municipalities will set standards for calculating compensation including for land, immovable property, and crops on the land." It specifies that when peasant housing is expropriated, these entities

> must, in accordance with a general principle of compensating prior to resettlement and improvement of living environment, heed the intentions of peasants and make fair and reasonable compensation via the relocation of housing sites,[19] the provision of property for resettlement, or monetary compensation.

It also stipulates that expenses for relocation stemming from expropriation and temporary resettlement should be reimbursed (Article 48).

3.1.4 Unique categories of compensation: resettlement subsidies

One of the categories of compensation described in Section 3.1.1 is a "resettlement subsidy." The term 安置 ("resettlement") has been used in China for a long time and means "to allocate to a person (work) that will allow them to settle (into a suitable location/occupation)." It relates to expropriation and encapsulates various elements including the assurance of occupation, housing and basic living needs and is an essential concept for the study of compensation for expropriation in contemporary China.[20] Resettlement compensation plays a major role in compensation for collective-owned land.

The concept of "resettlement" was used in law for the first time in Article 14 of the Regulation on Urban and Suburban Land Reforms promulgated by the Government Administration Council on November 21, 1950, which stipulated that "peasants cultivating land must be resettled appropriately." At the time, the planned economy system was in effect in China and all economic resources were distributed according to the state plan. Under the economic system, unlike under a capitalist economy, peasants whose land was expropriated were unable to purchase new land or invest in industry or commerce even if they were paid compensation. Hence, it was the responsibility of the government to guarantee long-term livelihood for those subject to expropriation, who were unable to secure the prerequisites of starting a new life. Once the planned economy changed to a socialist market economy, the basic nature of expropriation compensation as the livelihood compensation described as "resettlement" compensation did not change substantially due to the characteristics of China as a socialist state.[21] Nevertheless, thus far, neither the LAL nor any other law has defined "resettlement compensation." According to the judgment given on the 93rd case of first instance by the People's Court of Wulong County in 2006,

> the resettlement compensation is payment made to give necessary support to the production and basic living of the agricultural population from whom the country receives the source of its livelihood in the form of the main products of expropriated land.

Article 48 of the revised LAL stipulates that fair and reasonable compensation should be granted to maintain peasants subject to expropriation at their previous standard of living and ensure their long-term basic standard of living. However, the problem of just how much resettlement compensation should be paid to accomplish this goal continues. As discussed earlier, the revised LAL removed the upper limit of resettlement subsidy and the total amount of compensation; there is no clear standard for the calculation of these amounts. The actual practice varies from locality to locality and is obscure. The inadequacy of actual compensation to peasants has become a social problem, and although the 2019 amendment addresses the issue, it is not likely to resolve it at once.

3.2 "Fair compensation" for the expropriation of urban buildings

Article 13 of the Constitution states that compensation shall be made, but it does not specify any details. Article 58 of the LAL states that for expropriation in urban areas, "appropriate compensation will be provided to holders of usage rights to land," but standards for calculation of this compensation are not defined.

3.2.1 "Fair compensation"

Article 2 of the 2011 REC, as discussed in Section 2.2.1, stipulates that "fair compensation will be paid to owners of buildings subject to expropriation . . . in the event of the expropriation of buildings belonging to businesses or individuals on state-owned land" and defines the general principles of "fair compensation." The specifics of "fair compensation" used by the REC are distinctive in that they emphasize consistency with market prices. The term "fair compensation" is explained as follows:

> First, those subject to expropriation must be fairly compensated, and publicly-known, impartial, and reasonable compensation shall be made according to a specified plan. Second, fair compensation must be given for expropriation and all those subject to expropriation. Third, the standard of compensation will be consistent with and determined according to market value.
>
> (Wang et al. 2015, 287)

For urban buildings, the principle of "fair compensation" is used in lieu of "appropriate compensation," because a market exists for building ownership and land usage rights.[22]

3.2.2 The scope of and standards for compensation

The REC specifies three types of compensation: for the value of the building subject to expropriation, for eviction and temporary resettlement and for losses because of the ceasing of production or operations (Article 17). Generally, compensation for eviction and temporary resettlement is paid in cash for expenses incurred on relocation. However, if those subject to expropriation, in lieu of cash compensation, choose an in-kind compensation in the form of an exchange of building property rights, these parties must be compensated with a temporary resettlement subsidy or provided with temporary residence (Article 22).

Article 23 addresses compensation for losses because of the ceasing of production or operations. It states that:

> in the event that production or operation is halted due to the expropriation of a building, compensation for losses will be assessed according to factors such as effective profits prior to the expropriation of the building and the length of time production or operation is halted. Specific administrative measures[23] will be enacted by provinces, autonomous regions, and directly-controlled municipalities.

Article 19 of the REC specifies that compensation for the value of buildings subject to expropriation *must not be less than* the market value of comparable real estate (emphasis added). A real estate valuation agency assesses the value of a building subject to expropriation based on Measures for Expropriation of Buildings on State-Owned Land. In the words of Justice Bixin Jiang:

> Market value is a minimum standard of compensation regarding the value of a building. In Chinese practice, the composition of building ownership and other legal rights of most parties subject to expropriation represents a complex situation due to historical factors. As a general rule, it is not possible to compensate according to market value. Using the market value and other factors if reasonable, the expropriator is able to give compensation at an amount higher than market value. Due to particular factors (for example, a potential risk of natural disaster such as an earthquake and a resulting state of fear), the market value of a building subject to expropriation may be lower than the cost within a reasonable range of the building itself. In this case, it is possible for the expropriator to reasonably compensate the parties subject to expropriation at a higher standard than the market value of the building.
>
> (Jiang 2012, 185)

This interprets market value as a "minimum" for compensation and favors the setting of compensation at an amount exceeding market value as long as it is within a reasonable range.

In contrast, no clear standard has been set for the appraisal of interior furnishings, so negotiations between the relevant parties play a significant role. Article 14 of the Measures on Expropriation of Buildings on State-Owned Land holds that

> compensation will be determined through negotiations between the parties involved for the costs involved in relocating furnishings, machinery, and appliances from an expropriated building, for raw materials, and for losses in production or operations. Should such negotiations fail, a real estate valuation agency may make an appraisal.

Article 25 of the REC specifies that the department expropriating a building and parties subject to expropriation will enter into a memorandum on compensation concerning

> matters such as: the form, amount, and period of payment of compensation; the location, floor area, eviction compensation, and temporary housing as resettlement compensation offered in exchange for property rights; losses consequent to halting of production or operation; and the eviction period, form of relocation, and period over which relocation is to occur.

Article 22 of the REC also stipulates the provision of temporary resettlement compensation or temporary housing if the parties have chosen a relocation payment and exchange of building property rights. Article 23 requires, in addition to the value of the expropriated building compensation for relocation expenses, temporary resettlement payments and compensation for the suspension of business.

3.2.3 Forms of compensation: the selection system for cash or in-kind compensation

Article 21 of the REC specifies that parties subject to expropriation may select cash payments or may seek the exchange of building property rights as compensation. Unlike the single form of compensation (cash payments) prescribed for the expropriation of collective-owned land, these two forms can be applied in combination.

Resettlement compensation, which constitutes a substantial portion of the compensation for agricultural land, in the case of compensation for urban buildings, is not provided. To be sure, Article 17 of the REC addresses compensation for temporary resettlement, which is to serve as a bridge to new housing. However, these measures are only temporary. Unlike compensation for agricultural land, the compensation for expropriation of buildings barely has characteristics as a livelihood compensation.

4 Conclusion

This chapter discussed the dual structure of land-ownership rights in China and the course of the historical development of the land expropriation system, which was erected in parallel to the development of the socialist market economy, and local governments have strongly tended to expropriate rural agricultural land on a large scale in pursuit of enormous economic benefits. There are limitations to planned expropriation, which are deliberate and intended to restrain the practice, and the problem has arisen that the rate at which cities expand exceeds the rate at which peasants who lose their land are provided social welfare. For state-owned urban land, the 2011 REC established a system by which courts can review the practical and procedural requirements specified by the regulation and determine whether a project fulfills conditions of public interest, thus enabling them to regulate land expropriation. However, in studying actual court cases, we can see that this mechanism does not function adequately.

Systems pertaining to compensation for expropriation are premised on the existence of a dual ownership mechanism that differs between urban and rural areas. Expropriation compensation for agricultural land comprises land compensation paid to the agricultural collective that owns the land, resettlement subsidies for individual members of the collective and compensation paid to individuals for crops and immovable property on the land. The role of fulfilling resettlement subsidy payments as basic livelihood compensation to peasants is substantial, but the standard for doing so is unclear and we cannot say that this adequately helps stabilize the lives of those who lose their land. For urban state-owned land, the REC specifies compensation based on the market value of the land, and when compared to the situation with agricultural land, only a very limited component of livelihood compensation is specified.

Notes

1 Shu Jiao is the author of Part 2 and Yashu Yang is the author of Part 3. Part 1 and Part 4 are by both authors. This work is supported by JSPS KAKENHI Grant Number JP18KK0033.

2 See Wang, C. (2016) and Peng (2018) for the overall description of land expropriation and private property in China. Peng (2018) is particularly noteworthy in that the book questions "transition paradigm" and aims at a "contextualized description and immanent critique of China's rural land takings law, based on an internal and sympathetic understanding of its origin and evolution" (Peng 2018, 14, 26).

3 Article 15 of the '82 constitution.

4 The unit "*mu*" is a traditional Chinese unit of measurement equivalent to 1/15th of a hectare.

5 See 3.1.4 for more about "resettlement."

6 Peng (2018, 241) calls this "individual expropriation."

7 Peng (2018, 241) calls this "batched expropriation."

8 For an English translation, see www.lawinfochina.com/display.aspx?lib=law&id=8580&CGid

9 The requirements for compensation in the REC are omitted here.

10 This regulation also includes the introduction of a social stability risk assessment system as a procedural requirement for the decision to expropriate. However, the regulation does not provide specific details for the operation of this system, and because the social stability risk assessment systems as implemented in each locality differed in specifics, this chapter does not discuss them.

11 ZheJiang province High People's Court, Administrative Litigation, Appeal, Judgment No. 58, 2014.

12 In these cases, the plaintiff made such a claim and the court accepted it.

13 Supreme People's Court, Administrative Litigation, Retrial, Ruling No. 4693, 2014.

14 See note (18) for the ways in which collective-owned land may be used under the revised LAL.

15 "Tract development" refers to the comprehensive development and construction activities of a certain area of land, organized by local governments in the

centralized construction area determined by the national land and space plan. Cf. www.gov.cn/zhengce/zhengceku/2020-11/06/content_5557796.htm

16 In practice, the land compensation award and basic living allowance are not paid separately but are aggregated as a lump sum that is paid to the rural collective. It is typical for the collective to distribute money among its members.

17 The Property Rights Law of the People's Republic of China was enacted in 2007. Article 42 contained provisions addressing the expropriation of land and compensation thereof. However, when the Civil Code of the People's Republic of China entered into force on January 1, 2021, the current Property Rights Law was abolished forthwith.

18 Before the revision, the LAL stipulated standards of compensation for "arable land" and "land other than arable land," but the revised law established standards separately for collective agricultural land (land used directly for agricultural production including arable and forest land, grasslands, land used for irrigation of farmland and sites of aquaculture) and land used for nonagricultural purposes (construction and undeveloped land).

19 "Housing sites" (宅基地) refers to the land used exclusively for housing in rural areas. It is distributed free of charge to the collective.

20 If a peasant whose land is expropriated moves to a city and becomes a worker, "resettlement" leads to a change in their *hukou*, or household registration, which is effectively a change in their social status. (This author would like to thank Professor Mang Zhu (Shanghai Jiao Tong University) for pointing this out.) The dual nature of the *hukou* system limits the movement of population. It is extremely difficult to convert one's *hukou* from agricultural to nonagricultural, with conversions possible only under circumstances such as being hired at a state-owned enterprise, recruitment to the military or being subject to land expropriation.

21 This mode of dealing with "resettlement" appeared in the 2019 amendment of the LAL. Before the amendment, the law did not stipulate social welfare for those subject to expropriation, but Article 48 of the new law held that "people's governments at the county level and higher must make payments to those subject to expropriation through pensions and other social welfare systems. Social welfare expenses for peasants subject to expropriation are to be used mainly for social insurance such as pension insurance for peasants who meet requirements. Provinces, autonomous regions, and directly-controlled cities will establish administrative measures for the procurement, administration, and use of social welfare for peasants subject to expropriation." However, the revised law does not specify the details of the standard for calculating compensation.

22 Jiang (2009, 21, 2012, 48) holds that a "market value standard" must be used both in cities and in rural areas based on the standpoint of a principle of "complete compensation." However, it is not clear how this "market value" is to be calculated for agricultural land for which free transactions are not conducted.

23 In Chinese, 办法. This term refers to rules and provisions for implementing laws.

References

Chen, Yinrong (陈银蓉/Mei, Yun (梅昀)/Wang, Rumin (汪如民)/Zhao, Dong (赵冬) (2006), Consideration in Coordinating General Land Use Planning and Urban Planning during Urbanization (城市化过程中土地利用总体规划与城市规划协调的思考, *China Population, Resources and Environment*, 16(1), p. 32.

Gu, Jingtao (顾京涛)/Yin, Qiang (尹强) (2005), Survey of the New Round Comprehensive Land Use Planning From the Perspective of Urban Planning (从城市规划视角审视新一轮土地利用总体规划), *City Planning Review*, 9, pp. 9–13.

Jiang, Bixin (江必新) (2012), *Understanding and application of Regulation on the Expropriation of Buildings on State-Owned Land and Compensation* (国有土地上房屋征收与补偿条例理解与适用), China Legal Publishing House.

Jiang, Lihong (江利紅) (2009), Development and Challenges of Land Expropriation Compensation System in China (中国における土地収用補償制度の発展と課題), *Chuo University's Bulletin of Graduate Studies* (中央大学大学院研究年報), 39, pp. 3–27.

Jiang, Lihong (江利紅) (2012), Land Expropriation Compensation and Challenges in China (中国における土地収用の補償とその課題), *Evaluation*, 45, pp. 43–51.

Peng, Chun (2018), *Rural Land Takings Law in Modern China: Origin and Evolution*, Cambridge University Press.

Research Team of Ministry of Land & Resources on the Land Expropriation Reform, (2003), Report of the Land Expropriation Reform Research (征地制度改革研究报告), *National Land and Resources Information*, 11, pp. 48–55.

Wang, Chuanhui (2016), *The Constitutional Protection of Private Property in China: Historical Evolution and Comparative Research*, Cambridge University Press.

Wang, Keqiang (王克强)/Wang, Hongwei (王洪卫) /Liu, Hongmei (刘红梅) (2015), *Real Estate Law* (房地产法), Fudan University Press.

Ye, Bifeng (叶必丰)/Jia, Xiuyan (贾秀彦)/Gong, Jing (弓晶) (2004), How to Connect the Land Administration Law with Amendment to the Constitution (土地管理法怎样与修宪衔接), *China Land*, pp. 28–29.

Part III

Securing commons in the old and new property regime

9 Vacant properties in Japan

A new challenge for the study of the commons and land laws in Asia

Gakuto Takamura

1 Introduction

The study of the commons has long focused on the challenges posed by the overuse of finite resources (Hardin 1968; Ostrom 1990). Legal regulations are an important measure to solve the overuse problem. Furthermore, the primary function of land laws in Asia is to regulate this problem in the context of rapid development.

In Japan, however, where population decline is a constant problem, vacant properties such as abandoned houses have become notable. This issue has arisen from the underuse of resources, which has resulted in negative externality of surrounding communities. Although the vacant properties examined in this chapter are personal properties, those who use them should belong to the local community in which they are located and be joined to the comanagement of the various commons. Consequently, this is a new challenge for commons and property law studies.

Based on fieldwork in Fukui prefecture from 2011 to 2014 as well as further information that has been revealed since, how the community-based approach and theory of property law should evolve to solve the issue of underuse are examined in this chapter.

From 2010, most of Japan's local governments enacted ordinances that impose upon the owners of vacant properties the duty of appropriate management. Subsequently, the Act on Special Measures for Unoccupied Houses was enacted by the national government in 2014 (Kadomatsu 2020a). However, the governments' legal enforcement actions are infrequent. With reference to the municipal ordinance, often the neighborhood or community persuades owners to take appropriate measures. To avoid having to undertake legal action, municipalities rely on pressure from their respective communities.

Even though vacant properties often have the potential for habitability, the Japanese who are generally apprehensive around strangers have a tendency to avoid renting or selling these properties on the market. To reduce the owner's anxiety and assess a newcomer's personality, community-based organizations serve as mediators between the parties.

DOI: 10.4324/9781003170600-12

Although, to some extent, this community-based approach is effective, too much emphasis on the homogeneity of the community, which is often an inevitable consequence of such approaches, tends to exclude diversity. In this chapter, to relativize the Japanese community-based approach, we examine a rights-based approach of French Housing Law in which housing is regarded not as private property but as a condition of human rights and also the perspective of the American Landbank that relies on Heller (1998)'s anticommons theory.

2 Unoccupied houses and a challenge for legal theory

The origin of property arises from an intention and act of appropriating a thing in pursuit of economic value (Rose 1985; Carbonnier 2000:84). However, in Japan, where vacant properties, including abandoned houses, vacant lots and deserted cultivated lands, have become prominent, a new phenomenon where property owners who find no economic value in their properties and consequently, abandon them without selling or leasing them to others can be observed (Figure 9.1).

Property law is based on the assumptions that properties have active uses, and the role of property law involves the attribution of resources for efficient use and provision of legal rules for competitive use. A new framework to analyze the causes of the underuse of resources is imperative so as to solve this problem (Chilstein 2006; Dross 2012).

Since 2010, many of Japan's local governments have enacted ordinances that impose the duty of appropriate management on owners of vacant properties (Kitamura ed. 2012). Following this enactment of local ordinances, the national government passed an act on special measures for unoccupied houses in 2014. The act clarified the legal authority of local governments to order appropriate management by the owners and remove dangerous houses, thus subrogating the owners if they neglect this order (Kadomatsu 2020a; Kitamura 2014).

Houses that have been abandoned for a long time without management are extremely dangerous and produce a significant number of negative externalities for their surroundings. Consequently, the public law approach that has been noted is imperative. Furthermore, it is crucial to concretize the criteria that enable

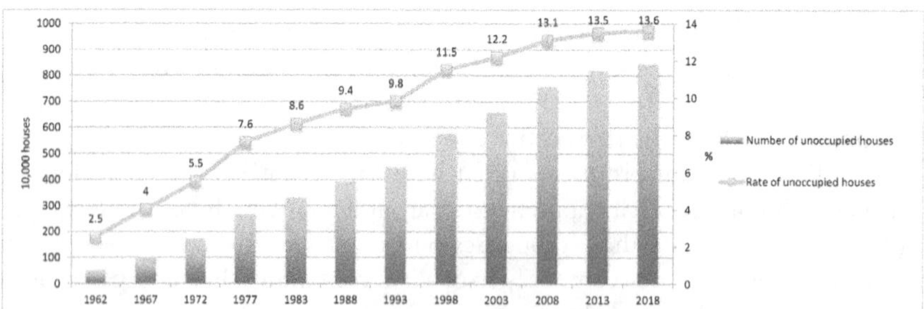

Figure 9.1 Percentage and number of unoccupied houses in Japan

the administrative subrogation measure to assist in the enforcement of this measure. However, this measure may be regarded as nothing more than an ex-post measure for extreme cases. Rather, it is of paramount importance to deepen the socio-legal analysis of why vacant properties are increasing, how Japanese property law and the Japanese attitude toward the law are related to this increase and how property law can be implemented to prevent vacant properties.

The Japanese civil law including its property law and the Japanese land use law were enacted during the period when capitalism was on the rise and land overuse was acknowledged as a social problem (Takamura 2014, 2015). Consequently, these laws focus mainly on the regulation of overuse and competitive use of resources and do not deal with the problem of underuse adequately (ibid.).

For 20 years, Japan has experienced economic stagnation. In addition, with the exception of Tokyo, population decline is problematic. In parallel with this economic stagnation and population decline, the percentage of vacant houses has increased: it rose to 13.5 percent in 2013 (Figure 9.1). Moreover, the number of young women is expected to halve in approximately 50 percent of local governments by 2040 (Japan Policy Council 2014). The myth of economic growth is no longer considered to be true in Japan. Anderson (2012:124) proposed the necessity to view urbanization in a life-cycle model where growth is followed by decline. Accordingly, the legal regulations to control the decline successfully should be examined.

There are two approaches related to the issue of unoccupied houses: a community-based approach and a rights-based approach. Most of the actions implemented in Japan's rural areas have adopted the community-based approach. Therefore, this chapter analyzes the reason why this approach is so popular and notes the limitations of this approach. In addition, a hybrid that incorporates a rights-based approach, drawing from French Housing Law that regards housing not as private property but as a condition of human rights (Melot 2020) as well as the American Land Bank system's perspective that relies on Heller's anticommons theory, are examined (Kelly 2020; Heller 1998; Alexander 2015).

Based on participant observations that we conducted in the communities and local governments of Fukui prefecture, the reason the community-based approach has been preferred in Japan is first explained and subsequently, the effects and limits thereof are measured. Second, the types of new rights-based approaches that are required will be described from French and American cases. Third, the theoretical implications of the issue of vacant properties are summarized and recommended future research outlined.

3 Why is the community-based approach so popular?

The increase in unoccupied houses has often been attributed to aging and the declining population of rural areas. Yoneyama (2012:8) verified that rural areas are experiencing problems related to an aging population and a diminishing number of children and added that at a macro level of analysis, depopulation correlates with an increase in the rate of unoccupied houses (Yoneyama 2012:8). However, micro-level field surveys have revealed another factor besides aging and a declining population involved in the percentage of unoccupied houses.

However, it is not as though there is no demand for vacant houses in rural areas. Rather, because of their historical and natural landscape as well as relaxed lifestyle, rural areas have appeal. Furthermore, most have tourist potential. Because of the shock of the COVID-19 pandemic, young people from urban areas have shown a tendency to prefer the lifestyle that characterizes rural areas.

One may question why the demand of vacant houses is far greater than the supply thereof. As detailed subsequently, the closed nature of the Japanese community is a factor that discourages transactions in vacant houses. Herein lies the reason for the popularity of the community-based approach in Japan.

3.1 *Law and economics approach to the market in existing houses*

Before considering the results of field research, it is necessary to examine policy measures briefly other than the recent national act for unoccupied houses and the theoretical model on which this policy relied.

The central government employed the theory of information asymmetry as a theoretical model to elucidate the policy for unoccupied houses (Akerlof 1970). In law and economics, a decrease in the number of transactions in existing houses may be explained as the information asymmetry between seller and buyer (Hatta 1997). Sellers know more about their houses than buyers do. This knowledge includes information about defects of the house, which the buyer can only guess. Thus, the price of the house may drop lower than the seller's expectation. Consequently, fewer transactions will occur. To prevent this market tragedy, the law should ensure that the seller is accountable.

In comparison to other developed countries, Japan has fewer regulations related to this accountability (Saito 2010). Furthermore, in 2018, the country's market share of existing houses (14.5 percent) was less than that of the United States (81 percent) and France (69.8 percent). Consequently, the Japanese central government has passed regulations that make the disclosure of information mandatory and strengthen realtors' code of professional conduct to protect consumers since 2010. Although it was necessary to improve these regulations, from the perspective of a sociologist in the field, it appears as though this market-oriented policy option does not concur with the sociological concept of property among the people of rural areas and is thus not effective.

3.2 *The sociological concept of property in the case of Kumagawa Community*

The question of what the sociological concept of property in Japanese rural society is may be posed. Key findings from a field survey I conducted in a local community in Fukui prefecture may be employed to answer this question. This community is located in Wakasa Municipality, Kumagawa district. As depicted in Figures 9.2 and 9.3, the population of the community is gradually decreasing and

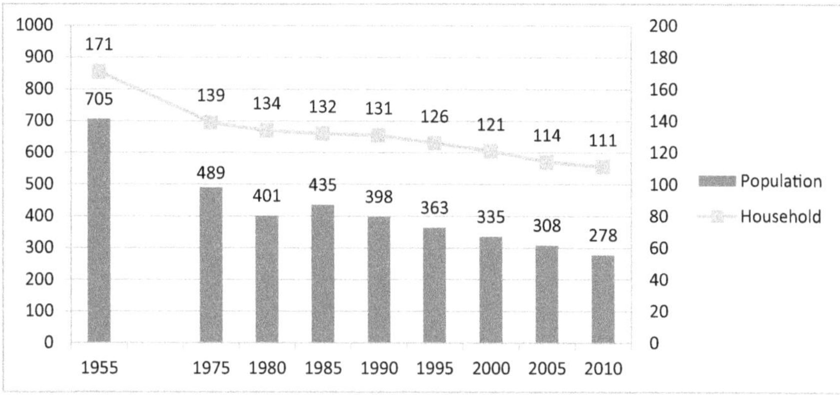

Figure 9.2 Population and household numbers of Kumagawa District 1955–2010

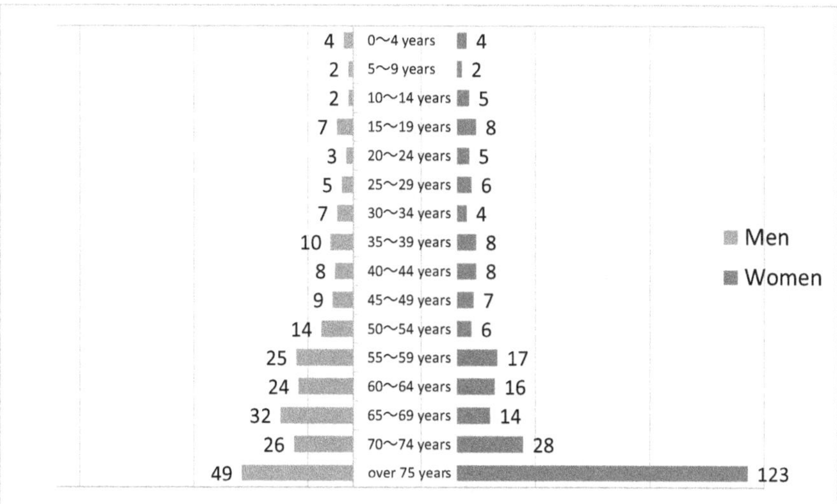

Figure 9.3 Age-sex pyramid of Kumagawa District in 2010

aging. Before motorization, Kumagawa flourished as an inn town on the route between Kyoto and the Japanese Sea. It was also a retail center for the surrounding rural area. Because of its many historical and high-quality wooden houses, in 1996, this district was designated as an Important Preservation District for Groups of Traditional Buildings. Despite this, the community's population has continued to decline. In 2010, 28 percent of houses in the district were unoccupied. Furthermore, of the 111 houses in Kumagawa, 31 were unoccupied (Figure 9.4). Most of Kumagawa's visitors are surprised at the shocking deterioration of the abandoned houses rather than being in awe of the historical landscape. The

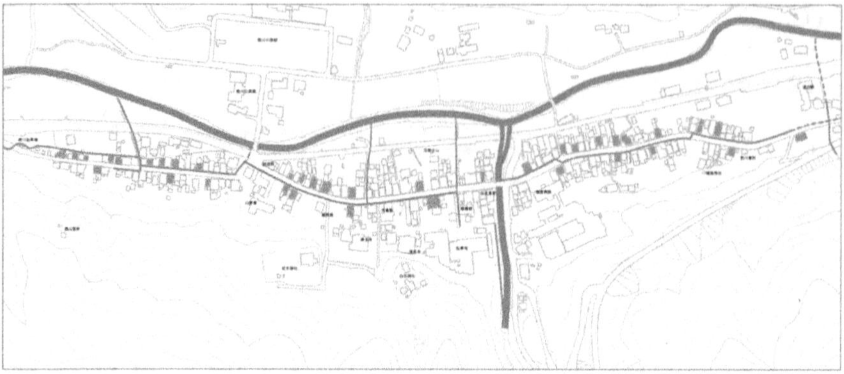

Figure 9.4 Map of vacant houses in Kumagawa

local government, namely, Wakasa Municipality, which incorporates Kumagawa, experiences this decline as undesirable because of the district's great potential to attract tourists to the municipality.

Anxiety related to market transactions in property may be regarded as the first characteristic of the sociological concept of property. According to a district bylaw of Kumagawa, owners are required to give notice to the community organization and receive advice from it when they want to sell or rent their property. This is indicative of the general anxiety related to outsiders. There are a number of community events and forms of mutual assistance in Kumagawa. The majority of residents participate in sustaining community life and are concerned that newcomers from urban areas are unlikely to adopt the same attitude.

It is rare for a community to have a bylaw that restricts transactions. However, in general, it is also unusual for outsiders to decide to live in a rural area. Most property acquisitions in Japanese rural areas have been inherited or gifted from parent to child. Although there are property transactions, they are conducted primarily through relatives or acquaintances and not realtors. Hence, property is perceived as a patrimony and component of the local community rather than an individual asset. It is regarded as shameful for ancestors if their descendants have to sell this patrimony in the market and put an estate sale sign in the front garden. This sociological concept of property reduces the number of property transactions that owners have no intention of using themselves. Accordingly, we conducted surveys to shed light on the influence of this concept on the transactions of existing houses in Kumagawa.

3.3 Method

Three types of questionnaire surveys were conducted to explore the thought processes of owners of unoccupied houses in relation to their properties and problems new inhabitants who moved to Kumagawa experienced.

First, a mail-in survey was conducted by Wakasa Municipality for all the owners of unoccupied houses in the municipality. The response rate was 75.4 percent and there were 132 valid responses. We performed a secondary analysis of the survey.

Second, a mail-in survey was conducted in 2012 and 2013 through the joint collaboration of Wakasa, Kumagawa and the author's seminar class for the owners of unoccupied houses in Kumagawa. While the response rate was 68 percent, there were 17 valid responses.

Third, a door-to-door survey was conducted in 2011 by the author's seminar class for those inhabitants of Kumagawa who were not born there. All nine such inhabitants responded, thus yielding a response rate of 100 percent.

3.4 Anxiety and expectations of the owners of vacant properties

The questionnaire conducted by the municipality for all the owners of unoccupied houses in Wakasa revealed that half of the respondents who had intentions of selling or renting their houses expected the municipality to be the intermediary in transactions involving unoccupied houses (Figures 9.5 and 9.6). They did not appear to trust the professional realtors because they were of the opinion that professional realtors would only pursue their own economic interests and were unconcerned about the new buyer or renter.

To shed light on what measures the owners found effective to advance the transaction, the owners of the unoccupied houses were required to provide more concrete answers in the second survey. The results showed that they would be more positive about selling their property if the community organization explained the local customs and community activities of Kumagawa to any new potential buyers beforehand and supported the process of their integration into community life (Figure 9.7).

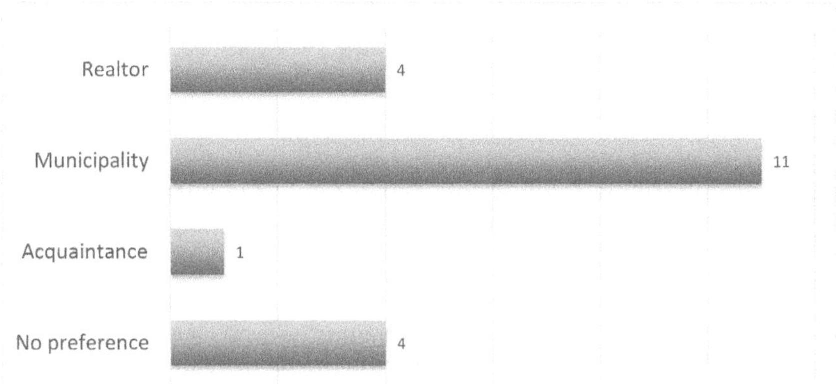

Figure 9.5 Owners' preferred intermediary to rent unoccupied houses in Wakasa, n = 15 (multiple answers allowed)

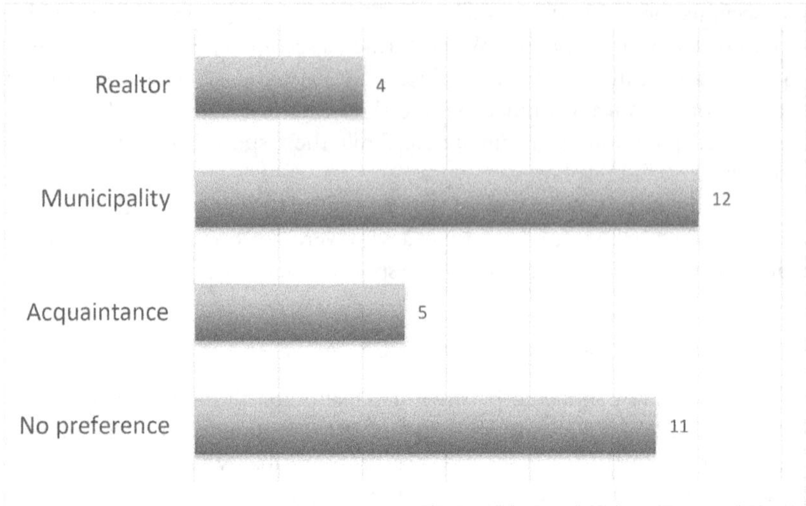

Figure 9.6 Owners' preferred intermediary to sell unoccupied houses in Wakasa, n = 24 (multiple answers allowed)

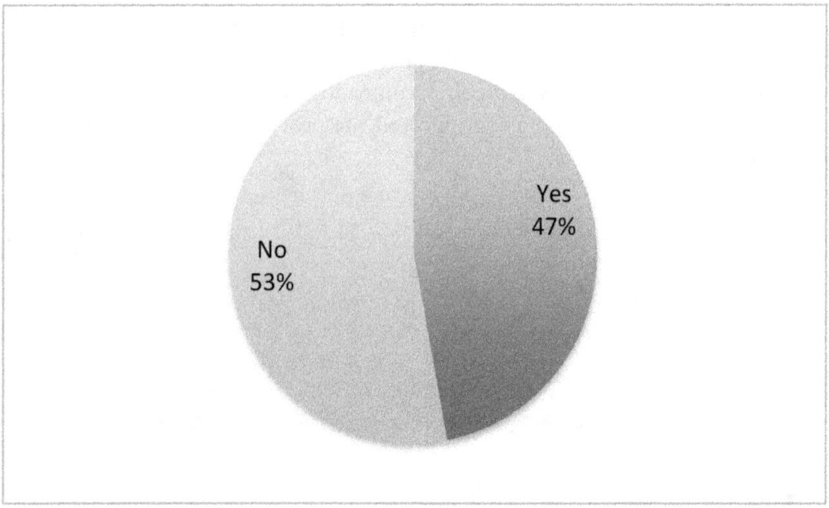

Figure 9.7 Question: Provided that Kumagawa Community Organization conducted an interview with a would-be buyer or tenant explaining the local customs and community activities beforehand, would you be willing to register your unoccupied house on the list of available properties of the Vacant Houses Bank of Wakasa Municipality? (n = 17)

These results revealed that the owners of unoccupied houses did not sell or lend their properties because they were afraid of the uncertainty of any newcomer's personality and did not want to cause problems for the community that were related to newcomers' lack of cooperation.

The results of the questionnaire survey that the inhabitants of Kumagawa who were not born in the district completed demonstrated the importance of the information with reference to how they should cooperate with the community. The results revealed that their main concern before moving to Kumagawa was whether they would be welcomed by the community and be able to adapt to community life (Figure 9.8). However, most of them expressed satisfaction with the current community life (Figure 9.9).

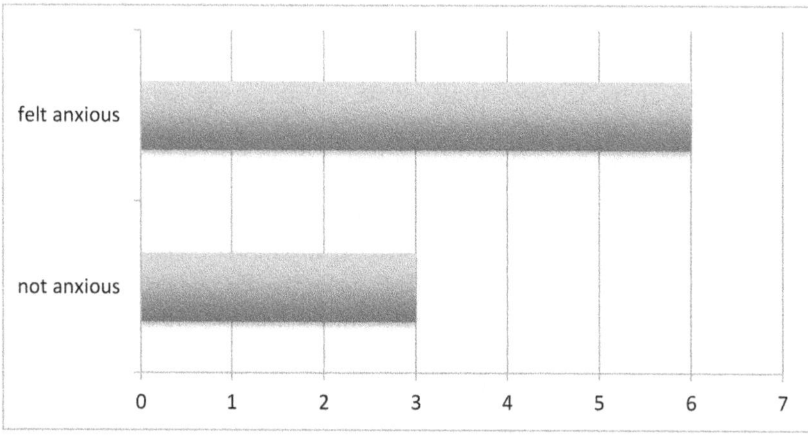

Figure 9.8 Question: Did you feel anxious about whether you would be welcomed by Kumagawa Community before you moved in? (n = 9)

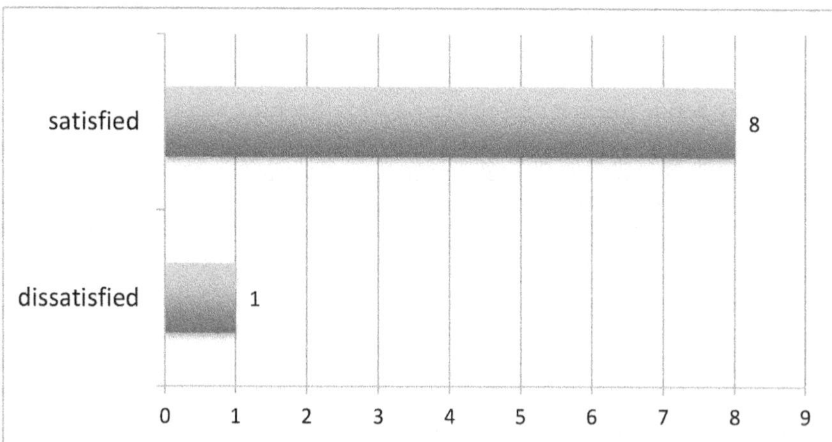

Figure 9.9 Question: Are you satisfied with the human relationships in Kumagawa Community now? (n = 9)

The results of the surveys provide new insight on the existing theory. The theory of information asymmetry posits two parties: a seller and a buyer. The information related to the quality of the housing unit is important. However, social reality revealed by the surveys demonstrated that both parties were very conscious of the community as a third party. They perceived how the community regarded them as important. Social psychologist Yamagishi and Yamagishi (1994) found that the Japanese tend to be wary of community outsiders and only trust members of their own community. This tendency was confirmed by the results of the surveys conducted in Kumagawa. The community's hyperconsciousness and the less up-front communication among these three parties are important social factors that prevent transactions of unoccupied houses.

3.5 Community-based organization as intermediary in transactions of unoccupied houses

To remove this inhibiting factor and facilitate up-front communication, Wakasa Municipality, Kumagawa District and the author's laboratory collaborated to set up a community-based organization that would act as an intermediary in unoccupied house transactions. This type of community-based organization, which is known as a Vacant House Bank (*Akiya Bank*), is growing in rural areas of Japan. The purpose of this community-based organization is to mediate between owners of vacant properties and new inhabitants in the place of professional realtors. Furthermore, it encourages the former to register their properties on the list of available properties and explains community life to the latter beforehand. Although the list of available properties is accessible on the Internet, the potential inhabitants are required to meet with the community organization to proceed with the transaction.

The organization is intended to help reduce the anxieties of owners and new inhabitants. The owners afforded the security of knowing that the new inhabitants will buy or rent their homes with an understanding of community life as well as an awareness that they are expected to join community activities. The new inhabitants are given the opportunity to feel that the community welcomes them. Moreover, they are made aware of what is expected of them in the community before they decide to enter into a contract with the owner.

Establishing the community-based organization has given the inhabitants of Kumagawa the opportunity to reflect on their community, clarify their community rules and expectations for new inhabitants and ensure Kumagawa was more open and welcomed them. They designed a brochure for the new inhabitants in which they described their community and hopes. Moreover, in the spring of 2013, they organized a community walking tour for those interested in living there.

Those owners of vacant properties who were negative about the sale of their property have since been changing their attitude and begun to register their homes on the list of available properties. There is no shame attached to this because it was the community that solicited the registration.

From 2013 to 2020, this community-based organization succeeded in accommodating 20 families in Kumagawa as new inhabitants who purchased or rented unoccupied houses. Most of these families are young couples with children and have their own businesses in Kumagawa as artists, web designers and restaurant and café owners. These new inhabitants have been able to attract more people to the community, which has become active with no fears of disappearing.

Other field interview surveys of community-based organizations for mediation in vacant house transactions, namely, at *Imai-cho* in Nara prefecture, *Ayabe* City and *Nishijin* District in Kyoto prefecture and *Onomichi* in Hiroshima prefecture, have revealed that they would perform very well if they could define their local identities and attractive aspects clearly and generate a positive message for new inhabitants (Takamura 2010). This defining process would ensure that the community was more open to others and clarify the procedure for vacant house transactions as well as the adaptation process of new inhabitants to the community.

It is for this reason that the community-based approach is so popular in Japan to resolve issues related to vacant properties. If the community acts as an intermediary between an owner and new inhabitant, both of them are likely to feel at ease. This attitude is related to the Japanese sociological concept of property, which regards property not as an individual asset but as a component of the local community, as well as to Japanese psychological anxiety about others in general.

4 Toward a rights-based approach: beyond the limits of the community-based approach

The community-based approach is effective even though too much emphasis on the community inevitably reveals the limitations of this approach. First, the Japanese community-based approach has been unable to link the issue of unoccupied houses to that of the poorly housed because the community selects only desirable people. Second, it has not been able to solve the problem of long-term abandoned houses that are severely dilapidated or the owners thereof who have been difficult to identify. Third, this approach supposes the growth of communities and does not respond to the problem of shrinking communities. To overcome these limitations, it is crucial to blend a rights-based approach with the community-based approach. A review of the policies and practices of other countries may facilitate in identifying the kind of rights-based approach that is needed.

4.1 Right to housing

While the number of unoccupied houses has increased in Japan, the housing conditions of the young and the elderly have worsened (Hirayama and Izuhara 2018). Young people without secure employment and the elderly who do not own their own homes experience difficulty securing adequate housing because it is assumed that they will be unable to maintain their rental or housing loan payments. The Japanese housing policy, which favors home ownership, does not provide enough support for those in their circumstances (ibid.).

One solution may be to furnish them with unoccupied housing through the government and thus improve their situation. However, the involvement of community-based organizations has inevitably led to the exclusion of these vulnerable people.

In the case of Kumagawa, civil servants of Wakasa Municipality are not in favor of receiving elderly persons from other local governments because of their dependency on the municipal welfare budget as well as the fact they do not pay income tax, which is the Japanese local governments' main revenue. Thus, new elderly residents would be a financial burden on the local government. Kumagawa community is particularly in favor of young families with children, which will enable it to keep a nearby elementary school open and help run community events. Other than this family model, they are reluctant to accept other potential residents.

Other communities also willingly receive young families who can contribute to the community. Furthermore, they too are reluctant to accept the elderly, foreigners and those with financial insecurities.

In this regard, the movement of the Right to Housing in France is noteworthy. Unoccupied houses became a social issue in France because a nonprofit organization, namely, the Right to Housing (*Droit au logement*) began to squat on vacant apartments so as to provide housing to vulnerable people. The movement demanded that the public authorities expropriate unoccupied properties to convert them into social housing and thus succeeded in linking the issue of unoccupied houses with that of the poorly housed (Péchu 2007).

The French government and housing authorities actively buy or expropriate vacant houses to provide remodeled social housing (Dietrich-Ragon 2011). France does not regard housing as private property but rather as a basic element of human rights. France is far more inclusive of the vulnerable and active in public intervention in relation to abandoned housing than Japan is. Furthermore, they convert deteriorated housing into good quality public houses (Melot 2020).

4.2 Public intervention in abandoned housing

It is imperative that unoccupied houses that can be sold through the community-based system are in relatively good condition and do not cost much to repair. Long-term abandoned houses are not transactionable goods even in communities where this system has proven to be successful. A rights-based approach is crucial to address these difficult cases.

The question of abandoned properties has not been addressed in Japanese property law. However, there is a section on dangerous abandoned buildings in the Japanese building code, which gives local governments the authority to remove dangerous buildings. Kitamura ed. (2012) noted that the application of this section has been very rare as most local governments do not know how to do so.

To clarify their authority and procedures involved in removing dangerous buildings, many local governments have enacted local ordinances since 2010. However, these local ordinances are symbolic because even after their enactment, municipal legal enforcement action has been rare. Often, by referring to the municipal ordinance, it is the neighborhood and community that persuade owners to take the appropriate measures. To avoid having to undertake legal action, municipalities rely on this social pressure.

The right of ownership is absolute, sacred and inviolable for Japanese municipalities. In relation to abandoned housing, they do not have enough confidence in the judicial legitimacy of public intervention. In comparison to other countries, this is most unusual.

In 1789, the Declaration of the Rights of Man and of the Citizen defined the right of property as sacred and inviolable in France. Moreover, a municipal police code for abandoned properties has existed since the French Revolution and has been applied often (Takamura 2014).

Most cities in the U.S. have municipal codes that impose upon the owners of properties the duty of appropriate management and give the city the authority to remove any dangerous building, thus subrogating the owners when they neglect their duty (Kelly 2020).

In both countries, the right of ownership is not absolute and can be exercised only if this right does not interfere with the rights of others. Furthermore, the rule of the appropriate exercise of property rights is ensured by police power and property rights have internal restrictions. On the contrary, in Japan, the notion that respect for the right of others belongs to moral or social manners rather than being a legal issue is upheld. Thus, in relation to property rights, the municipal code is less developed.

As noted previously, the national government enacted the Act for unoccupied houses in 2014, which gave local government legitimacy to public intervention in abandoned housing. This legislation resulted in local government becoming more active in undertaking legal action (Kadomatsu 2020a). However, given the traditional concept of property and the non-litigious orientation of the Japanese, it remains uncertain what the effect of such legal action on the situation of dangerous abandoned houses may be.

The dimension of private law, rather than that of public law, has remained unaltered by lawmakers. If a property has been abandoned for a lengthy period, intestate succession may occur and consequently, many co-owners may be difficult to contact. To transfer the property to an individual, the unanimous accord of co-owners is required and each has a right of veto. Heller (1998) described this as an anticommons situation. Thus, the transaction cost of overcoming this situation is very high. The recent policy framework of Unknown Land Owner Issue problematized the issue of a multiple number of co-owners and enacted the Unclaimed Land Act in 2019 to facilitate taking such land (Kadomatsu 2020b). However, no fundamental legal change to prevent this issue has been implemented.

In addition, in inner-city areas in Japan, each property is small. For the effective use of such a property, integrated redevelopment with the surrounding properties is necessary. To overcome this spatial anticommons situation, the unanimous accord of every property owner is required.[1] Because the transaction cost is so high, nothing has been done and buildings have been allowed to deteriorate.

In the U.S., under the influence of the theory of the anticommons, the reintegration of rights of properties has been conducted through a system of land banks (Alexander 2015). Working in conjunction with local governments and the courts, these hold the titles to abandoned properties so as to manage them and coordinate their future desirable use.

It is important that Japan follows this rights-based approach so as to prevent the problems associated with the anticommons and economize the transaction costs for future use.

4.2.1 A shrinking strategy and the paradigm shift of law

Heller's anticommons approach supposes that there will be effective utilization of land if multiple rights on the land are addressed. This approach is valid in areas where there is a high demand for land, including inner-city areas in metropolitan cities. Another approach is needed in rural areas: it is necessary that low growth is acknowledged and a shrinking strategy is adopted by converting residential plots to open spaces and returning urban zones back to nature.

In this regard, the challenge of Echizen municipality, which is located an hour's drive from Kumagawa, is interesting (Takamura 2012). The town subsidizes a neighborhood association that removes vacant abandoned housing and creates and manages open common spaces on the vacant plot. This subsidy encourages a community-based approach: a neighborhood association convinces owners of vacant properties, addresses multiple claims on the properties, settles any conflict related to the boundary of property lines, places the order to demolish vacant houses and manages the open common space.

Our survey of several neighborhoods in Echizen in 2012 revealed that 14 unoccupied houses were removed under this scheme and all the sites were well-maintained and utilized actively by the neighborhood as recreational spaces. The open spaces in which there were abandoned houses were transformed into local commons managed by the community. Such transformations could only be realized by the community-based approach. The example of Echizen illustrates an advantage of the Japanese community-based approach.

However, the fact that the municipality plays an active role in facilitating this scheme should not be ignored. The municipality concludes lease contracts for ten years with the owners of vacant properties free of charge and subleases vacant lots to the neighborhood for free. These lease contracts provide the legal structure that allows abandoned properties to be transformed into open commons space. Therefore, the legal solution is an indispensable condition for the community-based approach.

After a ten-year transitional period, the municipality and owner of the vacant property have to renegotiate how the land should be used. The town then has to consider the ownership of the land seriously: whether the municipality legally recognizes the property as abandoned and becomes the new owner by purchasing or claiming ownership of it. A serious discussion on the extinctive prescription of ownership may be necessary. In an era of underuse, a new theory of property law is imperative to consider this future problem.

5 Conclusion

The purpose of this chapter is to explain why the community-based approach has been employed in Japan to address the issue of vacant properties. While legal and economic analyses of the existing houses market only include a seller and a buyer in their models, the results of our field surveys revealed that both buyer and seller are extremely conscious of how the community may regard them and that enhanced up-front communication between the seller, buyer and community can resolve the social-psychological barriers that prevent transactions in unoccupied housing. It is for this reason community-based organizations for mediation in the sale of vacant houses have been established and are preferred in rural areas in Japan.

However, the community-based approach has various limitations: an exclusionary attitude toward outsiders and vulnerable groups, the absence of an adequate solution for long-term abandoned houses and the inability to adapt to the shrinking community. Consequently, a hybrid approach, which draws from the French view that regards housing not as private property but as a condition of human rights as well as the perspective of the U.S. that relies on Heller's anticommons theory and the pursuit of transaction efficiency and land use that can be combined with the Japanese community approach, is proposed in this chapter.

The problem of vacant properties presents a new challenge for the existing theory of property law that assumes that there are active uses of properties and that the primary role of property law is the provision of rules for competitive use. We can learn from the study of commons to manage vacant lots as new commons. The provision of a new framework in the era of the underuse of properties is imperative.

Japan has a more serious problem in comparison to the U.S. and France with the underuse of resources, and many countries of Asia will be faced with depopulation in the future (Iiguni et al. ed. 2018). Continual field surveys on this problem may be beneficial in the elaboration of a new theoretical framework for the study of land laws in Asia.

Note

1 Referring to Japanese Land Law and the situation in Kobe after the earthquake, Heller (1998:684) argued that the small parcel of each land plot in Japanese cities and too much respect for property owners, co-owners and tenants in Japanese Land Law have created an anticommons situation and prevented efficient land use.

References

Akerlof, George A. (1970). "The Market for 'Lemons': Quality Uncertainty and the Market Mechanism", *Quarterly Journal of Economics* (The MIT Press) Vol. 84, No. 3, pp. 488–500.

Alexander, Frank S. (2015) *Land Banks and Land Banking*, 2nd Edition, Center for Community Progress.

Anderson, Michelle Wilde (2012) "Dissolving Cities", *Yale Law Journal*, Vol. 121, No. 6, pp. 1364–1447.

Carbonnier, Jean (2000) *Droit civil -Tome 3 Les biens*, 19éme édition, P.U.F.

Chilstein, David (2006) "Les biens à valeur vénale negative", *Revue trimestrielle de droit civil*, pp. 663–689.

Dietrich-Ragon, Pascale (2011) *Le logement intolerable*, P.U.F.

Dross, William (2012) *Droit civil – Les choses*, L.G.D.J.

Hardin, Garrett (1968) "The Tragedy of the Commons", *Science*, Vol. 162, No. 3859, pp. 1243–1248.

Hatta, Tatsuo (八田達夫) (1997) "Housing Market and Public Policy (住宅市場と公共政策)", in: Iwata, Kikuo (岩田規久男) and Hatta, Tatsuo, ed., *Jyutaku no Keizaigaku* (住宅の経済学), Nihon Keizai Shinbunsha (日本経済新聞社).

Heller, Michael (1998) "The Tragedy of the Anticommons: Property in the Transition from Marx to Markets", *Harvard Law Review*, Vol. 111, No. 3, pp. 621–688.

Hirayama, Yosuke and Izuhara, Misa (2018) *Housing in Post-Growth Society: Japan on the Edge of Social Transition*, Routledge.

Iiguni, Yoshiaki (飯國芳明) et al., ed. (2018) *Hollowing Out of Land Ownership* (土地所有権の空洞化), Nakanishiya Syuppan (ナカニシヤ出版).

Japan Policy Council (日本創成会議) (2014) *Strategy for Reduced Birth Rate and Rural Revitalization (ストップ少子化・地方元気戦略)*, www.policycouncil.jp/

Kadomatsu, Narufumi (2020a) "Emergence of Unoccupied House Problem in Japan and Legal Measures Towards this Issue", in: Kadomatsu, Narufumi et al., ed., *Legal Responses to Vacant Houses: An International Comparison*, Springer, pp. 1–15.

Kadomatsu, Narufumi (2020b) "The Tragedies of the Commons and Anticommons in an Era of Underuse", in: Kadomatsu, Narufumi et al., ed., *Legal Responses to Vacant Houses*, Springer, pp. 61–81.

Kelly Jr, James J. (2020) "Municipal Responses to Vacant Properties in the United States", in: Kadomatsu, Narufumi et al., ed., *Legal Responses to Vacant Houses: An International Comparison*, Springer, pp. 17–34.

Kitamura, Yoshinobu (北村喜宣) (2014) "Commentary on the National Law of Vacant House (空き家対策特別措置法を読む)", *Jichi Kenkyu (自治研究)*, Vol. 90, No. 10, pp. 3–26 and No. 11, pp. 30–56.

Kitamura, Yoshinobu (北村喜宣) ed. (2012) *Local Ordinances on the Duty of Appropriate Management of Vacant House (空き家等の適正管理条例)*, Tiikikagaku Kenkyukai (地域科学研究会).

Melot, Romain (2020) "Expropriation of Vacant Property in France: The Case of Substandard Housing", in: Kadomatsu, Narufumi et al., ed., *Legal Responses to Vacant Houses*, Springer, pp. 35–43.

Ostrom, Elinor (1990) *Governing the Commons: The Evolution of Institutions for Collective Action*, Cambridge University Press

Péchu, Cécile (2007) *Droit au logement, genèse et sociologie d'une mobilization*, Dalloz.

Rose, Carol M. (1985) "Possession as the Origin of Property", *University of Chicago Law Review*, Vol. 52, No. 1, pp. 73–88

Saito, Hiroko (齋藤広子) (2010) "The Roles of Information and Experts on Buying and Selling an Existing House (住宅市場における住宅情報)]", *Fudosan Kenkyu (不動産研究)*, Vol. 52, No. 3, pp. 3–14.

Takamura, Gakuto (高村学人) (2010) "Essay for the Theory of the Contract Law on Real Estate in the Era of Population Decreasing (人口減少時代における不動産

契約法理論の試論)", *Syakaikagaku Kenkyu (社会科学研究)*, Vol. 61, No. 3–4, pp. 99–138.

Takamura, Gakuto (高村学人) (2012) "Creation of Pockets Park after the Removal of Abandoned Houses from the Case of Echizen Town in Fukui (空き家の解体・除去によるコミュニティの拠点づくり—福井県越前町のポケットパーク整備事業を通じて)", *Jyutaku (住宅)*, Vol. 61, September, pp. 24–28.

Takamura, Gakuto (高村学人) (2014) "Reconsidering Land Property Theory from the Era of Underuse of Real Estates: Revisiting French Modern Property Law's History (過少利用時代からの土地所有権論史再読—フランス所有権法史を中心に)", *Seisaku Kagaku (政策科学)*, Vol. 24, No. 4, pp. 81–131.

Takamura, Gakuto (高村学人) (2015) "Reconsidering Property Theory in the Era of the Underuse of Properties (過少利用時代における所有権論・再考)", *Housyakaigaku (法社会学)*, No. 81, pp. 64–75.

Yamagishi, Toshio and Yamagishi, Midori (1994) "Trust and Commitment in the United States and Japan", *Motivation and Emotion*, Vol. 18, No. 2, pp. 129–166.

Yoneyama, Hidetaka (米山秀隆) (2012) "Future Forecast of the Rate of Vacant House and Necessary Policies to Overcome this Issue (空き家率の将来展望と空き家対策)", *Fujitsu Research Institute Research Report*, No. 392, http://jp.fujitsu.com/group/fri/downloads/report/research/2012/no392.pdf

10 Securing *adat* land rights in Indonesia

From constitutional justice to legislation making

Rudy Lukman

1 Introduction

Indonesia's transformation to constitutionalism and democratic change is a critical phase in Indonesia's life as a nation. One transformation was the significant amendment of the Indonesia 1945 Constitution, beginning from the first amendment in 1999 to the fourth amendment in 2002. The amendment marked Indonesia's transition to constitutionalism and democratic society. Indonesia's transition to constitutional democracy is the effect of constitutionalism waves in the world (Carothers 1998).

The rise of constitutional democracy has been a world phenomenon followed by the new emergence and expanding role of constitutional courts in many countries as part of the institutionalization of each constitutional structure (Ginsburg 2003). In Indonesia, together with many other jurisdictions belonging to the civil law traditions, this constitutional democracy has taken the pattern of creating the constitutional court through the series of constitutional amendment process.

The result is the new provision of the Judicial Power constructed in articles 24–25 of the 1945 Constitution of the Republic of Indonesia. The judicial authority provided in Article 24 paragraph (2) confirms that judicial power vested in both the Supreme Court (hereinafter stated as "MA") and Constitutional Court (hereinafter stated as "MK"). With this constitutional arrangement, MK has an equal position with the MA, while both are defined as the judicial power holders who have different authorities. The construction of the MK has a purpose in strengthening the people's constitutional protection as the guardian of the Constitution.

Such a construction of the MK seems to be a natural phenomenon given the fact that the role of the Constitutional Court has long been associated with the two dimensions of the Constitution, namely, procedural and substantive objectives (Tate 1995). For example, Mauro Cappelletti (1970) explained the constitutional court's role as a method for validating the Constitution's positive values.

DOI: 10.4324/9781003170600-13

One of the aspects of the Indonesian Constitution in which the role of MK is tested is the matter of natural resources, which primarily involves the land-related questions (Robinson 2014). Land law in Indonesia has long been associated with the complexity, inconsistency, fragmented, injustice, and far from reality (Lindsey 1998). International financial agencies have long asked for the legislative reconstruction in this area of law.

At the same time, the constitutional amendment process has also covered the amendment on the provision on local government and local autonomy, including the provisions relating to the customary legal rights or "*adat.*" Namely, such a specific area of *adat* right provision as the constitution guarantee upon the *adat* law in Article 18B paragraph (2) of the 1945 Constitution has been debated in regard to the role of the State that recognizes and respects the societies with customary Law and traditional rights as long as they remain in existence, fit with social development and in harmony with the principle of the Unitary State of the Republic of Indonesia.

The establishment of the MK and the *adat* revivalism guaranteed by the Constitution have invited a wave of the petition calling for the *adat* rights recognition. Now is the era when Indonesian people have started to seek the agrarian justice under the MK judgments. This situation has brought it the new controversy of two different judicial powers in conflict. The MK has been deemed with a positive image in exercising judicial power, while the MA has a negative image of maintaining a conservative consistency through several judgments. Pompe, for example, gave a lousy assessment of the MA (Pompe 2005), even though the MA Reform since after the reformation period has not had much impact on the quality of the MA judgment (Djohansjah 2008).

On the other side, since its birth, the MK has been rendering the judgments favoring the agrarian constitutionalism, such as the ones for the protection of communal forest or known as the "Adat Forest," as well as the ones finding the unconstitutionality of the privatization on natural resources management. The recognition by MK of the Adat Forest triggered the *adat* revivalism calling for all the more recognition of *adat* issues, such as the institutionalization of the communal land rights into formal law. It stems back to the past when one of the Suharto New Order efforts was the enactment of Law No. 5/1979 on the Village Government. The Law systematically abolished the *adat*-based governance system by making all the Village Government uniformed throughout Indonesia, and thus destroyed the long-established basis of the *adat*-based community. This Law had also been the basis for the court to deny the legal capacity of *adat* community.

In the specific area of land law, the conflict between national law versus customary law is evident where the government has been destined to win based on the positive law. The defeat of *hak ulayat* (indigenous right) usually happened when the *adat* community made an agreement with private companies to create the right of use. After the right of use period ends, the land automatically becomes the state land under the provision of Basic Agrarian Law enacted in 1960 and the *adat* community lost its *hak ulayat*. This is due to the logic that they cannot any more prove the continued existence of *adat* community, which has been the result of the aforementioned Law No. 5/1979 on the Village Government. This result has been endorsed by the MA, which has withheld the positive law rather than take more account on *adat* claim.

The sinking of the *adat* system was changed by the agrarian justice given by the MK. It is proven by the series of judgments by MK, from constitutional recognition on *adat* democracies to the recognition of Adat Forest as *adat* people's constitutional rights. However, even agrarian justice has been given to the *adat* community. The number of agrarian conflicts involving *adat* rights has not been reduced.

In 2017, at least 659 agrarian conflicts are reported in various regions and provinces with a total accumulative conflict area of 520,497.87 hectares. The number of family heads involved in the conflict was at least 652,738. The 2017 conflict data show a significant increase of 50 percent when compared to 2016 data. That is, if averaged, agrarian conflicts occur two times per day (Konsorsium Pembaruan Agraria 2017). In 2018, there were at least 410 agrarian conflicts in various regions and provinces with a total accumulative area of conflict area of 807,177,613 hectares. The number of family heads involved in the conflict was at least 87,568. Based on the 2018 data, an accumulative 1,769 agrarian conflict occurred during the 2015–2018 period (Konsorsium Pembaruan Agraria 2018). In 2019, there were recorded at least 279 agrarian conflicts in various regions and provinces with a total accumulative area of conflict area of 734,239.3 hectares. The number of family heads involved in the conflict was at least 109.42, spread in 420 villages throughout Indonesia (Konsorsium Pembaruan Agraria 2019).

This increasing number of conflicts even after the constitutional judgments by the MK makes us question the fate of the constitutional justice in Indonesia, since it implies the fact that the governmental institutions or even the MA is not always following the constitutional judgments by the MK. In fact, MA judgments rarely follow the path of MK judgments, as many researchers have voiced about this problem (Bedner and Arizona 2019). In this situation, the judgment of MK is not sufficiently capable for making an immediate impact on the ground (Ardiansyah et al. 2020). More studies on the phenomenon should be awaited with the comparative exploration on the trend of the constitutional courts in the world.

At the same time, with the difficulties in applying customary rights in the Indonesian legal system, the formation of legislation has also been carried out. The effort to guarantee *adat* rights is currently being conducted through the drafting processes of the Bill on Hak Ulayat of Adat Community, Bill on Land and the Bill on Recognition of Adat Community. The following section of this paper will discuss how Indonesia is developing the perspective of the constitutional justice through the dynamic challenges, with a focus on the judicial as well as legislative development to secure *adat* land rights.

2 Constitutional justice on *adat* land rights

Indonesian MK is one of such typical products amid the third wave of democratization. Until the introduction of the Indonesian MK in 2003, neither sense of the rule of law namely the procedural sense of rechtstaat or the substantive sense of democracy was within the reach of the Indonesian people. Indonesia's constitutional doctrine that "Indonesia is rechtstaat but not machstaat" was only written in the Constitution elucidation and constitutional books but had never been realized. It is reasonable to assert that throughout Indonesian history, particularly at dictatorial rule periods, constitutional Law had been assigned a marginal role. The leading causes of the constitutionalism failures were the 1945 Constitution's weaknesses and the absence of an institution for safeguarding the Constitution.

All those experiences and the 1945 Constitution's weaknesses were the considerations that led to the MK establishment as one of the judicial power executors and the Supreme Court. The establishment of the MK was regarded as one of Indonesia's most significant constitutional reforms after President Suharto's fall in 1998 (Subekti 2008).

With the MK establishment, two branches of judicial power under the MA and the MK were established in Indonesia. Constitutional adjudication in Indonesia follows the path of civil law pattern by a centralized model like the Kelsen model of the constitutional court, outside of the regular judicial establishment (Rudy 2013). In this system, the MK stands as the independent branch of judicial power beside the MA with different jurisdictions pursuant to the Indonesian 1945 Constitution.

For many years, the Indonesian judiciary hardly played a legal evolution role, as it lacked the institutional devices to turn legal interpretation in single cases into a judicial doctrine (Bedner 2013). However, the establishment of Indonesia's MK in 2003, combined with the accessibility and acceptance of legal sources of international and translational origin, has changed this.

The birth of the MK is giving hope for agrarian justice. The MK has granted many petitions asking the recognition of *adat* rights. This Judgment covers many dimensions of *adat* rights, from the *noken* practice on voting to the Adat Forest. This section discusses the constitutional court judgment on the dimension of agrarian justice. Based on a search from the MK's official website in the range of 2005 to 2019, we found 25 Judgments related to land disputes. The highest number of Judgments was in 2015, with details in Table 10.1.

However, only a few MK Judgments related to *adat* land whose lawsuit was accepted by the MK from 2004 through 2019, namely, MK Judgment Number 45/PUU-IX/2011, MK Judgment Number 35/PUU-X/2012 and MK Judgment Number 95/PUU-XII/2014. Outside the ruling, several cases were tested at the court but rejected by it. The Judgment will be discussed next.

Table 10.1 Total number of land-related cases in the MK

Years	*Number*
2005	1
2006	0
2007	1
2008	0
2009	1
2010	0
2011	4
2012	2
2013	2
2014	3
2015	6
2016	2
2017	1
2018	1
2019	1

Source: Rudy (2020a).

2.1 MK Judgment

2.1.1 MK Judgment Number 45/PUU-IX/2011

The case adjudicated was the review of Law Number 41 of 1999 concerning Forestry. In this case, the applicant is the Kapuas Regency Government, Dr. Hambit Bintih, M.H., Regent of Katingan, Regent of East Barito, Regent of Sukamara and Dr. Akhmad Taufik, M.Pd. The plaintiffs challenged the constitutionality of Law on Forestry, stipulating that the Ministry of Forestry has the authority to stipulate rather than appoint land within the forest area territory. In this case, the MK found in favor of the plaintiffs and granted Judgment on this matter.

It held Article 1 paragraph (3) of Law 41/1999 on Forestry (as twice amended) to be inconsistent with Article 15 of the same Law and hence in contravention of Article 28D (1) of the Constitution, which guarantees legal protection and certainty. In the Judgment, the MK held that only if the full process of gazettement of an area is complete could this land be labeled as forest area. According to the Court, the contested Article 1 paragraph (3) must now read: *Forest areas are areas gazetted by the government to be maintained as permanent forest.*

In its Judgment, the MK stated that the phrase "appointed or determined" was contrary to the 1945 Constitution because it was not in sync with the provisions in a quo Law and caused legal uncertainty. The court in deciding this case is based on the rule of Law based on Article 1 of the Indonesian Constitution.

This Judgment is vital since many conflicts relating to the land within the forest area is caused by the appointment of land use given to many corporations by the Ministry of Forestry. This mere appointment by deliberation has pushed aside the *adat* community within the area and instigated the forest area's conflict.

2.1.2 MK Judgment Number 35/PUU-X/2012

The case adjudicated was the review of Law Number 41 of 1999 concerning Forestry. In this case, the petitioners are the Indigenous Peoples Alliance of the Archipelago (AMAN), the Kuntu Adat Community and the Cisitu Adat Community. In this case, the MK granted part of its petition for the review of Articles 1–6, Article 4 paragraph (3), and Article 5 paragraph (1) and paragraph (2) of Law Number 41 of 1999 concerning Forestry. The court determined that the word "state" should be erased from the said articles, and as a result, the Adat Forest would no longer be part of the state forest area. By this Judgment, the Ministry's stipulation shall not reach the Adat Forest area. However, MK also recognized the validity of the conditional recognition from Article 18B (2) of the Indonesian Constitution.

By this condition, the application of deciding Adat Forest is the question of proving whether the *adat* community is still existing. Therefore, without the Law that will be giving the mechanism of the *adat* land legal recognition within the forest area, this Judgment cannot be applied to protect *adat* land in the forest area.

2.1.3 MK Judgment Number 95/PUU-XII/2014

The case was the constitutional review of Law Number 41 the Year 1999 concerning Forestry. Petitioners in this case are Mr. Mawardi title Datuk Malin, Edi Kuswanto, Dato Perkasa, Murshid, Walhi, AMAN, Agrarian Reform Consortium (KPA) and several other parties.

This Judgment essentially gives *adat* people's rights as "people who have lived for generations in the forest," among others, to cut trees or harvest or collect forest products in the forest and herd cattle in the forest area as long as they are not for commercial purposes. This Judgment is trying to stop the criminalization of *adat* people who live in the forest and take a small portion of forest resources.

2.2 The Judgment of MA following MK Judgment

Our research on the Supreme Court (MA) Judgment supports our argument that the other institution, including the MA, does not always follow the MK Judgments. The data collected from the MA directory during years 2003–1019 encompassing Civil Law, State Administrative, and Judicial Review found a total number of 2,818 land-related cases in Judgments for Civil Law, 1,060 Judgments for State Administrative and 895 Judgments for Judicial Review.

Table 10.2 Total number of land-related cases in the MA

Supreme Court decisions about land disputes 2003–2019			
Year	*Total*		
	State Administrative	*Civil Law*	*Judicial Review*
2003	18	20	13
2004	32	11	11
2005	41	19	8
2006	47	71	28
2007	60	80	20
2008	102	75	27
2009	103	87	27
2010	75	99	45
2011	114	146	57
2012	51	207	55
2013	33	246	128
2014	125	312	100
2015	134	291	84
2016	46	359	63
2017	22	367	75
2018	38	262	85
2019	19	166	69
Total	**1,060**	**2,818**	**895**

After the classification of Judgments based on fields and years, the Judgments are analyzed. The Judgment analysis process is carried out in detail by reading one by one the Judgments that have been downloaded, to see the relationship between the MA Judgment and the MK Judgment. After analyzing each of the Judgments related to land in the private Law, administrative case, and Judicial Review, we found three Supreme Court Judges relating to the MK Judgment. They were primarily related to Adat Land in MA Judgment Number 47P/HUM/2011, Number 248K/TUN/2016 and Number 433K/PID.SUS-LH/2016. The following is the analysis of the MA Judgment.

2.2.1 *The Judgment of MA Number 248K/TUN/2016*

The Judgment of MA Number 248/K/TUN/2016 involves the Saumolewa Adat Peoples as petitioners against the Regent of South Buton and Satya Jaya

Avadi Corporation bringing a legal case against forest exploitation in Sampolawa District, South Buton District. Forest exploitation by Satya Jaya Avadi Corporation is based on South Buton Regency Government Decree Number 110 the Year 2015, dated June 20, 2015.

This Judgment justifies Makassar State Administration Judgment Number 01/B/2016/PT.TUN.MKS, rejecting the Representative of Adat Community representative who lives around the Saumolewa forest. The Judgment was rendered with the reasoning that there is no evidence of indigenous peoples' existence in the region. The rejection of the lawsuit was due to the absence of strong evidence that they were indigenous people whose interests had been impaired by the dispute.

MA Judgment 248/K/TUN/2016 is related to MK Judgment 35/PUU-X/2012, which has provided legal protection for indigenous and tribal peoples regarding customary forests. Juridically, indigenous peoples through a quo Judgment have obtained rights to their customary forests as long as the indigenous peoples concerned still exist and are recognized.

2.2.2 The Judgment of MA Number 433K/PID.SUS-LH/2016

The case decided in this Judgment was about the criminal conviction of Haji Mandau for illegal logging and illegal use of forest areas. Forests that have been illegally logged in this case are forests that have been determined in the Map of Forest Area and Water Conservation of Central Sulawesi No. 869/Menhut-II/2014 dated September 29, 2014. This piece of land is under the Defendant's control in Sampalowo Village, West Petasia District, North Morowali Regency, based on a quo map that is a protected forest area. The criminal charges imposed on the Defendant are the act of ordering, organizing or mobilizing illegal logging and illegal use of forest areas because they were not permitted by the authorities, both the Local Government and the Ministry of Forestry.

MA Judgment No. 433 K/PID.SUS-LH/2016 then provides guarantees to communities or individuals freedom from criminal threats because the land or buildings they have legally can already be claimed as holders of land rights in forest areas. The Defendant has a letter of land-ownership called SKPT owned by the Defendant originating from customary land whose existence is still recognized. This evidence follows the Letter of the Head of the Central Sulawesi Province Regional Office Number 1460/72/XII/2014 dated December 15, 2014, concerning the explanation of SKPT as proof of ownership of land rights.

This MA Judgment follows the Judgment of the Constitutional Court Number 35/PUU-X/2012 dated May 16, 2013, which in essence, in determining the status of the forest, the existence of customary rights must still be recognized.

2.2.3 The Judgment of MA Number 47P/HUM/2011

The case in this Judgment was a judicial review of the Decree of the Minister of Forestry of the Republic of Indonesia dated February 16, 2005, Number:

SK.44/Menhut-II/2005, concerning the Designation of Forest Areas in the North Sumatra Province Area. MA Judgment No. 47P/HUM/2011, in this case, contains consequences for right holders in forest areas.

This Judgment is in line with MK Judgment No. 45/PUU-IX/2011 of which constitutionally has corrected the Article 1 number 3 of the Forestry Law. In the application level, the Minister of Forestry enacted Decree No. 579/2014 as a substitute for Decree of the Minister of Forestry No. 44/2005 as a product of the MA Judgment No. 47P/HUM/2011, giving legal certainty to holders of land rights in forest areas.

3 Securing *adat* rights with legislation

From the previous examination of judgments, it is shown that the MK plays an important role and even legally has absolute legal superiority concerning institutions from other branches of power, such as the executive and legislative branches. This is because, in the development of practice, the MK acts as a negative legislator who cannot change the norms of the positive Law directly. The MK Law states that all Judgments of the MK are final and binding. All Judgments of the MK must be carried out by all Indonesian citizens, including the MA and all other state institutions.

The fundamental problem of the MK Judgment is the failure of the constitutional order to force law enforcers and legislators to comply. Although the words final and binding have been stated explicitly in the 1945 Constitution and the MK Law, they are often ignored by the State organs. Not all Judgments of the MK can affect the legislature and other state institutions or other nonjudicial actors. The execution of the MK Judgment emphasizes self-respect and legal awareness without coercion.

In addition, law enforcers are not aware of the MK Judgment. Many legal provisions that the MK has declared unconstitutional are not well documented in the lower level. The law enforcers, especially judges in the general court are not well informed with the Judgment. This fact has been known during the research on the consistencies of the Judgment between the MK and the MA. Based on the interview during the focus group discussion with judges in the general court, several judges said the Judgment of the MK was not disseminated in the region. In fact, this is happening because so many Judgments have been delivered by the MK making the gap of information on the substance of Judgment. Besides, judges usually follow the positive Law in the form of legislation not to be so well informed on the MK Judgment. They will prefer to learn the Law's application based on legislation in force rather than the Judgment given by the MK.

This is proven that still, so many criminalizations happen under the name of legal certainty. Based on Vote for Forest data, in 2018, there were 326 natural resource conflicts involving around 176 thousand indigenous peoples (Alaidrus 2020). Indonesian Legal Aid (YLBHI) noted that throughout 2019, 43 indigenous peoples were criminalized, mostly because of traditional farming and clearing land by burning. Most of them were caught in Article 108 in conjunction with 69 Law No. 41/1999 on Forestry and Law No. 18/2013 on Prevention of the Eradication of Forest Destruction (Nugraha 2019). As we know, MK Judgment Number 95/PUU-XII/2014 is protecting *adat* peoples from cutting trees or harvesting or collecting forest products in the forest and herding cattle in the forest area as long as they are not for commercial purposes.

The solution to this problem is not simple because it requires constitutional communication, primarily because the 1945 Constitution of the Republic of Indonesia does not provide a constitutional construction regarding the executorial institutional relationship for the MK Judgment.

The response to this difficulty is the making of legislation on *adat* rights. There are two development in this kind of legislation. The first is the *adat* court's recognition within the Law Concerning Special Autonomy, and the second is through legislation making on *adat* rights.

3.1 Recognition of adat *court in the law concerning special autonomy*

The recognition of customary courts in Indonesia's laws and regulations has been recognized in several laws, especially laws that regulate particular areas. There are four regions with special autonomy status in Indonesia, namely DKI Jakarta, Yogyakarta Special Region, Aceh Province and Papua Province. Of the four regions, only three regions accommodate *adat* rights in the content of their laws, namely Papua Province, Aceh Province and Yogyakarta Special Region.

3.1.1 Papua Special Autonomy Law

Papua Province is granted individual autonomy based on Law Number 21 of 2001 concerning Special Autonomy for Papua. The Law provides more space for the deliberation mechanism of indigenous peoples, including in determining their territory/land. The regulation regarding communal land in the Papua Special Autonomy Law provides space for customary law communities to carry out the management of their *ulayat* rights, which are operationally based on the provisions of laws and regulations.

By the Law, customary courts are recognized within specific customary communities. Papua's customary justice mechanism is given authority in cases of civil disputes and internal criminal cases of indigenous peoples. However, customary courts are not given the authority to impose imprisonment. Besides, Judgments are not final because they can be submitted to the First Level Court. Furthermore, customary courts are also defined as institutions for resolving *adat* disputes or cases in specific customary communities in Papua.

Regarding the types of sanctions in the Judgment of the customary court, it is described as consisting of customary fines and the traditional restoration ceremony's implementation. Judgments are made based on the customary law that applies to each indigenous community. *Adat* Judgments are binding if no objection is filed at the First Level Court.

3.1.2 Aceh Special Autonomy Law

The specialty of Aceh Province is granted through Law Number 11 of 2006 concerning the Aceh Government. Customary Law in Aceh, in this case, specifically refers to Islamic Law. The Law gives more room on the formulation of *adat* rights under the Qanun. This is also with regard to the existence of communal land and all those related to *adat* such as customary justice, communal land, customary institutions and so on.

The judiciary in Aceh, based on Article 128 of the Aceh Governance Law, is called the Syariyah Court. Unlike the customary courts in Papua, which are considered different from the state courts, the Syariyah Court, according to this Law, is considered an integral part of the national justice within the religious court.

Outside the Syariyah Court, based on the Aceh Qanun Number 9 of 2008 concerning the Development of Customary and Customary Life, the Gampong and Mukim Adat Courts are also recognized. The Gampong Customary Court, as the name implies, has a locus in each Gampong and Mukim (village). This court, in particular, carries out efforts to resolve disputes that occur at the village level.

Minor disputes resolved by the Gampong and Mukim Courts include domestic disputes, family disputes, disputes between residents, disputes over property rights, theft in the family, etc. The Gampong and Mukim Adat Courts have received legitimacy as agreed in the Joint Decree of the Governor of Aceh, the Head of the Aceh Regional Police and the Chairperson of the Aceh Adat Council concerning the Implementation of the Gampong Traditional Court and Mukim or Other Names in Aceh.

This Adat Court Judgment is final and binding so that it cannot be filed again by the general courts or other general courts. Regarding the form of sanction, the Adat Court Judgment is prohibited from imposing bodily sanctions such as imprisonment, washing with dirty water, cutting hair and other things that are contrary to Islamic values.

3.1.3 Yogyakarta special region law

Yogyakarta is one of the regions that have individual autonomy. In exercising land authority, the Sultanate and the Kadipaten in Yogyakarta are given a legal entity's status. Through this status, the Sultanate and the Kadipaten have rights to their own lands. The land coverage of the Sultanate and the Kadipaten itself is divided into two, namely, the Keprabon land and non-Keprabon land found in all districts/cities in the Yogyakarta region. The authority of the Sultanate and the Kadipaten in managing and utilizing their land oriented to the most significant possible development of culture, social interests and community welfare.

In the province of Yogyakarta, the prevailing judicial mechanism is the general court conducted by the judiciary under the MA. There is no customary justice mechanism in resolving land disputes.

3.2 *Securing* adat *rights through legislation making*

Following the call of *adat* revivalism, legislation makers are trying to draft several Laws related to *adat* rights recognition, including *adat* land rights. There are the Draft Law on Customary Land Rights or Hak Ulayat, the Draft Law on Land and the Draft Law on Adat Community.

3.2.1 Draft Law on Customary Land Rights

The Draft Law on Customary Land Rights was proposed by the Regional Representative Council of the Republic of Indonesia (DPD RI) on September 13, 2017. The proposal was initially included as part of the 2014–2019 national legislation program long list. Led by the famous scholar on land law Professor Maria Soemardjono, the Bill was drafted during 2018 and now waits for the next step on tripartite discussion among the Government, house of a representative and a regional representative assembly. The scope of *adat* land rights arrangements includes the following:

(1) recognition and confirmation;
(2) granting land rights above customary rights;
(3) transfer and imposition;
(4) compensation; and
(5) abolition of customary rights.

The provision in some ways is similar to the formulation of *ulayat* rights under the Draft Law on Land next.

3.2.2 Draft Law on Land

The Bill on Land proposal began on February 2, 2015, where this Bill was listed as one of the long lists of the 2014–2019 national legislation program. However, the end of Parliament periodization in 2019 cannot finish the draft.

The Government then asked the Indonesian Parliament to reenter the Draft Law on Land into the long list of the 2019–2024 national legislation program. This was then responded to by the inclusion of the Bill on Land as one of the bills that became the 2020 priority national legislation program, which means that the Draft Law on Land is carried over into the 2019–2024 long list national legislation program (Rudy 2020b).

Several provisions related to land dispute resolution were found in the draft, namely, the provisions regarding the settlement of land disputes and establishing a land court. In the chapter on dispute resolution, the provision of the Bill determines that Land dispute settlement prioritizes deliberation between parties to reach an agreement through mediation between the parties. The Minister will determine the Land mediation procedure in this formulation. Furthermore, dispute resolution through mediation shall be proven by a peace deed before the authorized official. The peace deed shall be registered at the local court to obtain a peace Judgment to gain executorial power.

However, if the deliberation to reach an agreement cannot be reached, the parties can resolve the dispute through the Land Court. The Land Court determines land cases, which include civil lawsuits, state administration, and land crimes. Then, the Land Court will be established by the Supreme Court no later than five years from the Land Bill's enactment.

The Bill also provides the recognition of *hak ulayat. Hak ulayat* is defined as land located in the territory of customary law community, which according to the fact, still exists. The bill orders the Government to make measurements and mapping and recording of *ulayat* land. This Bill also contains a declaration of rights to the holder of Land Rights over the field of *hak ulayat* that was owned before the Bill was enacted.

3.2.3 Draft Law on Adat Community

The Draft Law on Adat Community is a formerly formulated Bill in 2014 under the title Bill on the Recognition and Protection of the Rights of Indigenous Peoples (PPHMHA). However, it was not resolved until the end of the DPR RI position for the 2009–2014 period.

In 2017, the Draft Law on Adat Community was included in the Legislation Planning 2014–2019 and became the draft bill initiated by the DPR RI on February 14, 2018 (Rudy 2017). A working meeting between the Legislation Body and the Government was held. However, until the end of the term of office of members of the DPR RI for the 2014–2019 period, the Government did not submit an Inventory of Problems List (DIM) to the DPR, which resulted in the discontinuance of the discussion on the Draft Law on Adat Law Community.

Currently, the Adat Law Community Bill is included in the list of the 2020 Priority number 31. The Draft Law on Adat Law Community consists of 16 Chapters containing 57 Articles (www.dpr.go.id). It is in the process of tripartite harmonization among the Government, House of Representative (DPR) and Regional Representative Assembly (DPD).

The draft has the provision on the Adat Territory and Dispute Settlement. In this provision, the Adat Community, determined as a legal entity, is entitled to the Customary Territories they own, occupy, and managed for generations. Customary territories are communal and cannot be transferred to other parties. *Adat* communities have the right to manage and utilize natural resources in the Customary Territory according to local wisdom.

Suppose in a Customary Territory, there are natural resources that have an essential role in fulfilling the people's livelihoods. In that case, the State can manage it with the consent of the Adat Peoples. For management by the State, Adat Peoples are entitled to compensation. Apart from compensation, Adat Peoples are entitled to receive the main benefits in implementing corporate social responsibility.

Adat Institutions will be given the authority to resolve the settlement of problems related to Adat Peoples. The settlement of disputes that occur due to violations of Adat Law in Adat Territories is resolved through customary courts organized by Adat Institutions. Every person who is not a member of an Adat Community who violates Adat Law in a particular Adat Territory is obliged to comply with the Adat Institution's decision.

4 Challenges in legislation formulation

From the previous discussion, we found that recognition of *adat* rights has been guaranteed in the special autonomy legislation. However, the special autonomy law is given only for the particular region in Indonesia. Therefore, the impact of the recognition is not significant compared to the number of regions in Indonesia.

On the other side, the Parliament and Government are trying to draft several laws to solve the problem of the recognition of *adat* rights and land application problems. The formulation of these laws is not smooth and took a very long time to be stipulated. The main problem is that several norms are tough to be formulated. This norm is very related to the definition and classification applied to all the Adat Community in Indonesia. The vast diversity of the *adat* system in Indonesia makes it difficult to find the similarity line for forming the norm in the legislation.

5 Conclusion

Constitutionalism in Indonesia took ground after a series of 1945 Constitution amendments from 1999 to 2002. The establishment of the Constitutional Court (MK) and the guarantee of local autonomy have made the revival of the *adat* rights. The MK itself has been consistent for the recognition of *adat* rights with the famous Judgment on Adat Forest Land that is constitutionally separated from the State Forest. While many pundits have hailed the Judgment of the MK, its Judgment has a weakness. The weakness lies in the application of the Judgment in the ground. Many *adat* rights are still waiting for the positive Law for its application.

At the same time, with the difficulties in applying customary rights in the Indonesian legal system, the formation of legislation has also been carried out. Following the MK Judgment, Indonesia, through the Government and Parliament, is trying to draft several laws to uphold the guarantee of *adat* rights. There are two developments in this legislation making. The first one is using the special autonomy law in Aceh, Papua and Yogyakarta. The second one is drafting the Law on Customary Land Rights or *hak ulayat*, Law on Land, and Law on Adat Community.

With the difficulty in applying the MK Judgment on the ground and the slow development of legislation making on *adat*-related Law, especially on *adat* rights on land, it seems we will have to wait more years to see the widespread recognition on *adat* rights, especially *adat* land.

References

Alaidrus, Fadiyah (2020) "Discussion of the Stagnant Indigenous Peoples Bill, Ignored Citizens' Rights" *Tirto.id* (Jakarta, 25 January 2019) <https://tirto.id/de5s> accessed 14 August 2020.

Ardiansyah, Ardiansyah, Lalu, Sabardi, and Widodo, Dwi Putro (2020) "National Law Relations with Customary Law in the Establishing of Regulation of the Recognition of Indigenous Peoples Rights to the Land of Ulayat" *International Journal of Multicultural and Multireligious Understanding*, 7:5. http://doi.org/10.18415/ijmmu.v7i5.1695.

Bedner, Adriaan (2013) "Indonesian Legal Scholarship and Jurisprudence as an Obstacle for Transplanting Legal Institutions" *Hague Journal on the Rule of Law*, 5:2, 253–273.

Bedner, Adriaan and Yance Arizona (2019) "Adat in Indonesian Land Law: A Promise for the Future or a Dead End?" *The Asia Pacific Journal of Anthropology*, 20:5, 416–434. http://doi.org/10.1080/14442213.2019.1670246.

Cappelletti, Mauro (1970) "Judicial Review in Comparative Perspective" *California Law Review* 58:5, October 1970, 1017–1053.

Carothers, Thomas (1998) "Rule of Law Revival" *Foreign Affairs* 77:2 March/April 1998.

Djohansjah, J. (2008) *Reformasi Mahkamah Agung Menuju Independensi Kekuasaan Kehakiman* [*Supreme Court Reform for Judicial Independency*], Keisaint Blanc.

Ginsburg, Tom (2003) *Judicial Review in New Democracies*, Cambridge University Press.

Konsorsium Pembaruan Agraria (2017) *Catatan Akhir Tahun 2017: Reforma Agraria di Bawah Bayangan Investasi Gaung Besar di Pinggiran Jalan* [*End of Year 2017 Note: Agrarian Reform Under the Shadow of Big Echoes of Roadside Investment*], Konsorsium Pembaruan Agraria.

Konsorsium Pembaruan Agraria (2018) *Masa Depan Reforma Agraria Melampaui Tahun Politik: Catatan Akhir Tahun 2018* [*The Future of Agrarian Reform Beyond Political Years: End of Year Notes 2018*], Konsorsium Pembaruan Agraria.

Konsorsium Pembaruan Agraria (2019) *Dari Aceh sampai Papua: Urgensi Penyelesaian Konflik Struktural dan Jalan Pembaruan Agraria ke Depan: Catatan Akhir Tahun 2019* [*From Aceh to Papua: The Urgency of Structural Conflict Resolution and the Path for Agrarian Reform Ahead: End of Year Notes 2019*], Konsorsium Pembaruan Agraria.

Lindsey, Tim (1998) "Square Pegs & Round Holes: Fitting Modern Title into Traditional Societies in Indonesia" *Pacific Rim Law and Policy Journal* 7: 699–719.

Nugraha, Indra (2019) "Indigenous Peoples Bill Enters Prolegnas 2020, Following Input from the Parties" *Mongabay* (Jakarta, 13 December 2019). <www.mongabay.co.id/2019/12/13/ruu-masyarakat-adat-masuk-prolegnas-2020-berikut-masukan-para-pihak/> accessed 14 August 2020.

Pompe, Sebastian (2005) *The Indonesian Supreme Court: A Study of Institutional Collapse*, Cornell University Press.

Robinson, K. (2014) "Citizenship, Identity, and the Difference in Indonesia's" *Review of Indonesian and Malaysian Affairs* 48:1, 5–34.

Rudy, R. (2013) *Konstitusionalisme Indonesia Buku I Dasar dan Teori* [*Indonesian Constitutionalism Book I Basics and Theory*], Indepth Publishing.

Rudy, R. (2017) "Indigenous People's Bill" (*DPR*, 6 November 2017) <www.dpr.go.id/dokakd/dokumen/RJ2-20171106-094054-7086.pdf> accessed 14 August 2020.

Rudy, R. (2020a) "Analysis of MK's Judgment on Adat and Land Bill" (*MK*, 18 June 2020) < https://mkri.id/index.php?page=web.Putusan&id=1&kat=1&menu=5&jenis=PUU&jnsperkara=1> accessed 18 June 2020

Rudy, R. (2020b) "Legislation Plan Longlist" (*DPR*, 1 January 2020) <www.dpr.go.id/uu/prolegnas-long-list> accessed 14 August 2020.

Subekti, Valina Singka (2008) *Menyusun Konstitusi Transisi* [*Drafting Transition Constitution*], Rajawali Press.

Tate, Neal C. (1995) "Why the Expansion of Judicial Power?" in C. Neal Tate and Torbjorn Vallinder eds., *The Global Expansion of Judicial Power*, New York University Press.

11 History of Japanese common rights

Iriai-ken – social, judicial and academic overview

Sachihiko Muroi

1 Introduction

1.1 Purpose and methodology of this article

Although land disputes are observed all over the world, there is a common issue found in the background of all of them: how to harmonize modern property rights that have been transplanted from modern Western legal systems with the rights that have historically existed in the local legal system and society from the premodern era. Japan experienced this issue as well; numerous land disputes occurred related *Iriai-ken* (common rights) in the process of establishment of Japan's Civil Code in the early *Meiji* era (late 19th century), and some still exist after more than 100 years.[1] Similar issues are observed in recipient countries of Japanese legal system development assistance. Looking back at history, Western countries also experienced this issue. The second enclosure movement in 18th-century United Kingdom is one typical example. In other words, this issue inevitably occurs where modern property law is introduced.

This Article aims to examine the essence of the problems that have recurred with the expansion of modern property law, through an introduction to the social, legal and academic history of Japan's *Iriai-ken.*

1.2 Theory of property rights in the context of "law and development"

Scholars like Harold Demsetz and John Henry Merryman provided the theoretical backbone of the first "law and development" movement in the 1960s. Demsetz and Merryman's theory of property rights focused on the supremacy of property rights as seen in continental law. More than ten years before Demsetz and Merryman, Takeyoshi Kawashima of Tokyo University published the book *The Theory of Property Rights* in 1949. Kawashima's understanding was that (1) modern property rights are a reflection of social relationships; (2) capitalism is composed of private property rights (goods that are subject to an entity's intention), contracts (procedures for transactions) and personalities (the entities that decide the intention); and (3) capitalism stands above the conflict and contradiction between private property rights and contracts. Kawashima focused on the *Iriai-ken* issue

DOI: 10.4324/9781003170600-14

in his theory called the "Extinction of *Iriai-ken*," where communal customary rights like *Iriai-ken* are inevitably merged into the legal system of modern property rights and become extinct.

But such "extinction" did not actually occur in Japanese society as a "historical necessity" as Kawashima and the majority of Japanese socio-legal scholars predicted. In contrast to the "extinction" theories, *Iriai-ken* is focused on interdisciplinary research such as commons theories that address new agenda, sustainable use of natural resources, protection of local environment, local town planning and so on.

Legal system development assistance by multiple donors has been very active in the last three decades under the second "law and development" movement. The introduction and promotion of modern property laws is one of the pillars of such assistance, with new institutional economists such as Rafael la Porta and Andrei Shleifer providing the theoretical justification. But the continued existence of *Iriai-ken* through more than 100 years of development in Japan hints there is room for reconsideration of the practical implementation of legal system development assistance led by the new institutional economic theories of "law and development" and the modernization theories of Kawashima.

In this article, I would like to identify this room for reconsideration of law and development through an introduction to the social, legal and academic theoretical history of Japan's *Iriai-ken*.

2 Social and legal history of Japan's *Iriai-ken*

This chapter will take a historical look at the social and legal status of *Iriai-ken*. There were no specific statutory provisions or legal definition of *Iriai-ken* for more than 100 years after the introduction of the modern legal system in Japan. The purpose of this chapter is to identify and consider the present and future situation and social role of *Iriai-ken* by reviewing its history.

2.1 *Legal characteristics of* Iriai-ken

Iriai-ken are the rights for local community members to use local forests and fields based on local customs that have been maintained since the premodern era.[2]

Iriai-ken are defined in Articles 263 and 294 of Japan's Civil Code. The word *Iriai-ken* is a legal term and the name used for the lands that *Iriai-ken* are attached to differs by community. There is a difference between the legal term *Iriai-ken* and what people actually call "*Iriai*" in Japan's villages.

The definition and legal characteristics of *Iriai-ken* have accrued through case law and academic theories. The present common understanding of *Iriai-ken* is as follows.

2.1.1 Iriai-ken *as private rights*

Opinions have long been divided on the question of whether *Iriai-ken* are private rights or public rights. This is because of an inconsistency in which *Iriai-ken* have the characteristics of private rights both in the definition in Japan's Civil

Code and in practice, but in administrative statutes they can be regulated as local government assets. The private rights theory is based on Articles 263 and 294 of the Civil Code. The public rights theory is based on Article 209 of Local Autonomy Act, which provides for "old common use rights." On the one hand, the use and management of *Iriai-ken* land follows the customs and rules of local communities according to the private rights theory. On the contrary, the decisions of local government assemblies take priority over such local customs and rules according to the public rights theory. Thus, it means a local assembly can change or even abolish *Iriai-ken* by a majority vote according to the public rights theory (Article 238–6 (2) of the Local Autonomy Act).[3] Japan's administrative organs have followed the public rights theory for long time. But the controversy was ended by the Iriai Forest Modernization Act in 1966, which seems to follow the private rights theory.

Other notable characteristics of *Iriai-ken* that have been defined by court precedents are:

- *Iriai-ken* can be asserted against third parties without registration.[4]
- *Iriai-ken* accrue on land that is owned by the government (local or central).[5]

2.1.2 Principle of collective ownership

Iriai-ken are under "collective ownership" by local community members, which is not defined in the Civil Code.

Commonly, it is said the constituent entity of *Iriai-ken* is the "*Mura.*" The word *Mura* means "village" in Japanese. But, in this context, this "*Mura*" does not mean village as an administrative municipality but as a local community. Japanese socio-legal scholars largely use the term "Iriai Group" (*Iriai-Shuudan*) for such community groups that are the constituent entities of *Iriai-ken*, and this Article will follow this practice. An Iriai Group is understood as the "total of the local people" and is composed of equal membership by household units. Court precedents have also found that the unit of *Iriai-ken* members are not individuals but households.[6]

What is the difference between collective ownership and normal co-ownership that is provided by the Civil Code? In the case of normal co-ownership, each co-owner can dispose of his or her share in accordance with his or her intention, by way of sale, pledge or any other dealing. In the case of collective ownership, individual right holders do not have specific shares. Therefore, an individual holder of *Iriai-ken* cannot sell or pledge as collateral his or her *Iriai-ken.* No case law or academic theory recognizes shares of or the free disposition of *Iriai-ken.*

Iriai-ken cannot be inherited.[7]

Local community rules on the use and management of land subject to *Iriai-ken* are decided by unanimous vote. This point is different to normal co-ownership, where a majority vote is sufficient in the case of normal co-ownership.

2.1.3 Actual residence as a condition of Iriai-ken

Access to and termination of *Iriai-ken* is determined by actual residence, not by contract or any other legal action. The unit of a *Iriai-ken* rights holder is a household, not an individual, as described earlier.

In recent years, this principle has sometimes been relaxed because of depopulation and aging in rural areas.

2.2 Modernization policies in the early Meiji era and Iriai-ken

In the following part of this chapter, I will explain how *Iriai-ken* were treated after the reception of modern Western laws in Meiji-era Japan. In this section, I will focus on the following two points.

(1) Issue of land certificates, land tax reform and the public/private ownership separation policy, which seem to have been based on a Torrens-style system.
(2) How *Iriai-ken* were treated and survived through the Codification Controversy and the establishment of the Civil Code and land titling system.

2.2.1 Issue of land certificates

Land policies in the early Meiji era had a strong influence on *Iriai-ken.*

In 1868, land-ownership by commoners was permitted following the Meiji Restoration. In 1869, taxation by feudal lords was abolished. In 1872, restrictions on land transactions were abolished. These changes were the preliminary phase of land titling and taxation.

The first step toward land titling was the issue of land certificates, which started in 1871. The Japanese government issued a "Land Certificate" to people who claimed land-ownership or potential owners of the land. Documentary evidence was required for ownership claims; a contract deed or inheritance document are typical examples.[8] A land certificate indicated the landowner and the calculated land value. Thus, the landowner owed a tax obligation based on the land value. This was the aim of issuing such land certificates. Thus, the ownership and use of the land was uniform under the authority of the state.[9]

During this procedure, many lands, especially in the case of rural forests and fields, were found to be owned not by an individual but by a "*mura*" (village). The Japanese government categorized such land as "common land" (*ko-yu*) and issued a land certificate. The Japanese government was rushing the issue of land certificates, or to be precise, was rushing the imposition of taxation. Land titling by land certificates was finished and a *Land Title Book* was collated by 1873.[10]

2.2.2 Land tax reform and public/private ownership separation policy

The Land Tax Reform Act was promulgated in 1873. Taxation started based on the ownership and land value recorded in the *Land Title Book.* At this point, imposing land tax on "common land" like *Iriai* land faced difficulty because it was difficult to confirm who owed the tax obligation for such land. In 1874, the government abolished the "common land" category and the ownership of lands considered "common land" had to be reexamined; this time the only consideration was whether the land was public (i.e., government-owned) or private. This procedure was called the "Public/Private Ownership Separation Policy" (*Kan-Min Yu Kubun Seisaku*). Under this procedure too, local people bore the burden of proof and documentary evidence was required for confirmation of land title.[11] However, documented transactions concerning forests and fields were very rare at that time. Further, it was impossible to confirm inheritance of such rights because the lands were considered "common land" and under local community control. The government issued the 143rd Order on Land Title Examination in the same year. According to this order, "common lands" without documentary evidence of private ownership were to be merged into public land. Many lands merged into government-owned land under this procedure but continued to be used and managed by local communities as the base of their livelihoods. Many movements by farmers and residents who sought to claim back *Iriai* land that had been merged into public land arose, sometimes leading to riots. Yet despite such movements, the merged land remained government-owned, causing many land disputes over a long period of time. It is a problem that is similar to the problems that are presently occurring in many Asian countries.

In 1889, the Municipal System Act (presently the Local Autonomy Act) came into effect. Former "*mura*" became municipalities. Certain *Iriai* land called "*mura-mochi*" (village-held) merged into the municipality's property. Before the Meiji era, a "*mura*" was not only a municipal unit but also the unit of a local community, membership of which was indivisibly tied to local residence. After the introduction of the Municipal System Act, "mura" became simply a modern municipality that was unrelated to the local residents.

It is notable that some *Iriai* groups actively protected *Iriai-ken* using legal procedures. In one example, a local community leader registered the land title over *Iriai* land on behalf of the local community. Such action was not rare at that time.

2.3 *Investigation of* Iriai *customs and Japan's Civil Code*

2.3.1 *Investigation of* Iriai *customs*

There was great controversy upon the introduction of the first Civil Code in Japan; it came to be known as the "*Houten Ronsou*" (Codification Controversy) and the treatment of *Iriai-ken* was one major topic of the controversy. In 1890, the Civil Code drafted by Gustave Boissonade was once promulgated but it was never enforced. In 1893, a nationwide investigation of local *Iriai* customs was conducted, led by the famous legal scholar Kenjiro Ume. Today, we cannot find any evidence that a detailed analysis was conducted by the government, even though a large number of documents related to *Iriai* customs from all over Japan were collected during the investigation.[12]

2.3.2 Iriai-ken *within Japan's modern private law*

Japan's Civil Code came into force in 1899. It has two provisions on *Iriai-ken*, Articles 263 and 294. However, an Iriai Group cannot be registered as the owner of *Iriai-ken*. The Real Property Registration Act (which also came into force in 1899) has provisions on "registerable rights" in Article 3 but does not include *Iriai-ken*. Thus, *Iriai-ken* do not have a strong method of being published even though it is provided as a property right in the Civil Code.

2.4 Court judgments concerning **Iriai-ken** *over government-owned land*

The Japanese government maintained a policy of abolishing *Iriai-ken* throughout the prewar era, especially *Iriai-ken* over government-owned land. The judiciary followed this policy as well. It can be said a Japanese Supreme Court judgment in 1915 approved the land-grabbing policy.

Whether *Iriai-ken* existed over government-owned land was in dispute in this case. The local people of Higashiuchi village (now within Ueda city) of Nagano Prefecture filed a case to the court claiming confirmation of their *Iriai-ken* over government-owned land. Although the first-instance Nagano District Court recognized the *Iriai-ken*, the second-instance Tokyo High Court reversed the decision and denied the claim.[13] The Supreme Court affirmed the High Court's decision; the summary of the Court's judgment is as follows.

(1) All lands that fulfill the conditions to be privately owned have been registered as privately owned during the procedures under the Public/Private Ownership Separation Policy. The fact the land in question had been merged into government-owned land indicates a lack of fulfilling the conditions.
(2) During the procedure of land tax reform, land grants or leases were recognized, taking into consideration the daily life of local people. All people should have known this; thus, all private rights over government-owned land are assumed to have been extinguished.

This judgment is heavily criticized for its unfairness and bias toward the government, particularly by socio-legal scholars. Despite such criticism, the Japanese government and courts continued to deny *Iriai-ken* over government-owned land until 1973.[14]

2.5 **Iriai-ken** *in the postwar era and 50 years of the* **Iriai** *Forest Modernization Act*

2.5.1 Iriai-ken *and mountain and forest management after World War II*

The situation surrounding *Iriai-ken* has changed significantly after World War II. First, agricultural land reform was implemented in 1947 under U.S. military occupation. Tenant farmers and small farmers became landowning farmers and were released from the burden of paying rent. Thus, their dependence on crops harvested from *Iriai* land decreased. The role of *Iriai-ken* in agriculture was further reduced by innovation in farming methods and the development of chemical fertilizers as well.

Another notable point concerning postwar *Iriai-ken* is forestry. At the end of World War II, there were many bare mountains and forests in Japan's rural areas. One reason for this was excessive lumbering by local farmers, especially tenant farmers and small farmers.[15] Tax and other financial obligations were a burden too heavy for them because monetary economics was not widespread in rural areas in the prewar era. Such tenant farmers and small farmers often cut trees and sold the timber to pay monetary obligations. Another reason was World War II. Many trees were cut for military goods. After World War II too, there was a huge demand for timber for rebuilding the war-damaged country. Therefore, excessive lumbering of forests continued after World War II.

In 1947, a big pacific typhoon called Typhoon Kathleen struck Japan and caused heavy flooding and landslide damage. The importance of forest management was widely reacknowledged in Japan due to this occurrence. The function of *Iriai-ken* was revised to incorporate forest management including disaster management, and its value as a pure property right was recognized through such circumstances.

*2.5.2 Forest product cooperatives (*Seisan Shinrin Kumiai*)*

The Forest Act was amended in 1951 as a reaction to such societal demands for forest management. A Forest Product Cooperatives (*Seisan Shinrin Kumiai*, hereafter referred to as "Seishin") system was established by this amendment. Although creating a "trinity of ownership, management and labor" was the purpose of its establishment, Yano (2018) points out it was actually not the establishment of a new institution but the conversion of Iriai Groups into such cooperatives that was intended.

2.5.3 Iriai *Forest Modernization Act*

The *Iriai* Forest Modernization Act was established in 1966 and *Iriai* forest development projects were started. The "advanced use of *Iriai* forests" and the "promotion of utilization of Iriai forests for agriculture and forestry" were stated as the purpose of this law (Article 2). The "modernization of *Iriai* forests" meant the abolishment of *Iriai-ken* and conversion to private ownership or other rights provided by modern laws. In other words, the *Iriai* Forest Modernization Act was legislation that substantiated the "extinction of *Iriai-ken*" theory, which was discussed by Takeyoshi Kawashima and many Japanese socio-legal scholars.

Yano (2018) analyzes the text of the *Iriai* Forest Modernization Act as follows.

(1) Rejection of the public right theory: the *Iriai* Forest Modernization Act has provisions on "development projects in old common use forest" (Chapter 3, Articles 19 to 24). Article 20 requires the mayor of a municipality to conduct a hearing and confirmation process with local residents. This contradicts Articles 209 and 238 of the Local Autonomy Act, which the Japanese government has long argued provides the grounds for the theory of *Iriai-ken* as a public right. Through this, the *Iriai* Forest Modernization Act fixed *Iriai-ken* as a private right.
(2) Seishin as the replacement for extinguished *Iriai-ken*: Iriai Groups converted to Seishin in the majority cases during the process of *Iriai* forest development projects. This indicates that the *Iriai* Forest Modernization Act is part of the legal reform in reaction to the demands for forest management after World War II, in the same way as the Forest Act in 1951.

2.5.4 Iriai *forest development project*

The area subject to *Iriai* forest development projects reached its peak in 1974 and has been in decline since.[16] Japanese forestry is static at present, due to factors including the liberalization of the import of timber, the end of the era of high economic growth and the decline in demand for housing, as well as the change in construction methods from timber structures to reinforced concrete. Depopulation and aging in rural areas are also behind this change. In other words, it can be said that the government policy aimed toward the dissolution of Iriai Groups led to the decline of the Japanese forestry industry.

*2.5.5 Present situation of forest product cooperatives (*Seishin*)*

The Local Autonomy Act was amended in 1991. A system of "Approved Local Groups" (*Ninka Chien Dantai*) was newly established by this amendment; local groups can obtain juridical personality if approved by the mayor of the municipality (Article 206–2). Yano (2018) identifies that underperforming Seishin were dissolved and converted to Approved Local Groups in many cases.[17]

The Forestry Basic Act (established in 1964) was amended and renamed as the Forest and Forestry Basic Act in 2001. The word "*Iriai*" was erased from the text of this law by this amendment. It reflects government policy to remove *Iriai-ken* from the forestry industry.

The Forest Act was amended in 2016. According to Yano (2018), it was a radical review of the Seishin institution itself. Originally, Seishin were subject to strict regulations under the principle of cooperative unions, such as the duty to have full-time commitment to the work and regulations on the use of external people for labor. The 2016 amendment was the deregulation of these rules, with the intention of persuading the remaining Iriai Groups to convert to Seishin as well. The Japanese Forest Agency published the report "Present Situation of Forest Cooperatives" in March 2016. It recommended that Seishin should be classified into the following three groups and persuaded to undergo structural transformation.

Type 1: Seishin, which operate large projects, have a good performance history and active administration. These groups should be encouraged to convert to companies and aim to be globally competitive forestry businesses.
Type 2: Maintain present Seishin Statute.
Type 3: Underperforming Seishin should be encouraged to convert to Approved Local Group status and be relieved from the duty to conduct projects, tax obligations and so on.

Such transformation reflects a policy that abandons underperforming Seishin. In practice, the majority of Seishin will be classified into Type 3. In such case, how, what or who would maintain local mountains and forests that had been under projects? Yano (2018) expresses concern about the possibility of the administration of certain forests and mountains being abandoned.

The management of forests and mountains has a direct and strong influence on the local natural environment and local disaster management. Sustainable development of the present issues cannot be fulfilled under policies that only focus on "performance" or "global competitiveness."

3 Survey of research on *Iriai-ken*

This chapter will survey *Iriai-ken* research from the past to present with the purpose of reviewing how Japanese academics treat *Iriai-ken.*

3.1 Izutaro Suehiro: first research on Iriai-ken

Izutaro Suehiro is widely acknowledged as the first socio-legal scholar in Japanese history. His 1924 book *Legal Issues in Farming Villages* (*Nouson Houritsu Mondai*) covers almost all of the points of discussion on *Iriai-ken* raised in the following years. Suehiro did not give an answer on the following point: Should *Iriai-ken* be merged into capitalism and the market economy as a pure property right? Or do *Iriai-ken* exist separately from the market economy? The former discussion developed into the "extinction of *Iriai-ken*" theory by Takeyoshi Kawashima and many socio-legal scholars. It became the majority view in the discussion of Japanese socio-legal scholars in the postwar era. The *Iriai* Forest Modernization Act in 1966 seemed to be based on this theory. The latter was succeeded by Michitaka Kainou, and it formed the core part of Kainou's theory that connects practice and research.

3.2 "Extinction of Iriai-ken*" theory*

Iriai-ken is a remnant of the premodern era under feudalism. It should be merged into the frame of property rights under the modern legal system and inevitably become extinct. This is the basic understanding of the "extinction of *Iriai-ken*" theory. Takeyoshi Kawashima is the most notable scholar of this, and the majority of Japanese socio-legal scholars who researched *Iriai-ken* followed this theory.

Takeyoshi Kawashima, Toshitaka Ushiomi and Yozo Watanabe examined many cases from all over Japan between 1959 and 1968. They published a three-volume book titled *Extinction of Iriai-ken* (Kawashima, Ushiomi and Watanabe 1959–1968). In this book, Kawashima, Ushiomi and Watanabe criticized autocratic land-grabbing by the Japanese government. At the same time, Kawashima, Ushiomi and Watanabe discussed "Extinction of Iriai-ken" through merging into the modern legal system and market economy as a "historical necessity," especially in the postwar era because of the rapid economic growth in Japan.[18]

Kawashima, Ushiomi and Watanabe suggested the following major methods of extinction of *Iriai-ken*:

(1) Individualization of use.
(2) Incompatibility between the property rights system and *Iriai-ken*.
(3) Dissolution of *Iriai* Groups.

3.2.1 Individualization of use

Kawashima, Ushiomi and Watanabe (1959–1968) suggested the dissolution of the principle of collective ownership and the individualization of use of *Iriai* land. They pointed to three typical changes to *Iriai* land through their observations.

*Division of use

Division of *Iriai* land was observed, where *Iriai* land was divided and individual users use each area subject to the internal rules of the *Iriai* Group. In such cases, the substantial use itself is determined by the individual users. Thus, the internal rule and regulation by the *Iriai* Group was slowly weakened. This is one typical step in the "extinction of *Iriai-ken*."

*Weakening of direct control

Certain factors concerning *Iriai* land is under the direct control of the *Iriai* Group in many cases. The management and allocation of forestry and disaster management to prevent floods and landslides are the typical examples. In such cases, the *Iriai* Group directly makes decisions on land use. The provision of labor may be required from individual holders of *Iriai-ken*. Kawashima, Ushiomi and Watanabe (1959–1968) identified that monetary payments have replaced such rules in many cases; for example, payment for the individual use of an area under the direct control of an *Iriai* Group.

*Use under contract

Kawashima, Ushiomi and Watanabe (1959–1968) identified that contractual land use is observed in many cases. There is no limitation on who can use the land; even nonmembers of an *Iriai* Group can be the lessee. The intention of the *Iriai* Group is to obtain lease income. The contractual rights take priority to control by the *Iriai* Group. Thus, *Iriai-ken* become extinct.

3.2.2 Incompatibility between the property rights system and Iriai-ken

Kawashima, Ushiomi and Watanabe (1959–1968) identified incompatibility between the property rights system and *Iriai-ken*. Weakness due to the lack of public record is one example; *Iriai-ken* cannot be registered. *Iriai-ken* holders are disadvantaged in the case of opposing modern property rights. Denial of *Iriai-ken* over government-owned land, merging into public rights (old common use rights), enclosure by registered landowners, land use that conflicts with the management by *Iriai* Groups and offering security or usufruct with occupancy are notable examples. Claiming rights of exclusion based upon *Iriai-ken* is very hard in such cases. Thus, *Iriai-ken* are becoming extinct.

3.2.3 Dissolution of Iriai *groups*

Kawashima, Ushiomi and Watanabe (1959–1968) suggested *Iriai* Groups dissolve in many ways. The individual use of *Iriai* land accelerates as the products acquired from *Iriai* land increase in market value. *Iriai* Groups are sometimes converted into juridical entities.[19]

3.3 Michitaka Kaino and Iriai-ken

Michitaka Kaino is very distinctive among the Japanese socio-legal scholars who have conducted research on *Iriai-ken*. In his youth, Kaino was a member of the Investigation Group of Land-Use Customs in Northern China (*Kahoku Nouson Kankou Chousa*) alongside his mentor Izutaro Suehiro and got involved in the establishment of a land law system in Manchuria. His research on *Iriai-ken* is accomplished in the 1943 book *Iriai no Kenkyuu* (Research on *Iriai-ken*).

Afterwards, he got involved in the "*Kotsunagi* case" land dispute over *Iriai* land in *Iwate* prefecture as an attorney. He resigned from his position as a university professor and sold his house to support this movement. The result of his work is described in his 1964 book *Kotsunagi Jiken* (*Kotsunagi* Case).

3.3.1 "Livelihood right" theory

Kaino published much research on *Iriai-ken*. In almost all of those, he expressed *Iriai-ken* as a "livelihood right" or "basis of livelihood right" and focused on the importance of *Iriai-ken* in a farmer's life. On this point, Kaino is the successor of the essence of Suehiro's research on *Iriai-ken*.

3.3.2 Insufficiency of collective ownership theory

Kaino (1943) referred to Karl F. Eichhorn, Georg L. von Maurer and Otto von Gierke, whose theories were the basis for the legal theories of Japanese *Iriai-ken* in that era, and identified the limitations in the theories. Kaino pointed out that such German legal theories are based on feudalism and favor by feudal lords. Kaino described collective ownership in German law as not a type of modern ownership but a grant of occupation under feudalistic rule. Kaino rather focused on the process of how such a feudalistic system shifted to collective ownership under autonomic collective ownership by farmers.

Kaino's perspective was beyond comparison with the German theories. Kaino focused on Japanese court judgments for material for his examination and research on *Iriai-ken*.[20]

3.3.3 Michitaka Kaino and "extinction of Iriai-ken*" theory*

Kaino agreed with the "advanced use of *Iriai* forest," which is the purpose of the 1966 *Iriai* Forest Modernization Act, from the perspective of providing improvement to the quality of life of farmers.[21] At the same time, Kaino suggested that *Iriai-ken* by nature is appropriate for the collective use of land. He predicted the purpose of "advanced use of *Iriai* forest" would not be fulfilled if *Iriai* land is allocated to individual ownership.[22] The reason behind Kaino's prediction is that if *Iriai-ken* are converted to individual ownership, landowners cannot resist the attraction of the exchange value of the land. Individual landowners will sell to the buyer who offers the higher price or who will attract value-adding industries to his or her land rather than the advanced use of *Iriai* forest.

Kaino suggested an alternative solution to fulfilling the intention of "advanced use of *Iriai* forest." Kaino focused on actual residence as a condition to *Iriai-ken*. According to Kaino's solution, there should be qualification on entry; only local residents should be able to participate in *Iriai* forest development projects. Kaino suggested the development of *Iriai* forest cannot be fulfilled without recognition of who holds *Iriai-ken* rights. Actually, Kaino's suggestion did not consider government policy on *Iriai* forests.

3.3.4 Michitaka Kaino and Iriai-ken

Despite his detailed historical research in 1943, Kaino explains *Iriai-ken* itself in a simple way: *Iriai-ken* are rights to land for harvesting grass, fruits and firewood that are fundamental necessities for a farmer's life.[23]

Kaino's words are a reflection of his focus on the improvement of the quality of farmers' lives and the elimination of poverty in rural areas of Japan rather than a legal analysis of *Iriai-ken*. Kaino did not only focus on the preservation of *Iriai-ken* but also the possibility of a new role: local development based on *Iriai* Groups or *Iriai-ken* customs.

Kaino's study is inductive. He suggested the possibility of the role of *Iriai-ken* in modern society under capitalism and the market economy through his legal advocacy in the *Kotsunagi* case and his learning from coming into contact with the actual life of farmers. This is the specialty and distinctiveness of Kaino's study.

3.4 *Japanese commons theory*

Michitaka Kaino suggested a new societal role of *Iriai-ken* in capitalism and the market economy. I will next introduce how this point developed in later research. *Iriai-ken* in Japan have been regarded as "commons" since the 1990s and reconsidered from the aspect of their role in local environmental protection and the sustainable use of natural resources.

3.4.1 The Tragedy of the Commons

There is no consensus definition of the word "commons." Originally, this word refers to the British version of *Iriai* land. Presently, the meaning of the word "commons" has changed into a versatile term that is not necessarily linked to the original meaning (i.e., "commons" in a broad sense).

The word "commons" became widely recognized all over the world in 1968 through Garrett Hardin's Article published in *Science* magazine and titled "The Tragedy of The Commons." In this article, Hardin raised over-pasturing in British commons as one example of a moral hazard. In the grass fields of British commons, over-pasturing is widespread because each farmer who uses the land egoistically aims to maximize their own benefit. In such case, egoistical over-pasturing ruins the grass field as a result.

Hardin suggested two solutions to avoid "The Tragedy of the Commons": one is placing the land under the control of the government and the other is allocation of the common land to individual farmers. Environmental issues were seriously focused upon internationally during this era and "The Tragedy of The Commons" was read worldwide.

3.4.2 Elinor Ostrom and Commons Studies

In 1990, Elinor Ostrom published *Governing the Commons.* Ostrom inductively suggested commons is one type of autonomy for a local community and that it contributes to the management and sustainable use of natural resources by introducing many case examples from all over the world. Ostrom (1990) is taken as a counterargument to Hardin's model. Subsequently, many scholars have followed and started case studies of commons; in other words, it was the start of "Commons Studies."

Gakuto Takamura suggests there is a gap between the definitions of the word "commons" by Hardin and scholars of Commons Studies. Hardin discussed open access resources. The majority of present commons theories discuss the use of resources that is limited to members of a certain community (Takamura 2009, 2012).

3.4.3 Japanese Commons Studies

After Ostrom (1990) introduced a Japanese example in this book, many scholars, especially economists and sociologists, focused on Japanese *Iriai-ken* in the context of commons, which was the start of Japanese Commons Studies. Japanese *Iriai-ken* is a desirable version of commons; it contributes to environmental protection in each local community and the proper management and sustainable use of natural resources. *Iriai-ken* should be reexamined in this new context and social role. This is the core discussion of Japanese Commons Studies. Mitsumata, Morimoto and Murota (2008) examine the use of natural resources under the customary land use of *Iriai-ken*; it provides an environment where the community is able to recycle sustainably without depending on resources from other communities. Mitsumata, Morimoto and Murota (2008) suggest this contributes to the autonomy of a local community as well.

Inoue (2004) mentions the difference between Hardin's model (open access) and the Commons Studies' model (limited to a certain community); Inoue (2004) called the former "Global Commons" and the latter "Local Commons." Inoue (2004) mentions the size of the community and relationships based on trust as well. It is possible to make relationships based on trust between each member of a community when the community size is small. On the contrary, it is hard to establish such relationships in bigger communities; people tend to pursue individual, egoistic benefits rather than common benefits when in a bigger community. According to Inoue (2004), *Iriai* Groups in Japan are an effective size.

3.4.4 Japanese Commons Studies and the "extinction of Iriai-ken*" theory*

Japanese Commons Studies scholars mention the "extinction of *Iriai-ken*" that Kawashima and the majority of Japanese socio-legal scholars have discussed. Miyauchi (2001) mentioned the "Collapse of Commons," which includes a legal and political background that accelerates the extinction of *Iriai-ken*; that is, the denial of *Iriai-ken* over government-owned land by the bureaucracy and judiciary and enclosure by registered landowners. Suzuki (2009) mentioned Commons Studies from the perspective of socio-legal studies, especially the disaster risk in abandoned forestry areas.

Japanese Commons Studies suggest a solution for such "extinction of *Iriai-ken*" based on a comparison to the United Kingdom, namely, the involvement of urban people. Suzuki (2009) examined the U.K.'s system, where open space is regulated for the public interest and the recreation of community members is included in the scope of public benefit. Suzuki (2009) suggests the involvement of external nonmembers of *Iriai* Groups in the management of *Iriai* land as a solution in Japan. Suzuki suggests the following as conditions:

(1) Regulation of public interest land in general, not only *Iriai* land. Forests that are connected to the public interest, disaster risks, water resources and so on should be accessed by citizens.
(2) Institution building for the preservation of *Iriai-ken*.

Mitsumata, Morimoto and Murota (2008) also refer to the history of the U.K. that protected British commons (in the narrow sense) through open access to the public. Mitsumata, Morimoto and Murota (2008) also suggest "open commons" in Japan through the involvement of urban people.

Miyauchi (2001) also mentions that the respect given to "*Satoyama*" (which means "village forest" in Japanese) among people in modern urban areas may be the solution, despite recognizing the difficulty of rule building and the coordination of interests.

It may be a realistic solution to the involvement of urban citizens in the management of *Iriai* land by recognizing *Iriai-ken* as commons.

Meanwhile, Takamura (2009) suggests the risk of providing open access; newly accessing urban citizens may be free-riders rather than active in the new management. Takamura focuses on the nature of commons rather than the geographical location. Takamura's definition of commons is:[24]

(1) Property that has the nature of providing benefit to all beneficiaries as long as all beneficiaries access it moderately.
(2) Property that has the nature of being easily ruined if some beneficiaries access it selfishly.

My understanding of "commons" is based on this definition by Takamura. I expect the customs of *Iriai-ken* to achieve appropriate and effective access to commons. It may be the modern role of *Iriai-ken* that Kaino suggested in the 1960s.

4 Conclusion

I have summarized the social, judicial and academic history of Japanese *Iriai-ken* in this article. The majority of Japanese socio-legal study scholars in the postwar era followed the "Extinction of *Iriai-ken*" theory. Actually, *Iriai-ken* still exists and is expected to perform a new role as "Japanese commons," despite what many socio-legal scholars predicted.

Japan experienced significant economic growth after World War II. It is remarkable that *Iriai-ken* have been preserved from the premodern era to the present day in a developed country like Japan. The contribution of academia to the preservation of *Iriai-ken* is notable despite the Japanese government maintaining an abolitionist policy for a long time. In particular, Japanese socio-legal scholars' research on *Iriai-ken* has been referred to in court judgments and has contributed to the distinguishment of the legal characteristics of *Iriai-ken* in accordance with the large number of court judgments.

Michitaka Kaino made many suggestions for the new social role of *Iriai-ken* by observing the significant change in the social circumstances of *Iriai-ken* in the postwar era. His research still adds many suggestions on the methodology of studying issues related to *Iriai-ken* even in the present day.

Japanese socio-legal scholars are conducting interdisciplinary research through active collaboration with Japanese Commons Studies. Japanese Commons Studies expect *Iriai-ken* to be a model of commons that contributes to environmental protection in local communities and the sustainable use of local natural resources. In response, Japanese socio-legal studies have conducted experimental research connecting urban and rural areas. Such academic collaboration has been continuing for more than two decades. The academic value of this collaboration is remarkable. It surely contributes suggestions for sustainable development in Asian and African regions.

Notes

1 I will use the Japanese term "*Iriai-ken*" to refer to Japanese common rights in this Article to avoid confusion with those of other countries, such as common rights in the United Kingdom. Land that is subject to Iriai-ken is called "*Iriai*-land" in this article.
2 In the annual report of Japan's Ministry of Justice *Shihou-Kenkyu* in 1926, Judge Masahide Morozumi described the following: "The people of local communities have collectively used local forests and fields for their daily needs. The historical repetition of such land use became legal rights and the provision of *Iriai-ken* in Japanese law is a reflection of such."
3 Watanabe (1968) strongly criticizes this point; it is unacceptable under Article 29 of the Japanese Constitution to violate private property rights through a local assembly decision.
4 Japanese Supreme Court judgment November 28, 1921, Nagoya High Court judgment November 30, 1971, etc.
5 Japanese Supreme Court judgment March 13, 1961.
6 Japanese Supreme Court judgment March 17, 2006.
7 Nakao (2009) pp. 41–42.
8 Transactions using land certificates was recognized. See Hojo (2000) p. 18.
9 Hojo (2000) p. 46.
10 The Real Estate Registration Act was established in 1899 based on this.
11 Hojo (2000) p. 126.
12 Hojo (2000) p. 153.
13 Tokyo High Court judgment July 9, 1914.
14 Japanese Supreme Court judgment March 13, 1973.
15 There was media discourse that claimed rural farmers were the main cause of excessive lumbering of forests and the resulting disaster. Michitaka Kaino strongly criticized this and published a counterargument. See Kaino (2008) pp. 625–626 (originally published in 1966).

16 Yano (2018) pp. 202–203.
17 Yano (2018) p. 201.
18 Kawashima, Ushiomi and Watanabe (1959–1968) pp. 4–6.
19 Kawashima, Ushiomi and Watanabe (1959–1968) wrote during an era of great economic growth in postwar Japan. This growth caused great demand for labor in urban areas and great migration from rural areas. It was the start of the depopulation in rural areas that continues to the present. This is a significant factor for such conversion.
20 Kaino (1943) pp. 5–25.
21 Kaino (1964, 2008) p. 570.
22 Kaino (1964, 2008) pp. 571–572.
23 Kaino (1966, 2008) p. 625.
24 Takamura (2009) pp. 88–91, Takamura (2012) pp. 7–25.

Bibliography

Crowe, Beryl L. (1969) 'The Tragedy of the Commons Revisited' *Science*, No. 166

Demsetz, Harold (1967) 'Toward a Theory of Property Rights' *American Economic Review*, No. 157

Feeny, David, Fikret Berkes, Bonnie J. McCay and James M. Acheson (1990) 'Tragedy of the Commons: 22 Years Later' *Human Ecology*, Vol. 8, No. 1

Hardin, Garrett (1968) 'The Tragedy of the Commons' *Science*, Vol. 162, No. 3859, 1243–1248

Hayasaka, Keizo (2016) 'Kotsunagi-jiken Bunko; 20 seiki Nihon, Iwate-ken ni okeru Tasuu no Iriai-jiken Saiban kara Tairyo-Hikaku-Bunseki ni mukatte' *Iwate University Artes Liberales*, Vol. 96

Hojo, Hiroshi (1977) *Iriai-Rinya no Shiteki Kenkyuu*, Ochanomizu-shobou

Hojo, Hiroshi (2000/2001) *Iriai no Hou-Shakaigaku*, Ochanomizu-shobou

Hojo, Hiroshi (2014) *Iriai, Iriai-ken to Local Commons*, Ochanomizu-shobou

Inoue, Makoto (2004) *Commons no Shisou wo Motomete*, Iwanami

Japan Agency of Forestry (2013) "Shinrin oyobi Ringyou no Doukou"

Japan Agency of Forestry (2016) "Shinrin-Kumiai no Genjo"

Kaino, Michitaka (1943) *Iriai no Kenkyuu*, Nippon-Hyouron-sha

Kaino, Michitaka (1951–1973, 2008) *Houritsu-Jihyou 1951–1973*, Jigaku-sha

Kaino, Michitaka (1964) *Kotsunagi Jiken*, Iwanami

Kaneko, Yuka (2009) 'Tochi-hou Kaikaku ni okeru Houteki-Tagen-Shugi no Kokufuku: Indonesia to Cambodia no Hikaku Kentou' *Kokusai-Kyouryoku-Ronshuu*, Vol. 16–3

Kaneko, Yuka (2010) *Asia no Hou-Seibi to Hou-Hatten*, Daigaku-Kyouiku shuppan

Kawashima, Takeyoshi (1949) *Shoyuuken-Hou no Riron*, Iwanami

Kawashima, Takeyoshi (1968) *Iriai-ken no Kiso-Riron*, Iwanami

Kawashima, Takeyoshi, Yasuo Kondo and Toshio Furushima (1958) *Iriai-Kanshuuhou no Jittai*, Iwanami

Kawashima, Takeyoshi, Toshitaka Ushiomi and Yozo Watanabe (1959–1968) *Iriai-ken no Kaitai*, Vol. 1–3, Iwanami

Koyanagi, Shunichiro (1998) *Minpou-ten no Tanjo' edited by Toshio Hironaka and Eiichi Hoshino Minpouten no 100 nen*, Yuuhikaku

Kurumizawa, Yoshiki and Yoshihiko Nawata (1993) 'Chiiki-Chuukan-Shuudan no Hou-Shakaigaku; Toshi to Nouson ni okeru Juumin-Shuudan no Koukyouteki

Shakai-keisei to sono Seidoteki Kiban' edited by Nobuyoshi Toshitani, Tamio Yoshii and Takeshi Mizubayashi, *Hou ni okeru Kindai to Gendai*, Nippon-Hyouron-sha

Mamiya, Yosuke and Yuji Hirokawa, ed. (2013) *Commons to Koukyou Kuukan*, Showa-dou

McKean, Margaret A. (1992) 'Management of Traditional Common Land (Iriaichi) in Japan' edited by Daniel W. Bromley, *Making the Commons Work: Theory, Practice and Policy*, ICS Press

Mistumata, Manabu, Sanae Morimoto and Takeshi Murota (2008) *Commons Kenkyuu no Frontier*, Tokyo University

Miyauchi, Taisuke (2001) 'Commons no Shakai-gaku; Shizen Shigen no Shoyuu, Riyou, Kanri wo megutte' edited by Hiroyuki Torigoe, *Shizen Kankyou to Kankyou Bunka*, Yuuhikaku

Morozumi, Masahide (1926) 'Iriai-ken ni tsuite' *Japan Ministry of Justice "Shihou-Kenkyuu"*, Vol. 2, No. 3

Nakao, Hidetoshi (2003) 'Iriai-ken no Sonpi to Iriai-chi no Shobun; Iriai-ken no Kankyou-Hozen Kinou' *Seinan Gakuin University Hougaku Ronshuu*, Vol. 35, No. 3, 4

Nakao, Hidetoshi (2007) *Iriai-ken no Hanrei Sougou Kaisetsu*, Shinzan-sha

Nakao, Hidetoshi (2009) *Iriai-ken; sono Honshitsu to Gendai-teki Kadai*, Keiso-shobou

Ostrom, Elinor (1990) "*Governing the Commons*" Cambridge University Press

Suehiro, Izutaro (1924) *Nouson Houritsu Mondai*

Suzuki, Tatsuya (2009) 'Nihon no Iriai-ken no Kouzou; England no Iriai-ken tono Hikaku no Shiten kara' edited by Takeshi Murota, *Grobal Jidai no Local Commons*, Minerva shobou

Takamura, Gakuto (2006) 'Iriai Rinya kara Satoyama Commons he' *Hou to Minshu-shugi*, No. 143

Takamura, Gakuto (2009) 'Commons Kenkyuu no tameno Hou-Gainen no Sai-Teichi; Shakai Shogaku tono Kyoudou wo shikou shite' *Shakai-Kagaku Kenkyuu*, Vol. 60, No. 5, 6

Takamura, Gakuto (2012) *Commons karano Toshi Saisei*, Minerva shobou

Tanaka, Manabu (1990) 'Nihon ni okeru Nouchi-Kaikaku to Nougyou-Hou no Seiritsu' edited by Hiromitsu Umehara, *Tounan Asia no Tochi Seido to Nougyou Henka*, Institute of Developing Econony, No. 406

Ume, Kenjiro (1896) *Minpou Yougi*

Upham, Frank K. (1987) *Law and Social Change in Postwar Japan*, Harvard University Press

Upham, Frank K. (2018) *The Great Property Fallacy: Theory, Reality and Growth in Developing Countries*, Cambridge University Press

Wagatsuma, Sakae (1932) *Bukken-Hou*, Iwanami

Watanabe, Yozo (1968) 'Kindaiteki-Shoyuu-ken no Seiritsu' edited by Hiroshi Hojo and Akira Murata (2009), *Kansyuuteki-kenri to Shoyuu-ken*, Ochanomizu-shobou

Yamanaka, Einosuke ed. (1994) *Nihon Kindai-hou Ron*, Houritsu Bunka sha

Yano, Tatsuo (2018) 'Iriai-Rinya-Kindaika-Hou no 50 nen to Kenkyuu-sha no Kiseki' *Shudo-Hougaku*, Vol. 40, No. 1

12 The concept of juridical personality and the autonomy of villagers' committees in China*

Mikiko Matsumoto

Introduction

Residents' committees in urban areas and villagers' committees in rural areas are designated in the Constitution of the People's Republic of China (hereafter "the Constitution") as "mass organizations of self-government at the grassroots level."[1] Although they are not "state administrative organs" in positive law, they are responsible for implementing some state administrative tasks in addition to the governance of their citizens in their areas.[2] While various arguments about the legal characteristics of these committees remain, the General Provisions of Civil Law of the People's Republic of China (hereafter "the General Provisions"), enacted in 2017, provided for the first time that these organizations have a "juridical personality (法人资格)."[3]

Accompanied by the diversification of administrative roles, more non-state actors are now taking part in implementing administrative tasks in many countries. Under these circumstances, how to ensure fair and equitable administrative operations at the same time as protecting the rights and interests of these non-state actors from the intervention of the state becomes a common question.

Out of the mass organizations of self-government at the grassroots level, this paper focuses on villagers' committees and examines how the clarification of the juridical personality of the committees affects their autonomy and their relations with the government. For this purpose, Section 1 discusses the concept of a juridical person in China, and Section 2 examines the meanings and effects of the provisions on the juridical personality of the committees based on the results of Section 1.

1 The concept of a "juridical person" in China

After the establishment of People's Republic of China, the juridical person system was first provided in the General Principles of Civil Law of the People's Republic of China (hereafter "the General Principles") in 1986. This law remained in effect even after the General Provisions went into effect in 2017, but the General Provisions was superior to the General Principles when a contradiction arose between them. These laws were expired as the Civil Code of the People's Republic of

DOI: 10.4324/9781003170600-15

China (hereafter "the Civil Code") became effective in 2021.[4] However, the provisions on the juridical persons has not been changed from those of the General Provision. This paper mainly refers to the General Provisions rather than the Civil Code since it was the first law which clarified the juridical personality of the villagers' committees.

Although many of the functions of a juridical person are common between China and other countries, there are some unique aspects of China's concept of a juridical person.

Article 57 of the General Provisions as well as Article 36 Paragraph 1 of the General Principles provides that a juridical person is "an organization with capacity for civil rights and capacity for civil conduct which independently enjoys civil rights and assumes civil obligations in accordance with the law." Based on this provision, the following analysis of China's concept of juridical persons focuses on independence (1.1) and the civil personality of juridical persons (1.2).

1.1 The independence of juridical persons

The substance of the independence of juridical persons provided in the General Principles and the General Provisions can be analyzed according to two relations that juridical persons usually have: (1) the relationship between a juridical person and the state and (2) the relationship between a juridical person and its members (including natural persons and juridical persons).

1.1.1 The relation between a juridical person and the state

The relationship between a juridical person and the state has an intimate bearing on the historical background of why and how the Chinese legal system adopted the concept of a juridical person. Before the General Principles was enacted in 1986, the concept of a juridical person was regarded as a legal technique that was based on capitalistic private ownership[5] and was rejected and erased from laws and legal terms under the planned economy.[6] Additionally, all organizations, such as corporations, were under the jurisdiction of the state and carried out activities based on national planning. However, since the 1980s, when the reform and opening-up policies were enacted, some scholars began to insist on reordering the economy by constructing a legal system that secures independent properties and allows independent management for certain institutions.

A paper written in 1980 by Shuyi Gao,[7] for example, stipulated that a juridical person had independent properties and independent management and argued that its property could not be confounded with properties of the state or any other groups. He pointed out that the legal system of the juridical person adopted in each country's civil law since the end of the 19th century encouraged the bourgeoisie to expand their assets and support exploitation. On the other hand, he also noted that the system positively affected the promotion of productivity, the development of scientific technology and economic growth in capitalist societies. By claiming that the nature of the state and the laws of socialist countries are completely different from those of capitalist countries, and that enacting the legal system can develop enterprise initiatives and institutionally guarantee economic reform, he ultimately legitimized the adoption of a juridical person system in China.

Another paper, written in 1981 by Huixing Liang, specifically analyzed commercial enterprises and insisted on the significance of securing their independent property rights, using laws to achieve reforms.[8] Under the assumption that ownership by all the people equals ownership by the state, he argued that it is a requirement of the development discipline of the socialist economy to provide enterprises "relative property rights (相对所有权)" and let them engage in production and distribution with "independent enterprise juridical person qualification (独立的企业法人资格)." He acknowledged that the commercial enterprise juridical person system is a privilege for the bourgeoisie that allows them to enjoy the benefits of limited liability. However, he also argued that the system has another aspect as a new manufacturing system that promotes the concentration of capital while separating the power of product management from the bourgeoisie to develop a property of "associated producers (联合起来的生产者)." He concluded that the socialist system, based on the commercial enterprise juridical person, could develop socialist commodity productivity and constitute an enormous proportion of a communist society's material basis.

As seen earlier, scholars who insisted on the need for the juridical person system recognized it as something that would develop socialism and legitimized its adoption. In so doing, the juridical person's element of independence from the state became a theoretical and practical foundation to adapt the juridical system to China as it promotes the initiatives and activeness of institutions. In other words, to give a juridical person a certain degree of independence from the state was not just one of the characteristics of the Chinese version of the juridical person provided in the General Provisions but a purpose in itself.

Since then, in China's legal textbooks, it is generally stated that a juridical person is independently responsible and has independent assets.[9] That is, a juridical person conducts activities such as business based on their own will, the state shall not unfairly confiscate its assets, and at the same time, the juridical person cannot rely on state assistance to relieve debt. Therefore, although any juridical person must be legally established and the state inevitably interacts with it in that sense, once established, it must be endowed with a certain degree of independence, even under the Chinese legal system. By guaranteeing this legal status to juridical persons, business stability is guaranteed, and efficiency improves, both of which are essential for the country's economic development. Of course, this independence is also related to the economic system and property rights system in China and cannot be simply reduced to the effect of juridical persons.[10] However, considering the historical background and provisions of the legal system previously described, the idea of a certain degree of independence from the state is the essence of a juridical person in China.

Note, however, that the specifics of this independence from the state differ between types of juridical persons depending on societal needs. That is to say, they are determined in combination with the specific legal frameworks, such as establishment procedure, necessity of registration, taxation system, forms of government supervision, status in lawsuits and so on. This is because of how and to what extent the independence discussed earlier should be guaranteed varies depending on the purposes and business contents of the juridical persons and social situations of the moment. Therefore, one cannot categorically draw a certain conclusion about a juridical person's legal status and the substance of independence from the mere fact that they are a juridical person. These must be examined individually based on concrete legal frameworks.[11]

1.1.2 The relation between a juridical person and its members

Another aspect of the independence of a juridical person must be analyzed from the point of view of the relationship between a juridical person and its members. In Japan, one of the effects of recognizing an institution as a juridical person is to divide its property from its members' individual property.[12] This is also common in China as providing a juridical personality is equal to providing limited liability. All existing juridical persons in China have limited liability status, and the members are only responsible within the range of their investment.[13] On the other hand, "unincorporated organizations (非法人组织)," those first provided for in General Provisions, can conduct civil activities under their name, but the members and founders must take unlimited liability.[14] When comparing these two kinds of organizations, juridical persons and unincorporated organizations, it is safe to say that one of the meanings of juridical personality is to separate the nonexempt property of the juridical person from that of its members.[15,16]

1.2 The civil personality of juridical persons

1.2.1 Rights and obligations of juridical persons

Another feature of China's juridical persons is their ability to enjoy rights and obligations. Article 57 of the General Provisions as well as Article 36 Paragraph 1 of the General Principles provide that a juridical person "independently enjoys civil rights and assumes civil obligations in accordance with the law." Thus, juridical persons in China, as well as Japan, may be the subjects of rights and obligations that are independent of those of its members. However, there is a difference between the General Principles and the General Provisions regarding whether the subject of rights and obligations is limited to natural and juridical persons.

In the General Principles, only citizens (natural persons) and juridical persons were recognized as subjects of civil rights. Therefore, as a general rule, organizations without a juridical personality did not have their rights and obligations recognized. Only when there is a specific provision are rights and obligations recognized under special circumstances.[17]

In contrast, in the General Provisions, there is a new provision for an "unincorporated organization." Unincorporated organizations, which are not juridical persons, can engage in civil conduct under their name and be treated almost the same as juridical persons through registration.[18] Thus, whether an organization has a juridical personality does not necessarily determine if it is subject to rights and obligations, and the role that juridical personality plays in judging the subjectivity of an organization becomes more relative.

1.2.2 The civil personality of juridical persons

A characteristic feature of juridical persons in China is that the designation can only be used when the subject is engaging in "civil conduct." This is directly expressed in the General Principles and General Provisions as "capacity of civil rights" or "capacity of civil conduct" but can also be observed from the whole of the legislative system and academic discourse.

In the General Provisions, for example, the "state organ juridical persons (机关法人)" are defined.[19] Article 97 provides: "An independently funded state organ or a statutory institution assuming administrative functions shall have the status of a state organ juridical person from the date of its formation, and may engage in civil conducts necessary for performing its functions." In this provision, the status of a juridical person is a "qualification" for engaging in civil conduct. A member of the Legislative Affairs Commission of the Standing Committee of the National People's Congress, the lawmaking organ, explains this provision as follows:

> state organ juridical persons are organizations that are set up according to provisions of laws and administrative decisions and entitled with public authority to engage in state public administration activities as primary work. This kind of organization implements public administrative tasks representing the state and has the status of state organ juridical persons when it engages in civil conduct. The reason why the status of juridical persons is necessary for these state organs is that they sometimes need to engage in certain civil conducts to implement public administrative tasks.[20]

In other words, the state organ juridical persons which are typically state administrative bodies such as the state council, local governments and courts[21] have the status of a juridical person as long as they are engaging in civil conduct; when they engage in state administrative activities, they cannot be considered juridical persons.[22]

In Japan, the legal status of a juridical person is not related to the nature of the activities that the organization is engaging in. The state and local autonomies, for example, have the status of a juridical person, regardless of whether they engage in administrative or civil conduct.

In contrast, juridical personality is a "qualification" for engaging in civil conduct in China. The legal status of a juridical person is not recognized when engaging in administrative activities.[23,24] In other words, whether the organization has juridical person status changes depending on its field of activities, even if it is the same organization. This paper calls the kind of capacity to enjoy rights and obligations limited to civil conduct "civil personality."

2 Meanings and effects of the clarification of the juridical personality of villagers' committees

Villagers' committees in rural areas of China are defined in the Constitution as "mass organizations of self-government at the grassroots level." The Constitution also provides for the election of commissioners by the villagers, and the committees establish subcommittees for people's mediation, public security, public health and other matters, to manage public affairs and social services in their areas, mediate civil disputes and help maintain public order. Besides the Constitution, the Organization Law of the Villagers' Committees of the People's Republic of China (hereafter "the Organization Law") designates their organizational structure and roles.[25] Article 2 of the Organization Law provides that villagers' committees are mass organizations "in which villagers administer their own affairs, educate themselves, and serve their own needs, and in which elections are conducted, decisions adopted, administration maintained, and supervision exercised by democratic means."[26] Although, in general, villagers' committees are not considered state administrative organs, their work is closely related to the tasks of the state. Indeed, some laws require them to conduct public affairs such as land administration[27] and community correction (社区矫正).[28] They must also cooperate with the local government's operations according to the Organization Law, and their expenses are fully or partly covered by a grant from the local government. While they are subject to the supervision and direction of the state and local government concerning these kinds of work, the Constitution and the laws require that the activities of villagers' committees must have a certain level of autonomy. However, there is no legal mechanism to secure this level of autonomy, and it is often said that villagers' committees are merely working for the government.

Under this circumstance, how meaningful was it that the General Provision stipulated that villagers' committees were juridical persons? This section examines the effects of this provision on securing the autonomy of villagers' committees and the relationship between the committees and the state based on the substance of the concept of the juridical person as described in the previous section ((2.1)–(2.3)). In addition, it also explains the impact of the provision on the property separation between villagers' committees and other actors (2.4).

2.1 Arguments during the lawmaking process

The General Provisions states that "An urban residents' committee or a villagers' committee has the status of a basic self-governing mass organization juridical person, and may engage in civil conducts necessary for performing its functions" (Article 101, Paragraph 1). In the process of legislation, some grassroots leaders reported that although villagers' committees must sometimes engage in some civil conduct to fulfill their functions, the law (the General Principles) did not designate the villagers' committees' status as civil entities; hence, they were unable to engage in civil conduct successfully.[29] From these details, we may assume the main point of clarifying the juridical personality for villagers' committees was to clarify their civil personality, namely, the ability to enjoy rights and obligations in civil activities. Without civil personality, the villagers' committees could not know if and how their civil activities would be legally protected.

However, granting juridical personality should not be the only way to clarify the civil personality of the villagers' committees. The law can also stipulate the legal status of organizations without juridical personality. The General Principles did not have such provisions, but they were included in the General Provisions. The General Provisions has established a new category of civil subjects: "unincorporated organizations." Unincorporated organizations are civil entities that can carry out activities under their names and are treated just like juridical persons if the organizations are registered. To achieve the goal of clarifying the civil personality of villagers' committees, it seems unnecessary to give them a juridical personality. Instead, they can register as unincorporated organizations. Why did legislators choose to give them a juridical personality?[30]

As mentioned before, a decisive difference between a juridical person and an unincorporated organization is that while the former accepts limited liability, the latter takes on unlimited liability. However, this cannot be the sole explanation because it is difficult to determine whether the liabilities of the villagers' committee members are limited. Villagers[31] elect the commissioners of the committee, but they do not take a stake in its activities.

As such, the reason why a juridical personality was given to villagers' committees needs to be examined from the point of view of independence from the state, which is one of the facets of the juridical person concept in China, as already described in Section 1.

2.2 *The juridical personality of villagers' committees and independence from the state*

The system of juridical persons was adopted in China under the circumstances in which all institutions were under the control of the state during the period of the planned economy to establish organizations with a certain degree of independence and scope of autonomy from the state. On the other hand, unincorporated organizations were not defined in the General Principles. They were defined for the first time in the General Provisions because the forms of organizations that were assumed when the General Principles were enacted had diversified along with the development of the market economy and there was a need to place organizations without juridical personality in law.[32] In other words, the main assumption of unincorporated organizations was that they were various organizations formed by private persons of their own free will and under their freedom of association. Thus, organizations generated from within the structure of the state are not in the same category[33] because they are given juridical personality during the separation processes.

Regarding the villagers' committees, these organizations were formed voluntarily by villagers in the first part of the 1980s and were not generated from within the state structure. However, after the villagers' committees were defined in the Constitution in 1982, they retained their position as part of the state organization while remaining separate from administrative organs.[34] One of the reasons legislators chose to give villagers' committees a juridical personality rather than registering them as unincorporated organizations could be that, in their mind, the traditional way of using the concept of juridical personality in China fits with the villagers' committees' current fixed status as a state organization. They consciously or unconsciously might have believed that it was suitable to give them a juridical personality to secure their independence and autonomy from the state in accordance with the Constitution and the Organization Law of Villagers' Committees.[35] If so, the clarification of villagers' committees' juridical personality is not simply a clarification of civil personality but can also be considered as a step toward a legal framework that institutionally secures the autonomous space for villagers' committees.

However, the concept of a juridical person in China is used only for civil conduct. Villagers' committees have a status of juridical persons as long as they engage in civil conduct, but what about when they engage in other activities, such as administrative operations? The work of villagers' committees includes various activities, such as exercising autonomy and conducting state administration. The question is how to distinguish so-called "civil conduct" from other activities and treat a villagers' committee as a juridical person.[36]

Moreover, even when it is clear that the committee is acting as a juridical person and has a certain degree of independence, the nature of that independence must be interpreted based on a specific legal system. As part of this process, the next section of this paper examines the nature of villagers' committees' juridical personality by analyzing their position in the General Provision's classification of juridical persons.

2.3 *The position of villagers' committees in the General Provision's classification of juridical persons*

The General Principles classified juridical persons into two categories: commercial enterprise juridical persons (Section 2 of Chapter III, "Juridical Persons"), and state organ, institution and social organization juridical persons (Section 3). It did not have provisions for the villagers' committees' juridical personality. In contrast, the General Provisions classifies juridical persons into three categories: for-profit juridical persons (Section 2), nonprofit juridical persons (Section 3) and special juridical persons (Section 4). It positions villagers' committees in the category of special juridical persons as basic self-governing mass organization juridical persons (see Table 12.1).

Table 12.1 Juridical persons under General Principles and General Provisions

General Principles (1986)	General Provisions (2017)
III Juridical Persons	III Juridical Persons
§1 General Rule	§1 General Rule
§2 Enterprise as Juridical Person	§2 For-Profit Juridical Persons
§3 State Organ, Institution and Social Organization as Juridical Person	§3 Non-Profit Juridical Persons
	§4 Special Juridical Persons
	IV Unincorporated Organization

The difference between for-profit juridical persons and nonprofit juridical persons is based on whether the juridical person aims to distribute its profit to its members. This criterion has been adopted since the first draft of the legislative process before the category of special juridical person existed. The category was added in the third draft, responding to examples referred to by the experts, such as when the commerciality of the juridical person is hard to judge, or when the method of establishing and dissolving the juridical persons is not the same as for either for-profit or nonprofit juridical persons, making classification difficult.[37] Under the present law, the category of "special juridical person" includes state organ juridical persons, rural collective economic organization juridical persons (农村集体经济组织法人) and urban and rural cooperative economic organization juridical persons (城镇农村的合作经济组织法人), in addition to basic self-governing mass organization juridical persons. These juridical persons are considered to be juridical persons that cannot be classified as either a for-profit or nonprofit juridical person.

A member of the Legislative Affairs Commission of the Standing Committee of the National People's Congress explains why villagers' committees are added to the category of special juridical persons by defining five features of villagers' committees that are not seen in other types of juridical persons.[38] First, their formation: villagers' committees are formed directly by law. Second, their termination: they will not be terminated unless the village is incorporated or its border is changed. Third, their function: they manage public affairs and public welfare. Fourth, their organizational structure: they are generally composed of leaders of the village and the commissioners are elected by villagers. Fifth, discharging liability: they cannot dispose of the collectively owned land to discharge their liability.

There is criticism of the category of special juridical persons, asserting that for-profit and nonprofit juridical persons should have a dichotomous relationship and that this is theoretically inconsistent with establishing a third category of special juridical persons.[39] In a sense, this criticism sounds correct. Arguments that support the need for a third category are not related to the classification methods of for-profit and nonprofit juridical persons. Issues such as the method of establishment, relation with the public interest or public purposes are not about whether the juridical person aims to distribute profits.

However, legislators seem to have assumed that the juridical persons classified as special juridical persons are different from the typical for-profit or nonprofit juridical person in the General Provisions. Professor Yang Lixin of Renmin University, a legislative expert of the Legislative Affairs Commission of the Standing Committee of the National People's Congress who took part in drafting the General Provisions, stated in his book detailing the background of the provisions that "special juridical persons are also established for a public purpose or other non-profit purposes, but without investors or founders, and differ from non-profit juridical persons because they are established by national law or government order."[40] In other words, for legislators, nonprofit juridical persons are established based on the free will of private persons whose intent is not to acquire and distribute profit. This suggests that a juridical person established by the state, even if it was established without the purpose of profit acquisition and distribution, might not be a nonprofit juridical person. This indicates an awareness on the part of legislators that there was a need to distinguish between juridical persons established by private persons and those established by the state.

Villagers' committees are not administrative organs but do have status as part of the state organization. Additionally, they are organizations directly established according to Organization Law. Accordingly, it is not surprising that they are classified as special juridical persons based on their establishment by "national law or government order."

However, the legal effects of the classifications of a juridical person as a for-profit, nonprofit or special juridical person are inherently unclear. In the legislative process, another approach to classification, such as corporate juridical persons and foundational juridical persons, was also proposed. However, the classification of for-profit and nonprofit was considered "more suitable for the legislative tradition" of China since the former civil law, the General Principles, had adopted the classifications of commercial and noncommercial enterprise juridical persons (state organ, institution and social organization juridical persons).[41] These classifications are not used in other laws besides the General Provisions, and they are not linked to other legal systems, such as the tax system. Under the current system, a juridical person's concrete legal status is not derived from these classifications and is solely determined by the organizational law and individual legislative systems.

Under this situation, the issue of whether other legal systems will be systematized based on the categories of for-profit, nonprofit or special juridical persons through future legislation deserves attention. For special juridical persons in particular, how juridical persons established by the state should be theoretically normalized compared with juridical persons established by private persons is likely to be an important issue because the norm may affect the autonomy of villagers' committees.

2.4 The separation of properties by a juridical personality

According to the earlier analysis, the clarification of the villagers' committees' juridical personality originally aimed to clarify that villagers' committees have civil personalities. Not only that, it turned out to contribute to distinguishing and separating their property from the property of others.

Regarding the expenses of villagers' committees, Article 37 Paragraph 1 of the Organization Law provides that "Expenses necessary for villagers' committees to accomplish the tasks assigned by the relevant departments of the people's governments shall be paid by the departments which assign the tasks." Paragraph 2 provides that "Expenses needed by a villagers' committee for the public welfare undertaking of the village shall be provided by the villagers' assembly with the funds paid by the villagers or with the labor provided by the villagers. Where it is difficult to cover such expenses, the local people's government may provide proper financial support." In addition to these cases, villagers' committees usually manage both the village's collectively owned land and any related fiscal revenue and expenditure.

In China, under "the system of socialist public ownership," land in rural and suburban areas is owned by collectives except for those portions that belong to the state in accordance with the law.[42] Farmers do not directly own land but use the land allocated by a rural collective economic organization that manages the collectively owned land in the village in line with a family-based contract. Rural collective economic organizations, however, are not set up in every village, while villagers' committees are. In areas where a rural collective economic organization does not exist, a villagers' committee manages the land instead. Moreover, there are cases in which even though an organization has been set up, its members are the commissioners of villagers' committees.

Under these circumstances, the budget of a villagers' committee may be easily mixed up with that of a rural collective economic organization, which creates a situation in which unfair accounting is likely.[43] At least in some areas, the clarification of the juridical personality of villagers' committees, accompanied by the clarification of the juridical personality of rural collective economic organizations, succeeded in dividing these budgets. According to my field investigation conducted in Shanghai villages in 2019, the commissioners of a villagers' committee also worked for a rural collective economic organization. However, after these committees and organizations were incorporated, their financial management became strictly separated. Villagers' committees' expenses are paid by local government, and those of rural collective economic organizations are paid from profits from collectively owned property. Villagers' committees spend money only for civil administration, while rural collective economic organizations do so only for something related to collectively owned property. As the forms of villagers' committees and rural collective economic organizations are diverse, this investigation's results cannot be easily generalized. However, it can be said that clarification of property relations in this way is appropriate for the ideal juridical person's independence.

3 Conclusion

This paper has examined the concept of a juridical person in China and analyzed the effects of clarifying the juridical personality of villagers' committees on their autonomy and their relationships with the government.

One feature of China's concept of a juridical person is how the concept has been adopted to ensure that organizations that have been under the control of the state have a certain degree of independence and autonomy. Another is that juridical persons' ability to enjoy rights and to assume obligations is only possible for civil conducts.

Based on these features, this paper examines the juridical personality of the villagers' committees. First, regarding the explanation in the legislative process that the clarification of the juridical personality of villagers' committees is to clarify its civil personality, I focused on the question of why legislators chose to give them juridical personality instead of registering them as an unincorporated organization. As a result, I proposed a hypothesis that the legislators recognized that it suited the Constitution and Organization Law to provide villagers' committees with a juridical personality to ensure they had a certain degree of independence from the state, considering the historical use of a juridical person to spin off an organization from the state.

Furthermore, regarding the position of villagers' committees in the General Provision's classification of juridical persons, I pointed out that legislators distinguish nonprofit juridical persons and special juridical persons by whether a private person or the state established the organization. As such, villagers' committees were positioned in a category of special juridical persons as organizations established by the state. It is necessary to clarify in what way the juridical persons established by the state should be theoretically normalized in comparison with juridical persons established by private persons, as the General Provision's classification of juridical persons is not lined with other legal systems, and positioning based on this classification does not lead categorically to specific legal status.

Finally, based on the results of field investigations, I demonstrated that the clarification of the juridical personality of villagers' committees also contributed to distinguish between and keep separate the property of villagers' committees and that of rural collective economic organizations.

However, these are still hypotheses derived from limited information rather than a fully proven thesis. To analyze the relationship between the thought behind legislators' decisions and their ideological background, further investigation regarding the reality of villagers' committees' work is necessary in the future.

Notes

* This work is supported by JSPS KAKENHI Grant Number JP19J22411 and JP18KK0033.

1 Article 111 of the *Constitution of the People's Republic of China*, enacted in 1982 and amended in 2018.

2 Regarding the historical and institutional position of residents' committees and villagers' committees, see Matsumoto (2019).

3 As will be explained later in this paper, the concept of "juridical person" in China is not the same as in Japan. Japan and China share many legal terms as both countries' languages use Chinese characters. However, the translation of "juridical person" is slightly different in each language. The Chinese word for "juridical personality" is "法人资格," the literal translation of which is "juridical person (法人) qualification (资格)," while it is called "法人格" in Japanese, which may be literally translated as "legal (法) personality (人格)."

4 The *General Principles of Civil Law of the People's Republic of China*, enacted in 1986, the *General Provisions of Civil Law of the People's Republic of China*, enacted in 2017 and the *Civil Code of the People's Republic of China* enacted in 2020.

5 Some scholars have pointed out that juridical persons were originally created as a system for autonomous cities and colonies in Rome, followed by universities and monasteries in the medieval age. Therefore, they may not necessarily be related to capitalism, and arguments that regard them as a capitalistic legal technique based on capitalistic private ownership are questionable. See Iwai (2003:64).

6 According to Chen Wang, the second draft of *Civil Law in China* made in 1964 had no "capitalistic civil law terms" such as rights, obligations, real rights, claims, natural persons, juridical persons and so on (Takamizawa and Suzuki (eds.) (2017:124)).

7 Gao (1980). Among academic articles about the juridical person system written after the foundation of the People's Republic of China, this is the oldest Article that I have found. Gao was a director of the Communist Party in Jilin University School of Law from April 1984 to September 1985.

8 Liang (1981).

9 For example, Wang (2018:61).

10 For example, provisions in the General Provisions such as "The personal rights, property rights and other lawful rights and interests of the persons of the civil law shall be protected by law and shall not be infringed by any organization or individual" (Article 3), and "When engaged in civil activities, all persons shall observe the principle of voluntariness, and establish, alter or terminate civil juristic relations according to their own free will" (Article 5) established a basis for the protection of property rights and the principle of free will. These provisions protect property rights, and the autonomous decisions of juridical persons as well since "persons of the civil law" or "persons" in these provisions generally include juridical persons.

11 After all, this is nothing but a question of what "independence" of a juridical person means. However, this is not a question unique to China. In Japan, for example, the balance between the requirement for supervision by the state (or a local government) and the independence of the juridical person has been discussed in cases in which whether administrative actors, such as designated corporations, have the right to sue the state or local government becomes a problem. After all, this kind of problem cannot be answered categorically or unambiguously, and the interpretation of certain laws is needed according to each case. See Matsudo (2017, 2018), Yamamoto (2011).

12 Yamamoto (2017:450–451).

13 S. Li (ed.) (2017:167ff).

14 Article 104 of the General Provisions.

15 In the case of Japan, some juridical persons, such as general partnership companies, accept unlimited liability. Thus, limited liability is not always a feature of a juridical person. For a critical analysis of a theory that regards limited liability as one of the features of a juridical person, see Hoshino et al. (1971).

16 However, there are some exceptional cases when members of a juridical person must accept unlimited liability. For example, the doctrine of "piercing the corporate veil" is also accepted in China.

17 For example, Article 2 of the *Copyright Law of the People's Republic of China*, enacted in 1990 and amended in 2010, states that "Works of Chinese citizens, juridical persons or other organizations, whether published or not, shall enjoy copyright in accordance with this Law." Also, Article 3 of *the Civil Procedure Law of the People's Republic of China*, enacted in 1991 and amended in 2017, states, "The provisions of this Law shall apply to civil actions accepted by a people's court regarding property or personal relationships between citizens, between juridical persons, between other organizations or between citizens and juridical persons, citizens, and other organizations or juridical persons and other organizations."

18 See Articles 102 to 108 of the General Provisions.

19 Generally, in Japan, organs (機関) are components of a juridical person and not independent legal persons in themselves. On the other hand, in China, the concept of an organ (机关) does not necessarily mean the organization is under the jurisdiction of a juridical person. Therefore, while the term "state organ juridical persons" sounds like a contradiction in Japan, it is not the case with China.

20 S. Li (ed.) (2017:301–302).

21 S. Li (ed.) (2017:304).

22 As the body text illustrates, there is an idea that state organs need a juridical personality to engage in civil conduct in China. Whether this idea relates to socialist thought needs to be analyzed in the future.

23 Ge (2007) points out that although China's legislation and jurisprudence adopt many concepts and theories from Civil Law, they have misunderstood juridical persons as a concept only used for civil persons, and as a result, failed to explain administrative persons by using the concept.

24 However, the concept of an administrative person (行政主体) in China has some mutual features with the concept of a juridical person. It is generally said that an administrative person can act under its own name and take responsibility independently (see Jiang (ed.) (2016:85)). This is similar to juridical persons that have the ability to act under their name and to take responsibility independently. Regarding differences between the concept of an administrative person in Japan and in China, see Matsumoto (2019:392 ff).

25 The *Organization Law of the Villagers' Committees of the People's Republic of China*, enacted in 1987 and amended in 2018.

26 It is not clear from the law who the members of a villagers' committee are. The Organization Law uses the term "成员," which is usually translated as "members" in English, to express the commissioners. However, villagers are expressed as agents in the village in Article 2 of the law as cited in the body text, and it is the villagers who elect a villagers' committee. Thus, this paper interprets the members of a villagers' committee as a juridical person as being the villagers.

27 Article 11 of the *Land Administration Law of the People's Republic of China*, enacted in 1986 and amended in 2019, states that "villagers' committees operate and manage the collectively owned land in the village."

28 Article 12 of the *Community Correction Law of the People's Republic of China*, enacted in 2019, states that "villagers' committees shall assist community correction institutions in effectively completing the community correction work according to the law."

29 Zhang (2016).

30 As far as I have been able to find, this point is not really discussed even among Chinese scholars.

31 See note 26.

32 About the reason why unincorporated organizations are provided as a civil person in General Provisions, Jianguo Li (a Vice Chairman of the Standing Committee of the National People's Congress) explains that "accompanied with the development of economic society in our country, many organizations that do not have juridical personality engage in civil conduct under its name in reality. To give them a status of civil person will contribute to the expansion of their activities and also fits other laws" (J. Li (2017)).

33 Article 102 of the General Provisions gives individual proprietorships (个人独资企业), partnerships (合伙企业) and professional service providers (不具有法人资格的专业服务机构) as examples of unincorporated organizations. The *Partnership Enterprise Law of the People's Republic of China*, enacted in 1997 and amended in 2007, provides for partnership enterprise; this law refers to the "general partnership enterprises" formed by general partners and "limited liability partnership enterprises" formed by general partners and limited partners. General partners shall bear unlimited joint and several liabilities for the debts of the partnership enterprise, while limited partners bear the liabilities for its debts to the extent of their capital contributions (Article 2). Wholly state-funded companies, state-owned companies, listed companies, public-welfare-oriented public institutions or social organizations may not become a general partner (Article 3).

34 The provision related to villagers' committees is positioned in "Chapter III The Structure of the State" of the Constitution.

35 S. Li (ed.) (2017:314) argues that "villagers' committees . . . are organizations of self-government at the grassroots level whose main job is to manage public affairs of the village and carry out some administrative works delegated by the government. They are not designed to be pure civil persons."

36 In general, China's court precedents and jurisprudence exceptionally regard a villagers' committee as an "administrative person" when there is an authorization by laws, administrative regulations (法规) or ministerial rules (规章), and otherwise regard it as a "civil person." However, as this argument is based on provisions about a proper defendant ("standing to be sued") in Administrative Litigation Law, whether this criterion can also be used any time other than the situation of litigation seems to be up for debate. See Article 2 and Article 26 of the *Administrative Litigation Law of the People's Republic of China*, enacted in 1898 and amended in 2017.

37 See Du (ed.) (2017:257) and "*Report on Modification of 'General Provisions of the Civil Law of the People's Republic of China (draft)' by the Law Committee of the National People's Congress*, (全国人民代表大会法律委员会关于《中华人民共和国民法总则(草案)》修改情况的汇报)," promulgated by the 25th meeting of the Standing Committee of the 12th National People's Congress, December 19, 2016.

38 S. Li (ed.) (2017:322–323).

39 Tan and Ying (2017).

40 Yang (2017:236).

41 S. Li (ed.) (2017:157).

42 Article 10 of the Constitution.

43 S. Li (ed.) (2017:314) points out that the replacement of rural collective economic organizations' functions by a villagers' committee has led to outflows of collective assets and corruption by making the difference between these two organizations unclear and creating conditions under which a few leaders control all the assets.

References

Du, Tao (杜涛) (ed.), *Birth of General Provisions of the Civil Law* (民法总则的诞生), Peking University Press, 2017, p. 257.

Gao, Shuyi (高树异), Actual Effects of Juridical Person System on the Four Modernizations in China (法人制度对我国实行四化的现实意义), *Chinese Journal of Law*, 1980 (No. 4), pp. 15–17.

Ge, Yunsong (葛云松), Restructuring the Theories of Juristic Person and Person of Administration (法人与行政主体理论的再探讨), *China Legal Science*, 2007 (No. 3), pp. 77–99.

Hoshino, Eiichi (星野英一), Hasui, Yoshinori (蓮井良憲), Ueda, Tetsuichiro (上田徹一郎), Yamaguchi, Masaru (山口賢), and Ueyanagi, Katsuro (上柳克郎), Theory of Juridical Person (Joint Symposium of Civil and Commercial Law) (法人論（民商合同シンポジウム）), *Private Law*, 1971 (No. 33), pp. 3–69.

Iwai, Katsuhito (岩井克人), *What Will Happen to Companies from Now?* (会社はこれからどうなるのか), Heibonsha, 2003, p. 64.

Jiang, Mingan (姜明安) (ed.), *Administrative Law and Administrative Litigation Law* (6th edition) (行政法与行政诉讼法 [第六版]), Peking University Press, 2016, p. 85.

Li, Jianguo (李建国), An Explanation on 'General Provisions of the Civil Law of the People's Republic of China (Draft)': The 5th session of the 12th National People's Congress on March 8, 2017 (关于《中华人民共和国民法总则(草案)》的说明 – 2017年3月8日在第十二届全国人民代表大会第五次会议上) (www.npc.gov.cn/zgrdw/npc/xinwen/2017-03/09/content_2013899.htm; last accessed on September 8, 2020)

Li, Shishi (李适时) (ed.), *Explanation on General Provisions of the Civil Law of the People's Republic of China* (中华人民共和国民法总则释义), Law Press China, 2017.

Liang, Huixing (梁慧星), Discussing Enterprise Juridical Persons and their Property Rights (论企业法人与企业法人所有权), *Chinese Journal of Law*, 1981 (No. 1), pp. 26–31.

Matsudo, Hiroshi (松戸浩), Diversification of 'Administrative Actors' and its Integration by the Courts (1) (2) (「行政主体」の多様化と裁判所による統制（一）（二・完)), *St. Paul's Review of Law and Politics*, 2017 (Vol. 95), pp. 45–73, 2018 (Vol. 99), pp. 26–62.

Matsumoto, Mikiko (松本未希子), Legal Characteristics of 'The Primary Mass Organization of Self-Government' in China: The Public/Private Divide by the Theory of 'Administrative Bodies'? (中国における「基層群衆性自治組織」の法的性質ー「行政主体」論による公私の二分化？), *Kobe Law Journal*, 2019 (Vol. 69, No. 2), pp. 371–407.

Report on Modification of 'General Provisions of the Civil Law of the People's Republic of China (draft)' by the Law Committee of the National People's Congress (全国人民代表大会法律委员会关于《中华人民共和国民法总则(草案)》修改情况的汇报) promulgated by the 25th meeting of the Standing Committee of the 12th National People's Congress, December 19, 2016.

Takamizawa, Osamu (高見澤磨) and Suzuki, Ken (鈴木賢) (eds.), *Vital Issues in Chinese Law* (要説中国法), University of Tokyo Press, 2017, p. 124.

Tan, Qiping (谭启平) & Ying, Jianjun (应建均), Examination on issues of 'Special Juridical Person' ('特别法人'问题追问), *Journal of Social Sciences*, 2017 (No. 3), pp. 82–91.

Wang, Liming (王利明), *Civil Law* (7th edition) (民法（第七版), China Renmin University Press, 2018, p. 61.

Yamamoto, Keizo (山本敬三), *Civil Law Lecture I General Provisions* (3rd edition) (民法講義I総則(第三版)), Yuhikaku Publishing, 2017, pp. 450–451.

Yamamoto, Ryuji (山本隆司), Actors in Administration (行政の主体), in Isobe, Tsutomu (磯部力), Kobayakawa, Mitsuo (小早川光郎), and Shibaike, Yoshikazu (芝池義一) (eds.), *New Framework of Administrative Law I* (行政法の新構想I), Yuhikaku Publishing, 2011, pp. 89–113.

Yang, Lixin (杨立新), *General Provisions of the Civil Law: Stories and Difficult Problems behind the Provisions* (民法总则－条文背后的故事与难题) Law Press China, 2017, p. 236.

Zhang, Cong (张璁), The Standing Committee of the National People's Congress Discussed the Draft of General Provisions of the Civil Law: Adding a Category of Special Juridical Person to a Chapter of Juridical Persons (全国人大常委会审议民法总则草案：法人一章增加特别法人类别), *People's Daily*, December 20, 2016, 4th edition.

Part IV

Land law toward alternative "development"

13 State-centered land regimes and the struggle for customary land in East Asia

John Gillespie

1 Introduction

This chapter explores how East Asian states integrate customary claims[1] to land into statutory land tenure systems. Studies show that state-centered land systems, which connect legal recognition of property rights to state territorial authority, often fragment and subordinate customary possessory claims to land (Fu and Gillespie 2014; Sikor 2004; Upham 2018: chpts 1 & 2). Attempts by states to project their sovereignty over farmland results in a diverse range of highly contested land disputes. This chapter investigates this phenomenon by comparing two types of statutory land systems, title by registration in Cambodia and socialist land use rights in China. It explores whether state-centered property law creates legal understandings of property that conflict with the social reality of customary land practices.

Land law reforms in East Asia have generated paradoxical outcomes. Instead of promoting uniformity, order and predictability, their stated objectives, they have often generated fragmentation and disputation (see authors in this volume). Land claims and state property rights often conflict, producing unpredictable and multilayered disputes. As the authors in this volume demonstrate, highly ambiguous and contested patterns of land rights persist in many East Asian countries long after land reform programs have supposedly harmonized land tenure rights. Adding to the fragmentation, courts and administrative agencies struggle to use land laws to find lasting solutions to land disputes. Far from state-centered land law dominating, no single actor or set of regulatory traditions can gain the upper hand in many land disputes.

State-centered land law – typified but not limited to Torrens systems – stipulates that private land-ownership (or land use rights) arise by grant from the state. They tie legal understandings of property to the projection of state territorial authority (Singer 2009; Sikor and Müller 2009). Land laws enable governments to claim eminent domain and draw legal boundaries around the resources and people within particular territories. Governments can use land law to legally fence off common or customary property, turning landholders into trespassers. Much has been written about the use of Torrens systems in East Asia to undermine customary claims to land by privileging registered over unregistered interests (see Yuka

DOI: 10.4324/9781003170600-17

Kaneko and Issei Sakano in this volume; also see Upham 2018: chpt 3). This chapter argues that state-centered land laws in socialist Asia (China, Vietnam and Laos) have produced similar results.

This chapter investigates a core question: How do landholders assert possessory claims to land? Franz von Benda-Beckmann and Keebet von Benda-Beckmann (2010: 175) observed that many farming communities in East Asia "treat property relations as only one aspect or strand of more encompassing categorical relationships, in which kinship relations, property relations and relations of political authority are largely fused in a many-stranded or multiplex relationship." These possessory rights can be recognized and enforced as land rights by customary societies or by governments through law (Rose 1994; Sikor and Lund 2009). This tension between state and customary recognition of land right raises two research questions: (1) Do state-centered laws provide meaningful procedures that recognize customary rights to land? (2) Do state institutions recognize and support the customary institutions that determine who obtains land rights and how land rights are transacted and protected?

In many East Asian societies, multiple institutions (state and non-state) compete to define and enforce property rights and determine access to land. To understand this competition between different land tenure systems, we need to investigate the quality of the land rights that people acquire and the effectiveness of the institution(s) that guarantee them.

2 Economic explanations for title by registration

International reform projects during the last four decades have invoked economic growth and social stability to justify the introduction of land titling projects (Sikor and Müller 2009). Formal legal titles are assumed to promote optimal levels of agricultural productivity that increase living standards and benefit societies. Klaus Deninger (2003: 3), a senior land economist at the World Bank, summarized this approach:

> [T]he benefits of well-defined and secure property rights and the advantages of public provision of such rights have, over history, led virtually all economically and politically advanced societies to establish state-managed systems for regulating land ownership and land transfers.

The connection between economic development and land titles is not new. European colonial powers during the 19th century imported title by registration systems into Indochina and Indonesia to encourage industrial agriculture (Benton and Ross (eds) 2013). Reflecting this development objective, the French Colonial Inspector of Native Affairs in Vietnam opined that:

> The establishment of property ownership will be the prosperity of the country: the rights to sell, to buy, to mortgage – to execute all the conveyances of

> property will augment the country's wealth in circulating the capital which is now frozen by many cultivators.
>
> (Bassford 1984: 129–130)

Reprising colonial enthusiasm for land titling, international donors such as the World Bank have more recently promoted robust private property rights throughout the developing world (Sikor and Müller 2009; Upham 2018). Donors were influenced by Harold Demsetz's (1967) assertion that private property is the solution for resource tragedies (also see Upham 2018: chpt 2). According to Demsetz, the privatization of property offsets negative social costs, such as exclusion from natural resources, because the individual pursuit of self-interest increases overall social welfare. This assumption that societies are better off when people can reap what they sow dates back to the classical economics of Adam Smith. The World Bank has added the neoliberal economic objective of minimizing government oversight and maximizing Coasian (1960) bargaining between private property holders.

The central economic justification for title by registration is that state recognition provides assurances that investors can benefit from returns on their investments (Sikor and Müller 2009; Upham 2018: chpt 2). State-backed titles enable investors to divert resources from defending property claims to investing in the productive use of land. They are also thought to provide collateral to secure borrowings that might fund land and other productive investments. In theory, virtuous investment cycles emerge because increasing land values provide further incentives for investment and exchange.

From a developmental perspective, effective property rights need to adapt to political processes, technological innovation and most importantly to economic pressures. The standard economic explanation for adaption and variation is that title by registration regimes lower transaction costs so that potential gains in value can be realized (Merill 2002). Demsetz postulated that state-administered land titles lower transaction costs by reducing information costs about the rules governing property (Merrill and Smith 2011). He argued that because rules about property must be communicated to a large and diverse audience, this information must clearly identify the nature and extent of property rights so that potential violators can avoid the consequences of infringement. Title by registration, which is the simplest form of exclusionary entitlement, is supposed to provide the clearest message about who is entitled to benefit from property. This theory further postulates that information costs are reduced if land laws grant states exclusive power through registration to confer land-ownership. Following Demsetz, international donor programs urged developing countries to upgrade their land regulation systems by replacing customary informality with land titling systems.

3 Torrens system land titling in Cambodia

The World Bank's land titling program in Cambodia reveals shortcomings in Demsetzian economic theory. Enacted in 2001, the Cambodian Land Law 2001[2] created "hard edged" property rights to displace collective and customary property ownership. The program adopted Hernando de Soto's (2000) metaphor of a bell jar to explain the difference between registered and unregistered land rights. Those within the bell jar enjoyed state protection of their registered property rights, while those outside the bell jar must fend for themselves. The assumption underlying this metaphor is that state regulators and courts would protect land titles more effectively than preexisting customary land systems.

The Cambodian Land Law 2001[3] created a default system in which land that belonged to no one was deemed to belong to the state (see Issei Sakano in this volume for details) (also see Upham 2018: chpt 6). This meant that only the state could create land-ownership rights – an eminent domain policy that displaced preexisting customary land rights.[4] Further strengthening state power over land, the Law provided that legal rights in land could only be conferred by registration of title. Landholders were required to apply for certificates of possessory rights before they could convert informal customary claims over land into ownership.[5] The state only recognized registered land titles (and other state entitlements such as economic land concessions). By equating property rights to state sovereignty, the Law delegitimized rights to land (such as customary rights) that resided beyond the administrative systems of the state.

Land titling reforms dispossessed large number of Cambodian farmers who claimed possessory rights to land (Springer 2013; Diepart 2015). Although colonization, and especially forced collectivization under the Khmer Rouge, caused widespread social disruption, in many areas access to land remained socially negotiated between households and village/commune leaders (Luco 2002). Most farmers continued to regard appropriation "by the plough" as a legitimate mode of land acquisition. Customary claims to land were not confined to rural areas. A UN-Habitat survey found that approximately 75 percent of unregistered landholders in Phnom Penh thought they were the legal owners of their land (United Nations Human Settlements Programme 2003).

Tensions between land titling and possessory claims to land are illustrated by the Koh Kong sugar dispute. In August 2006, the Ministry of Agriculture, Forestry and Fisheries granted two Economic Land Concessions (ELCs) of nearly 10,000 hectares in Koh Kong Province to two Cambodian companies – Koh Kong Plantation Co. Ltd. (KKPT) and Koh Kong Sugar Industry Co. Ltd (Hodal 2013; Rob 2013). Through their foreign owners, the companies supplied sugar to Tate and Lyle Sugar – a British multinational.

To clear the land for the ELCs, the government forcibly dispossessed 465 families who had farmed the land for generations. The farmers argued the ELCs were illegal and should be canceled. They held well-documented possession rights, which should have made them eligible for land title certificates. According to Article 243 of the Cambodian Civil Code 2011, ownership titles are granted where farmers can prove continuous occupation for more than five years. The farmers further claimed that the ELCs did not follow the procedures that required public consultation for social impact assessments and resettlement plans for dispossessed landholders. According to some farmers: "When the company came in May 2006, they bulldozed without consultation or any environmental impact assessment. . . . They bulldozed the fields and streams. They shot our animals" (Hodal 2013).

After years of legal and extralegal protests, only 23 of the original 465 families had received compensation. Having exhausted domestic avenues of complaint, in 2013 farmers filed a civil lawsuit against Tate and Lyle Sugar in the U.K. High Court (commercial division).[6] The statement of claim alleged that Tate and Lyle Sugar purchased sugar that was produced on land that was wrongfully taken from farmers. Farmers secured an out-of-court settlement that implicitly recognized their customary claims to the land. However, years later in 2019, they claimed that Tate and Lyle Sugar had not yet paid them the compensation promised (Sokun 2019).

Rather than improving land tenure security for ordinary Cambodians, a key aim of the drafters (Biddulph 2014), the Land Law 2001 gave the government a legal basis for displacing customary claims to land (Diepart 2015). Over the last two decades, the government has dispossessed more than 500,000 farmers and allocated 2.2 million hectares of fertile agricultural land constituting 10 percent of the landmass to domestic and foreign investors (Human Rights Watch 2015). The state institutions that were supposed to protect the farmers instead made dispossession possible by supporting land clearing for wealthy investors. Although it is estimated that approximately 75 percent of land allotments have been registered (see Issei Sakano in this volume), preferential land registration has resulted in less than 1 percent of the population owning more than 30 percent of the privately held land. Since the Land Law 2001 was enacted, dispossessions, landless farmers and rural poverty have steadily increased (Brinkley 2013; Licadho 2015).[7] Cambodia is now one of the most economically unequal societies in East Asia.

Over the last two decades, the governing elite in Cambodia have used the Land Law 2001 to territorialize claims over farmland and forests and accumulate resources primarily for their own benefit. Land reforms have denied farmers access to reliable and cost-effective processes that might have converted possessory customary land claims into land titles. Rather than facilitating private markets, which was the economic justification for land titling, state officials used the Land Law to maximize elite control over land. By giving authorities exclusive powers to grant rights to land, the reforms inserted the government into the lives of the people. Land reform and resettlement affirmed the authority of government institutions and thus formed a central aspect of state formation in Cambodia.

4 Socialist land rights reforms

Following economic reforms during the 1980s, socialist countries in East Asia (China, Vietnam and Laos)[8] incrementally recognized private land use rights. They ignored advice from international donors to adopt Torrens Law systems and instead developed their own unique land tenure systems (Lund 2011; Chen 2014; Le and Quang 2014). Party leaders created hybrid land laws that retained some features of orthodox socialist land law systems, such as state ownership of land, but also extended private land use rights to citizens and corporations. They accepted the economic argument that long-term growth depends on the possibility of allocating property rights to those who have the ability to put resources to more effective use. However, party leaders rejected calls to restore private landownership as a betrayal of the revolution.

Socialist land tenure systems lack the hard-edged legal distinctions between registered and unregistered land found in Torrrens systems, in theory allowing more latitude for farmers to assert customary rights. In practice, farmers in socialist Asia have struggled to assert possessory rights against the state (Gillespie 2017; Upham 2018).

Most societies impose restrictions on state sovereignty over land because private and community property would have little meaning if governments could expropriate or exclude customary rights at will (Upham 2018: chpt 2). How such restrictions are calibrated depends on the political treatment of property rights. At one end of the spectrum, Torrens systems create a regulatory space for registered land titles that is largely, although never entirely, free of state interference. At the other end of the regulatory spectrum, socialist land systems promote state management and planning and discourage the enforcement of private (and especially customary) land rights against the state.

Asian socialist legal systems absorbed a highly positivist Soviet understanding of law that regarded traditional customs as a cultural residue that progressive socialism should sweep aside (Clarke 2014; Gillespie and Tran 2021). Marxist–Leninist theory locates law and customs in the "superstructure" and, as a consequence, the interaction between social customs and law is considered inappropriate. Land law systems in China, Vietnam and Laos reflect this socialist antipathy toward customary land rights.

Chinese land reforms illustrate this tension between state ownership of land and customary rights (Clarke 2014). Following Deng Xiaoping's rise to power in 1978, China searched for ways to grant farmers more autonomy in using agricultural land. A series of reforms, beginning with the household responsibility system (HRS) was launched in 1978. Under the HRS, villages owned the land and allocated contractual rights that allowed farmers to work and profit from agricultural land (Shitong 2016). The HRS ended decades of state collectivization in favor of private contractual rights. Land use rights remained with the village authorities, giving them significant management powers over land use and disposal. Attempts to individualize rights over agricultural land in the Land Law 2007 were blocked, ensuring the retention of strong state management powers over rural land. Contrasting with the tight state control over rural land, in 1990 the State Council legalized the transfer of 70-year urban land use rights among private citizens – opening the way for private urban land markets (Clarke 2014).

Rapid economic development in China has converted large areas of farmland into infrastructure and housing projects. To make this development possible, the Standing Committee of the National Party Congress issued a resolution titled "Requisition of Land by the State for Construction." It empowered local and national governments to requisition agricultural land (Shitong 2016). The 1982

Constitution was amended in 2004 to allow the state "in the public interest and in accordance with the provisions of law, to expropriate or requisition land for its use" (Zhou and Banik 2014: 257). Requisition powers were further strengthened by the Land Administration Law in 2004, which confirmed that farmers leased but did not own land. This ensured that farmers could not acquire propriety interests in land that were enforceable against the state.

In what Annette Kim (2004) termed fiscal socialism, local governments used their requisitioning powers to acquire inexpensive rural land that could be profitably developed. As the Chinese land boom gained momentum during the 1990s and 2000s, the incentive for local governments to requisition rural land increased. It is estimated that 1.5 million farmers lost their land annually in the last decade, and the number is expected to reach 100 million by the end of 2020 (Zhu 2015).

Farmers in China have responded to compulsory land acquisitions by engaging in "rightful resistance" (O'Brien and Li 2006; Pils 2014). This involves the use of both legal and extralegal means to protect customary and contractual land rights. Many disputes reveal conflicts in the ways the state and farmers conceptualize land tenure rights. The state treats land as a commodity in the service of the national economy. Whereas for many Chinese farmers, property relations remain embedded in relational and/or spiritual practices and have not yet re-embedded into legal relationships (Pils 2014). Traditional farming communities remain a common form of social organization in rural China, Vietnam and Laos, and community structures continue to shape the degree to which state law can provide a useful framework for resolving disputes.

Chinese farmers have creatively used state institutions, such as petitioning and litigating to press their claims. It is estimated that 70 percent of China's land petition cases are related to public land acquisition (Liu and Sun 2014). A bourgeoning literature dealing with land-taking disputes in Chinese courts and grand mediation (*da tiaojie*) reveals the difficulties that citizens have in challenging the state (He 2014; Pils 2014). After reviewing more than 200 land-taking decisions in China between 2004 and 2011, Cheng Jie (2014) found that judgments closely followed government policies. Judges were placed in a difficult position:

> on one side, a powerful government agency may have demolished houses or occupied land for policy purposes; on the other side are a group of people who are angry, helpless, but ready to demonstrate in front of the court if the court's decision is considered unfair.
>
> (Cheng 2014: 107)

She concluded that courts were unsympathetic toward individual land claims and routinely interpreted the land law to favor the state. Land users have fared no better in Vietnamese courts, which rarely (if ever) find against the state in land-taking cases (Gillespie 2017).

Against this backdrop of institutional failure, aggrieved land users are turning in increasing numbers to more confrontational strategies to improve their bargaining position. As Xin He (2014: 202) concluded, "when litigation is conducted with coordinated demonstrations, the dynamics take a drastically different form." Extralegal protests have proved more effective than petitions and litigation in asserting customary rights against the state. For example, nail house protests involve farmers who locked themselves into their houses to prevent eviction. A prominent illustration of this method of resistance occurred in 2007 when Wu Ping and Yang Wu bolted their doors and resisted bulldozers working to demolish their home (Shin 2017). After weeks of confrontation that attracted widespread media attention, the couple gained more compensation but were unable to prevent eviction. The state refused to recognize possessory claims to the land.

Another example where public protest forced the state to reconsider the appropriation of customary land without compensation occurred in the southern village of Wukan. During 2011, villagers forced the entire local government and police out of the village to protest farmland that was sold to developers without just compensation (He and Xue 2014). In China, as in other socialist countries, the state is not required to base compensation on market values.

Mass protests in Wukan eventually forced the state to reverse land sales, even though they had been carried out in accordance with the Land Administration Law 2004. Exercising rights under grassroots democracy, villagers dismissed local officials and then elected new officials who agreed to respect customary claims to the farmland (Fu 2014). The protests were only partially successful in preventing further land takings, and the dispute reemerged in 2016 when local authorities once again sold village land without compensation.

In most cases, public protest and rightful resistance do not produce lasting recognition of customary claims to farmland. Officials respond by increasing compensation and/or suspending land takings but do not change the underlying legal and policy settings. What has changed over time is the quality of the land tenure rights conveyed to citizens. Urban land use rights now resemble private ownership in many respects. Amendments to the Land Administration Law 2020 now allow some farmers the right to transfer farmland – a significant change from past land policies. However, this right is subject to the veto of local village authorities and does not recognize customary claims to land.

Widespread public resistance to state-centered land laws in socialist Asia undermines the official line that the state is the sole institution determining and enforcing property rights (Kerkvliet 2019: chpt 2). In practice, property rights are not autonomous legal ideals, but rather closely tied to a broad range of political, social and economic forces. This story of property rights is very different from state-centered narratives that place laws and state officials in charge of defining rights and duties. It shows that rights in land are subject to a larger contestation over how land should be valued and who should exercise authority over land. To understand how property rights are conceptualized in everyday practice, it is necessary to search well search beyond legal texts and official pronouncements.

5 Conclusion

This chapter began by posing two questions about state recognition of possessory claims to land: Do state-centered laws provide meaningful procedures that recognize customary rights to land, and do state institutions recognize the customary institutions that determine who obtains land rights and how land rights are transacted and protected? The review of land law in Cambodia and China reveals the importance of regulatory institutions that support farmers in asserting customary land claims against the state. Farmers in the first instance require processes that enable them to convert customary claims into formal land rights. Absent a "rule of law" where legal institutions are willing to enforce private land claims against the state, conversion processes are most likely to work in favor of farmers where the state extends political recognition to the non-state institutions that generate customary land rights.

The Cambodian Land Law 2001 provided pathways for farmers to convert possessory claims into legal titles. Problems occurred when farmers attempted to gather evidence of possession and convince government officials to issue land titles. Cambodia lacks legal institutions that are willing to enforce possessory land rights against the state. Farmers in China face the additional hurdles of a land law that does not recognize customary land rights and a polity that is hostile to non-state institutions that generate such rights. In this unsupportive legal environment, farmers in both countries found extralegal avenues, especially public protest, the most effective way to assert their customary claims.

In Cambodia, the hard-edged legal distinctions between registered and unregistered land in the Torrens system worked against the farmers. Not only did the creation of land titles over farming land extinguish any residual legal rights to possession, it also disrupted any social obligations developers might have owed to dispossessed farmers. In contrast, the "fuzzy" land tenure rights in China gave farmers room to maneuver with state officials (Verdery 1999). For example, farmers persuaded local officials to treat property rights as contingent entitlements rather than rigid legal categories (Shitong 2016; Gillespie, 2017). Officials in some cases responded by temporarily suspending state law and flexibly accommodating community perceptions about just access to land and compensation (Hurst, Liu and Tao 2010). However, these informal processes were context specific and offered few possibilities of scaling-up into state recognition of customary land rights (see generally Gillespie 2014).

The findings suggest that land law regimes that give the state exclusive power over land disadvantage small-scale farmers. For example, until recently farmers in Indonesia could not claim customary land rights. For decades, Indonesia applied the Basic Agrarian Law 1960 and Basic Forestry Law 1967 to claim "unused" forestland for the state – a legal prerogative that abrogated long-standing customary (*adat*) land rights (see Rudy Lukman in this volume). In 2013, the Constitutional Court ruled in favor of the Alliance of Indigenous Peoples of the Archipelago by grating them customary rights over "unused" forest land (Butt 2014). This landmark decision found that "[m]embers of customary societies have the right to clear forests belonging to them and use the land to fulfil their personal and family needs."[9] It deemed the state's eminent domain claim to unused forestland unconstitutional.

Although there are limits to the practical effectiveness of this constitutional ruling, it recognizes a form of legal pluralism in which state-centered land laws coexist with customary land tenure. How legal pluralism might work in other East Asian countries will depend on the nature of customary land rights. For example, some ethnic minority communities in China and Southeast Asia have retained "living customary laws" with functioning institutions that could regulate land tenure independently from the state-centered land system (Michaud 2009). In other areas, farmers assert possessory rights based on traditional land systems that have been completely or partially displaced by state and market institutions. In these circumstances, the state would have more say in recognizing and protecting customary claims. This observation returns our focus to the underlying political nature of land law. Unless states are willing to extend property rights to customary claims, formal and informal institutions are unlikely to offer much support to farmers.

Notes

1 Customary law refers to the non-state norms and practices that shape the accepted and expected conduct in discrete communities. See Merry (1988) and Zenker and Hoehne (2018).

2 Land Law promulgated by Royal Kram No. NS/RKM/0801/14 dated August 30, 2001. See World Bank 2007 Cambodia rural sector note and business plan, World Bank: East-Asia and Pacific Region, Sustainable Development Department. See generally Hel, Chamroeun 2012, "Introduction to the Land Law of Cambodia," in Hor Peng, Kong Phallack and Jörg Menzel (eds.) *Introduction to Cambodian Law* (Phnom Penh, Konrad-Adnauer Stiftung); Frank Upham, 2018. *The Great Property Fallacy: Theory, Reality, and Growth in Developing Countries* Cambridge: Cambridge University, chapter 6.

3 The Law on Application of the Civil Code 2011 integrated the most substantive provisions of the 2001 Land Law into the Civil Code.

4 Land Law of 2001, art. 30. The rule of "special acquisitive possession" requires possession that is unambiguous, nonviolent, notorious to the public and in good faith: (arts. 32, 38). See Springer (2013).

5 Art. 242 Civil Code Cambodia 2011.

6 The High Court of Justice (U.K.), Queen's Bench Division, Commercial Court Claim No. 2013 Folio 451 Between Song Mao and (1) Tate and Lyle Industries Limited (2) T & L Sugars Limited, Defence and Counterclaim of the First and Second Defendants, available at www.business-humanrights.org.

7 According to data collated by the Cambodian Human Rights and Development Association (ADHOC), more than 770,000 Cambodians have been affected by land grabs and resulting conflicts over natural resources (See ADHOC 2014).

8 Land Law in Laos differs from China and Vietnam as "people's ownership" has become "community ownership" and the Land Law provides for title by registration. North Korea has not reformed its land regime and is consequently not included in this study.

9 Court Ruling No. 35/PUU-IX/2012, available at http://Www.Forestpeoples.Org/Sites/Fpp/Files/News/2013/05/Putusan_Sidang_35%20PUU%20 2012-Kehutanan-Telah%20ucap%2016%20Mei%202013.Pdf.

References

ADHOC (2014). "Land Situation in Cambodia 2013" Cambodian Human Rights and Development Association (ADHOC).

Bassford, Jean Louis (1984) *Land Development Policy in Cochin China Under the French (1865–1925)*, University Michigan Microfilms.

Benda-Beckmann, Franz von and Keebet von Benda-Beckmann (2010) "Multiple Embeddedness and Systemic Implications: Struggles over Natural Resources in Minangkabau since the Reformasi" *Asian Journal of Social Science* vol. 38, pp. 172–186.

Benton, Lauren and Richard J. Ross (eds) (2013) *Legal Pluralism and Empires, 1500–1850*, New York University Press.

Biddulph, Robin (2014) *Cambodia's Land Management and Administration Project*, WIDER Working Paper 2014/086, UNU-WIDER.

Brinkley, Joel (2013) "Private Property Public Greed Cambodia" *Politico*, June 5, www.politico.com/story/2013/05/lawyer-works-to-put-end-to-land-grabbing-90985.html.

Butt, Simon (2014) "Traditional Land Rights Before the Indonesian Constitutional Court" *Law, Environment and Development Journal* vol. 10, no. 1, pp. 57–69, www.lead-journal.org/content/14057.pdf.

Chen, Lei (2014) "Legal and Institutional Analysis of Land Expropriation in China" in Hualing Fu and John Gillespie (eds), *Resolving Land Disputes in East Asia: Exploring the Limits of Law*, Cambridge University Press, pp. 59–85.

Cheng, Jie (2014) "Judicial Role in Land-Taking Cases" in Hualing Fu and John Gillespie (eds), *Exploring the Limits of Law in Resolving Land Disputes in East Asia*, Cambridge University Press, pp. 86–114.

Clarke, Donald (2014) "China's Stealth Urban Land Revolution" *American Journal of Comparative Law* vol. 62, no. 2, pp. 323–366.

Coarse, Ronald (1960) "The Problem of Social Cost" *Journal Law and Economics* vol. 3, pp. 1–44.

Davies, Rob (2013) "Cambodia Farmers Launch Action Against Tate & Lyle" April 12, www.thisismoney.co.uk/money/markets/article-2308269/Cambodia-farmers-launch-action-Tate – Lyle.html.

Demsetz, Harold (1967) "Toward a Theory of Property Rights" *American Economic Review* vol. 57, no. 2, pp. 347–359.

Deninger, Klaus (2003). *Land Policies for Growth and Poverty Reduction*, World Bank Policy Research Report, World Bank Group.

de Soto, Hernando (2000) *The Mystery of Capitalism: Why Capitalism Triumphs in the West and Fails Everywhere Else*, Black Swan, pp. 47–62.

Diepart, Jean-Christophe (2015) *The Fragmentation of Land Tenure Systems in Cambodia: Peasants and the Formalization of Land Rights*, Paris: Country Profile No 6 Cambodia, The Technical Committee on Land Tenure and Development, pp. 6–7.

Fu, Hualing (2014) "What Does Wukan Offer: Land-taking and Dispute Resolution" in Hualing Fu and John Gillespie (eds), *Resolving Land Disputes in East Asia: Exploring the Limits of Law*, Cambridge University Press, pp. 173–193.

Fu, Hualing and John Gillespie (eds) (2014) *Resolving Land Disputes in East Asia: Exploring the Limits of the Law*, Cambridge University Press.

Gillespie, John (2014) "Social Consensus and the Meta-Regulation of Land-Taking Disputes in Vietnam" *Journal of Vietnamese Studies* vol. 9, no. 3, pp. 91–124.

Gillespie, John (2017) "Transforming Land-Taking Disputes in Socialist Asia: Engaging an Authoritarian State" *Law & Policy* vol. 39, no. 3, pp. 280–303.

Gillespie, John and Hong Quang Tran (2021) "Legal Pluralism and the Struggle for Customary Law in the Vietnamese Highlands" *American Journal of Comparative Law* vol. 69, no. 4.

He, Shenjing and Desheng Xue (2014) "Identity Building and Communal Resistance against Landgrabs in Wukan Village, China" *Current Anthropology* vol. 55, no. s9, pp. 126–137.

He, Xin (2014) "Protest-Supported Housing Demolition Litigation and Social Change in China" in John Gillespie and Hualing Fu (eds), *Resolving Land Disputes in East Asia: Exploring the Limits of the Law*, Cambridge University Press, pp. 194–221.

Hodal, Kate (2013) "Cambodia's Sugar Rush Leaves Farmers Feeling Bitter at 'Land Grab'" *The Guardian*, July 10, www.theguardian.com/world/2013/jul/09/cambodia-sugar-land-grab-claims.

Human Rights Watch (2015) *World Report: Cambodia*, www.hrw.org/world-report/2015/country-chapters/cambodia.

Hurst, William, Mingxing Liu and Ran Tao (2010) "Reassessing Collective Petitioning in Rural China: Civic Engagement, Extra-State Violence, and Regional Variation" Paper Presented at the American Political Studies Association, Toronto.

Kerkvliet, Ben (2019) *Speaking Out in Vietnam: Public Political Criticism in a Communist Party Ruled Nation*, Cornell University Press, chapter 2.

Kim, Annette (2004) "A Market Without the 'Right' Property Rights: Ho Chi Minh City, Vietnam's Newly-Emerged Private Real Estate Market" *Economics of Transition* vol. 12, no. 2, pp. 275–305.

Le, Toan and Nguyen Hung Quang (2014) "An Historical Overview of Vietnamese Land Law and Dispute Resolution" in Hualing Fu and John Gillespie (eds), *Resolving Land Disputes in East Asia: Exploring the Limits of Law*, Cambridge University Press, pp. 275–290.

Licadho (2015) "Renewed Surge in Land Disputes Must be Addressed Not Denied" *Licadho*, www.licadho-cambodia.org/pressrelease.php?perm=374.

Liu, W. and M.X. Sun (2014) "The Occurrence and Management of Mass Disturbance Concerning Land Acquisition" *Public Management Journal* vol. 11, no. 2, pp. 101–113.

Luco, Fabienne (2002) *Between a Tiger and a Crocodile: Management of Local Conflicts in Cambodia. An Anthropological Approach to Traditional and New Practices*, UNESCO.

Lund, Christian (2011) "Fragmented Sovereignty: Land Reform and Dispossession in Laos" *Journal of Peasant Studies* vol. 38, no. 4, pp. 885–905.

Merrill, Thomas W. (2002) "Introduction: The Demsetz Thesis and the Evolution of Property Rights" *Journal of Legal Studies* vol. 31, no. 2, pp. 331–359.

Merrill, Thomas W. and Henry E. Smith (2011) "Making Coasean Property More Coasean" *Journal of Law and Economics* vol. 31, pp. 34–62.
Merry, Sally Engle (1988) "Legal Pluralism" *Law & Soc'y Review* vol. 22, no. 5, pp. 869–996.
Michaud, Jean (2009) "Handling Mountain Minorities in China, Vietnam and Laos: From History to Current Concerns" *Asian Ethnography* vol. 10, no. 1, pp. 25–49.
O'Brien, Kevin J. and Lianjiang Li (eds) (2006) "Rightful Resistance" in *Rural China*, Cambridge University Press, pp. 35–38.
Pils, Eva (2014) "Ownership in Urbanizing China" in Hualing Fu and John Gillespie (eds), *Resolving Land Disputes in East Asia: Exploring the Limits of Law*, Cambridge University Press, pp. 115–172.
Rose, Carol (1994) *Property and Persuasion – Essays on the History, Theory and Rhetoric of Ownership*, Westview Press.
Shin, Hyun Bong (2017) "How Stubborn 'Nail Houses' Take a Stand against China's Rapid Urbanisation" *The Conversation*, March 20, https://theconversation.com/how-stubborn-nail-houses-take-a-stand-against-chinas-rapid-urbanisation-72990.
Shitong, Qiao (2016) "Politics of Chinese Land, The Politics of Chinese Land: Partial Reform, Vested Interests and Small Property" *Columbia Journal of Asian Law* vol. 29, no. 1, pp. 70–113.
Sikor, Tomas (2004) "Conflicting Concepts: Contested Land Relations in North-western Vietnam" *Conservation & Society* vol. 2, no. 1, pp. 75–95.
Sikor, Tomas and Christian Lund (2009) "Access and Property: A Question of Power and Authority" *Development and Change* vol. 40, no. 1, pp. 1–22.
Sikor, Tomas and Daniel Müller (2009) "The limits of state-led land reform" *World Development* vol. 37, no. 8, pp. 1307–16.
Singer, Joseph William (2009) "Democratic Estates: Property Law in a Free and Democratic Society" *Cornell Law Review* vol. 94, no. 4, pp. 1009–1069.
Sokun, Khut (2019) "Villagers Accuse UK Firm of Failing to Pay Compensation in Sugar Dispute" *VOD News*, December 26, https://vodenglish.news/villagers-accuse-uk-firm-of-failing-to-pay-compensation-in-sugar-dispute/.
Springer, Simon (2013) "Illegal Evictions? Overwriting Possession and Orality with Law's Violence in Cambodia" *Journal of Agrarian Change* vol. 13, no. 4, pp. 520–546.
United Nations Human Settlements Programme (2003) *The Challenge of Slums: Global Report on Human Settlements*, UNDP.
Upham, Frank (2018) *The Great Property Fallacy: Theory, Reality, and Growth in Developing Countries*, Cambridge University Press.
Verdery, Katherine (1999). "Fuzzy Property Rights, Power and Identity" in Michael Burawoy and Katherine Verdery (eds), *Uncertain Transition: Ethnographies of Change in the Postsocialist World*, Rowman and Littlefield Publishers, pp. 53–81.
Zenker, Olaf and Markus Virgil Hoehne (2018) "Processing the Paradox: When the States has to Deal with Customary Law" in Olaf Zenker and Markus Virgil Hoehne (eds), *The State and the Paradox of Customary Law in Africa*, Routledge, pp. 1–40.
Zhou, Chao and Dan Banik (2014) "Access to Justice and Social Unrest in China's Countryside: Disputes on Land Acquisition and Compensation" *Hague Journal on The Rule of Law* vol. 6, pp. 254–275.
Zhu, Qian (2015) "Land Acquisition Compensation in Post-Reform China: Evolution, Structure and Challenges in Hangzhou" *Land Use Policy* vol. 46, pp. 250–257.

14 Administrative court in Vietnam in solving land disputes

Legal and political boundary

Pham Duy Nghia

Being in place since 1996, administrative court contributes to diversify the channels to settle land disputes between the socialist party state and its citizens. Administrative lawsuits may arise as consequence of land-taking disputes when the government grants land use right, decides on land conversion or decides on how to compensate for land taking. Despite efforts to improve the legal framework for administrative court and procedure, the court could only play a marginal role in land dispute settlement in Vietnam. This chapter analyzes the development of administrative court and procedure and their role in Vietnam. It also highlights the legal and political constraints, which undermine the significance of administrative court as an adjudication channel for land disputes within the Vietnam political context.

1 Administrative court in Vietnam: overview and current state of development

Ordinary Vietnamese people now have the legal means to force the government to pay compensation for its wrongdoings or to rescind unlawful decisions. Since 1986, as the country embraced market-oriented reform and integrated deeper into the global economy, numerous international recognized norms, practice, institutions and legal approaches have been received into the country. The legal reception began with, first and foremost, commercial, investment and business law, but inevitably was also followed by procedural, administrative and constitutional law. The spiral of legal reform is indeed widening and deepening over the years. Administrative court emerged in Vietnam since 1996 within this transitional economic, political and legal context.

Historically, although there has been always some form of oversight and inspection of the bureaucracy practiced by traditional Vietnam dynasties (Phan Dien, 2014), the administrative court and procedure were unknown in feudal Vietnam. Under the colonial rule, French administrative procedure was installed in 1885 for the first time, with limited application to French and foreigners only (Phan Dien, 2011; Republic of Vietnam, 1962). As the country was divided during three decades of Vietnam war, South Vietnam created the administrative procedure that followed essentially the French model. By contrast, North

DOI: 10.4324/9781003170600-18

Vietnam, and later the unified Vietnam, became part of the socialist block. Within socialist legality doctrine, there was theoretically no demand for administrative court within the socialist regime. Instead of litigation, citizens should have the right to petition, file a complaint, or denounce state agencies in case of discrepancy of view and interest (Asia Foundation, 2009). Under the circumstances that all economic activities were managed strictly under central state command, the individual right was extremely narrowed. Without economic foundation for individual right and independent judiciary, there was in fact no demand in Vietnam for creating administrative court and procedure during the time of war and then under the command economy.

The situation changed gradually since the 1986 economic liberalization, particularly after the issuance of the first wave of laws on foreign direct investment (1988), private business (1990), the revision of constitution (1992) and the recognition of private land use rights (1993). In responding to the growing number of grievances that inevitably arose as interests became diversified among various actors, the first rule on administrative court was adopted in 1996, which carefully inserted into the existing court system a new division and new procedure, with very narrow jurisdiction (to hear only a handful of certain categories of disputes as listed by the law). Land disputes, for example, were initially not included in the administrative court jurisdiction; they were added by the 1998 revision but removed again by the subsequent 2006 revision (Dao Thi Xuan Lan, 2019).

Based on experiences learned during the implementation of this 1996 Ordinance, the proved rules and practice of administrative court and procedure were then codified in the Law on Administrative Procedure in 2010. But this Law was also rather short-lived. It was soon replaced by the 2015 Law on Administrative Procedure, the existing law on administrative court and procedure in Vietnam.

As previously summarized, administrative court and procedure were subject to frequent minor changes over the last 20 years, but the changes are not fundamental. The administrative court is not designed as a separate court system with the power to hear disputes between citizens and public authorities. On the opposite, it is rather an extended division of the existing ordinary court system. Its mandate is not to replace but at best, to supplement the existing political-social mechanism of grievance settlement.

Since the 2016 court organization reform, the Supreme People Court (SPC) was substantially reduced from 105 to 17 judges. Its jurisdiction is also narrowed to hear only revision cases and to decide on recognition of so-called case law. The former three SPC branches in Hanoi, Da Nang and Ho Chi Minh were transformed into three new High Courts (for Northern, Middle and Southern Vietnam). High Courts are courts of appellation for cases heard by 63 province courts (Vietnam Supreme People Court, 2016).

At the regional level, in each of 63 province courts throughout the country, jurisdiction is separated into six divisions: criminal, civil, economic, labor, administrative and, most recently, the division for family and minors. The province court is the court of appellation for cases heard by lower district courts. There are 713 district courts in Vietnam.

At the district court level, the lowest level within Vietnam's judiciary system, although the separation into six divisions is not mandatory by law, district court leadership usually practices some form of specialization among judges. Individual judges are selected, additionally trained to become specialized in administrative or economic cases. That is in a nutshell the current organization of administrative court in Vietnam.

For the year 2018, SPC reports that the entire court system in Vietnam received a total of 580,000 cases. Out of this number, the court system was able to settle only 76 percent of all cases filed (420,000 cases settled). Among them, there are only 6,708 administrative cases, which include 4,011 first instance, 1,296 appellation and 51 revision cases (Than Quoc Hung, 2018). Accordingly, the administrative cases make only 1.16 percent of all court cases. At least from a statistical perspective, the workload and importance of administrative court within Vietnam's judiciary system are very marginal.

From a broader perspective, the administrative court is also insignificant within the existing mechanism to settle citizens' grievances. Particularly, the administrative court has less influence in settlement of land grievances that spread throughout the country. Land disputes may vary from recognition of land use rights, to land taking, and compensation (Vietnam National Assembly, 2018). Statistically, among these different disputes' settlement channels, the traditional ways of filing complaints and petition to public authorities are preferred and more frequently used than lodging a lawsuit with the court. For 2018, for example, there were 27,580 complaints that had been handled by the public authorities, which greatly outnumbered the 6,708 administrative court cases (Vietnam General Inspectorate, 2018).

Furthermore, the distribution of administrative cases among 63 provinces is also not proportional. Depending on population density, economic growth and potential grievances, particularly those arising during land taking and compensation, the demand on administrative court procedure differs from province to province. Understandably, most lawsuits are handled by the courts in Ho Chi Minh City (HCM), Hanoi and provinces with rapid economic growth. For the year 2017–2018 about ¼ of all lawsuits in Vietnam are heard by the court in HCM (Tạp chí Tòa án 04/09/2019), followed by the court in Hanoi (with 697 administrative cases). By contrast, courts in remote, backward areas still have little practice with administrative procedure (Báo Pháp luật 17/10/2018). If so considered, experience in dealing with administrative procedure also differs from province to province, from district to district.

Out of 63 provinces in Vietnam, the court in HCM had the most extensive practice in dealing with administrative cases. Because of the shortage on personnel, the workload of judges in HCM is extremely heavy. The current working environment of judges in HCM is described by its chief judge as follows: on average, from receiving the case to finalizing the verdict, each judge in HCM must handle 298 cases annually, that is, on average, ten cases in a month. Consequently, he or she has only two working days for settlement of a case (Tạp chí Tòa án 07/07/2018). This heavy workload is not properly honored: the average monthly salary of judges is less than USD 400, much lower than the salary paid in the private sector, compatible at manager level (Navigos Search, 2019). Consequently, the judiciary in Vietnam cannot attract talented lawyers. In the year 2018, 51 judges mostly in HCM left their job to enter the private sector. Shortage of personnel, inappropriate compensation, absence of societal recognition for judges, lack of independence, lack of integrity and other organizational, legal, and procedural weakness – all those may explain the limited role of administrative court in Vietnam (Tạp chí Tòa án 05/09/2019).

2 Legal constraints narrowing the jurisdiction of administrative court in Vietnam

As distinct from criminal and civil procedure (so-called ordinary court procedure), the administrative court and procedure are unique. For Vietnam, the administrative court is unique because of the following characteristics:

- So far nurturing a good relationship with public authorities is still inevitable for individual and business success; lodging a lawsuit against a public authority appears as only a last resort from the plaintiff's perspective. The plaintiff, individual or organization is subject to be regulated by government agencies. Because of this asymmetry of information and power, the plaintiff in an administrative procedure is most likely in a disadvantage compared to the defendant.
- Beyond the court procedure, the defendant (a government agency) is a policy regulator or executor (granting license, approval, permit, accepting or rescinding of public procurement, conducting inspection etc.). The defendant has such a wide range of possibilities to intervene and to pressure the plaintiff in and beyond the court procedure.
- Not only the plaintiff's, but the court's position is also weak in comparison to defendant. Although judicial independence is recognized formally by the Constitution and law, the government can influence the court's operation through various channels (budget allocation, participation in appointing process of judges, personal influence etc.). In administrative procedure, the government is the potential and permanent threat to judicial independence. In case a government agency refuses to implement the court's order (for instance, representatives of public authority refuse to appear in court hearing or refuse to provide evidence), or in case public authority refuses to implement the court's judgment, the court cannot execute it properly.

A mindful design of administrative court and procedure should reflect and respond properly to these unique features. The following part discusses the main legal enduring obstacles that limit the success of administrative court in Vietnam: (1) inappropriate court organization, (2) inappropriate court procedure and (3) weakness in executing the court's order and verdicts.

2.1 Inappropriate court organization

Back in the 1990s when drafting the first rule on administrative court procedure, Vietnam lawmakers were already aware of the risk within the country's political system. It is almost impossible for a district judge to make judgment contrary to the will of the district government (Nguyen Quang, 2004). It is unrealistic to expect that a judge, appointed for a term of five years and in most cases being a party member (member of Communist Party Vietnam) who must obey the party discipline, will dare to challenge decisions made collectively by the party and state authority supervising his court at the same district level. Suggestion to establish regional administrative court separating from the existing ordinary court system was discussed among lawmakers in the early 1990s before the Law on Court Organization and Ordinance on administrative court procedure were adopted in 1995 and 1996, respectively. But this suggestion was not supported by majority of policy- and lawmakers (Vnexpress 16/11/2005).

Since then, the discussion on separating the court system from the existing administrative boundaries never stops. According to the party's strategy on judiciary reform by 2020, a court system shall base on jurisdiction, and not on geographic affiliation (Cao Mai Phuong 2006). This discussion seems to gain additional momentum once again during the process of revising the Constitution in 2013. Session 2.3, 102.1 of the Vietnam 2013 Constitution provides that judicative power is vested with the court, that is, the court is theoretically empowered to control the legislative and executive power. In addition, the wording of Session 102.2 of the Vietnam 2013 Constitution appears that the court protects justice first, followed by the protection of socialist regime and citizen right. These rules are new in Vietnam's political context.

According to the party strategies, the court system does not need to follow strictly the existing geographic and administrative structures. However, the resistance from provinces and from the existing political system remains strong. So far, all attempts to separate the court system from the existing administrative boundaries, for instance to establish regional court of first instance, possibly responsible for several districts, or to relocate the jurisdiction to hear administrative cases from district to province court, all were not yet successful. By majority, the legislator still favoring a court system follows strictly the local political and administrative substructures of the party state (Vnexpress 23/6/2015).

The 2015 Law on Administrative Procedure modifies the jurisdiction of administrative court only slightly. According to Sessions 31.1 and 32.8 Law on Administrative Procedure, the district court is still responsible for hearing administrative cases challenging acts made by the district government at the same level, except those adopted collectively by the District People Committee (PC) and by the PC Chairman, and except those considered important and will be heard by the higher province court.

As verified by SPC Vice Chief Judge Le Hong Quang and other National Assembly members (Committee for Judiciary), the influence of the district government on district judges is obvious. Within the party-state hierarchy, the district

PC Chairman is cum vice party secretary. As party member, a judge hardly can escape the personal influence of his supervisor in the party hierarchy. Therefore, when being sued, the district government as defendant mostly wins in first-instance procedure (Vnexpress 4/6/2015).

The plaintiff may have little chance to win in appellation procedure, when the province court may fully or partly accept the plaintiff's request and rescind unlawful decisions made by the lower district government (Vnexpress 27/09/2019). For one reason, judges at the higher province court may be less sensible to influence of the lower district government. But another reason may also lead to this outcome. In sensible cases against the local government, for instance, when a court's verdict may affect land acquisition and compensation at a larger scale involving mass disputes, judges are best advised to consult guidance from the court leadership, then later again may consult guidance from the local party leadership, at least from the committee for internal affairs (Báo Chính phủ 15/11/2018). This informal practice contradicts the court's independence formally provided for by Constitution and law. However, the practice also indicates that there are different internal channels operating within the party-state structure to adjust local policy. The court verdict, in some of those cases, appears only as the formal decision presenting the consensus among local elites that has been already made within the party apparatus.

In summary, from an organizational perspective, the current administrative court is ill-designed. As extending division of the current people court system, the administrative court is subject to influence of local substructures of the party state. Therefore, it couldn't be independent to exercise judicial review over local government. To overcome power fragmentation at a district or province level, regional separate administrative court could be the more mindful model.

2.2 *Inappropriate court procedure*

In addition to court organization, procedural rules are also inappropriate. Although the jurisdiction of administrative court was gradually widened over the last two decades (Tran Viet Dung, 2014), other procedural constraints still endure. Consistently from 1996 to present, the administrative court in Vietnam has jurisdiction to hear only lawsuits concerning individual decision, and not generally applicable normative act. Concerning land disputes for example, land price in any province is determined by resolution of the province elected body (PPC: province people council). According to Vietnam law, a PPC resolution is normative, generally applicable, and therefore is not subject to judicial review. On the contrary, the compensation for an individual land plot is individual, decided by the PC Chairman in the form of an administrative decision. Consequently, this individual decision may be challenged at the administrative court (SPC Guideline No 02/2018/QD-TANDTC). Similarly, businesses may challenge individual decisions made by a certain tax authority, but they cannot challenge normative ministerial circulars on tax policies in administrative court procedure.

This boundary substantially narrows the scope of power of the administrative court. The court can correct certain administrative wrongdoings, but it isn't designed to exercise judicial power over the entire administrative system. In Vietnam party state, administrative acts must follow state policies, then later follow party program and guidelines. Limiting on individual acts, the administrative court has no power to correct injustice incurred by unlawful policies and party directions. In land-taking disputes, for example, the administrative court doesn't have the jurisdiction to review unjust policies adopted by the local people council to convert land use (from agricultural land to residential or commercial use) or to determine policies on land price in case of compulsory acquisition. In addition to the absence of a clear mechanism for constitutional review, the fact that the court does not have the power to exercise judicial review over normative acts (Session 119.2 of 2013 Constitution) seriously weakens the judiciary in Vietnam.

In addition to a narrowly defined jurisdiction, the administrative procedure remains burdensome, time consuming and clearly in disadvantage to the claimant and even to the trial panel at the court. The rules on representation of public authority as defendant remain somewhat inflexible and irrational. In a lawsuit against local government (local PC: people committee), only its PC Chairman or its PC Vice Chairman is authorized by law to represent the defendant before the court (Session 60.2.d and Session 60.3 of the Law on Administrative Procedure 2015). If these local politicians are absent, the trial panel must postpone the hearing. And that is the common practice at the administrative court in recent years (Đoàn Thị Ngọc Hải, 2018). Only when duly summoned for the second time, and these local politicians still don't appear in the hearing, then the trial panel may conduct the hearing in their absence (Session 157 of the Law on Administrative Procedure). However, without the active participation of the defendant, prior-hearing reconciliation and adversary proceeding cannot be productive (Session 130–145 of the Law on Administrative Procedure). Given the complexity of facts and circumstances leading to an administrative act, the court seems to be very reluctant to proceed with the hearing in the defendant's absence.

The court procedure is also unpredictable because of the intervention of the procuracy. This unique role of the public prosecutor (in Vietnam: people procuracy) is a relic from the Soviet party-state heritage. Although the party strategies on judiciary reform by 2020 envisages that people procuracy shall be transformed and limited within the public prosecutor's role, in fact people procuracy still enjoys the unique power to supervise the judiciary. Thus, the procuracy is authorized by law to attend actively any court procedure, including administrative. By doing so, the procuracy is entitled to present legal opinions, to make suggestions during the hearing, consequently taking immense influence on the court's outcome. Finally, the procuracy may file a protest against the first-instance verdict, such as initiating the appellate procedure by itself, independently from the plaintiff and defendant (Session 211 of the Law on Administrative Procedure). Currently, there is no clear trend in Vietnam on how to restructure this Soviet-styled people procuracy and transform it into public prosecutor. The interference of procuracy during the administrative procedure is certainly a constraint not only to the parties' autonomy, but it also challenges the independence of the court.

Without a profound change in procedural rules to widen the court's jurisdiction, to ensure the party autonomy and to limit intervention from third parties, the administrative court can only play a minor role in supplementing the existing mechanism to settle administrative disputes between individual/organization and the party state in Vietnam.

2.3 Weakness in enforcing court's order and verdicts

In Vietnam, the defendant may be any agency within the traditional administrative hierarchy. From grassroots, there are 11,142 wards, 713 districts, 63 provinces (*Vietnam Government Statistics Office*) and agencies of the central government (22 ministries and regional offices of the government). This administrative bureaucracy has a long tradition and enjoys the respect of the Vietnamese people. In the party-state hierarchy, the administrative bureaucracy continuously remains the strongest power branch at all levels.

In contrast to this traditional government branch, the court system in Vietnam is relatively new and quite weak. The party state continues this tradition. At the local level, heading the local government is the deputy party secretary, that is, the second strongest person in the local party organization. He and his subordinates form the majority within the inner circle of local party leadership. Compared to that, the chief judge of district or province court doesn't belong to this inner circle of party leadership. He or she is considered at the same rank as head of department, subordinated to the local PC chairperson. Likewise, at the central level, among 16 politburo members, the highest organ within the party hierarchy, five serve in Government (executive) and two at the National Assembly (legislative); none of them serve in the judiciary. The SPC Chief Judge is not a politburo member, indicating that in the lenses of the party state, the court system is less important than the executive or legislative branch.

Based on this power structure within the party hierarchy, the district or province court can neither order the representative of public authority at the same locality to appear in the hearing nor demand the representative to provide evidence needed in an administrative procedure. This power structure is reflected in existing law accordingly. A province court does not have the power to order a local politician or minister to attend in person at a court's hearing.

The rule on execution of administrative judgments and rulings is also ill-designed. Once the verdict is given, formally the public agency as so-called judgment debtor must implement the rulings. In case it fails to obey this rule voluntarily, at the judgment creditor's request, the court may order the compulsory execution of judgment. However, the agency in charge is the *local civil judgment execution department*, a subunit of the Ministry of Justice (Session 312.2 of the Law on Administrative Procedure). Like the postman, this execution agency is only authorized to request the local government to obey the court's judgment or to report to the supervisory level in case the local government fails to do so.

Obviously, this rule is meaningless to compulsorily enforce the court's judgment against the local government. The staff working as executors also don't have the motivation to act against their supervisory local government (Báo Pháp luật 28/7/2018).

It is always like an adventure to initiate a lawsuit against public authority with the court in Vietnam; it is extremely difficult to win. Rarely then, when winning the case, the plaintiff faces impossibilities to get the judgment compulsorily executed. The court has no meaningful power to force the defendant to obey the verdict. In case a verdict is made against the public authority as defendant, the defendant frequently disregards the court verdict and refuses to implement it properly (Vnexpress 10/10/2019). According to a recent MOJ report, for the year 2018, the number of verdicts that could not executed increased three times compared with the previous year (Báo Chính phủ 15/11/2018).

3 Conclusion and the way forward

Thirty years after the first wave of economic liberalization, Vietnam is nowadays a success story in the developing world. Deeply integrated into the global economy, it is party to many new generations of free trade agreements, including with the EU, Japan and the regional CPTPP. Unusual for a country with such a large population, Vietnam ranks fifth among the most open economies in the world, with total trade more than double the size of GDP.

Following economic liberalization, the spiral of legal, judicial reform in Vietnam is widening and deepening. The administrative court was adopted in a move to empower individuals and organizations with the right to challenge illegal acts and wrongdoings conducted by public officials and agencies. It was an experiment, testing the boundary of the court as a supplementing channel to adjudicate public grievances, which inevitably arise as interests become diversified in a more open society.

Twenty years have passed from the time this new concept of administrative court and procedure was inserted into the existing court system of Vietnam. The success and failure of the administrative court attest to how foreign legal concepts when incorporated into the socialist party state context may evolve under the local institutional environment of recipient countries.

Overall, this transplantation is far from being a success. The administrative court is still insignificant in Vietnam. It cannot supplement the existing mechanism of lodging administrative complaints and denunciation to settle disputes with public authorities. The court is not in the position to correct injustice caused by public authorities.

Although the laws on administrative court and procedure are frequently changed over the last 20 years, the fundamental guiding principles endure. The party state eyes in administrative court are only a supplement, supporting the existing mechanism of complaints and denunciation. The administrative court is not separate but only an extension of the ordinary people court system. Although its jurisdiction was widening over the years, the administrative court is only authorized to hear individual acts and not allow to review normative rules or policies that are generally applicable. The party state doesn't see in administrative court a judicative power capable of enforcing constraints on the administrative bureaucracy. It is not designed for the purpose of check and balance of power.

Instead of using the court, there are other formal and informal party internal channels to exercise oversight over the bureaucracy. The party discipline, the party internal affairs committee, vote of confidence, party survey of public opinions, etc. are some examples of these channels. They replace the role of the court in adjudicating over policies and acts of public authorities.

This situation is unlikely to change in the near future. The institutional setting, in which the administrative court operates, endures and reinforces itself. Revised in 2015, the law on administrative procedure cements the weakness of the court in comparison to local and central government as defendant. The court is neither in a position to force the defendant's representative to appear in a court hearing nor to execute its own verdict.

On the other hand, in accordance with international commitments, Vietnam is obliged to make any interference to the court seemingly illegitimate and illegal. Formally, the party state recognizes the independence of the court and is committed to protect citizens' rights. Once the Vietnam public become aware of their legitimate rights and learn to demand their implementation, additional momentum to judicial reform may emerge. Under those changing circumstances, it is to be seen how the party state in Vietnam may reinvent the administrative court and procedure to cope with these changes.

References

Asia Foundation, 2009: *The Mechanism to Settle Administrative Complaints in Vietnam*, www.asiafoundation.org/resources/pdfs/VNAdminComplaintSettleReportEnglish.pdf

Báo Chính phủ 15/11/2018: http://baochinhphu.vn/Tin-noi-bat/Thi-hanh-an-la-khau-cuoi-cung-de-cong-ly-duoc-thuc-thi/352141.vgp

Báo Pháp luật 28/7/2018: https://plo.vn/phap-luat/kho-nhu-thi-hanh-an-hanh-chinh-784629.html

Báo Pháp luật 17/10/2018: https://baophapluat.vn/ha-noi-hotnews/ha-noi-con-gap-nhieu-kho-khan-trong-thi-hanh-an-hanh-chinh-418118.html

Cao Mai Phuong, 2006: *Party Resolutions on Judiciary Reform, Vietnam Law and Legal Forum*, https://vietnamlawmagazine.vn/party-resolutions-on-judicial-reform-3425.html

Dao Thi Xuan Lan, 2019: *Jurisdiction of Administrative Court over Land Disputes*, https://tapchitoaan.vn/bai-viet/nghien-cuu/ky-nang-giai-quyet-vu-an-hanh-chinh-trong-linh-vuc-quan-ly-nha-nuoc-ve-dat-dai

Đoàn Thị Ngọc Hải, 2018: *Những vướng mắc, bất cập của Luật Tố tụng hành chính và hướng đề xuất hoàn thiện*, Tạp chí Tòa án Nhân dân, 12/10/2018, www.tapchitoaan.vn/bai-viet/phap-luat/nhung-vuong-mac-bat-cap-cua-luat-to-tung-hanh-chinh-va-huong-de-xuat-hoan-thien

Navigos Search Salary Report 2019: www.enworld.com.vn/blog/2019/03/jobseeker-salary-report-in-vietnam-in-2019

Nguyen Quang, 2004: *The Organization and Operation of Administrative Courts in Vietnam*, www.academia.edu/1501963/The_organisation_and_operation_of_administrative_courts_in_Vietnam

Phan Dien, 2011: *Legislation in French-Ruled Vietnam*, Vietnam Law & Legal Forum, February 24, 2011, http://vietnamlawmagazine.vn/legislation-in-french-ruled-vietnam-4504.html

Phan Dien, 2014: *Ethos of State Power Supervision in Feudal Vietnam*, Vietnam Law & Legal Forum, July 03, 2014, http://vietnamlawmagazine.vn/ethos-of-state-power-supervision-in-feudal-vietnam-4472.html

Republic of Vietnam (1962) *Judiciary*, Việt Nam Cộng hòa, *Chế độ tư pháp* (1962).

Supreme People Court 2016: Prior to 2016, the Supreme Court had 105 judges, structured in five divisions (criminal, civil, economic, labor and administrative) and had the jurisdiction both in appellation and revision cases. There was no rule to recognize case law. Instead, the SPC Council adopted annual summaries or guidelines as orientation for lower courts in handling of cases. Currently, this organization had been changed. SPC has now no jurisdiction to hear appellation cases, its jurisdiction is limited only to revision cases. The appellation jurisdiction is provided for the three high courts being established in 2016. Instead of issuance of annual summaries, SPC has now the power to select and recognize certain court decisions and publish them as case law, and this case law is applicable to all lower courts in Vietnam. The body of SPC judges is also reduced from 105 judges to 17 SPC judges. www.toaan.gov.vn/webcenter/portal/tatc/thanh-vien-hdtp

Supreme People Court Guideline No 02/2018/QD-TANDTC dated September 19, 2018 on implementing of administrative procedure, https://tapchitoaan.vn/bai-viet/phap-luat/giai-dap-15-vuong-mac-ve-to-tung-hanh-chinh

Tạp chí Tòa án 07/07/2018: *Interview HCM City Chief Judge Ung Thi Xuan Huong*, https://tapchitoaan.vn/bai-viet/suy-ngam-cuoi-tuan/ap-luc-doi-voi-tham-phan

Tạp chí Tòa án 04/09/2019: https://tapchitoaan.vn/bai-viet/thoi-su/toa-an-thu-ly-tang-63-949-vu-so-voi-cung-ky-nam-truoc

Tạp chí Tòa án 05/09/2019: *Interview SPC Vice Chief Judge Le Hong Quang*, https://tapchitoaan.vn/bai-viet/thoi-su/nguyen-nhan-ty-le-giai-quyet-an-hanh-chinh-thap

Than Quoc Hung (2018): *Quality of Handling of Administrative Cases by the Court*, https://hcma.vn/Uploads/2018/5/8/LA%20_%20Hung%20_cap%20HV_.pdf

Tran Viet Dung, 2014: *New Administrative Procedural Rules – An Analysis from Judicial Reform Perspective*, Chonnam National University Law Review, 34 (1), 2014

Vietnam General Inspectorate 2018: Report of Vietnam General Inspectorate (Báo cáo của Tổng Thanh tra Chính phủ trước Quốc hội) dated November 14, 2018, http://baochinhphu.vn/Utilities/PrintView.aspx?distributionid=352065

Vietnam Government Statistics Office: www.gso.gov.vn/

Vietnam Law on Administrative Procedures 2015: An unofficial English is available at WIPO Website: www.wipo.int/edocs/lexdocs/laws/en/vn/vn082en.pdf

Vietnam National Assembly 2019: Land disputes accounted in 2018 for 67.7 percent of administrative complaints; see Report of General Inspectorate to the National Assembly, dated September 12, 2019: http://quochoi.vn/tintuc/Pages/tin-hoat-dong-cua-quoc-hoi.aspx?ItemID=41808

Vnexpress 16/11/2005: Interview of former SPC Vice-Chief Judge Dang Quang Phuong, https://vnexpress.net/phap-luat/se-thanh-lap-toa-an-khu-vuc-2062215.html

Vnexpress 4/6/2015: *Đại biểu Quốc hội: Quan xử quan, thế nào dân cũng thua*, https://vnexpress.net/phap-luat/dai-bieu-quoc-hoi-quan-xu-quan-the-nao-dan-cung-thua-3229147.html

Vnexpress 23/6/2015: https://vnexpress.net/chuyen-an-hanh-chinh-len-tinh-la-chat-chan-nguoi-dan-3238152.html

Vnexpress 27/9/2019: *A Company Win the Case against Government of Danang City*, https://vnexpress.net/phap-luat/da-nang-bi-doanh-nghiep-khoi-kien-3988297.html. An overview about administrative cases in which claimants win: https://vnexpress.net/topic/dan-kien-co-quan-cong-quyen-11988

Vnexpress 10/10/2019: https://vnexpress.net/phap-luat/bo-tu-phap-than-lanh-dao-dia-phuong-phot-lo-an-hanh-chinh-3994718.html

WTO Center at VCCI: www.wtocenter.vn/fta

15 Land law and disputes in Myanmar

A historical struggle for redefining the property rights

Yuka Kaneko and Ye Naing Lin

1 Introduction

Since after the establishment of the 2008 Constitution regime of Myanmar, roaring protests of national people have raged against the "land grabbing" that occurred during the military reign. The union parliament set up a special committee in 2011 to receive the petition for land disputes investigation, which resulted in the President's report in April 2014 with the finding of a total of 7,600 cases of land-grabbing incidents amounting to total 120,000ha. The governmental response to the settlement of land disputes has attracted the keen eyes of foreign observers as a touchstone to test the reach of Myanmar's democratization.[1]

Behind the unsolved democratic claims in contemporary scenes, however, we can also pierce the negative heritage of colonial land law regime. The land law in the late 19th century made the Burmese land into a marketable commodity, resulting in the dramatic increase of landless farmers and the concentration of lands to the absentee landowners as the result of large-scale deprivation of subsistent farmlands. The postindependence enactment of the 1953 Land Nationalization Act was an attempt to overcome the colonial land law by securing the land cultivators' right through the restriction of land transfer. The implementation of the 1953 Act was, however, frustrated with political disturbances and compromises between social classes, resulting in a halfway reform. After the collapse of the Burmese way of socialism upon the coup d'état in 1988, the military reign added the confusion to the disparity of land regime by the revived use of colonial waste land management, inviting numerous land-grabbing incidents. Some survey reports the ratio of landless farmers amounted to 90 percent as a result.[2]

Even after the 2008 Constitution (art. 23) declared the protection of farmer's right, the 2012 Farmland Law took a pro-development stance by liberalizing the free transaction of farmland, a revival of the legal design of colonial land law. Indeed, Myanmar is the most prominent example of a country that contains the genealogy of colonial land law within the present system. The land regime brought by British colonial rule still forms the basis of today's system (Table 15.1).

DOI: 10.4324/9781003170600-19

Table 15.1 Genealogy of Myanmar Land Law since the colonial era

	Colonial land laws	*Laws applied post-independence period*	*Laws currently applied*
Land Revenue	**1876 Lower Burma Land and Revenue Act** **1889 Upper Burma Land and Revenue Regulations** **1899 Lower Burma Town and Village Act** 1881 Forest Act→1909	1953 Land Nationalization Act 1963 Tenancy Law 1963 Law Safeguarding Peasant Rights 1977 Land Management Law **1876 Lower Burma Land and Revenue Act** maintained **1889 Upper Burma Land and Revenue Regulations** maintained **1899 Lower Burma Town and Village Act** maintained	**2012 Farmland Law** **2013 Law Safeguarding Peasant Rights** **1992 Forest Law** **1876 Lower Burma Land and Revenue Act** maintained **1889 Upper Burma Land and Revenue Regulations** maintained **1899 Lower Burma Town and Village Act** maintained
Registration systems	– Title Registry: 1876 Land and Revenue Act, etc. – Deed Registry: 1909 Registration Act	– Land Record System under 1953 Land Nationalization Act – Deed Registry: 1909 Registration Act maintained	– Title Registry: **2012 Farmland Law** revived the title registration – Deed Registry: **2018 Registration of Deeds Law**
Waste Land Management	1863 Waste Land Claims Act (~1992)		1991 Notification No. 44/1991 on Vacant, Fallow and Virgin Lands Management Procedure **2012 Vacant, Fallow and Virgin Lands Management Law**
Land Expropriation	1894 Land Acquisition Act	1894 Land Acquisition Act	**2019 Land Acquisition, Resettlement and Rehabilitation Law**
Property Transaction Law	**1882 Transfer of Property Act**	**1882 Transfer of Property Act** maintained +1947, 1953, **1987 Transfer of Immovable Property (Restriction) Act**	**1882 Transfer of Property Act** maintained **1987 Transfer of Immovable Property (Restriction) Act** ↔ **2016 Investment Law**

Source: Collated by the author. Bolded entries signify the laws that are currently in effect as of 2020.

Upon the lifting of land transaction restriction by the 2012 Farmland Law, speculative transactions have occurred as if reminding us of the phenomenon in the late 19th century, particularly in the outskirt of the large cities, inviting illegal changes of land use categories from farmland to non-farmland (La Na 39), causing ten times higher speculation of land price together with the ugly city sprawling phenomenon.[3]

This dilemma of land policy is not a sole challenge for Myanmar, but many of other developing countries in Asia are more or less facing similar struggles.[4] World Bank and the IMF have encouraged the land law reforms as part of the development policy via the promotion of foreign investments, or the "Washington Consensus" model,[5] centering on the land titling project as well as the compulsory land acquisition for economic purposes. Along with such reform, many developing countries across the world have been caught in a similar type of policy dilemma as the result of increasing confrontation on lands between investors and local residents and farmers. The complexity is added by the current trend of the investors increasingly resorting to the Investor-State Dispute Resolution (ISDS), a procedural framework incorporated in many bilateral investment treaties (BITs) for an investor to sue the government of a host country in an international arbitration, particularly at the International Centre for Settlement of Investment Disputes (ICSID), a part of the World Bank Group that has a tendency of arbitral awards emphasizing the investor's interest. When the government listens to the local protest calling for the suspension of investments, it has to face the risk of tremendous compensation claims in the ISDS.[6] If the government instead chooses to treat the investors to prevent the ISDS claim, the local criticisms might amount to trigger the international mechanisms of human rights claims against the government.[7]

To mitigate this land policy dilemma, in 2016, the Myanmar's new government led by Daw Aung San Suu Kyi adopted the "National Land Use Policy," which involved several hints toward the solution of land policy dilemma, including the land dispute settlement (section 6(d)) and the community participation (section 6(e)). Toward the general election in November 2020, to impress the successful achievement of the "National Land Use Policy," her government expedited the overall conclusion of land disputes through the Scrutinizing Committee for Acquisition of Farmland and Other Land, an administrative dispute mechanism established nationwide in each layer of local administration, starting from the bottom of village tract level committee.

In this chapter, to comprehend the legal causes of roaring land disputes in Myanmar and obtain hints toward a desirable direction of future reform of land law, the authors will first review a historical path dating back to the precolonial days up to the present in coming Sections 2 through 5, and then examine the legal characteristics of the contemporary land disputes in Section 6, based on the authors' interview surveys conducted from March 2016 to January 2020 with the parties to the disputes as well as the members of the Farmland Management Committees in Dawai and Myeik districts in Tanintharyi Region or former Tenasserim, where the British colonial law took the first step in the early 19th century;

the outskirts of the union capital Naypyitaw representing the Upper Burma terroir, where local farming households maintain a stable land order for centuries; and the outskirts of the city of Mawlamyine in Mon State, where increasing areas of farmlands are left fallow due to the population outflow of ethnic minorities seeking jobs abroad; each represents a typical environment of contemporary land disputes in Myanmar.

2 Precolonial vs. colonial land orders

There is an accumulation of prior research in Japan regarding the characteristics of land law in colonial Burma (Takemura 1976; Okudaira 1985; Saito 1985, etc.). The basic question held in the research is why the prompt dismantling of the agricultural order occurred during the British colonial rule, turning an originally homogeneous independent farming in precolonial Burma into a sharp increase in a class of landless farmers. Among them, Saito (1985) doubted the common theory that the British introduced the Ryotwari system of Indian land taxation in Burma as a means of protection of landowning farmers but resulted in the loss of land due to the ignorance of the Burmese farmers (Furnivall 1956: 92 etc.). Rather, she focused on the fact that, while the private rights traditionally held by Burmese subsistent farmers already had the exclusiveness and absoluteness compatible to modern ownership, they were relegated to the weak status of "landholder's rights" by the colonial law, and as a result, they lost the land due to the inability of paying highly exploitative land revenue or the financial burden to borrow for such revenue payment in cash (Saito 1985: 152–153).

The question was whether it was actually a Ryotwari system protecting landholding farmers, or rather a systemic framework for exploiting them disguised under the cover of the Ryotwari system. Although the research of Saito raised a keen issue, research gaps still remain as it did not identify the legal nature of the property rights that Burmese farmers traditionally had. Saito's research was based only on the documents written by the British rulers recorded during the process of forming the colonial land law, without paying attention to the analysis of inherent Burmese law as contained in the established code such as the *Manugye Dhammathat*, even though that was explored in depth by Okudaira (1985). Also, a section-by-section analysis of the British colonial law should have been done to clarify in what exact legal mechanisms the British colonial law caused the deprivation of farmers' rights. We should start with covering these issues left behind.

First, what were the property rights in Burma before British rule? Initial observations by the British rulers were contradictory. Maingy, the first British governor of Tenasserim (1825–1833), reported that farmers had private ownership rights over the land that they cleared by their own labor, and for that reason the Government of India once decided to impose the Ryotwari system of direct taxation on landowning farmers. However, Blundell, the second governor of Tenasserim (1834–1842), reported that there was no rationale for a land register due to the low degree of farmers' attachment to the land, and accordingly, the "squatter" system of taxation on the farmers who are in yearly possession was introduced.[8]

But then, as British rule extended to all over Lower Burma and the pressure to export Burmese rice via Suez Canal arose, British interest in a land register reignited. Phayre, the first Chief Commissioner of Burma (appointed in 1862), wrote that Burmese farmers had a complete allodial title including the freedom of disposal. At the same time Colonel Ardagh, the Commissioner of Rangoon District (appointed in 1862), insisted that farmers lacked attachment to the land and suggested the introduction of the ownership concept to educate local farmers to change their behavior.[9] These contradictory observation records by the British rulers have confused Japanese researchers on Burmese law, and they have held a hypothetical view that there was a custom of "*da ma u cha*" where a mere provisional cultivation right was acquired by clearing the land.[10]

It might be wrong, however, to conclude only on the observation records of British colonists, that the legal nature of the *da ma u cha* custom did not exceed the provisional rights of a squatter. The codified laws of the dynasty period before British colonization should be revisited. When the last Konbaung dynasty came under British rule as the result of the Third Anglo-Burmese War, the conquerors found a large volume of legal material in the royal library, including numbers of versions of the codified laws *Dhammathat*; among these, the *Manugye Dhammathat* was translated into English[11] and utilized by the British colonists in early judicial processes.[12] Looking at Chapter 8 of the *Manugye Dhammathat*, *myay-thay* or perfect titles over land and *myay-sheng* as still disputable rights in the process of development into a *myay-thay* were defined. While the land that has come by hereditary succession for the cultivation use or *bo bwa paing myae* (grandfather's land) comes under a category as *myay-thay*, other lands are *myay-sheng*, including the land that had been inherited, purchased, openly cultivated for ten years without interruption, cleared forest or officially allotted (Chapter 8, 1st section). It is notable that the land obtained through inheritance, purchase and adverse possession for ten years, which are naturally recognized as "ownership" under modern property law, did not provide sufficient grounds alone for an established title under Burmese law, therefore continued occupied cultivation for three generations of ancestors was necessary until a *myay-thay* is claimed. It is also remarkable that the Burmese law lacked the concept of "sale" of land in the sense of immediate transfer of the land, while the right of redemption of the heirs remained as of the succeeding transfer of the land by the first buyer (Chapter 8, 1st section; also Chapter 7, art. 36). Even when there was an outlook of a sale, its legal nature was a provisional transfer of land to mortgagee with the right of repurchase attached (Chapter 3, 4th section). This implies the highly stable nature of once established land rights either *myay-thay* or *myay-sheng*.

Thus, the legal nature of *da ma u cha* under the inherent law was an exclusive property right *myay-sheng* that farmers acquired through clearing forests, and it was a right that could mature into an absolute private right *bo bwa paing myae* through the inheritance for a few generations. Such *myay-sheng* land rights under Burmese law sufficiently corresponded to modern Western ownership in terms of exclusiveness. Colonial land law should have recognized the title of "proprietary rights" to these *myay-sheng* as well as to *myay-thay*. Nevertheless, a mere "landholder's right" was given to Burmese farmers, which was the de jure deprivation of property rights under the inherent law.[13]

3 Nature of colonial land law

3.1 Land law as a means of revenue collection

Then what were the mechanisms of the British colonial law that resulted in the deprivation of farmers' rights? Its entirety was developed as a system for the collection of land revenue. Originating in the village contracting system and squatting system applied in the 1820s and 1830s, followed by the 1839 Waste Lands Grants Act introduced in Tenasserim (present Tanintharyi Region) and Arakan (present Rakhine State), which Britain acquired in the First Anglo-Burmese War of 1824, and a series of trial and error in Lower Burma such as the 1858 Lease Act, 1863 Waste Lands Claims Act, the Hatta System, the 1862 squatter system, etc. that were applied after the 1852 Second Anglo-Burmese War, the colonial land law regime was collated in the 1876 Lower Burma Land and Revenue Act. Then, after the entire territory was consolidated including Upper Burma, following the end of the 1886 Third Anglo-Burmese War, the 1889 Upper Burma Land and Revenue Regulations and the 1899 Lower Burma Town and Village Act were introduced. In addition to this, British Indian laws such as the 1882 Transfer of Property Act, the 1894 Land Acquisition Act and the 1909 Registration Act came into effect through the application of the "Indian Code" that accompanied Burma's position as a state of India. Most of these laws still apply today.

The essence of 1876 Lower Burma Land and Revenue Act, as the basis of land revenue collection, was a squatter system, by construing the land rights of farmers as "landholder's rights," instead of the ownership or proprietary rights. The basis for collecting tax was a "land revenue," which had a nature of a license fee paid to the government for annual use of the governmental land. As stated earlier, since not only *myay-thay* absolute right but also *myay-sheng* rights were comparable to the modern Western concept of ownership, it should have been a legally accurate way to treat both *myay-thay* and *myay-sheng* as proprietor's rights and imposing "tax" through democratic procedure instead of "land revenue" unilaterally decided by the government. In fact, such assertions were made at the tax law drafting committee of the time.[14] However, in response to the policy of British India to treat the farmers as the "tenants" of the state land for paying "rent," Ashley Eden, the first civilian governor of British Burma (1871–1877) took on an intermediate expression of "land revenue" collected against "landholder's rights" (Saito 1985: 153), which was not different from annual "rent" of squatters in substance.

Another tax basis was the collection of "rent" via the method of waste land grants under the 1889 Upper Burma Land and Revenue Act. All fallow land in the colony was ascribed as government-owned land by the unilateral declaration, and the government granted fixed-term leasehold (grants, leases and licenses) and imposed rent. This system was established in the 1839 Waste Land Grant

Rules in Arakan, the 1861 Waste Land Grant Rule in Pegou, the 1863 Rules for the Sales of Waste Land and, finally, the 1889 Upper Burma Land and Revenue (art. 23–26), and the same method was incorporated in the 1876 Land and Revenue Act (art. 18–19) and the 1899 Lower Burma Town and Village Act (art. 12, 16–21), penetrating the entire colony.

The design of these colonial mechanisms was developed by the British East India Company using its discretionary legislative function, during the Company's constant expansion until its abolition in 1858. Since the Zamindari system, which utilized feudal landowners as tax collectors in the governance of British India, was difficult to implement as a method of exploiting agricultural resources in Southeast Asia characterized by liberal cultivation practices of homogeneous independent farmers in the delta area as well as the communal customary law in mountainous areas, in Burma, the 1876 Lower Burma Land and Revenue Act established the two pillars of expropriation mechanisms: a registration system of a land user title on national land, and the waste land management. What is now known as the Torrens system of title registration was said to be introduced in South Australia in 1858 and then reimported back to Britain as the Land Registration Act of 1925, which led to the current law of 2002, but its institutional design is recognized by Torrens himself as a product of gradual institutional exploration that accompanied the development of British colonialism (Torrens 1882).

3.2 *Landholders' rights subject to resolutive conditions*

Saito (1985) as aforementioned casted a doubt that the colonial land law brought by the British intentionally defined the farmers' rights as weak "landholders' rights." To further identify its legal nature, we should examine the substance given by the 1876 Lower Burma Land and Revenue Act.

The landholder's right was defined as "a permanent heritable and transferable right of use and occupancy" (art. 8), which was not compatible to ownership or a fee simple absolute in the British common law terminology. It was designed to be acquired by proof of completion of the 12-year prescription period (1876 Act, art. 7), which at a glance reminds us of the traditional *myay-sheng* rights acquired through acquisitive prescription after free land clearing *da ma u cha*, instead of *myay-thay* right. But this "landholder's right" was further subject to numbers of obligations set by the Act and was destined to be easily canceled by the government due to the violation of such obligations, namely, payment of land revenue (art. 8), continual cultivation (art. 11) and maintenance of registration (Lower Burma Land and Revenue Act art. 15–17; Upper Burma Land Revenue Ordinance art. 30, 53). Also, a system of temporary relinquishment of land to the revenue officer was set up, where the land was nationalized if relinquishment continued for more than 12 years (art. 12–14), and where the land was immediately auctioned after 30 days of delay following notice, the old right was extinguished, whose outcome equated to a declaration of nationalization (Land and Revenue Act, art 48; Upper Burma Land and Revenue Ordinance, art. 42; Lower Burma

Town and Village Act, art. 11–15). Severe penalties such as payment of five times the amount of tax and imprisonment were available for breaching eviction orders after nationalization (Land and Revenue Act, art. 22A; Lower Burma Town and Village Act, art.19).

Thus, the "landholder's right" was configured as vulnerable as a tenancy interest to be created by the government and subject to its unilateral cancellation. It lacked the exclusiveness that the precolonial *myay-thay* or *myay-sheng* had as comparable to the modern concept of ownership, and rather reminds us of the layered structure of the British feudal land relation. Nevertheless, the "landholder's right" was designed to be a transferable title as a commodity, which made its legal nature something other than a contractual tenancy. We might be able to support the aforementioned hypothesis of Saito (1985) that the British colonial policy intentionally made the legal nature of "landholder's right" ambiguous, by inventing a colonial land right that is transferable but subject to the state's upper authority in the multilayered land relations.

At that time, "ownership" concepts had already been introduced in neighboring Asian colonies, as seen in art. 570 of Indonesia's Civil Code brought in 1848, art. 48 of the Philippines' Civil Act of 1902, art. 49–50 of the 1920 French Indochina Civil Code and art. 1333 of Thailand's 1934 Civil Code. The "ownership" in these codes was a basis of capitalist acquisition of absolute title by land transactions, while traditional private rights of farmers often kept outside the scope of ownership registration systems.[15] Nevertheless, later on after independence, this "ownership" provided a conceptual foothold in each unique attempt to establish the exclusive right of farming population to secure their basis of livelihood. It is noteworthy that the modern land law of Burma started with an unexclusive right concept under the state control, which has been maintained up to the present as its fundamental characteristic.

3.3 Torrens-style title registration

The registration system brought by the colonial land law (Lower Burma Land and Revenue Act art. 15–17; Upper Burma Land Revenue Ordinance art. 30, 53) was what is presently known as the Torrens-style title registration, a system where the administrative entry in registry takes effect as the conclusive evidence of complete title to exclude judicial review after a certain objection period has lapsed (mirror principle), and the defects of such registration is otherwise compensated without affecting such once established title (indemnity principle), and this has the effect of eliminating all historical rights and interests in the land unless such notice is explicitly entered in the registry (curtain principle). It was a mechanism of land expropriation in the British colonies of the 19th century, since the colonists easily established an absolute and conclusive land title by way of simple registration free from all existing rights and interests and placed such a brand-new title to a free market transaction.

Torrens-style registration was said to be initiated by Sir Robert Torrens with the enactment of the 1858 Real Property Act of South Australia that was a mechanism to establish a conclusive title of a fee simple absolute, after an objection period lapsed. In colonial Burma too, the 1876 Land and Revenue Act (art. 15–17) adopted a typical Torrens-style title registration system that established a conclusive title within five years after registration, and thereafter the existence of the title could not be contested even in judicial review. However, a fundamental difference here was the legal nature of title established by the registration in Burma, which was a "landholder's right" that could be canceled by the government by many reasons, instead of a fee simple absolute that was envisaged in the South Australian model.

3.4 *Waste land grant*

Another legal system of land deprivation of colonial land law was the waste land management, that was elaborated in the 1863 Waste Land Claims Act and 1889 Upper Burma Land and Revenue Regulations. The first stage was the declaration as state land, which deprived farmers of their lands that had not been cultivated for more than two years before the enforcement of the law, including land of unknown ownership (Upper Burma Land and Revenue Regulations, art. 23(e), art. 24 para. 1). Objections by interested parties were finalized with a single appeal against the revenue officer to his superior, while judicial review was obstructed (art. 24, para. 2), and these objections were subject to a short time bar period of one-year from the state land declaration (art. 3).

The second stage was the process of waste land grant, that was the procedure of grants of such nationalized lands to the private sector (Land and Revenue Act, art. 6 (a), 18; Upper Burma Land and Revenue Regulations art. 25; Lower Burma Town and Village Act, art. 16). At this time, the interested parties who originally used the land were "evicted" without compensation, and the new right holder who was granted or leased the state-owned land had the right to self-relief of evicting these interested parties (Upper Burma Land and Revenue Regulations, art. 25–26).

This state-land declaration method was indeed a tool for colonial conquest by the European powers dating back to the 16th century, where all land for which private rights could not be proved were regarded as state land. Here the question is whether it is still a valid justification under the modern law. If land that was fallow for just two years is deemed as state-owned land, all land areas under the local agricultural practice of leaving land fallow for several years for the fertilization purpose, which is still widely found in various areas of rural Myanmar in present time, are destined to be ignored. There are also collectively managed pasture and forestry land for common use. It can be said that "state land declaration" was nothing more than the institutional framework of deprivation of land without compensation.

3.5 *Compulsory expropriation*

Another deprivation mechanism was the compulsory expropriation procedure based on the 1894 Land Acquisition Act, which was part of the "Indian Code" drafted by the Indian Law Commission that adopted the "eminent domain for public use" principle in the colonies. According to the 1894 Act, either the "public purpose" of a government project (art. 6, para. 1) or the purpose "useful to the public" of a private development project (art. 40, para. 1) was a requirement for compulsory expropriation; it was confirmed by presidential declaration and not subject to judicial review. Here it is notable that this unilateral expropriation process is available not only in national projects but also in private projects.

For interested parties, there was a system of appeal to the revenue officer, but appeals were only allowed within 30 days from the presidential declaration, and it did not allow appeals relating to the "public purpose" and was strictly limited to disputes about the measurement and the compensation only (art. 11–12, 23–24). Interested parties who could not prove a right for compensation were not entitled to appeal (art. 3 (g)), and if they objected to the eviction, they were subject to imprisonment or fines, and the compulsory execution applied (art. 46–47).

Later, the 1932 Land Expropriation Ordinance and the 1947 Land Acquisition Manual that are still applied in administrative practice today added an inspection procedure on the "public purpose" requirement (art. 18 (b)). However, this was merely a self-checking system inside the administration, with no room for appeal by interested parties.

While the compensated expropriation for public projects such as railways only began to occur in British law in the 19th century, when the theoretical limits of expropriation and the principles of compensation were still debated issues, the Indian Code went ahead as a model for colonies throughout Asia, where the parties were deprived of their private rights without given the opportunity to question the appropriateness.

3.6 Liberalization of land transactions

As another mechanism of land exploitation, the 1882 Transfer of Property Act can be mentioned, which sets the freedom of trade as the fundamental principle (art. 6) and emphasizes the protection of interests of a "bona fide third party for consideration" in the course of transactions (art. 38 to 44) prioritizing the goal of land mobilization by eliminating the complexity of existing land relations. But it also can allow malicious investors to fraudulently obtain farmland by intentionally creating a chain of transactions involving a good faith purchaser as an intermediary.

Further, the same Act (art. 53A) provides that the defect of registration doesn't affect the bona fide third party with consideration. This reminds us of the aforementioned principles of the Torrens-style registration.

The Act also introduced a mortgage system that provides for the power of sales type enforcement that completes a transfer of title immediately upon default. This design of mortgage law must have contributed to the rapid concentration of land in the hands of capitalists. In traditional Burma's law, it is said there was no concept of outright "sale" or "foreclosure" of land (Hla Aung 2008: 81–82). Even if a certain contractual relationship presents the appearance of a real estate sale, it was interpreted as collateral to be transferred for borrowing, the seller continued to cultivate the land and repay the debt with the harvested goods, and even where the buyer-mortgagee intended to enforce the right to resell the land, there was a priority "redemption right" of the heirs of the former owner.[16] When the 1882 Transfer of Property Act suddenly introduced the notion of outright sales and mortgages, and the priority of "bona fide third party for consideration," it extinguished the traditional owner's redemption right. A natural consequence was farmers suffering severe loss of land.[17]

4 Postindependence farmland reform

4.1 Land Nationalization Act

The 1953 Land Nationalization Act was a postindependence attempt to overcome the deprivation mechanisms of colonial land law. While securing the retention of farmlands to farmers up to certain standard areas (e.g., 50 acres for a standard household of four adults) (art. 6), the possession of land beyond this standard was nationalized (art. 5) and was expected to be redistributed to landless farming households to secure a standard portion of land (*Ta-ton-Hton*, an area of land that can be cultivated with two heads of cattle) (art. 7).

Not only in Burma at that time, but many countries that had gained independence from British colonial rule had each embarked on similar agricultural land reforms. In India, land reform in the 1950s aimed at the abolishment of the Zamindari system of large landholders and land redistribution on the base of purchase was developed, with the declaration that only one class of rights (*maliks*) should be recognized over all farmlands. This reform did not stop at establishing new rights that equated the land user as owner but was also designed to subsequently maintain this status with long-term stability. However, the reality of implementing such reformist land law has been shaken by various exceptions.[18]

Also in the design of the Land Nationalization Act in Myanmar, there was a sense of compromise with the class of capitalist landowners. If one person in a household is continuously engaged in agriculture, the household is considered an "agricultural household" and exempted from nationalization (art. 6); further, in addition to the standard area, there were various added concessions that considered even nonagricultural households (Schedules I and II). These design features of Burma's 1953 Land Nationalization Act provided certain rooms for eased implementation toward existing landed class. During the U Nu regime, less than 6 percent of the total farmland was redistributed, and in the following Ne Win era, there were few results of redistribution.[19]

4.2 Ambiguous nature of farmers' rights

Even if the results were limited for the redistribution, the 1953 Land Nationalization Act did play a role in securing the existing farmers within the land holding limit (art. 6). Then, what was the nature of such property rights of farmers? It was expressed as the right to possess, cultivate and profit from land, and to sell, transfer or gift land to farmers and nonfarmers who promised to use the land for agriculture, and to divide and exchange land (art. 9).

On the other hand, the Act clearly prohibited the provision of land for mortgage, sale or other transfer or division that violated the law or regulations (art. 4), unless an approval is given by the President (art. 9). Thus, the structural design of a farmer's right under the 1953 Act was similar to those of other Asian postindependent land reforms with the protective design of farmland owner-and-cultivators, such as Japan's 1952 Farmland Act.

However, the decisive difference is in the vulnerable legal substance of such farmer's right that ceases to exist subject to the state's unilateral cancellation up on the violation of various obligations. Namely, any violations to the prohibitions of mortgage and transfers, as well as the failure to meet with obligations of continual usage of the land, payment of taxes and revenue, maintaining agricultural household or not to leaving the land fallow without valid reason were the grounds for confiscation of the land (art. 29 to 32). This legal design closely resembles the "landholder's right" under colonial land law, which was easily extinguished for breaches of tax obligations, abandonment of cultivation for two years and violation of registration obligations, etc.

It is a preface to modern ownership rights that the state must compensate for the public taking, putting aside police purpose regulations. Also in the traditional Burmese law before colonization, the established property title of *bo bwa paing* could even resist the king's taking. But the 1953 Land Nationalization Act did not choose to reinstate such traditional characteristic of the land right and rather, succeeded the colonial design as weak as a tenancy of state land that was destined to cease when conditions failed.

In the following decades, as social criticism against unsatisfactory result of the redistribution roared, the late U Nu government pushed the protection of tenancy rights to the front, which seemed to be an attempt to pacify the gap between independent farmers and tenant farmers, by narrowing the gap of legal natures between their rights.[20] The 1963 Tenancy Act and its 1965 revision emphasized the protection of tenancy rights by measures such as controlling rents.

The closeness between small-scale farming and tenant farming became more prominent in the Ne Win era, particularly since the declaration by the Central Agricultural Committee in 1970, which expressed both the rights of independent farmers and tenant farmers equally as "*loat paing kwint*" or right to use for cultivation purposes.[21] It is ironic that the choice of tenancy policy in Burma for pacifying the social criticisms against the compromised implementation of land redistribution was the path to lower the status of small-scale farmers closer to that of tenants.

5. Contemporary land law reform in Myanmar

5.1 Cultivation rights under the 2012 Farmland Law

In a struggle to get away from the controlled agriculture under the Ne Win regime, followed by the unarranged land policies by the military government after the 1988 coup d'état, there has been a series of land law reform under the current 2008 Constitution guided by international donors. That is, the 2012 Farmland Law (Law No. 2/2012) and its implementation rules (including the Ministry of Agriculture and Irrigation Notification No. 62/2012) and the 2012 Vacant, Fallow and Virgin Lands Management Law (Law No. 10/2012) and its implementation rules (including Ministry of Agriculture and Irrigation Notification No. 1/2012) appeared with great fanfare. Along with these, the 1953 Land Nationalization Act, the 1963 Tenancy Law and the 1963 Law Safeguarding Peasant Rights were abolished.

The highlight of the land reform was the nationwide simultaneous registration of farmland title conducted under the 2012 Farmland Law. It is often said farmers' rights have been strengthened through this reform that made the agricultural system shift to a free market economy. However, as for the legal nature of thus registered title, the 2012 Farmland Law adopts the same expressions as the 1953 Land Nationalization Act, as *loat paing kwint*, that is, the right of cultivation use. It is neither a modern "ownership" nor the *bo ba paing* land title established in traditional Burmese law. It is stated that the state as the original owner of all lands gives permission for cultivation use in conformity with this law and related regulations so that agricultural production capacity develops (art. 3 (d)). Also noted is the appearance of words *loat paing kwint* (usage right) and *aton pyaw kwint* (profit right) in the 2012 Vacant, Fallow and Virgin Lands Management Law (art. 4) that inherited the system of waste land grant of colonial law. Even though the 2012 Farmland Law has established the freedom of transfers, it cannot be said that the right is strengthened, if the substantive basis of the right is unchanged.

Indeed, *loat paing kwint* has uncertainties in its substantive details. While individual farmers are obliged to continue the farming according to the law (art. 6 (a), art. 7 (a), art. 12 (a)), such provisions do not apply to the organizations or companies, which makes the individual households disadvantaged in the title contests with the investors. Such title conflict is left to the dispute resolution procedure through the Agricultural Land Management Committees of each administrative layer (art. 22 to 25).

Loat paing kwint is designed to be easily lost due to breaches of public obligations (Farmland Act, art. 19; Vacant, Fallow and Virgin Lands Management Law, art. 16), which exactly follows the structure of the colonial "landholders' right" under the 1876 Land and Revenue Act (art. 8, 11, 15–17), which was inherited by the 1953 Land Nationalization Act (art. 4, 11, 29–32). It is noteworthy that the 2012 Farmland Law further adds opportunities for farmers to lose rights beyond those in the previous acts. Namely, in addition to tax violations (art. 12 (b)), abandonment of cultivation (art. 12 (b)(i)) and registration deficiencies (art. 12 (c) and (d), art. 13), which were also prescribed in the 1953 Act, the 2012 Farmland Act goes as far as being reminiscent of the agricultural control system in the Ne Win era, such as violations of permits for nonagricultural use and violation of crop-changing permits.

With this vulnerable legal nature as a property right close to a tenancy of the state land, which reminds us of the layered structure inherited from the British feudal law, the 2012 Farmland Law cannot be deemed as the donors' attempt to secure the status of farming population but looks more as an attempt to promote capitalist transactions of farmland.

5.2 *Revival of title registration system*

Myanmar's current land registration system for farmland has succeeded a binary structure since the colonial law, implementing a deed registration system that gives the effect of public notice under the 1909 Registration Act (recently substituted by the 2018 Registration Act with nominal change), and also a title registration system by the 2012 Farmland Law, which took over the land record system under the 1953 Land Nationalization Act.

In regional areas, both registrations are under the jurisdiction of the registry office belonging to the district-level Department of Farmland Management and Statistics under the Ministry of Agriculture, Livestock and Irrigation. Among them, the deed registration system for town land is managed by seven types of Books based on the Registration Act, in which all deeds relating to contracts on land and buildings are transcribed into the Book-1 register in chronological order. The contents of the deed are transcribed word-for-word by hand by the registrar, the signatures of all parties are confirmed and two registration certificates (Form 105) are prepared, with one certificate attached to the register. Under the practice of the 1953 Land Nationalization Act, the data contained in this Book-1 register were used for ex officio entry to the land records compiled for each right holder (1A register) as well as the records compiled by geographical area (1B register).

But the 2012 Farmland Law has newly obliged farmers to participate in the simultaneous registration carried out nationwide from 2012 to 2013 as one of the requirements for the *loat paing kwint* to be effective (art. 4).[22] All inheritance and assignments after the simultaneous registration must also be registered by each party under the Farmland Law (art. 12 (c) and (d)).[23] Failure to register will see the right extinguished as a violation of the requirement of *loat paing kwint* (art. 19). Registration is definite evidence and cannot be judicially reviewed (art. 13). Thus, the registration of farmland is a necessary requirement for the emergence of and subsequent changes to *loat paing kwint*, similar to the Torrens-style registration system under the colonial law.

However, this registration system under the 2012 Farmland Law has an aspect that differs from the colonial law. The registration under the colonial 1876 Land and Revenue Act (art. 15–17) established a title five years after registration, and thereafter the existence of the title could not be contested in judicial review. In contrast to this, under the 2012 Farmland Law, farmers who failed to prove their right at the time of the simultaneous registration and could not obtain a registered title are still given the opportunity to object without time limit (art. 22 to 25). The real practice of implementation of this procedure will be investigated in Section 6.

5.3 *Vacant, Fallow and Virgin Lands Management Law – reviving waste land grant system*

The contemporary land law reform is expected to address to the problem of "land grabbing" or the forced seizure of farmland by state or military power, which occurred frequently in the 1990s according to the legal basis of the 1991 Vacant, Fallow and Virgin Lands Management Procedure (Notification No. 41 of 1991) introduced by the military government after the coup in 1988. It was a revival of the colonial method of waste land grant, as discussed earlier with the 1861 Waste Land Management Act and the 1889 Upper Burma Land and Revenue Regulations.

Law on Vacant, Fallow and Virgin Lands Management adopted in 2012 is, however, a confirmation of this method of waste land grant. The Central Committee for Vacant, Fallow and Virgin Lands Management, established by the President under the Ministry of Agriculture and Irrigation (art. 3), in consultation with the Myanmar Investment Committee (MIC) (art. 7), is a mechanism for granting rights to use land (*loat paing*) and to receive benefits (*aton pyaw*) (art. 4) to the joint ventures between Myanmar investors and foreign investors (art. 5). Although "land grabbing" has been heavily criticized as an act by the military government, it is ironic that Myanmar's parliament reenacted this 2012 Law that follows the same legal basis used by the military for land grabbing.

In 2018, an amendment was made to this 2012 Law with a campaign to mitigate the law's exploitative effect. But its essence was the extended coverage of forestry and waterfront areas (amended art. 2 (f)) without changing the substance of wasteland management mechanism, except a minimum chance of local participation (amended art. 3 (a)). While the emphasis is made for the encouragement of local landless population to apply for the wasteland grant (art. 5 (a)), the criminal penalties were increased on those who resist the eviction (art. 27), which only reveals the policy of further strengthening this colonial-inherited land exploitation mechanism.

5.4 *Land Acquisition Law reform*

While waste land grant method is the deprivation of land without compensation, the compulsory expropriation procedure is a mechanism for the compensated requisition of property rights. The colonial 1894 Land Acquisition Act has recently been substituted by the 2019 Land Acquisition, Resettlement and Rehabilitation Law, as the result of guidance by the international donors,[24] to reflect art. 356 and art. 372 of Myanmar's 2008 Constitution.

But the 2019 Law still maintains the same structure as colonial law. The essence of the acquisition procedure under 1894 Land Acquisition Act was a unilateral declaration of land acquisition by the President (art. 6), which could not be appealed against. Prior to this declaration, a survey is performed without a court warrant (art. 4), and an objection against the survey is finalized by the

President's administrative judgment, which cannot be contested. Once the President's unilateral declaration of acquisition is in place, this is definitive evidence of its "public purpose" (art. 6, sec. 3), and the court shall not give substantive consideration (art. 24). The 2019 Land Acquisition, Resettlement and Rehabilitation Law, as the result of the donors' involvement, has maintained such basic structure of the 1894 Act.

It is true that the 2019 Law incorporates new procedural improvements, such as requiring the compensation plan to be included in the initial scrutiny (art. 9 (f)); incorporating the Parliament's involvement for certain cases (art.15); obliging the "public purpose" of the acquisition to be explained in the declaration (art.16 (b)(ii)) as well as the socio-environmental considerations to be disclosed (art. 16 (c)); prioritizing the voluntary sales negotiation to the compulsory taking (art. 16 (d)); prolonging the objection period from 30 days under the 1894 Act to 45 days (art. 18 (a)); clarifying the range of those who can raise an objection by defining the term "affected persons" that includes not only the land title holders but also the crop-sharing tenants, fixed rent tenants, joint venture partners and the peaceful land user for 12 years or longer (art. 18, art. 3 (k)); and explicitly referring to the possibility of the cancellation of once made declaration after the hearing of objection (art. 19, 20, 28). However, the basic nature of unilateral declaration (art. 16) and the finality of governmental decision uncontested by the judicial review (art. 28) are firmly maintained.

Another noteworthy point of the 1894 Act was the public acquisition process for private companies, for the construction of corporate housing by companies (art. 39) and construction activities "useful to the public" (art. 40). The 2019 Land Acquisition, Resettlement and Rehabilitation Law has even enlarged the possibility of public acquisition for private projects by newly introducing a list of eligible projects for the acquisition for "public purpose" (art. 2, art. 3 (h)), which widely covers the development projects under the National Economic Policy and the National Planning Law, urban development and infrastructure building, the projects for resettlement and rehabilitation and other acquisitions under existing laws except for the Vacant, Fallow and Virgin Lands Law and the Farmland Law.

In sum, the newness of the 2019 Land Acquisition, Resettlement and Rehabilitation Law is limited to the "early participation" to incorporate an objection procedure prior to the finalization of the effect of the declaration of acquisition (art. 28). The 1894 Act already had a similar administrative objection procedure, but the 2019 Law is understood to have detailed it as a participatory procedure (art. 21–23), which may vest a chance for an affected group of people to exercise an increased bargaining power to influence the proportionality contest between the public purpose and the adequate compensation.

It should be noted, on the other hand, that the land acquisition under the Farmland Law and the Vacant, Fallow and Virgin Lands Law are exempted from the application of the 2019 Law. The 2012 Farmland Law has a single provision (art. 29) regarding the decision of compulsory acquisition by the Union Government based on the advice of the Central Agriculture Committee, while the 2012 Regulation No. 67 provides for the standard for compensation,[25] which is almost similar to the standards under the 2019 Law (art. 42), but one substantial difference is that the 2019 Law (art. 36) vests the affected persons a wider choice of the mode of compensation, such as monetary compensation, substitution of land, resettlement and rehabilitation projects and a swap to the investment shares to the project.

An implication is that the policy tendency of the 2019 Land Acquisition, Resettlement and Rehabilitation Law, a result of elaboration of international donors, has after all been the promotion of land acquisition for the furthermost of economic development, while emphasizing the early participation and the increased choices of compensation as the means to soothe the local objections.

5.5 *Prioritization of land transactions*

The 1953 Land Nationalization Act exercised control over the creation of mortgage on land from the viewpoint of controlling the loss of farmland, which occurred during the colonial time to the degree making the historian J. S. Furnivall lament as aforementioned. Since this restriction by the 1953 Act was removed by the 2012 Farmland Law, farmland mortgage has revived, which has been professed as freeing farmers from illegal high-interest loans. However, such argument is inaccurate without considering the exploitative structure of the mortgage provisions still maintained under the 1882 Transfer of Property Act.

The 1882 Act defines five types of financial mortgages, whose enforcement can be done through "power of sales" or private enforcement (art. 69 (1)) if explicitly defined in the security contract or as a matter of course for contracts in urban areas such as Yangon. The entire sum received from the sale by private enforcement is received by the security holder, and there is no obligation to account to the debtor (art. 69 (4)). In practice,[26] the Mortgage by Deposit of Title Deeds is overwhelmingly used among five choices, as it allows the flexible enforcement, including the illegal high-interest lenders to conveniently enforce their security privately via the power of sale without going through the courts (art. 69 (1)). Even in case of enforcement though a judicial foreclosure proceeding (art. 67), a "power of sales" acts in parallel as a pressure to prevent the debtor to slow down the judicial process.

The fact that the 19th-century structure of mortgage law is maintained today gives excessive superiority to financial capitalists, which not only distorts rural finance but also hinders debtors' freedom to diversify their access to finance and utilize their assets.

6 Land dispute resolution under the Myanmar National Land Use Policy

6.1 *Redefining the rights of farmland*

While the 2012 land law reform was thus dedicated to the farmland fluidization through the revival of title registration, liberalization of land transfer and promotion of waste land management, the reform naturally invited the furtherance of land disputes. The Union President announced the "Myanmar National Land Use Policy" in February 2016, with an intention to overcome the social disturbance. This Policy showed struggles to balance the two opposing policies of farmland protection and the economic developmentalism as shown in its Foreword defining controversial objectives, namely, the sustainable land use aimed toward the future (para. 1, paras. 6 (a), 8 (a)), separation of the state and private rights (para. 3), stabilization of land titles as the foundation of livelihoods (para. 4, para. 6 (b)), and the respect of customary rights (para. 6 (c)), while emphasizing economic methods such as utilization of market mechanisms, promotion of land title registration and utilization of land tax reduction (para. 8 (d)(f)).

It is notable that the final version of the Policy added emphasis to the issuance of new title certificates to the actual cultivators, regardless of whether they have been registered (para. 16 (e)), and community consultation and participatory land use mapping methods should be used in performing such titling (para. 17 (f)).

Then, how has the identification of actual cultivators been done for this new title issuance? The 2012 Farmland Law vests the title of cultivation right *loat paing kwint* to individual households by the criteria of "legally occupied and cultivated" (art. 6 (a)), and to the organizations and companies when they receive farming permit (art. 6 (b)). But this determination is left to the dispute resolution procedures (art. 22 to 25), which are detailed in the Farmland Rule (art. 59–63) through a four-tiered system: with the Village-Tract level Farmland Management Committee conducting the first instance hearing, and appeals are to be heard at the Township, District, and State/Region levels. Then, what is the substantive basis for this base level Farmland Management Committee members to resolve the title disputes? It seems to be a work of redefining the cultivation right *loat paing kwint*, which is the fundamental right on farmland under the 2012 Farmland Law, but which has never been clearly defined. As a result, the base level Farmland Management Committees are entrusted with the hard task of deciding to whom the land title certificate of *loat paing kwint* (Form 7) should be issued, especially when the conflict occurs between a farming household and an investor. The same decision is entrusted to the Committee when an investor seeks for the conversion from farmlands to town lands (art. 30 or the La Na 39 certificate), necessitating the confirmation of the *loat paing kwint* of such party as a premise.

In January 2017, the authors had a chance of on-site interview with the support of the General Administration Department of the Ministry of Home Affairs of Myanmar (at that time) and hosted by the Region's agriculture minister and the district commissioners in Dawei and Myeik districts in Tanintharyi Region, the very historical place where the British colonial reign first started in the early 19th-century Burma. According to the data disclosed, the annual number of farmland title disputes that rise to the Tanintharyi Regional-level Farmland Management Committees was as few as four cases in 2012 when the simultaneous registration was started under the 2012 Farmland Law, but it dramatically increased thereafter (detailed number was not obtained), and in 2016 had eased

Table 15.2 Number of disputes handled by Farmland Management Committees in Tanintharyi Region

	Region Farmland Management Committees	*District-level Farmland Management Committees (3 districts)*	*Township-level Farmland Management Committees (10 townships)*
2012	4	7	11
2016	19	30	32

Source: The authors' interview with the Tanintharyi Region's Farmland Management Committee, January 2017.

Table 15.3 Land-related disputes in Myeik District (2012)

	District	*Township*	*Ward/Village Tract*
Farmland Titling Disputes (by Farmland Management Committees)	3	4	20
Number of expropriations of farmland (by Scrutinizing Committee for Acquisition of Farmland and Other Land)	3	n.a.	234

Source: The authors' interview with the Myeik District Commissioner, Tanintharyi Region, January 2017.

at 19 cases. However, the further down the administrative chain toward the District and Township levels, the more of fresh farmland disputes are continuing (Table 15.2). As seen in the number of disputes in Myeik District (Table 15.3) on cases concerning the land titling (handled by the Farmland Management Committees) as well as cases concerning land acquisition (handled by the Scrutinizing Committee for Acquisition of Farmland and Other Land), most objections occur at the village-tract level, which is at the front line of disputes. Interestingly, the appeal rate is remarkably low since the vast majority of disputes are settled at this base level.

As for the composition of the Farmland Management Committees, while all administrative levels of State/Region, District, Township and Village-Tract Committees are headed by the administrative chief under the vertical control by the General Administration Department, and the deputy chief is sent by the Department of Agricultural Land Management and Statistics, only in the base level of Village-Tract, each committee has three publicly selected members in addition to two administrative representatives.

The authors interviewed four of such publicly selected members who were retired civil servants or intellectuals such as former teachers. When asked about the methods of dispute resolution, they emphasized upon a "mediation" having an adversarial structure with the parties facing each other and asserting their opinions in open forum so that any local residents can listen, which often continues day and night in order to extensively progress debate until all parties are satisfied, as the hearing period at this base level is limited by the Farmland Law to 15 days. The members never hold closed caucuses with each individual party, nor press mediation proposals upon them. Unlike mediation in normal facilitative sense, the goal of this procedure is not the facilitation of any compromise, but the fact-finding in an open forum, and it does not demand unreasonable compromise. The secret of dispute resolution with a high success rate at the base level seems to be the fair method for fact-finding.

Asked about the basis of fact-finding on the existence of *loat paing kwint*, all of the interviewed members of the Village-Tract level Farmland Management Committee responded that it is very simple. The core of such investigation is the fact of who is actually cultivating the farmland, according to the fundamental requirement of a continuous cultivation for a minimum of five years, based upon the continued operational practice under the 1953 Land Nationalization Act.

When this standard is applied, the logical consequences seem to be that perpetual tenant farmers can claim a *loat paing kwint*, while a temporary lessee less than five years cannot obtain such a right. The question is if this *loat paing kwint* is being established as the highest right on farmland, or if it is considered merely as a tenancy interest that is subject to the upper layer of control by either the state or private absentee ownership. On this point, the ideal of farmland security for actual cultivators was firmly held between the Committee members, and in their belief, *loat paing kwint* is equal to ownership. But the author's question of how many years of recess of cultivation for the purpose of fertilization makes a *loat paing kwint* cease to exist was not clearly answered, while some of the Committee members referred to the fact of tax payment and local custom.

It was also notable that, although the Farmland Law (art. 25 (c)) provides that the State/Region-level decisions are final and that they even bind the courts, a view is held among all level Committee members that this "finality" is subject to the Supreme Court's prerogative writs. This implies a stance of the administration placed on the ultimate satisfaction of the parties, rather than the promotion of land transactions through quick confirmation of title as originally envisaged in Torrens-style registration.

In August 2018, the authors also had the other opportunity to interview the chairman and members of a village-tract level Farmland Management Committee in Lawei district on the outskirts of the capital Naypyidaw, as an example of upper Myanmar. It was obvious from the historical land records and maps at the land registry office that a stable farmland order has been maintained since the British colonial period in this area. Of the total 1,500 households, 40 percent are landed farmers and 60 percent are from the so-called landless class though they actually have left farming and work in office or business. There were only a few cases of direct objection to the title certificate issuance under the 2012 Farmland Law, but there are some cases in which siblings have disputed the title certificates in connection with inheritance disputes. The dispute resolution method is similar to Myeik District described earlier, a fact-finding with thorough discussion in the presence of both parties through a public, adversarial "mediation" process. Some of these disputes were appealed and further disputed in court, but the courts tend to respect the results of fact-finding by the base-level Farmland Management Committee.[27] The same tendency of deciding on the fact of actual cultivation by a continuous cultivation for five years was obvious in this interview.

6.2 *Torrens-style title registration modified in practice*

It is also interesting to see that the Farmland Management Committees have been hearing the disputes over title even after many years had passed since the simultaneous title registration in 2012. While one of the main features of the original Torrens-style title registration system is a short time limitation for filing objections as aforementioned with the aim of quickly finalizing the absolute title, the Myanmar's 2012 Farmland Law does not clearly indicate a time limitation for claims, and ceaseless objections are being heard at the forefront of farmland administration. In the authors' interviews, the publicly elected members of the Committees even showed their enthusiasm to determine the truth until the last stroke. We may conclude that the registration system of the 2012 Farmland Law has not revived the same Torrens-style title registration as the colonial time, at least at the grassroots administrative level of dispute resolution. Rather, attention should be focused on the fact that a title is being established over time according to the social norm of upholding the actual cultivator.

Another notable aspect is the operation of land registry. According to the authors' interview survey with land registry officers in January 2017 in the Dawei and Myeik districts of Tanintharyi Region, and in August 2018 in the Lewei Township in Naipaytaw, the current administrative operation of land transfer maintains the approval system by the Farmland Management Committee. In particular, a cautious view is taken by the Committees to the land transactions involving the change from agricultural use to other use (issuance of so-called La Na 39 certificate). Also, the registry office has not yet commenced the administrative work of registering mortgages over farmland due to the delay of implementation rules. As long as the administrative workplace maintains the farmland protection policy, and unless "top-down" projects are brought about in political line, the liberalization of transfer of *loat paing kwint* under the 2012 Farmland Law is limited to land liquidity among cultivators.

6.3 *Resolving the "land-grabbing"*

Among the problems that have been generally criticized as "land-grabbing," the National Land Use Policy refers to different spheres, namely:

(1) Land acquisition under the 1894 Land Acquisition Act, which does provide for compensation to cultivators who have titles, but there are battles over the procedures and the amount of compensation: for which the Policy refers to

the amendments that stipulate public participation from the project planning stage, countermeasures against corruption, optimization of compensation standards and strengthening livelihood recovery measures (para. 40), while learning from international best practices (para. 38). This aspect has been met by the introduction of the 2019 Land Acquisition, Resettlement and Rehabilitation Law.

(2) Problem of evicting short-term residents or so-called squatters who do not have registered titles capable of resisting the waste land nationalization for grant. Legally speaking, they should not be simply named squatters if they were the cultivators deprived of farmland while it was left unused for fertilization purposes, or if they collectively manage the communal land that lacks the means of public notice at the registry. But the Policy does not differentiate them and instead emphasizes an environmental and social impact assessment (ESIA) on squatters: in case of projects for "public purpose," it emphasized the resettlement through consultation and participatory procedures (para. 32 (a)); while for "private purpose" projects, the intention of residents is given priority (clauses (b) and (c)). It also refers to the land redistribution for the landless class (clause (f)).

(3) Problem of illegal confiscation of fallow land by the military pursuant to Notice No. 41 of 1991, which looks similar to the previously mentioned squatter relocation problem but separately treated. Mechanisms for land dispute resolution is considered a topic of future research (para. 80 (n)), such as dispute resolution involving the participation of farmers' associations (para. 41), establishment of a new special tribunal separate from existing administrative and judicial procedures as well as a monitoring system (para. 42).

(4) Restitution of land that was lost during the civil war, which was a newly added topic in the 2016 final version of the "National Land Use Policy" (para. 74), regarded as a topic for future research (para. 80 (n)).

To investigate and resolve these categories of land-grabbing cases, under the auspices of a presidential order issued in 2016, a "Scrutinizing Committee on Acquisition of Farmland and Other Land" was established at each level of local administration. As for such committees' formation, the authors found a certain degree of local participation in the aforementioned survey conducted in January 2017 in Tanintharyi Region, where the base-level committee at the Ward and Village Tract level had three publicly nominated members from the community and two administrative representatives. Positioned above this are the Township and District levels, which in addition to the members of Farmland Management Committee, also have one member from the local assembly, one public member and three NGO delegates participating as members.

In 2019, the Central Scrutinizing Committee on Acquisition of Farmlands and Other Lands issued the revised principles for policy, process and performance for the lower committees in solving land-grabbing cases, with an expectation to expedite the nationwide settlement of land disputes before the general election scheduled in November 2020. It consists of 52 principles for settling farmland return cases, particularly when the claimer has a genuine right on farmland or the *loat paing kwint*.

Namely, the 2019 principles first declared the goal of settling all disputes on land acquisition from genuine right holders that occurred after the 1998 military coup (section 1(a)). The point of whether the claimant has a genuine right over farmland is decided by ex officio investigation of documentary evidence such as tax receipts and also by the testimonies (section 3(a)). The title registration is not a necessary nor final evidence in here, and rather, the acquisition based on unlawfully issued title certificates (such as Form 7 for *loat paing kwint* and La Na 39 for farmland use change) has to be canceled and sent back to the original farmer (section 1(j)). If a genuine right is not established in this stage, the context will be turned to a squatter on a waste land.

The 2019 principles made it the rule to return all acquired land for private development projects that were granted for excessively long periods, and also the land once acquired for public purpose but such a public purpose has ceased to exist (section 1(b)). The adequacy of length of grant is decided by the consideration of proportionality between the purpose and the effect (section 3(d)).

It also sets a rule that a land acquisition for public purpose that was conducted lawfully can be maintained if the payment of compensation and damage is completed (section 1(c)), while the cases acquired for public purpose but conducted unlawfully (section 1(d)), and the cases lacking the public purpose even if conducted lawfully (section 1(e)) cannot be sustained and the land should be returned. In here, the point of whether the "public purpose" exists is decided not only by the original intention but also by the actual effect (sections 3(c), 4(e)). The point of whether the acquisition was conducted lawfully is decided by the legal procedures then applicable (sections 3(b), 4(a)). The point of whether the proper compensation was made is decided by the laws then applicable (section 4(a)) and decided based on the governmental records or other evidence (section 4(b)(c)). If the farmer did not accept any compensation since the time of acquisition, he or she is entitled to the compensation based on the current market price (section 1(g)).

Thus, the 2019 principles of the Union-level Scrutinizing Committee have focused on the land acquisition cases raised by farmers claiming land title. The land-grabbing cases by the military are also targeted as aforementioned. The basic policy stance is straightforward to confirm the farmers' cultivation rights and return the land unless the acquisition projects maintain the public purpose and the procedure is lawful, including the adequate compensation payment. However, the actual implementation of such principles must include varieties of delicate considerations on what is the genuine cultivation right, what is the public purpose, what is the lawful procedure and what is the adequate compensation. The reality of dispute settlement involves a political compromise.

Such a political nature of land dispute settlement is particularly evident in the acquisition cases for urbanization and commercial development purposes, which the 2019 principles specially entrust to the State/Region government through a tripartite negotiation (section 1(i)). This reminds us of the National Land Use

Policy that emphasized the participatory approach particularly for the land use change from agriculture to commercial or industrial use, often known as La Na 39 (para. 19 (c)), and the urban land use planning (paras. 21 (d), 22, 27). Here, the ideal of farmland protection suddenly turns under a logic of political negotiation at around the urban peripheral. Such a participatory approach without identifying the substantial rule for urbanization control is questionable and could result in an indulgence for the development projects.

Another characteristic of the 2019 principles is the straightforward stance on land-grabbing cases involving the military (aforementioned (3) category), which has been the overall denial of the military's commercial operations outside the national security purpose, and the immediate return of lands to original holders. However, illegal confiscation of fallow lands is not the only matter of the military, but the current 2012 Vacant, Fallow and Virgin Lands Management Law openly legalizes the operation of the government to nationalize fallow lands and grant them to investors, to succeed the waste land management method of the colonial land law. The logic is weak in that the implementation of the National Land Use Policy keeps silent on the land grabbing by the actors other than the military.

In August 2019, some of the authors' team had the opportunity to interview with the leaders of four villages near Mawlamyine city in Mon State. They were Mon ethnic minority and had a dispute with the local administration over their ancestry farmland, which the government suddenly confiscated without compensation and granted it for development projects. The disputed farmland was registered in the land record system under the 1953 Land Nationalization Act, had the certificates of cultivation rights and had retained tax receipts, but it failed to be registered when the simultaneous title registration was conducted under the 2012 Farmland Law due to the lack of knowledge on such new Law. The disputed land had been left fallow, and as a result, it seems the land was confiscated as vacant land. But in the firm belief of the villagers, it is the established custom that the rights inherited from their ancestors should not be disturbed, no matter how many years land has not been cultivated. They also insisted that ceasing of cultivation is unavoidable in Mon State because of a shortage of labor due to the young migrants' outflow to Thailand. This seems to be a typical case of land grabbing by nonmilitary actors under the 2012 Vacant, Fallow and Virgin Lands Management Law, which the government's 2019 principles did not focus on.

6.4 Need to reform the Transfer of Property Act

Even if participatory procedures are established and the substantive content of private rights are strengthened, the farmland will not be secured unless the 19th-century style property transaction law is reformed. The 1882 Transfer of Property Act brought from India during the British colonial era is maintained in Myanmar, which promotes the land transactions by prioritizing the interests of bona fide third party with considerations. Substantive law reform that balances the interests of investors and the people's rights will be awaited. For example, after a land sale with registration, can a tenant farmer assert his or her right for cultivation or a lease that existed on such land against the new buyer?

It is also essential to restructure the financial mortgage system in harmony with agricultural and housing policy. At the very least, establishing a rule for the return of surplus funds after the enforcement of a mortgage is necessary. To develop the fair financial practice to make the Simple Mortgage as the primary means of mortgage publicity in order to overcome the abuse of the Mortgage by Deposit of Title Deeds, the integration of the land record system and the deed registration is another crucial issue.[28] Without such reforms of law on property transactions, the National Land Use Policy will remain an abstract theory.

7 Summary and conclusion: dispute resolution toward the redefining of land rights

This chapter tried to understand the causes of contemporary land disputes in Myanmar through a historical review of the land law changes across time. It seemed to be a drama of conflicting legal policies between the two main axes, namely, the policy to secure the subsistent basis of livelihood on farmland, on one hand, and the policy prioritizing the free transactions of land as commodity as represented by the British colonial land law, on the other. The colonial land law featured a series of exploitative legal mechanisms including the derogation of farmer's status into an ambiguous "landholder's right," which was transferable but as weak as a tenancy, introduction of Torrens-style title registration system that finalized the title free from existing rights and interests, the waste land management system that nationalized untitled lands for grants to investments, the compulsory land acquisition applied to private projects, as well as the transaction law prioritizing the status of a bona fide purchaser. The postindependence Land Nationalization Act in 1953 attempted to overcome such colonial apparatus toward the farmland securing policy by restricting the land transfer, but its implementation came under excessive governmental control, which gradually made the nature of a farmer's title as weak as a tenancy interest. The contemporary land law reform guided by the international donors has brought about a series of legislations that featured the liberation of land transactions, revival of title registration system to facilitate land fluidization, deregulation of farmland use change to commercial purposes, legalization of waste land management and land acquisition law to utilize public taking for private projects, which seemed to be a revival of the colonial land law mechanisms meant for the commoditization of land. Table 15.4 gives a summary of these legal changes over time.

In Section 6, the authors observed legal causes of contemporary land disputes in the light of the aforementioned features of land law designs that have been historically fluctuating between the two policy axes. One of the common implications from these cases has been a need to redefine the farmers' land right. The British colonial land law defined it as "landholder's right" with an ambiguous legal nature that was easily canceled by the discretionary will of the state maintaining the upper authority over land, as if reflecting the layered structure of the

Table 15.4 Summary of historical changes of land law designs in Myanmar

	Precolonial era (Manugye Dhammathat, etc.)	*Colonial land law (1876 Land and Revenue Act, etc.)*	*Postcolonial era (1953 Land Nationalization Act)*	*Contemporary land reform (2012 Farmland Law, etc.)*	*Modification through land dispute settlement*
Land Title	*Bo Ba Pain* as *myay-thay* (full title); and *myay-sheng* such as purchased land, and a cleared forest land during acquisitive prescription	*Landholder's right* with ambiguous legal nature (transferable tenancy or lease), obtained by registration	*Farmer's right to cultivation* later called *Loat Paing Kwint* full title subject to resolutive condition of continued cultivation, regardless of registration →weakened	*Loat Paing Kwint* transferable but undefined legal nature, obtained by registration	*Loat Paing Kwint* interpreted as full title subject to resolutive condition of continued cultivation, regardless of registration
Registration	Land record	Final evidence of title	Land record	Final evidence of title	Disputable
Land Transfer	Communal order	Free	Restricted	Free	Communal order
Waste land management	None	Nationalization of unregistered land	None	Nationalization of unregistered land	Squatters' prescription context
Land acquisition	Rare	Unilateral discretion for both public and private projects	Unilateral discretion for both public and private projects	Unilateral discretion for both public and private projects + participatory procedure	Stricter consideration on "public purpose" and due procedure

Source: summary by the authors.

traditional British land law. Such a layered system was something that was eliminated in other jurisdictions in Asia, which chose to establish an exclusive type of land right equivalent to the "ownership" concept in the continental civil code. In Myanmar, the postindependence attempt of the 1953 Land Nationalization Act was to reestablish the farmer's land right as a firm title, but the Act succeeded the same layered structure as the colonial law in terms of the state authority of conditional cancellation maintained over the private rights. Even after the repeal of the 1953 Land Nationalization Act, the 2021 Farmland Law succeeded the same layered structure.

In the forefront of land dispute resolution, however, the authors have found the fact that both the members of the Farmland Management Committee and the disputing parties shared a notion that the right of actual cultivator is firm and perpetual and should not be confiscated by the governmental discretion nor granted for investors. The authors understand that such commonly held notion on the nature of a farmer's right indicates a right concept equivalent to the exclusive title of either *Myay-thay* or *Myay-sheng* in the Burmese tradition, which the British colonial rulers intentionally avoided to recognize for the convenience of colonial exploitation.

Perhaps, the ultimate settlement of contemporary land disputes will not be possible without facing the fact of farmers' perpetual claims for full title, toward reestablishing their highest perpetual right on farmland. Some of the overseas cases of successful farmland security against land fluidization, such as Japan under the 1952 Farmland Law, which has maintained the small-scale farming even after recognizing a full ownership title for them, will alleviate the fear of Myanmar lawmakers regarding land fluidization as a result of full title offering.

The recent endeavors of the Aung San Suu Kyi government aiming at the settlement of all land disputes before November 2020 election should be a critical chance for such a redefinition of a farmer's exclusive title. The 52 policy principles established by the Central Scrutinizing Committee on Acquisition of Farmlands and Other Lands in 2019 distinguished various cases of disputes into two categories, namely, the category with a firm title and the category without such, while the latter cases are handled in the context of squatters in the waste land management. Thus, the existence of a firm title is the sole fundamental test that decides the ultimate conclusion. This campaign should not end up with a quick administrative settlement putting off the problems to another routine of endless claims management in the future, but it should be the last and decisive chance to incorporate the people's normative belief into the formal law.

Notes

1 See Crouch and Lindsey (2014), Cheesman and Farrelly (2016), Harding (2017), etc.
2 See USAID (2013: 8).
3 See Sai Thet Naing Moe and Zaw Zaw Aye (2019).
4 See Benda-Beckmann et al. (2006), Fu and Gillespie (2014), etc.

5 See, for example, World Bank (1975), World Bank (2005), Bruce et al. (2006), World Bank (2011), UNDP (2008) etc.

6 The recent trend of ISDS tribunals on the land policy issues is fluctuating. In Abengoa & Cofides (Spain) vs. Mexico case (ICSID Case No. ARB(AF)/09/2 awarded on April 18, 2013), for example, the municipal government council in Mexico withdrew the once-offered land use license for toxic waste disposal project due to the local protest, where ICSID found Mexico liable for US$30 million damage to the Spanish investor according to the Mexico-Spain BIT. On the other hand, the ICSID annulment award on Álvarez & others vs. Republic of Panama (ICSID Case No. ARB/15/14 awarded on October 12, 2018) declined the jurisdiction and dismissed all claims on the grounds that the investors violated the Panamanian land law that extends special protections for indigenous communities, and therefore not qualified as investors to obtain protection through ISDS.

7 See, for example, JICA Examiner for the Guidelines for Environmental and Social Considerations (2014) for an objection raised by a group of local farmers against the Thilawa Special Economic Zone (SEZ) Development Project funded by JICA (Japan International Cooperation Agency).

8 Saito (1985: 143–146).

9 Ibid., 147–148.

10 Ibid., 134.

11 The English translation of *Manugye Dhammathat* was published by D. Richardson (1847).

12 See Okudaira (1986: 42–44).

13 See Hla Aung (2008: 81).

14 LSP Committee (1922: 42–43), referred to in Saito (1985: 152).

15 In French Indochina, a registration system for occupancy rights in agricultural villages was implemented in parallel outside of the ownership system (Jalzot 2019). In Thailand, as ownership registration system operated from the 1900s land revenue law, farmers' occupancy rights (*chap chorng*) have gradually been expelled (Kitahara 2002).

16 *Manugye Dhammathat*, Chapter 8, Sections 1–2.

17 See, for example, Furnivall (1939, 1956) for the phenomenon of acute securitization of land after the introduction of the Land and Revenue Act.

18 See Saxena (2020) at p. 70 for the post-independence Indian land law reform.

19 The survey of Village "Z" by Takahashi (1991) clarifies the situation that more than half of the villagers were landless during Ne Win period.

20 See Takahashi (1991: 75).

21 Takahashi, ibid.

22 An application is first submitted to the Farmland Management Committee at the village-tract level, which is sent up to the township-level Farmland Management Committee, which checks the status of land records at the township registration office, and is then elevated to the district-level Farmland Management Committee; after approval is received from this district level, the township-level Farmland Management Committee performs the registration by issuing permit (Form 7) to the township registration office within its jurisdiction (art. 5–6).

23 According to the author's survey as of January 2017, the succeeding entry of mortgages and seizure orders had not yet been started nationwide, lacking the administrative regulations for such operations.

24 See World Bank (2017). Also see Jayewardene, Ruwani and Nanayakkara (2018) for donors' guidance involving the European Union and Australia, Denmark, France, Ireland, Italy, Luxembourg, the Netherlands, New Zealand, Sweden, Switzerland, the U.K. and the U.S.A.

25 The acquisition procedure is performed by the General Administration Department using the Land Acquisition Manual succeeded from pre-independence according to the 1894 Land Acquisition Act (art. 23), which applies a market value evaluation of the property and adds 15 percent as consideration for the compulsory taking; in addition, there is compensation for three years' worth of cropping income and double the value of any buildings.

26 The information obtained in the author's interviews with the bank officers of Small Medium Industries Development Bank (SMIDB) Yangon Branch and C B Bank Magwe Branch as of August 2017, and Myanmar Livestock & Fishery Development Bank (MLFDB) Yangon Branch in January 2018, and also the author's interview as of February 1, 2018, with the Land Record Office at the City Planning and Land Administration Department, Yangon City Development Committee.

27 This is probably the result of the 2012 Farmland Law (art. 25c) prescribing the finality of administrative decisions on land titling.

28 According to the author's interview as of February 1, 2018, with the Land Record Office at the City Planning and Land Administration Department, Yangon City Development Committee.

References

Benda-Beckmann, Franz von, Benda-Beckmann, Keebet von, and Wiber, Melanie G. (2006) *Changing Properties in Property*, Berghahn Books.

Bruce, John W., Geovarelli, Rene, Rolfes, Jr. Leonard, Bledsoe, David, and Mitchell Robert (2006) *Land Law Reform: Achieving Development Policy Objectives*, World Bank Law, Justice, and Development Series, World Bank.

Cheesman, Nick and Farrelly, Nicholas (2016) *Conflict in Myanmar: War, Politics, Religion*, ISEAS.

Crouch, Melissa and Lindsey, Timothy, eds. (2014) *Law, Society and Transition in Myanmar*, Hart Publishing.

Fu, Hualing and Gillespie, John, eds. (2014) *Resolving Land Disputes in East Asia*, Cambridge University Press.

Furnivall, John Sydenham (1939) "The Fashioning of Leviathan", *Journal of the Burma Research Society*, 29 (1), pp. 1–137.

Furnivall, John Sydenham (1956) *Colonial Policy and Practice a Comparative Study of Burma and Netherlands India*, Cambridge University Press.

Harding Andrew, eds. (2017) *Constitutionalism and Legal Change in Myanmar*, Hart Publishing.

Hla Aung (2008) *Law and Justice in Myanmar*, Yangon, Thida Press.

Jalzot, Beatrice (2019) "Civil Law in French Asian Colonies", in Kaneko, Y. ed., *Civil Law Reforms in Post-Colonial Asia: Beyond Western Capitalism*, Springer.

Jayewardene, Ruwani and Nanayakkara, Ananadalal (2018) *Technical Review of the Draft Myanmar Land Acquisition Law 2017*, Land Core Group.

Kitahara, Atsushi (2002) "The Path to Land Policies that Create Small-Scale Farming in Modern Thailand (Parts 1 and 2)", *Economic Studies*, 50 (2), pp. 21–40 and (3), pp. 21–39.

LSP Committee (1922) *Report of the Committee Appointed to Examine the Land Revenue System of Burma, Vol. 1*, Superintendent Government Printing.

Okamoto, Ikuko (1997) "Land Revenue System and Land Ownership in Colonial Burma (in Japanese)", in Mizuno, H. and Shigetomi, S. eds., *Economic Development and Land System in Southeast Asia*, IDE-JETRO.

Okudaira, Ryuji (1985) "On the Process of British Colonialization and the Social Changes in 19th Century: A Study of the Changes of the Traditional Legal System in the Colonialization Process (in Japanese)", *Southeast Asian Studies*, 23 (2), pp. 125–141.

Okudaira, Ryuji (1986) "Burmese Dhammathat", in Hooker, M. B. ed., *Laws of South-East Asia, Vol. I*, Butterworths.

Richardson, Manu D. (1847) *Dhammathat: Or the Laws of Menoo Translated from the Burmese*, Maulmain Baptist Press.

Sai, Thet Naing Moe and Zaw Zaw Aye (2019) *Land related Laws and Policies in Myanmar*, SPRI Program Report by 3rd Period Myanmar Fellows, GRIPS.

Saito, Teruko (1985) "The Initial Land Systems in British Burma 1826–1876 (in Japanese)", *Southeast Asian Studies*, 23 (2), pp. 142–154.

Saxena, Astha (2020) *Land Law in India*, Routledge.

Takahashi, Akio (1991) "Farmland Holding and Commercialization of Agricultural Products in Upper Burma Irrigated Villages: A Comparison with Lower Burma Villages (in Japanese)", in Umehara, H. ed., *Land System and Agricultural Changes in Southeast Asia*, IDE-JETRO.

Takemura, Masako (1976) "Farmer's Debts and Land Concentration in Lower Burma Delta Area in 1920–302 (in Japanese)," *Asian Economy*, 17 (10).

Torrens, Sir Robert Richard (1882) *An Essay on the Transfer of Land by Registration: under the Duplicate Method Operative in British Colonies*, Cassell (MOML edition).

UNDP: United Nations Development Program (2008) *Making the Law Work for Everyone I &II*, UNDP.

USAID (2013) *Country Profile: Property Rights and Resource Profile of Burma*, USAID.

World Bank (1975) *World Bank Land Reform* (World Bank Sector Policy Paper), World Bank.

World Bank (2005) *World Development Report 2005: A Better Investment Climate for Everyone*, World Bank.

World Bank (2011) *Land Policy: Securing Rights to Reduce Poverty and Promote Rural Growth*, World Bank.

World Bank (2017) *Towards a Sustainable Land Administration and Management System in Myanmar: Land Sector Needs Assessment Thematic Policy Notes – Policy Note 5 Property Valuation and Taxation*, World Bank.

16 Asian land conflicts and the Great Transformation

Fallacy of the law and development long-term view

Brian Z. Tamanaha

In *The Great Transformation* (1944),[1] Karl Polanyi described the modern era in terms of a dual movement. One movement involved 19th-century European philosophers, social theorists, economists and politicians advocating and implementing a free market as the basic organizing principle for society – the liberal agenda epitomized by Ludwig von Mises and Friedrich Hayek. In no previous age had most people obtained their daily needs for food, clothing and shelter through buying and selling. People lived off the land, hunting, gathering, tilling, fishing, herding and creating shelter within communities that provided whatever was necessary for their collective existence. The most far-reaching and consequential modern change, Polanyi observed, was the transformation of labor, land and money into market commodities. Thereafter, markets became central to people's activities and needs: they earned income as wages and purchased their food, clothing and housing in the market. Under the liberal vision, society is organized through the self-regulating mechanism of the market based on prices, wages, rents and interest. Wealth in society is increased by providing incentives for people to engage in productive activities, and voluntary exchanges leave all parties better off. Thus was the "market society" born, first in the West, then spread across the globe through colonization and global trade.

However, the creation of market society was accompanied by a countermovement to slow the spread of the market and ameliorate the social harms caused by the destruction of traditional societies, Polanyi elaborated. In feudal and traditional societies everywhere, labor and land were integral elements of social organization, embedded in family, clan, tribe, social status, political power, social relations and obligations, spirituality, the entire social arrangement, all functioning in accordance with customary law and tradition. Starvation seldom occurred in subsistence agricultural societies because land and community provided daily sustenance, and security and support in hard times. The emerging market society and its consequences swept much of this away. The enclosures of commons – wealthy landowners seizing common land previously used for subsistence by those lacking land – and the prospect of earning wages prompted agricultural laborers to move to industrializing cities, where they lived in squalid hovels, worked long hours in unsafe workplaces for low wages and remained mired in poverty and food insecure. To counter the harmful consequences of market

DOI: 10.4324/9781003170600-20

society, legislatures across industrializing Europe in the late 19th and early 20th centuries enacted a host of social welfare reforms to help improve the conditions of workers.

Thus, this dual movement involved the pervasive penetration and reworking of society along the lines of the market, which in turn prompted efforts to slow the process and ameliorate the harms that followed. Polanyi recognized that markets provide desired goods and increase wealth in society and that people often choose to work for wages – though many were compelled to do so owing to the enclosures and punitive poor laws. He acknowledged the social benefits of the industrial and technological revolution. He was not a nostalgist naively calling for a return to a bygone age. He was not against capitalism and markets per se. What he opposed was the nigh total destruction of traditional communities that had given meaning to peoples' lives and the dismal conditions and economic insecurity of laboring masses in unfettered market societies. The market should serve society, not dictate to society. Maintaining the supremacy of society over the market, he believed, can be accomplished in all political systems – democratic, aristocratic, constitutional, authoritarian and ones yet to be created.

He advocated tempering market imperatives to ensure justice and fairness, education, food, shelter and security for people.[2] Jobs should be guaranteed to everyone who wants to work, and minimum wages should be legally set at levels sufficient for their needs. Land should be connected with essential social institutions, including "the homestead, the cooperative, the factory, the township, the school, the church, parks, wildlife preserves, and so forth,"[3] and removed from or restricted in the market when necessary. Markets for labor and the private ownership of land will continue to exist, in his vision, and no single formula applies to all societies. The guiding principle is that the ends of achieving a meaningful and humane society must establish the parameters for the market.

To guard against abuses from government involvements, Polanyi emphasized the importance of legally enforceable rights to protect freedom of conscience and choice of how to live, along with other rights and civil liberties.

> Every move toward integration in society should thus be accompanied by an increase in freedom; moves towards planning should comprise the strengthening the rights of the individual in society. His indefeasible rights must be enforceable under the law even against the supreme powers, whether they be personal or anonymous.[4]

More than a half century after its publication, central elements of Polanyi's account are playing out today across the terrain of Asian land disputes. The modern incarnation of liberal economic theory is neoliberalism of the "Washington Consensus," involving titling property, enforcing contracts, removing market restraints and other reforms, promoted across the Global South in the name of economic development, attached as conditions to loans – wrapped together as "rule of law development." Special emphasis has been placed on the need for formal, individually held land rights under state law, along with free transferability.

In theory, this produces security, predictability and certainty; transforms land into capital; allows property to serve as collateral for loans; and facilitates the transfer of land to more economically productive uses.[5]

Things have not worked out as neoliberal theory and rule of law development predicted,[6] however, as the chapters in this collection show across a number of Asian settings. In location after location, the introduction of formal property rights has exacerbated uncertainty and insecurity over property. State legal regimes have been juxtaposed on social arenas with preexisting customary and community-based understandings of land tenure, creating conflicts between state and customary systems, resulting in masses of people being dispossessed. Even when economic development occurs, the results have been socially unjust, enhancing the rich on the backs of the poor (though it bears saying that liberal theory does not promise otherwise, at least in the short run). Far from building the rule of law for everyone in society, as rule of law development seeks, all too often the law has been an instrument serving elite interests. Residential and agricultural properties in urban and rural areas are being expropriated by governments and transferred to private enterprises. The conflicts and dislocation resulting from land titling and expropriation are justified by governments as a necessary short-term price to pay to achieve long-term economic development.

The essays in this collection also reveal the countermovement Polanyi identified, slowing and countering market liberalism, efforts to preserve commons, to provide protections for people and communities in relation to land. In socialist as well as capitalist societies, we see a continuous battle between liberal market forces promoting economic maximization and countermovements for social justice, shaping the resultant social-economic-political-legal arrangements.

With this background in mind, let us now examine several themes raised by essays in this collection. It is not possible to discuss every topic raised in each chapter. Instead, the discussion is organized in terms of Polanyi's argument, along with related developments he did not discuss (the consequences of depopulation, state law monism). After covering these themes, I critically examine the long-term view that underpins liberal law and development land initiatives and close with a few generalizations drawn from this collection about equitable land development.

1 Subsistence versus productivity ideologies

"Origin of Land Disputes," by Yuka Kaneko (Chapter 1), is a sweeping overview of a two-centuries-long clash between contrasting ideologies about land: agricultural subsistence ideology revolving around families and communities versus maximizing the economic value of land as a productive asset. The origins of this clash began with colonial land policies in Africa and Asia oriented toward using land for commercial plantations for export crops, which required the formalization of property titles and seizing large tracts of land. Three main mechanisms were utilized: introduction of Torrens land registration with title vested in individual owners; nationalization of "wasteland" without compensation; and expropriating land (with compensation) that is turned over for private uses.[7] Various allowances were made for customary land rights, particularly in rural areas, but colonial property regimes applied to land utilized for economic purposes.

To fully appreciate the implications of the contrasting ideologies identified by Kaneko, it is useful to draw a general contrast in social understandings common across many development contexts (though the details differ with respect to each location). In advanced capitalist societies, land is an economic asset individuals utilize for various purposes: a place to live or to obtain rents from, an investment that appreciates in value, an asset to use as collateral for loans or to sell, a container of wealth to pass on to loved ones upon death. Land is univocal – an economic asset with multiple uses. Land in much of the Global South, particularly in rural areas, is far more complex and a central component of their lifeworld. Land involves a basis of political power, social status and wealth, a place to live and source of subsistence, a part of cultural and ethnic identity, an aspect of kinship and community relations, a locus of spirituality and an ongoing link to ancestors that is held in trust for future generations.[8] Land is multivocal – with multiple meanings, uses and implications for manifold aspects of social existence.

Owing to these contrasting roles property plays within the social system, customary land tenure is carved into different layers and slices inconsistent with transplanted liberal property regimes. Liberal property law and registration systems treat real property as individually held economic assets, with variations: fee simple, joint tenancy or tenancy in common, servitudes on the land, usufruct, life estates and remainders and contractually based lease rights and trusts. Customary land tenure often revolves around communal property that accords different rights and responsibilities to people, the family, kin group, lineage or community to occupy or possess; to be consulted about; to seek permission from; to use for planting, hunting or grazing; to reap present or future benefits from; to pass on after death; and to dispose of. Thus, ownership titles and land registration recognized by state law do not capture the full gamut of customary land tenure rights and responsibilities. When titles are granted and land is registered, customary land tenure rights may be officially extinguished, and the official records may not reflect actual possession and understandings within the community.

When colonization ended after the Second World War, newly independent states made efforts to accord greater recognition to customary land tenure. However, in recent decades, neoliberal law and development initiatives have once again pushed land laws and policies focused on enhancing economic productivity, which resemble colonial laws and policy. Kaneko describes contemporary Asian land conflicts in five contexts: (1) the Torrens system; (2) recognition of collective ownership to preserve communal villages; (3) state nationalization of land deemed unproductive without compensation and handed over to developers; (4) expropriation for private interests; and (5) the conversion of agricultural land for urban development in growing cities. These problematic situations are also covered in "Land Law and Disputes in Myanmar," by Kaneko and Ye Naing Lin (Chapter 15). These chapters detail how these situations produce significant iniquities in Cambodia and Myanmar. Only the Torrens system will be discussed briefly here, as the other topics are taken up later.

The Torrens land registration system originated in the mid-19th century as a means to establish title in colonial Australia. Property registered in a Torrens registry is conclusive evidence of title, not subject to challenge in court once a limited statutory challenge period expires, which provides certainty for land transactions like mortgages and sales. However, the Torrens system also operates to extinguish all other ownership claims (though a party losing land may make a case for compensation via insurance). Most countries do not use the Torrens system; more commonly, title is determined through property deeds (title is based on the deed, not registration itself).

After decolonization, a number of Asian countries discontinued the colonially implemented Torrens systems, but the World Bank and other law and development donors have revived it once again, promoted as a means to provide security and certainty for land titles, facilitating productive investments and transfers. Kaneko describes conflicts that resulted in Cambodia, where 80 percent of the population live in subsistence agricultural communities, many without required documents. The two alternative ways in the land law to demonstrate title for registration are either five years of continuous, open, uncontested possession *or* documentary evidence of purchase for consideration. Farmers who have not registered can lose their land to a good faith purchaser and be evicted, with no judicial opportunity to establish their superior claim.

"Registration of Land-Ownership in Cambodia," by Issei Sakano (Chapter 2), an attorney in the Cambodian Ministry of Justice who participated in drafting land provisions, details the interaction between the 1992 property system, which provided certificates, and the 2001 Torrens-style land registration law pushed by international development organizations. Although a significant number of certificates were issued pursuant to the 1992 land law, relatively few titles have been registered pursuant to the 2001 law. Currently, there are people who possess 1992 certificates and 2001 registration, 1992 certificates without registration, and people in the possession of land with neither form of official land recognition, all of whom engage in transactions. On the surface, these formal property systems purportedly allowed customary land-ownership rights to be protected as state recognized ownership; but the effect, as John Gillespie points out in his chapter, was to delegitimize customary land rights based on working the land, ultimately dispossessing a half million farmers, handing their land to the government or to wealthy Cambodians and foreign investors for commercial uses. Two egregious examples involved government expropriation of agricultural land of thousands of family farmers to accumulate vast tracts of land for a transnational sugar plantation, and expropriation of hundreds of plots in the heart of Phnom Penh for a property developer.[9] Following the implementation of the land law, landlessness has increased, while land uncertainty and conflicts continue.

Development agencies, heeding input from NGOs and Japanese development specialists familiar with local land conflicts, have made efforts to preserve and accommodate local property understandings, though with limited success. As

Kaneko describes, even provisions specifically designed to protect village communities from private ownership claims, enacted with the support of international development agencies, have not advanced this purpose. A community that desires to achieve special protected designation for collective ownership must demonstrate the existence of a sociocultural "unity," a continuous traditional way of life, collective agriculture, demarcation of land subject to use and membership in the collective. Even after these significant procedural hurdles are overcome, individual members may choose to separate and dispose of their share.

The clash highlighted by Kaneko involves, on the one side, Asian states (capitalist and socialist) advised by development agencies pursuing private ownership and economic maximization of land (the liberal market imperative); on the other side, people resisting the destruction of their ways of life and struggling for fair treatment. "They are not fighting over the exchange value of a piece of land," Kaneko tells us.

> Land use and its surrounding integrated ecosystems are the foundation of subsistence that the people have continued to protect for generations, and their rational lifestyle compatible with the ecology, is asserted as the basis of survival. If we call this ideology, it may be an ideology that concerns the minimum of human dignity.

Polanyi insisted that human dignity and communities must take priority over the maximization of wealth.

2 Socialist liberal market economies

An ongoing transformation fraught with complexity and conflict is the incorporation of neoliberal market reforms by Asian socialist countries, Laos, Vietnam and China (to a lesser extent). Socialist-liberal market economies might appear to be a contradiction, a mash-up of opposites. Yet as Polanyi observed, markets can operate within a variety of political-economic arrangements. The ultimate test is not a matter of theoretical consistency, but whether the market operates for the benefit of society, for the good of the people. The challenge in these Asian settings is to combine government ownership of land with liberal property rights as an economic asset, encouraging business investments in factories, urban development and commercial agriculture for export, while also protecting rural farming families that remain a significant proportion of the population and land use. Whether socialist governments can thread this needle remains to be seen – especially because significant economic pressure and momentum is on the side of prioritizing liberal reforms.

The supportive as well as highly problematic role played by development organizations pushing the liberal economic-legal agenda is made plain in Kenzo Okawa's chapter, "Civil Code and Land Law Debate in Laos." Desiring to improve its economic performance and participate in the global economy, Laos, a socialist country, opened a market economy in 1986. A full set of liberal market legal regimes were introduced in the 1990s, followed by a number of amendments and additions in the 2000s, culminating in the 2020 adoption of the Lao Civil Code. A potpourri of development organizations have provided assistance drafting laws in the past several decades: World Bank, United Nations Development Program, Swedish International Development Cooperation Agency, Asian Development Bank, German International Cooperation Agency, USAID, AUSAID, International Finance Corporation and the Japan International Cooperation Agency. Many cooks using different ingredients were in the kitchen helping Laotians draft liberal laws and the recently enacted Lao Civil Code. During the drafting of the Civil Code, the drafting committee referred to the French Civil Code, German Civil Code, Anglo-American laws, the Japanese Civil Code, Vietnamese Civil Code and Thai Civil Code. One of the goals of the drafters of the Civil Code was to provide family farmers with legally protected use rights (superficies and usufructs) on land owned by the state. Not surprisingly, Okawa writes, significant questions exist about overlaps, gaps and inconsistencies among various enacted legal provisions still in place. A major open question is the relationship between buildings and land, as well as inconsistencies between the official property regimes and social understandings and community land tenure practices.

At the final stage of drafting the Code, the International Finance Corporation (IFC), a World Bank entity, strongly urged a specific set of changes to security rights procedures in connection with bankruptcy. IFC pressured the government that if the amendments it proposed were not made, Laos's Doing Business score (a World Bank rating system of business friendliness) would be significantly reduced. The Laotian government was keen to improve its score to attract international investment, so provisions proposed by IFC were included. The problem this creates, Okawa explains, is that the Civil Code applies not only to businesses, but more generally to ordinary citizens, and the effect of the last-minute changes potentially obviates protections for subsistence farmers.

Vietnam also prioritizes foreign investment and economic development, using easements, usufruct and superficies to provide legally protected use rights to occupiers of land owned by the state. In this largely rural country, the majority of agricultural production remains household subsistence farming. In "Land Law Reform and Civil Code Drafting in Vietnam," Nguyen Hong Hai, a leading member of the drafting committee of the 2015 Civil Code, details numerous unresolved questions in the interaction between the Land Law, the Housing Law and the Civil Code. But the overall import is a clear government commitment to open land fully to the market. The Communist Party recently announced a commitment to treat land use rights in ways that constitute de facto ownership, as capital assets to serve as collateral for mortgages and freely transferable, as well as to encourage large-scale commercial agriculture and forestry – the full commoditization of land for economically productive purposes.

Countries like Laos and Vietnam, and their citizens, undoubtedly want, need and can benefit from economic development. The importance of this goal is not in question. Rather, the questions are whether household farmers and local communes that populate the countryside will be protected during the inevitable dislocations and deterioration of their lifeworlds that follow from the expansion of commercial agriculture; whether people pushed or pulled off the land are provided with housing, food and employment; and whether the benefits of economic development are equitably distributed to all sectors of society. There is value in slowing the process of commoditizing land, building in protections for traditional ways, Polanyi argued, because it allows people time to adjust to new modes of social economic existence. Shock therapy should be avoided. It is also important to keep in mind that collectively oriented rural communities provide meaning, security and value to people's lives that cannot be measured in economic terms. Rather than structure society to satisfy market mechanisms, which is the orientation of international development organizations, the market should be constructed in ways that work for society. This is the balance that socialist governments implementing liberal reforms purport to be seeking, but to achieve it will require not giving in to all demands of global capitalism.

3 State expropriation of land for private uses

State expropriation of private land for public purposes, with compensation provided to owners, commonly involves seizing property for government buildings like schools and government offices, and for public infrastructure, like roads, bridges, railway lines, sewage pipes, telecommunications cables, and so forth. These forms of state expropriation of land are widely accepted as legitimate, though private landowners subjected to expropriation often contest the amount of compensation and the need to take their particular parcel.

A far more controversial form of expropriation involves state seizure of private land that is given over to private parties for the claimed public benefit of enhancing economic development. What justifies these takings is the view that maximizing economic productivity is a general social good. However, this use of expropriation clashes with liberal commitments to the protection of property rights and market exchanges. In liberal economic theory, if property has higher use value, a free market should result in voluntary exchanges that produce the economically maximizing outcome. But reality does not follow liberal economic theory.

The chapters in Part II involve state expropriation for private development in Japan (Chapter 5, Narufumi Kadomatsu), Korea (Chapter 6, Jin-Sik Yoo and NooRI Se), Taiwan (Chapter 7, Ming-Chih Lee) and China (Chapter 8, Shu Jiao and Yashu Yang). Similar questions arise about the appropriateness of taking and adequacy of compensation across these very different political-economic systems. Asian capitalist countries have practiced state-led capitalism with significant state involvement, while China has implemented significant liberal market reforms, bringing them closer from both directions. This is a reminder of Polanyi's point, recently emphasized by sociologist Mark Granovetter,[10] that "capitalism" and "markets" are not abstract systems that take the same institutional forms everywhere, but rather are embedded within and shaped by the surrounding culture, society, polity, customs and laws.

Asian countries are in different phases of expropriation and utilize it in different ways. During the takeoff stage of its postwar economic ascent, Japan expropriated land from large landowners and redistributed ownership to former tenant farmers,[11] and it took land for private usage in the 1950s and 1960s within urban planning initiatives, creating industrial development parks and residential facilities. This is seldom done anymore. Today, Kadomatsu tells us, takings involve urban redevelopment projects in which new buildings are constructed and floors are allocated to previous landowners and businesses, who thus remain while presumably benefiting from higher economic values (or at least not losing value). Takings today also involve using abandoned or unclaimed property with limited economic value owing to declining population and migration to cities (more on this later).

Taiwan and South Korea continue to actively engage in expropriation today in close cooperation with private enterprises. Taiwan utilizes the controversial practice of "zone appropriation," Ming-Chih Lee explains (Chapter 7); the government seizes a substantial area of land, a major part of which is provided to private developers, while the original landowners are relocated to other locations of the area seized. Since the land appreciates in value and productive usage, in theory all parties benefit from newly commercialized land: the government benefits from increased revenues from employment and property taxes, private developers profit from the project, and higher land values benefit relocated landowners. However, Lee points out that no clear showing of "public interest" is made to justify evicting people from their land, completely uprooting their lives and destroying the community, while the government obtains revenues and property developers reap the greatest share of the economic benefit. As Yoo and Se detail (Chapter 6), land expropriation in South Korea, which has been used for entertainment parks, golf courses, resorts and spas, occurs with even greater direct involvement of private developers, a limited showing of public interest and significant questions about adequate compensation. The Korean Supreme Court has recently taken action to restrain takings of this sort, but the legislature strongly supports it, and hence it is likely to continue.

These chapters show that utilizing the coercive power of the state is an easier and more lucrative path for property developers than negotiating with the landowners to willingly sell their property; and they demonstrate the willingness of governments to trump the rights of citizens to obtain revenues and to wring more economic productivity out of land. Governments should keep in mind, however, that the social dislocation that occurs is not always followed by the promised economic benefits, as development projects regularly do not materialize or are not successful.[12]

In China, the state owns all the land in the city, while collectives own rural and suburban land (except when claimed by the state). When China opened up to the market, it provided greater formal protections of property usage rights; along with these protections came limitations on expropriation and specifications on compensation, elaborated by Shu Jiao and Yashu Yang in "Land Expropriation and Compensation in China" (Chapter 8). Private developers wishing to develop agricultural land must go through a two-stage process involving changing its official designation and securing use rights through expropriation; urban land use rights can be obtained directly. On paper, the law looks protective, but in practice, it has been abused. Shu Jiao and Yashu Yang reveal that local governments obtain significant revenues from expropriating land for private developments, so they have strong incentives to grant approvals; the criteria are vague and broad ("cultural project," "science and technology"); and what counts as the public interest is unspecified. Concerns about fairness and adequacy of compensation are greater for rural residents whose land is taken than for urban residents (the latter have the near equivalent of private property rights). Tens of millions of rural farmers have lost land as large swaths of property have been taken to build housing for rapidly growing cities (though rural collectives and their members have significantly benefited financially in certain locations from de facto illegal arrangements.[13]

Another crucial problem is the absence of a genuine judicial check on expropriations. The Supreme People's Court has indicated that approval of local congress and committees and the approval of the majority of the community provide conclusive support for an expropriation. The situation in China raises a fundamental tension for socialist governments that implement liberal legal regimes: liberalism requires legally enforceable rights (property, contract, etc.) with respect to other citizens as well as *against the government*, while socialism takes an instrumental view of law serving the government in advancing the interests of society (as determined by the Party). What this requires, at the very least, are independent courts with the power to hold government accountable to violations of legal rights. Polanyi emphasized the necessity of enforcing rights against government if the market is to serve the interests of society. While this can be accomplished in socialist systems, the government must be committed to legal accountability. Significant doubts exist about this commitment in practice. Chinese judges rarely rule against the government in cases challenging land acquisition, as Gillespie describes in his chapter.

"Administrative Court in Vietnam in Solving Land Disputes," by Pham Duy Nghia (Chapter 14), exposes institutional reasons for barely existent protection of property rights against the government in Vietnam. Government decisions granting land use rights, expropriating land and compensating for expropriations are considered administrative decisions subject to challenge in administrative courts. However, there are no administrative courts in remote areas and a shortage of administrative judges exists because they are very poorly compensated (below $400 per month). Pham Duy Nghia details further barriers to accountability: it is nearly impossible for judges to rule against district government land actions because that would rule against the Party, as well as against Party officials who are above the judge within the Party hierarchy; the procuracy (public prosecutor) has the power to take positions in individual cases as well as appeal decisions, which puts significant pressure on judges to conform; and judges have no enforcement power, but must request the local government to comply with an adverse decision. Under these circumstances, property rights are not protected against government land actions.

When property is expropriated for private economic development projects, as mentioned at the outset, the adequacy and fairness of compensation is often a contested issue. Market value can be measured at the time of the sale or based on the appreciation of land values that occur after expropriation. The former option dictates that former owners must accept a price they already rejected, while the latter option enables them to benefit from land they were forced to relinquish. Since prior to expropriation the land may have little or no market value because there is no economic demand or the land could not be legally sold (as with rural agricultural land in China prior to re-designation), landowners would obtain minimal compensation.[14] Socialist countries with collective ownership rights in villages raise additional questions about equitable payments to family farmers of individual plots. In addition to compensation for the loss of the land itself, there are also resettlement costs and the need for dispossessed people to find new livelihoods in a different location – a serious concern for displaced family farmers who lose their housing as well as means of subsistence.

Kadomatsu (Chapter 5) also raises costs rarely considered in these discussions: the loss caused by the collapse of a long-standing community and web of social relations that previously bound the lives of people together. Polanyi brought attention to this as the destruction of communities wrought by liberal markets, a harm that cannot be measured monetarily. The best way to account for it is *before* the decision is made, as a significant factor weighing against expropriation, which the government can overcome only by showing genuine necessity and substantial, concrete social benefits.

4 The survival of community

It is often said that Asian societies are communitarian, whereas liberal societies are individualist. Put in broad strokes, liberalism centers on the primacy of rights bearing individuals free to pursue their own vision of the good, structuring their activities through contractual relationships with others; communitarianism centers on the primacy of traditions, families, communities, which provide extended webs of relationships that people are born into and from which they obtain their life meaning. These ideal types do not exist in pure forms and every society involves various combinations of both sets of characteristics; yet as cultural generalizations, it may capture certain basic differences between Western and Asian societies (setting aside other societies). However, the spread and penetration of Western-derived market liberalism has also pervasively influenced Asian societies. Market liberalism, as Polanyi described, carries a set of imperatives with the capacity to destroy traditional communities and reorganize society along its own lines. Whether communitarianism in general, and traditional communities in particular, can survive the spread of market liberalism remains an open question. Can a communitarian culture be maintained if, outside immediate families and friends, social communities are replaced by largely economic ties?

Indonesia today has many communities following customary laws and practices, giving rise to numerous conflicts with modern economic initiatives, elaborated by Rudy Lukman in "Securing *Adat* Land Rights in Indonesia" (Chapter 10). National and regional laws recognize customary law and traditional tribunals at the village level. However, Rudy Lukman explains, *adat* communities have lost significant amounts of land because it is difficult to meet rules on the recognition of *adat* communities; and *adat* communities that utilize forest resources in the same traditional ways they have for generations (cutting trees, herding, clearing land for farming) have been subjected to criminal charges for infringing on local government grants to corporations of rights to harvest forests, as well as other problems that threaten traditional communities and ways. The Constitutional Court has issued rulings to protect customary communities, but lower courts and legal authorities do not consistently follow these decisions. A key feature of the continuance of these communities are customary tribunals applying local customary law and Islamic law in villages, which exist in many rural locations. Thus far, traditional communities remain cohesive, at least when their actions and customary land rights do not directly conflict with government-encouraged large-scale commercial activities.

China recently utilized the concept of juridical personality to help preserve resident communities in villages and urban areas. The notion of legal or juridical personality in many legal systems confers independent legal existence on recognized entities, attaching rights and responsibilities, including the right to hold property and enter contracts, as well as separating the assets of the entity from its members, and insulating members from liability for the actions of the entity. The recognition of juridical persons was an essential part of opening China to the market because it allows business entities to function independently of the state. Legislation was passed in 2017 that made villagers' committees eligible for this status, as Mikiko Matsumoto describes in "The Concept of Juridical Personality and the Autonomy of Villagers' Committees in China" (Chapter 12). In the early 1980s, villagers voluntarily formed committees across China composed of leaders of the village to help manage their affairs, which have remained outside the government structure. Rural and suburban land is collectively owned and managed by collective economic organizations (families are allocated land for use); but where these organizations do not exist, the land is managed by villagers' committees. With the conferral of juridical personality, the assets of collective economic organizations and villagers' committees are now more clearly separated. Providing villagers' committees with juridical personality should help maintain their vitality and functional capacity apart from the state, Matsumoto suggests, enhancing their ability to engage in legal transactions going forward.

Two chapters about contemporary Japan show the resilience of community in an advanced capitalist society, at least in certain settings. In "History of Japanese Common Rights" (Chapter 11), Sachihiko Muroi explains that despite government policy from the late 19th century through the postwar period to abolish traditional common lands (*Iriai-ken*), and contrary to declarations by scholars several decades ago that they had become extinct, forms of Japanese commons continue to exist today. *Iriai-ken* recognized the rights of members of local communities to use collectively held and managed forests and fields according to customs; access is based on actual residence, individuals do not own shares, it cannot be inherited and management decisions are made unanimously. In many locations, *Iriai-ken* did not acquire legal personality and did not fit public or private characterizations. Yet a significant number have survived. Contrary to the popular economic theory that commons are inevitably destroyed through over-exploitation by individuals for their own benefit, recent studies have shown that Japanese commons practice sustainable use of natural resources and may serve an important role in forestry management and environmental protection. The error of economic theory is that in close-knit communities, people do not behave like egoistic economic maximizers (which is a creature of market liberalism), but rather have a strong sense of community obligation and responsibility, maintained by social sanctions.

"Vacant Properties in Japan," by Gakuto Takamura (Chapter 9), describes the situation in towns with significant numbers of vacant homes, a growing problem in Japan. Kadomatsu discussed this as well in his chapter (Chapter 5) in terms of government taking of unclaimed land, used for public purposes like parks, public squares and shopping facilities. Japan has aging and declining rural populations and has experienced two decades of economic stagnation. When the economic value of a house is not worth the cost of keeping it up, people who inherit a family home may choose to abandon it. Takamura conveys a case study of a small town with a substantial elderly population, Kumagawa, with nearly 30 percent of houses unoccupied, scattered along the main road through town, many deteriorating. What he discovered is that about half of the owners were reluctant to rent or sell their houses to outsiders through realtors, while outsiders interested in renting or buying were concerned about whether they would be welcomed in the community. Insular communities can be seen as less welcoming to outsiders, even when they need an infusion of people to revitalize the community and support the tax base. A possible solution in rural areas of Japan is the formation of community-based organizations that serve as intermediaries (replacing realtors) between owners and potentially interested new inhabitants. Community-based organizations in small depopulating towns are also taking a more active role in demolishing abandoned properties and utilizing them as recreational spaces (while owners retain title). These community-managed solutions reflect collective responsibility and trust-based strengths of local communities, even as they undergo decline.

5 State law monism versus community customary law

The preceding analysis has conveyed the chapters in this book through Polanyi's framework of the spread of market liberalism and its impact on reshaping society in accordance with economic imperatives. The implementation of neoliberal legal regimes heavily promoted by international development agencies in recent decades has been the key mechanism for the extension of the market throughout society, from local and national markets, extending to global markets. This process and its deleterious consequences for community are what Polanyi warned about. While his focus was on society becoming sublimated to the market, creating the market society, today we also see governments increasingly sublimated to the market – the market-driven state. Asian state-led capitalism (Korea, Taiwan, Cambodia) bears significant resemblances to Asian market socialism (China, Vietnam, Laos), particularly government expropriation of land for private development and its disparate consequences for rich and poor.

Another fundamental transformation is occurring in conjunction with the spread of market liberalism: the expansion of state law monism. State law monism is the notion that the state has a monopoly over law and is supreme within society.[15] This vision, however, is not the reality. In many rural societies across the Global South, people arrange their affairs and live in accordance with customary and religious law, particularly on land matters. A report issued by the World Bank legal department observed:

> In many developing countries, customary systems operating outside of the state regime are often the dominant form of regulation and dispute resolution, covering up to 90% of the population in parts of Africa. In Sierra Leone, for example, approximately 85% of the population falls under the jurisdiction of customary law, defined under the Constitution as "the rules which, by custom, are applicable to particular communities in Sierra Leone." Customary tenure covers 75% of land in most African countries, affecting 90% of land transactions in countries like Mozambique and Ghana. . . . In many of these countries, systems of justice seem to operate almost completely independently of the official state system.[16]

As many as a billion people around the globe, according to one estimate, claim property rights and conduct property arrangements on terms inconsistent with official state law, ranging from urban squatter settlements (like favelas) where families have lived without official titles for generations (though still exchanging and passing on property), to peri-urban areas in rapidly growing cities, to rural areas where people follow customary land tenure.[17]

The granting of land deeds or certificates and the implementation of title registration systems, and the conferral of transferable land usage rights in socialist countries, involve more than just the commoditization of land for the market. What these actions also do is claim that the state alone determines what counts as property. This is state law monism asserting dominance over customary law and community understandings. (In China, this occurs through the state bureaucratic order more so than the legal order.) In "State-Centered Land Regimes and the Struggle for Customary Law in East Asia" (Chapter 13), John Gillespie sheds light on this process, offering examples from Cambodia, China and Indonesia. Since state requirements for land rights frequently differ from customary requirements for land rights followed by subsistence farmers, the dominance of state law all too often results in people losing their land.

The exertion of state law dominance over customary tenure is explicit in Myanmar's recent land reforms promoted by international development agencies, as explained in "Land Law and Disputes in Myanmar," (Chapter 15) by Ye Naing Lin and Yuka Kaneko. A consequence of the new title registration law is that farmers who fail to register stand to lose their property (though they can raise their claim later). Another law empowers the state to seize land deemed wasteland without compensation; this is problematic because under customary practices, farmers rotate their planting locations, leaving tracts of land fallow for a period of time to recover fertility, which the government may choose to deem wasteland. State law thereby imposes its own framework on social life. Significantly, however, what state law officially dictates is not necessarily what people actually do. At the grassroots level, when dealing with disputes over land, the authors found that local decision-makers tended to support customary cultivation rights and to resist transactions of farmland based on the title registry.

Both chapters suggest that one way to protect rural farmers and villages is to support local decision-making based on customary understandings of land. This is the situation described in Rudy Lukman's chapter on Indonesia (Chapter 10), where state law recognizes customary law and tribunals, but it can also exist where the state does not officially recognize customary law. As the earlier quote from the World Bank reveals, customary law and tribunals are utilized in many societies, particularly in rural areas, on land issues as well as other conflicts. It occurs where village communities remain cohesive and people utilize customary law generally on matters like property, personal injuries, debts, marriage and divorce, inheritance and other basic rules of social intercourse.[18] Law and development organizations, aware of the shortcomings of formal legal systems, have recently begun to appreciate the value of customary systems, offering measured support for their functional value.[19]

Nonetheless, even where customary land tenure operates, when state law articulates property rights, people everywhere want state recognition if they can obtain it. People hold up whatever arguments and evidence available to support their legal claims – long-term residence or cultivation, old grants or deeds, tax payments, family records, sales agreements or leases, etc. – even if they do not count as legally valid title.[20] Once the state proclaims that property is determined by state law, people in possession of land without state legal recognition are vulnerable to eviction by those with official legal titles, who can invoke the coercive force of the state on their behalf.

6 The fallacy of the long-term view

A pernicious assumption behind contemporary law and development actions and ideologies must be exposed and dislodged. However socially disruptive, legally uncertain and inequitable things might look in the short run, this assumption holds, we must take the long view. All transitions are messy, but in the long run, once the transformation to liberal legal and economic systems has finally occurred, society will be wealthier and more productive and the populace will be happier, justifying the pain suffered along the way. This claim brings to mind the old saying, "one must break a few eggs to make an omelette"; although the promised omelettes will come to unspecified future generations. For reasons I elaborate next, the long view argument is a fallacy that serves to rationalize away blatantly harmful consequences in the present.

Liberal proponents of the long view regularly invoke the English enclosure movement, which dispossessed serfs of their traditional use rights over commons, transforming them into landless wage earners, while solidifying private property rights of wealthy landowners. The short run ushered in human suffering, the liberal story goes, but the long-run establishment of individually held private property rights was a spectacular success, creating the conditions for Western prosperity.[21]

The fallacy of the long-term view can be illustrated through Frank Upham's recent book, *The Great Property Fallacy* (2018), which examines land issues in Japan, China and Cambodia, as well as the English enclosure movement and 19th-century American law. His discussion of Asian land conflicts covers a number of the issues raised in this collection, thus supplying an informative comparison. Professor Upham presents a sophisticated critique of the assumptions informing neoliberal rule of law development initiatives. He details the unjust dispossession of poor in favor of indigenous elites and foreign investors that resulted in Cambodia from land titling; the reality that Chinese economic development occurred largely in the absence of formal legal property protections; and the choice in postwar Japan to sacrifice economic productively in land by redistributing land from feudal landowners to farmers working the land, restricting the market in agricultural property and propping up the livelihood of farmers by erecting barriers to the importation of rice (at the expense of consumers). A prominent theme running through his book is that state property law operates to *destroy* property rights, contrary to the claim that formal recognition secures property. Based on these arguments, one might think that Upham would be resoundingly critical of liberal law and development land programs, but that is not his position.

Upham withholds a negative assessment of neoliberal property reforms on the grounds that it is necessary to take a "long-term, dynamic perspective to the study of property rights and development."[22] If displacing the poor from their land in Cambodia results in greater economic development for society in general, then it might have been justified, though he acknowledges that question is more complicated than mere improvement in GDP. This justification faces a high burden when one considers, as Gillespie indicates, that since the 2001 enactment of the land law to secure property, over 500,000 family farmers, constituting 10 percent of the landmass, have been dispossessed in favor of local developers and foreign investors. Economic development can increase wealth in society overall while leaving the masses in poverty.

Professor Upham offers hard-nosed realism fully cognizant of the harms inflicted. Economists and development practitioners, he advises,

> should be searching for a way to replace the old property regimes [customary land tenure] with the more productive ones, but they should do so while

> constantly being aware that creating the new requires the destruction of the old and that the cost of progress can be high.[23]

Continuing this stance, he suggests that the fate of the poor sacrificed in this transformation process

> cannot be ignored or dispensed with by a self-serving admonition [from development organizations] to poor states to redistribute any economic gains to compensate for the losses of the weak. Effective redistribution from the successful to those left behind simply will not happen.[24]

Law and economic development specialists must accept the fact that mass dispossession and injustice may result, regrettably, and move forward. What makes Professor Upham's tough-minded resignation especially compelling is his thoughtfulness and genuine appreciation of the complexity, human cost and unfairness of these situations.

His advice should not be followed. Owing to two factors, the long-term perspective is profoundly indeterminate and flawed. To be clear, Upham is correct that developments play out over time and one cannot expect immediate results, and one must make decisions today based on expectations about what consequences will follow in the future. What is incorrect is the suggestion that speculative long-run benefits can justify substantial injustice today. The long-term view is a pseudo-stance: (1) it is indeterminate because the historical framework is indefinite and cannot be closed; and (2) the complexity and interconnectedness of social causation precludes sound conclusions. Owing to these factors, taken up in order next, analysts can defend whichever position they prefer. Both are evident in Upham's own analysis.

When asked about the consequences of the French Revolution, Chinese Premier Zhou Enlai responded, "Too early to say." Alas, this pithy answer did not actually happen as reported. A translator present at the time revealed much later that Enlai thought the question was about the French student revolts of 1968, not the two-century-old Revolution. However, a deeper truth revealed by this misunderstanding stands: there is no way to definitively frame historical events to render conclusive assessments about their consequences.

Upham inadvertently exposes this flaw in his long-term view at two key points in his analysis. Japan's postwar redistribution of property from large landowners to family farmers and restrictions on the land market intentionally restricted the economic productivity of land and was followed by decades of political stability (tied to steadfast support from farmers) and the rise of Japan as a global economic force. Given so many decades of peace and prosperity, one might consider these land policies successful. To the contrary, Upham asserts, they "distorted the agricultural sector in ways that damage the sector itself and the economy as a whole."[25] Evaluated in light of aging and dwindling rural populations today, Upham says, the policy has been "a disaster."[26] People are departing "for the more dynamic possibilities of the city."[27] He likewise applies a long-term view to raise skepticism about the successes of China. China's unparalleled economic progress took place largely without formal private land rights, lifting hundreds of millions of Chinese out of poverty, apparently refuting the common assertion of development theorists that liberal property rights are necessary to economic development. Invoking the long-term view, however, Upham warns that "it is simply too early to be certain about the final destination."[28] Perhaps the lack of legal formality will stunt further economic advancement, he suggests, or perhaps it has enabled too much corruption, which will rot the political system.

The flaw in this reasoning is that no "final destination" exists, no moment in time to close the books on the past to make a conclusive determination of the consequences of historical events. This indeterminacy is hidden from view in liberal assertions that the English enclosures were positive because the implicit time horizon of the evaluation is Western capitalist countries *today*. A couple of centuries from now, however, if runaway global warming inflicts catastrophic consequences on life on earth, the evaluation of the industrial revolution and global capitalism may well be decidedly negative. The long-term perspective allows any evaluation to be positively reframed or undermined, as Upham does, by responding that, although things might have worked well for decades, it is "too early to say" that ultimately it was good; just as the response to current social harms from land titling programs is, "Don't be dissuaded by the short term upheaval and injustice – the long-run results from enhanced productivity will be worth it." Wait longer and things will look differently, both responses insist, worse or better, depending on the position one wants to assert.

The long-term view is an untethered abstraction that distracts from immediate reality. Since political, economic and legal actions occur continuously, with consequences playing out in real time, and since changes can be made when harmful or undesired results occur, short-term evaluations are critical and can provide sound bases for decisions, while long-term evaluations are chimerical.

The second flaw is Upham's suggestion that specific long-term social, economic or political consequences can be causally linked to particular legal initiatives or regimes. Economists still do not know whether formal legality is necessary for economic development or whether economic development is necessary for formal legality. Pronouncements cannot be made about such causal links because all aspects of society are interconnected – culture, social structure, demography, polity, economy, law, technology, ecology and everything else – extending internally within society and externally beyond national borders in myriad mostly invisible ways.[29] Interconnectedness renders long-term causal judgments impossible because too many factors are involved and everything affects everything else. The uniqueness of each context, interconnectedness, multiple causal factors that interact with one another, feedback loops and random events, internally and externally, changing at each moment in time, combine to make this impenetrable to reliable causal analysis.

Upham's long-term view analysis is filled with counterfactuals with head-spinning possible outcomes, all hopelessly speculative. Counterfactual reasoning plays out the consequences that would have followed from a different course of action. He asks, for example, whether Cambodia would have developed as quickly economically over the long run had land not been taken from the poor and used for a sugar plantation and an urban development project.[30] But this is unanswerable. Changing one thing affects everything connected with it, and the possible long-term consequences are multiple and numerous, branching off in different directions, as social, economic, legal and political choices and actions take place continuously in micro and mezzo settings. Had Cambodia actually respected the rights of small landowners, for example, that might have engendered public trust in the law and government (rather than anger and suspicion), which in turn might have enhanced political stability and economic progress going forward. There is no way of knowing. What we do know is that the Cambodian government took land from lots of poor people who suffered and gave it to wealthy developers who benefited.

The interconnectedness of society renders Professor Upham's causal assertions and counterfactual analysis implausible and unverifiable. For example, his suggestion that Japan's agricultural land and rice policies might have contributed to aging and depopulating rural communities does not account for the fact that across the world people are leaving the countryside for cities,[31] and populations are significantly declining (aging) in many countries, especially in Eastern Europe.[32] Judging from these general trends, rural aging and depopulation likely would have occurred for a complex of social and economic reasons regardless of Japan's agricultural land policies. Moreover, if China's economic advancement slows, which seems inevitable given its stunning pace for several decades, it is doubtful that formal legal regimes would make a significant difference. As Upham notes, the Chinese government obtains its legitimacy by delivering positive economic results. Thus, a loss of economic steam created by a global economic contraction would diminish government legitimacy, which a working formal legal system would not prevent.

The point here is not to dispute Professor Upham's particular counterfactual analyses about possible long-term outcomes of pursuing different courses of action, but to demonstrate that this analysis lacks rigor. Analysts who invoke it can argue for various scenarios and there is no way to determine which is correct, or even likely. This hypothetical reasoning is presented as analysis from which one might draw valid conclusions, but it is not empirical and not falsifiable. As stated at the outset, the effect of this analysis is to enable development actors to rationalize away the immediate social harms that result from proposed legal interventions in the promise of long-term benefits. Short-term legal uncertainty, conflict, mass dispossession and social injustice are justified because in the long term, everyone in society will eat omelettes.

John Maynard Keynes wrote, "In the long run we are all dead." Keynes emphatically did not deny the importance of long-terms goals and actions to achieve them, and he did not assert that one should myopically focus on the short term. Rather, he warned against reasoning away immediate social harms for speculative future benefits:

> Burke ever held, and held rightly, that it can seldom be right . . . to sacrifice a present benefit for a doubtful advantage in the future. . . . It is not wise to look too far ahead; our powers of prediction are slight, our command over results infinitesimal. It is therefore the happiness of our own contemporaries that is our main concern; we should be very chary of sacrificing large numbers of people for the sake of a contingent end, however advantageous that may appear. . . . We can never know enough to make the chance worth taking.[33]

Law and development specialists engaged in developing liberal legal regimes must keep this admonition in mind.

7 Guidelines for equitable land development

Since each situation is unique, no universal formula exists. Instead, I offer a handful of general guidelines gleaned from this collection on Asian land conflicts. Above all else, the guiding objective for land programs should be equitable economic development. A program exclusively aimed at increasing the economic productivity of land frequently has deleterious social consequences. For this reason, initiatives to enhance the productive uses of land should be designed to achieve fair and socially beneficial results. A number of concrete implications for land titling programs and for expropriation of land for private uses follow from this general proposition.

A critical implication is that land titling programs should not entail blanket implementation across an entire country. Rather, they must be implemented selectively in relation to specific contexts. Where rural populations largely engage in household subsistence agriculture, the potential harms outweigh the limited economic benefits from state titling programs. These programs create conflicts between two systems – customary tenure versus state land tenure – and increase land insecurity. Land titling and registration programs frequently operate to divest the poor of their land because obtaining state recognition is difficult for people with limited education who lack the required documentation. The Torrens system, in particular, is a trap for the poor and uneducated, who often lack the resources and know-how to successfully establish title and register. Even when blanket titling and registration programs are implemented by the government, people are often unable to make the required showing and do not register anew following transfers or inheritance, rendering their ownership vulnerable to third-party claims. Another set of problems are created by the fact that customary land tenure is often collective and distributes rights and obligations in ways that are inconsistent with, and extinguished by, liberal land tenure regimes.

In these situations involving rural agricultural areas with subsistence farmers, there should be a presumption in favor of maintaining customary land tenure – against introducing formal titling – unless and until specific protections are implemented that effectively substitute customary security with formal legal security. Titling systems might work well in cities, although with protections against dispossessing people. Indeed, these programs make it possible to confer rights on people like squatters who have lived on and improved the land for years without official title. The point, again, is that the appropriateness of titling programs must follow careful examination of necessity and likely consequences on an area-by-area basis.

Government expropriation of land for public purposes like public infrastructure, with fair compensation, creates unhappiness by the dispossessed, but not systematic injustice. However, government taking land from one set of private landowners and handing it to other private parties for economic development purposes has great potential for social harm and should not be allowed absent compelling necessity and justifications. If the land has higher economic value than current uses, the developers should be expected to negotiate with landowners to buy the land. After all, that is what liberal market theory says should occur.

Redistributions to private parties occur in two distinct ways with different implications, one far more justifiable than the other. Breaking up large landholdings (with compensation), then distributing small plots of land to occupiers, can be justified as providing housing and equitably distributing assets to a greater number of people in society. Taking land from small landholders and consolidating it in single owners, in contrast, removes housing and sources of sustenance from people and allocates wealth upward, producing social harms that cannot be justified solely by promised increases in economic productivity of the land. Increasing gross domestic product is less beneficial to society when the economic gains are obtained by a narrow elite. A grossly unequal distribution of wealth in poor societies creates many social and economic problems and should not be worsened by land policies.

Finally, when land is taken and handed to private parties for economic development, the amount of compensation provided should be based on the increased economic value after the taking. That is a fair way of sharing economic benefits with the people whose rights were sacrificed to obtain it.

This handful of guidelines will not resolve all problems, and it would be naïve to think they will be followed in situations in which corruption among government officials is rampant. Nonetheless, they provide a concrete alternative template for development organizations to replace the neoliberal land market paradigm, which seldom works as promised and often results in social hardship and injustice. These guidelines will help make the market for land serve society, rather than have society serve the dictates of the market.

Notes

1 Polanyi (2001 [1944]).
2 Id. Chapter 21.
3 Id. 260.
4 Id. 264.
5 See Upham (2012) Chapter 2. An influential promoter of these views is de Soto (2000).
6 See Tamanaha (2011).

7 Another common tactic not mentioned is the assertion by colonial states of mineral rights, granting mining concessions to private parties for royalties.
8 A sense of the integral social role of land is conveyed in Abubakari, Richter and Zevenbergen (2019).
9 Upham (2018) 116–130.
10 Granovetter (1985).
11 See Upham (2018) 73–78.
12 In the controversial *Kelo* case in the United States, decided in 2005, the Supreme Court upheld the expropriation by a private development organization (delegated authority by the local government) of an entire neighborhood for a planned project next to a Pfizer facility. Pfizer thereafter relocated its facility elsewhere and the area remains empty to this day. See *Kelo v. City of New London*, 545 U.S. 469 (2005).
13 Upham (2018) 95–98.
14 Upham (2018) 93–95.
15 See Tamanaha (2021).
16 Chirayath, Sage and Woolcock (2005) 3.
17 Fitzpatrick (2016). An illuminating exploration of these issues in Indonesia is Lund (2020).
18 See Tamanaha (2021).
19 See Harper (2011) and Wojkowska (2006).
20 See Lund (2020).
21 See, for example, Dam (2006).
22 Upham (2018) 133.
23 Id. 134.
24 Id. 141.
25 Id. 78.
26 Id. 78–80.
27 Id. 79.
28 Id. 103.
29 See Tamanaha (2011).
30 Upham (2018) 126–130.
31 See Population Facts (2018).
32 Kiersz and Hoff (2020).
33 Keynes, quoted in DeLong (2016).

References

Abubakari, Zaid, Christine Richter, and Jaap Zevenbergen (2019) "Plural Inheritance Laws, Practices and Emergent Types of Property – Implications for Updating the Land Register," *Sustainability*, Vol. 11, 1–17.

Chirayath, Leila, Caroline Sage, and Michael Woolcock (2005) *Customary Law and Policy Reform: Engaging with the Plurality of Justice Systems*, World Bank Legal Department Paper.

Dam, Kenneth (2006) *The Law-Growth Nexus: The Rule of Law and Economic Development*, Brookings Institute.

DeLong, Brad (2016) "Why Did Keynes Write in the Long Run We are All Dead?" *Washington Center for Equitable Growth*, April 7, 2016, https://equitablegrowth.org/a-note-on-niall-ferguson-why-did-keynes-write-in-the-long-run-we-are-all-dead/

de Soto, Hernando (2000) *The Mystery of Capital: Why Capitalism Triumphs in the West and Fails Everywhere Else*, Black Swan.

Fitzpatrick, Daniel (2016) "Fragmented Property Systems," *University of Pennsylvania Journal of International Law*, Vol. 38, 137–194.

Granovetter, Mark (1985) "Economic Action and Social Structure," *American Journal of Sociology*, Vol. 91, 481–510.

Harper, Erica (2011) *Customary Justice: From Program Design to Impact Evaluation*, International Development Law Organization.

Kiersz, Andy and Madison Hoff (2020) "The Twenty Fastest Shrinking Countries in the World," *Business Insider*, July 16, 2020, www.businessinsider.com/the-fastest-shrinking-countries-in-the-world-declining-populations

Lund, Christian (2020) *Nine-Tenths of the Law: Enduring Dispossession in Indonesia*, Yale University Press.

Polanyi, Karl (2001 [1944]) *The Great Transformation: The Political and Economic Origins of Our Time*, Beacon Press.

Population Facts, The Speed of Urbanization Around the World, Population Facts (2018) *United Nations Department of Economic and Social Affairs*, https://population.un.org/wup/Publications/Files/WUP2018-PopFacts_2018-1.pdf

Tamanaha, Brian Z. (2011) "The Primacy of Society and the Failures of Law and Development," *Cornell International Law Journal*, Vol. 44, 209–248.

Tamanaha, Brian Z. (2021) *Legal Pluralism Explained: History, Theory, Consequences*, Oxford University Press.

Upham, Frank K. (2018) *The Great Property Fallacy: Theory, Reality, and Growth in Developing Countries*, Cambridge University Press.

Wojkowska, Ewa (2006) *Doing Justice: How Informal Justice Systems Can Contribute*, United Nations Development Programme.

Index

Page numbers in *italics* indicate a figure and page numbers in **bold** indicate a table on the corresponding page. Page numbers followed by "n" indicate a note.

For Product Safety Concerns and Information please contact our EU
representative GPSR@taylorandfrancis.com
Taylor & Francis Verlag GmbH, Kaufingerstraße 24, 80331 München, Germany

www.ingramcontent.com/pod-product-compliance
Lightning Source LLC
LaVergne TN
LVHW021119300926
849160LV00010B/780

* 9 7 8 0 3 6 7 7 7 2 7 9 6 *